Look at the World Through Women's Eyes

PLENARY SPEECHES FROM THE NGO FORUM ON WOMEN, BEIJING '95

Edited by Eva Friedlander
Foreword by Irene M. Santiago

Look at the World Through Women's Eyes:
Plenary Speeches from the NGO Forum, Beijing '95
Edited by Eva Friedlander
ISBN 0-9651556-0-9
Library of Congress Catalogue Number 96-67821

Distributed by Women, Ink.
777 United Nations Plaza, 3rd Floor
New York, New York 10017 USA
Telephone: 212-687-8633; Fax: 212-661-2704
E-mail: WINK@IGC.APC.ORG

Translated into French and Spanish

Book design by Dolores Dwyer
Cover design by a.piccolo graphics
NGO logo design by Sisco & Evans

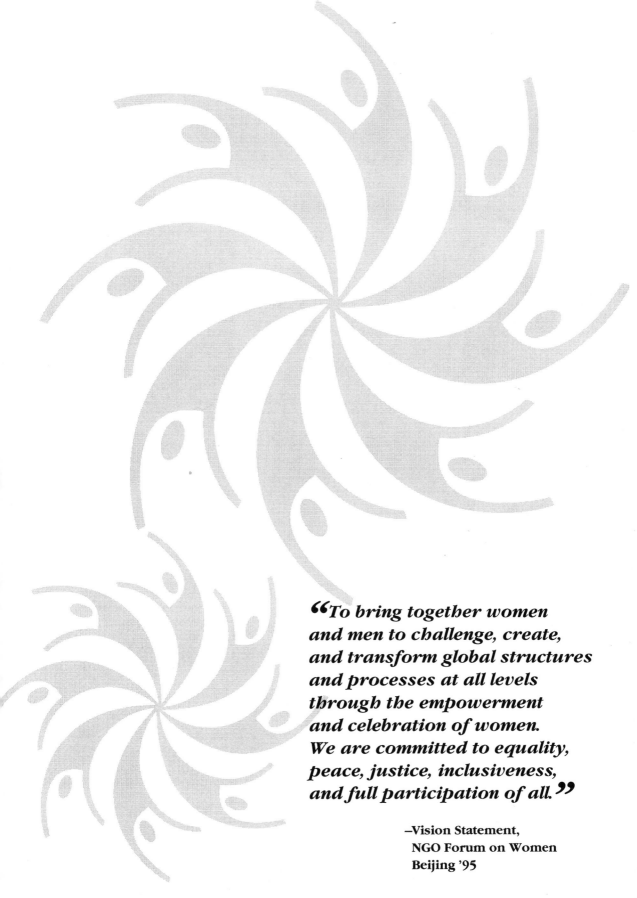

"To bring together women and men to challenge, create, and transform global structures and processes at all levels through the empowerment and celebration of women. We are committed to equality, peace, justice, inclusiveness, and full participation of all."

–Vision Statement,
NGO Forum on Women
Beijing '95

ACKNOWLEDGEMENTS

This volume of Plenary Proceedings was put together in record time, a feat possible only with the cooperation of a large number of people. Our thanks, of course, go first to the contributors. The speeches reflect their lives of courage, of thought, and of commitment to bring about a better world. They are responsible for the high quality of the plenary sessions. In addition, their patience and good humor in preparation for, and in the course of, the plenaries kept us inspired during what were often trying circumstances. In compiling this volume, their rapid response to our multiple requests for papers and other miscellaneous information that were required was greatly appreciated.

For the program itself, foremost thanks go to Chandra Budhu, the Coordinator of the Plenaries, for her commitment and dedication to making it happen. Charlotte Bunch, Rounaq Jahan, and Margaret Schuler played critical roles in shaping the program and we are very grateful to them for giving generously of their thought and time to consult with us on its design. We also want to express our appreciation to Sanae Kora, who was tireless in her efforts both during the preparations and in China at the Forum. The plenaries could not have happened without her. There were additionally many people, too many to be named here, who were essential in communicating with the contributors and providing them advice and assistance where necessary, whose cooperation we would like to acknowledge.

Special thanks go to the rapporteurs for their diligence, patience, and ability to put up with working conditions that were far from ideal. They were Linda Basch, Ramabai Espinet, Suzanne Hanchett, Faye Harrison, Kalpana Kannabiran, Aileen Kwa, Païvi Mattila, Joan Mencher, Ngozi Obinani, Teresa Valdés and Dessima Williams. The Chinese volunteers are to be thanked as well for making it possible to be in several places at once when necessary, and always being attentive to our needs.

The editors, Dolores Alexander, Dolores Dwyer, Sushma Kapoor, and Avis Lang, worked with lightning speed under pressure of extremely tight deadlines to produce this volume as quickly as humanly possible. Similarly we acknowledge the very valuable work of Tanya Selvaratnam, who assisted with every phase of the compilation and made herself available at short notice whenever required.

The Forum staff, particularly Rita Gibbons and Marian Urquilla, provided valuable assistance and important moral support throughout.

We thank the International Tribune Centre for their very valuable help with distribution.

Finally, we acknowledge the assistance of the United Nations Population Fund (UNFPA) with this publication, as well as the governments of Spain and France for their generous financial contributions, making possible the translation of the manuscript into Spanish and French.

EDITOR'S NOTE

The idea of a program of plenaries was an ambitious one and the speeches are impressive in the range of issues covered, the richness of substance, and the variety of perspectives presented. Nevertheless, issues close to the heart of some will undoubtedly be felt to be missing or only referred to in passing. The speed with which the plenaries had to be organized, the limitations of space, and unavoidable last-minute changes to the program meant that some issues fell by the wayside. Among the casualties, the most regrettable was a scheduled panel at which women heads of United Nations agencies were to be interviewed by Judy Woodruff of CNN. These included Catherine Bertini of the World Food Program (WFP), Elizabeth Dowdeswell of the United Nations Environment Programme (UNEP), Noeleen Heyzer of the United Nations Development Fund for Women (UNIFEM), and Nafis Sadik of the United Nations Population Fund (UNFPA). Unfortunately, a combination of bad weather and logistical problems made it necessary to cancel the panel.

Also missing here are the reports from the regions presented in Part III. These were too numerous to include, but syntheses can be found in the final report, and we encourage readers to look for them there.

As for the presentations that appear in this volume, many are written papers that were provided by the speakers, while others are transcriptions from the tape-recorded speeches. The presentations were only lightly edited, and then only for clarity and consistency to make for ease of reading. We felt it important to convey the passion and vitality that the speakers brought to their subjects; every effort was made, therefore, to maintain the voice of the speaker, to retain the individuality and energy of each presentation.

In spite of any shortcomings, this collection of speeches is one which enables us to hold a mirror up to ourselves and assess more clearly where as a movement we are today, and where our agenda will take us tomorrow. It is sure to be seen as a period piece.

–E.F.

CONTENTS

III • Approaches to Governance
(including Questions of Citizenship and Political Participation)

IV • Obstacles to Peace and Human Security
(including the Effects of Militarization, Violence and Poverty)

V • Challenges Posed by the Globalization of the Economy
(including the Impact of the Technological Revolution on Work)

VI • The Rise of Conservatism in Its Various Forms
(Religious, Nationalist, Racial/Ethnic and Homophobic)

VII • Media, Culture, and Communication
(Challenges and Opportunities)

PART II • STRATEGIES AND MECHANISMS

VIII • Governance, Citizenship and Political Participation — Strategies

XIII • Media, Culture and Communication: Challenges and Opportunities — Strategies

XIV • Institutional Mechanisms and Financial Arrangements — Strategies

XV • United Nations Agencies: Gender Equity Strategies

PART III • COMMITMENT TO THE FUTURE: Acountability and Action

by Irene M. Santiago
Executive Director, NGO Forum on Women '95

The NGO Forum on Women '95 was an extraordinary event. It drew more than 30,000 participants, making it the largest international gathering on women ever. Like previous NGO Forums, participants came because it provided tremendous opportunities for networking and learning from one another.

But the NGO Forum was also an occasion for agenda-setting for the global women's movement. The Fourth World Conference on Women, of which the NGO Forum was a parallel event, occurred at an important historical moment. It was five years before the end of the 20th century and the beginning of a new millenium. It was 20 years since the International Women's Year Conference was held in Mexico City, where the UN Decade for Women was launched. It was also 10 years after the Nairobi Conference and NGO Forum where, for the first time, a truly global women's movement started to emerge.

In those 10 years, women's NGOs and other groups concerned with women's issues began to play an increasingly important role in United Nations conferences. At these conferences, their governments made decisions on matters that affected their lives and those of their families and communities. Women believed, therefore, that it was important to make their voices as women heard consistently in all UN conferences. They contributed their knowledge and expertise on issues such as the environment, human rights, population and development, children's rights, and the future of small island developing states. But more than that, they challenged existing frameworks, proposing and lobbying for the inclusion of a women's perspective in all the critical issues of the day.

While UN conferences provide an arena for NGO input in international issues being discussed by governments, NGO Forums have always provided the space for articulation of new and emerging issues, or evaluation of strategies used in dealing with current problems in order to increase the effectiveness of NGO work at all levels. As in the past, the NGO Forum on Women '95 was an occasion for women to reflect on lessons learned from past work and struggles, and to create new agendas for the future.

At each of the five regions of the world where a regional NGO Forum was held from 1993 to 1995, an unprecedented number of women came to discuss their regional problems and priorities. Asia and the Pacific, while identifying 12 issues of concern, challenged the development model being pursued in the region where development has been most uneven. Latin American and Caribbean women gave priority to violence against women, democracy, and political participation, and structural adjustment. European and North America women focused on, among other issues, peace, women's human rights, political participation, and the economy.

In the countries of Central and Eastern Europe there was also concern about women and NGOs. Arab women saw peace in their region as well as in their homes, the environment, political participation, and economic development as their major issues. African women gave priority to peace, poverty, human rights, and the girl child. The regional NGO Forums were powerful occasions for sectoral groups and networks to discuss their common concerns and to plan common strategies. However, it soon became evident that many of the problems facing women were global in their reach and therefore needed an interregional response.

Consultations were held with various women to explore how such an interregional response might be articulated. Women discussed their hopes and fears about the future in the midst of the rising tide of conservatism and the globalization of the economy, including the speed and nature of the technological revolution, the breakdown of old political systems and alliances and the emergence of new ones, the increasing homogenization of culture through media that now reach almost every corner of the world, the continued violations of women's human rights and the fear that this engenders among women of all classes and ages.

Although the consultations brought out the need for analysis of the global forces that are affecting women's lives, women also expressed a strong need for "tools," or practical solutions to problems. They expressed the need not so much to be seen as victims but to be recognized as problem solvers. The plenaries were planned in order to "look at the world through women's eyes" both in terms of problem analysis and solutions.

It was decided to use the Program of Plenaries to stimulate a strategic planning process, starting with an analysis of the global forces affecting human communities, especially women, in order to understand their root causes and manifestations, to draw lessons from strategies used to respond to these global forces, and to plan actions from regional, sectoral and intergenerational perspectives.

The program brought together outstanding women leaders from all over the world. They came from indigenous communities, grassroots groups, academe, research institutions, media, youth groups, international agencies, churches, trade unions, government, lesbian organizations, older women's groups, and organizations of women with disabilities. They were all activists who had made possible many of the profound changes in women's lives over the past decades.

The plenary hall was packed every day for nine days. Unfortunately, many people who wanted to attend the sessions had to be turned away because of the size of the plenary hall. This book has been published to make sure that a broad range of interested people will have access to the excellent speeches that were given there.

The agenda-setting objective of the NGO Forum on Women '95 was accomplished not only through the plenaries but also through a rich program of more than 4,000 work-shops, panels, tribunals, congresses, exhibits, video screenings, and cultural activities.

As in past NGO Forums, the impact of the agenda-setting and networking activities will be felt at all levels when participants return to their communities and organizations to connect what they learned in Huairou to their work back home. The speeches and dis-cussions at the plenary sessions pointed to the need to connect across issue lines and national boundaries. For example, the responses to the problems created by the global-ization of the economy and the technological revolution must engage NGOs involved in human rights, the environment, health, education, politics, media, youth, trade unionism, and all other issues.

Looking at the world through women's eyes demands a holistic response to the global challenges that define women's lives today. An even stronger women's movement, global in its scope and rooted in the lives and struggles of women in the villages, towns, and cities of this increasingly small world will bring about significant and lasting social change not only for women but for the rest of the human community as well.

INTRODUCTION

By Eva Friedlander

As women gathered in Huairou, China for the NGO Forum on Women, the world was learning that nuclear testing had once again started in the Pacific and that Europe was once again the site of genocide, ethnocide, and dislocation not seen since the Second World War. It was learning of refugee crises and violent anti-immigrant campaigns. International trade agreements such as NAFTA, and the mergers of major financial institutions were in the headlines—as were currency crises and job relocations. Unemployment and migration were reported to be on the increase—along with declines in social supports and safety nets. The world was hearing about oil spills and the destruction of natural resources, endangered species, and habitats.

These images flooded our minds from television screens and newspaper headlines that presented them as unrelated, even isolated events—the products of such natural processes as deep-seated ethnic rivalries, or the inevitable results of development and free-market forces.

Women came to Huairou from every corner of the world to give their firsthand accounts of these events, to let one another and the world know just how their lives and those of their families and communities were being affected, often devastated by these policies and events. They came as leaders and activists in their societies, to exchange ideas and strategies for dealing with the difficulties they face.

The speeches presented here from the Program of Plenaries reflect the vitality these women brought to the Forum. The Program was organized to reach beyond the superficial and sensational, to provide critical analyses and a new understanding of the interconnections between seemingly unrelated parts of the world, of the structural changes taking place and what they mean for women and consequently for all people.

Not surprisingly, when we explore the world as seen by women, the picture shifts: isolated events become connected and new aspects come into view. Women, positioned at the intersection of production and reproduction, offer a perspective that is crucial to making sense of the world and acting to change it.

GLOBAL FORCES AND THEMES

This Forum was the fourth international gathering of women to take place in conjunction with a United Nations conference on women. Each gathering has reflected the times during which it took place, and focused the world's attention on a somewhat different facet of the problems facing women and the critical international issues of which these were a part. This Forum was distinct from the others in that it included the Program of Plenaries—panels that could inform an agenda-setting process to be undertaken by nongovernmental organizations in each region of the world.

The plenaries were organized thematically around five global issues: the globalization of the economy, including the impact of the technological revolution on work; obstacles to peace and human security, including the effects of militarization, violence, and poverty; approaches to governance, including questions of citizenship and political participation; the rise of conservatism in its various forms—religious, nationalist, racial/ethnic and homophobic; and media, culture, and communication.

The panels took up these questions with critical analysis in Part I, starting with an overview from the perspective of each region. Part II highlighted strategies for change and the lessons to be learned from them. Part III focused on commitment to the future, culminating in an intergenerational dialogue with women leaders of different ages exploring commonalities and differences and looking to ways of working together in the future.

Emerging from the plenary presentations and discussions were certain cross-cutting themes with broad implications for the future of the women's movement. These included issues of identity; of human rights; the respective roles of the state, civil society, the private sector, international organizations and NGOs; and institutional transformation. The significance of these themes can be fully appreciated only in the context of the global changes taking place today, and together constitute a map on which the future of the women's movement can be charted. It is this configuration of elements, as they are expressed in the realities of women's lives, that this time brought women together from around the world on new and significantly different ground.

The numbers and diversity of attendees at this Forum were truly impressive and would alone mark the event as a watershed in the history of the international women's movement. The groundswell of support that this meeting garnered can be gauged in comparison with the three conferences that marked the Decade for Women. At the Mexico City Tribune there were 6,000 participants; for the Mid-Decade Forum in Copenhagen there were 8,000 participants; and at the End of the Decade Conference in Nairobi there were 15,000 persons. Ten years later in Huairou there were 30,000 participants.

Then there was the composition of the attendees. It was obvious to those present at Huairou that there was far greater representation of women along ethnic and class lines than ever before. The outlines of the future, therefore, begin to be seen as much in the radical change in the patterns of commonality and difference among the women at the Huairou gathering.

By briefly looking back at the first three gatherings held during the Decade for Women, and at the changing situation since that time, one can see how the stage was set for what was to take place in China.

LOOKING BACK

The International Women's Tribune held in Mexico City in 1975 in conjunction with the International Women's Year conference launched the United Nations Decade for Women with the themes Equality, Development, and Peace. Sharp differences separated women from the North and South, and women from capitalist and noncapitalist worlds. This was also the UN's Second Development Decade and there was growing recognition of increasing gender disparities resulting from the development process.

Uppermost on the Mexico City conference agenda were concerns with women's integration into development, a questioning of the conventionally accepted gender division of labor, and the recognition of the equal value of women's work. While first world feminists were most concerned with issues of equality, third world women'saw such issues as divisive, as driving a wedge between men and women who needed to combine forces to deal with the bread-and-butter issues they faced. For them this was yet another example of a neocolonial agenda, with Northern priorities being imposed on the South. At the same time, women from the second world were concerned primarily with peace, considering capitalism and militarism as at the root of women's problems.

At the 1980 Forum held in association with the Mid-Decade Conference in Copenhagen, the North-South, capitalist-socialist divides again sharply framed the discussions, sparking heated exchanges over such international questions as the Israeli-Palestinian debate about Zionism as racism.

Only with the NGO Forum '85 was there a sense that a women's movement had finally taken off that could be recognized as truly international. Peace became a major issue and the development paradigm was fundamentally challenged by a growing network of Southern women and an increasing number of Northern voices. Although superpower politics continued to have a grip on the events there, for the first time the final document of the UN Conference, the Forward Looking Strategies, was passed by consensus.

THE CHANGED CONTEXT

The ten years since the end of the Decade for Women have seen a political, economic, and social transformation affecting millions of lives and creating a new and very different context for the conversations, confrontations, and exchanges that took place in Huairou.

The demise of the socialist world and the disappearance of balanced—if tenuously so—superpower politics has opened the way for shifting alliances and the emergence of new lines of differentiation and conflict. Trade agreements were renegotiated and trade barriers removed, resulting in economic globalization at an unprecedented rate. Speeded by new technology that enabled instantaneous capital transfer around the globe, financial expansion reached new heights.

Often unimpeded by national boundaries and legal constraints, transnational corporations have greatly exptended their operations, with Export Processing Zones providing many of the necessary footholds. The result has been a very uneven development, a growing inequality between and within nations, as well as between women and men, highlighting ever more clearly the relationship between development and underdevelopment, between wealth and poverty.

Incorporated into increasingly unstable labor markets, women are subject to rapidly shifting labor demands and are vulnerable to the whims of employers unaccountable to governments and laws of state. And, as social supports and safety nets have disintegrated in the path of privatization and the imposition of structural adjustment programs by governments and international financial institutions, poverty has markedly increased. For the women of the former socialist countries of Central and Eastern Europe, these and other problems previously associated primarily with the developing world have emerged as part of their entrance into the global economy.

Ecological devastation has been wrought by economies based on unencumbered growth and unlimited consumption for a few, placing at risk the biological and cultural diversity of the planet essential to its very survival, and taking a disproportionate toll on women and children. The past decade has seen growing awareness that new and sustainable strategies for survival are required, ones that are firmly rooted in the needs of the planet as a whole.

Growing insecurity and loss of control over livelihoods has turned many people in the direction of a strict conservatism. In the shape of religion this has dictated a subordinate domestic and maternal role as natural for women and a growing homophobia. Embracing a politics of divisiveness, it has fueled local conflicts, and provoked wars over national, religious, racial, and ethnic claims, wreaking violence on civilians—often in the name of the very women most victimized by the brutality of rape and domestic abuse.

Such local wars have become endemic, decimating populations and destroying resources. In spite of the decline in superpower politics, militarization has continued to be nourished by a thriving international arms trade and is supported by massive expenditures that divert funds from social needs. Unprecedented displacement of populations for reasons of economics, politics, or war often has meant that women and children have been left behind to fend for themselves or forced to flee in search of viable livelihoods.

Globalization of the media, in spite of its potential to bring about better understanding across cultures and nations, has instead pushed ever further an increasingly homogeneous view of the world that entails—in image and text—a message for and about women at once exploitative and demeaning.

New technology has revolutionized communications, along with productive and reproductive processes—offering undreamed of scientific progress—but also posing moral and ethical questions with implications for women that could barely have been foreseen a few years ago. Such is the case with biotechnologies introduced by international businesses and organizations raising such new issues as rights over intellectual property and genetic endowments.

Amid all of these changes has emerged a very new configuration of players. The relationships among governments, nongovernmental organizations, civil society, international organizations, and the private sector are very much in the making. Each claims the right to formulate policies with far-reaching implications, affecting persons in every corner of the world. In this arena of contention women are clearly staking a claim *as women*, to try to ensure that what takes place there is responsive to the conditions of over one half the population of the world, and thereby to all people.

Recent Gains

In the context of a fluid and shifting political environment, women have been able to organize internationally and regroup. Differences once experienced as irreconcilable are being bridged as women are perceiving common interests across what was previously a hard ideological divide. Issues of violence against women, the feminization of poverty, and sexual and reproductive rights, among others, today are bringing women together. Similarly, there is growing recognition of the South that exists in the North and vice versa, and a focus on gender rather than on women exclusively, with the necessity to see women's issues not as separate from, but in relation to, men. That gender roles are socially constructed, not natural, is more widely accepted, and there is growing agreement that it is necessary to work together with men in order to create better lives for all. These and other changes have laid a groundwork on which to build a common agenda.

Women had already come center stage in the international arena, as major players in the four most recent post-decade UN conferences leading up to Beijing. At each of the world conferences after Nairobi, by making the critical connections between the situation of women and the subjects under discussion, women were able to shift the discourse from narrowly defined concerns and bring attention to the complex interrelationship among issues and the importance of a holistic and human-centered perspective.

At the UN Conference on Environment and Development (UNCED) in Rio de Janeiro in 1992, the women's caucus made it clear that environmental sustainability for life on this planet was unthinkable and unfeasible without considering the women who make up more than one-half of the world's population. Consequently Agenda 21, the document produced in Rio, made reference to women in each of its chapters. The Human Rights Conference in Vienna in 1993 saw violence against women become a major issue, along with acceptance of the idea that women's rights are human rights. At the International Conference on Population and Development (ICPD) in Egypt in 1994, women's empowerment became critical as the issues of control over fertility and reproduction were placed on the table. Women gained a major victory by moving the discussion beyond contraception and achievement of numerical targets to that of reproductive rights broadly conceived, having social, cultural, and economic dimensions, and as requiring the involvement of men. Finally, in Copenhagen in 1995 at the World Summit for Social Development (WSSD), women were able to bring worldwide attention to the fact that the majority of people living in poverty are women and that the majority of women are poor, highlighting that women must be involved in decision-making to bring about the necessary change.

The gains established in the course of the past three years enabled the women's movement to emerge as a new, enlarged, and international force, with a legitimacy it did not have before. Unprecedented numbers of women were involved in the preparatory process leading up to the meetings in China. Attending regional Forums held in tandem with the official UN preparatory meetings, they learned about the UN process and developed their objectives for the events that would take place in China. By the time of Beijing the attention of the world had been brought to the decisive role that women could and would play in the international arena.

NEW AND EMERGING THEMES

This Forum would, then, deal with a very different world than that which existed at the time of the Nairobi meeting. After the successes of the other UN issue-based conferences and forums, it was now time to take stock, to examine strengths and weaknesses, to reflect on where the movement had come, and to look to the future.

Given these changes, it was not surprising to see certain themes come to the fore at the plenaries and take on a salience they did not have during the Decade for Women: issues of identity and of difference; of human rights; of the responsibility and accountability of governments, nongovernmental and international organizations, and questions of institutional transformation.

Identity

With the rise of conservatism, the politics of identity have become particularly important. While any individual clearly has multiple identities, people are being forced into increasingly narrow definitions of self, such as those based on gender, race, ethnicity, or religion—with characteristics assumed to be essential to them and self-evident rather than being the political, social, and cultural constructs of a given historical time and place. Whether for purposes of work, as subjects of legislation, of privilege or participation in any arena, women, lesbians, indigenous women, disabled women and others find increasingly that they must assert their rights and stake their claims on the assumption of an identity often defined by those who would stigmatize and marginalize them.

The speeches reflect the ways in which identities are played off one another to create multiple levels of similarity and difference, unity and divisiveness. As differentiation and inequality bring benefits to some while marginalizing others, the question of how to create unity while accommodating difference becomes a central problem for the future of the women's movement. Strategies of resistance against such narrow definitions of self were described, along with efforts to break out of and/or redefine identities in order to establish broader commonalities and more inclusive forms of action.

Human Rights

The move over the last decade from a concern with women's needs to an assertion of women's rights is reflected throughout the speeches. The concept of human rights, initially raised as a moral issue to circumvent restrictive legal definitions of rights as construed by particular governments, today is being fashioned by women as a tool by which to hold all governments accountable across a broad spectrum of women's rights deemed morally and ethically inviolable.

Fortified by the gains made at the UN Conference on Human Rights in Vienna, where wide recognition was gained for women's rights as human rights, panelists spoke of the erosion of such rights resulting from the wide range of negative circumstances now facing women: unregulated labor markets; the failure of development policies to provide sustainable livelihoods; the ascendance of repressive politics which threaten women's reproductive rights and access to health care; the rise of homophobic, racist, and nationalist assaults, which target the most vulnerable; violence against women, including that resulting from warfare and ethnic conflict, domestic abuse, and sex trafficking across national borders; and last but not least, the commodification of women in the media.

In speeches addressing indigenous rights, discussion of human rights issues was extended beyond questions of individual rights to those of collective rights, with the broader implications such a perspective brings to bear. This was particularly evident when viewing human rights abuses as a measure of continued colonial subjugation, and looking at the loss of indigenous collective rights that come with appropriation and destruction of natural resources through nuclear testing and other forms of environmental devastation.

Roles and Responsibility of Government and Nongovernmental Organizations

The growing power of transnational forces, and rapidly changing relationships among governments and people, NGOs, the private sector, and international organizations such as financial institutions, donor agencies, and judicial and regulatory agencies, has created serious concern about their respective roles and responsibilities.

There is renewed concern regarding the nature of the contract between governments and civil society, and how and for whom civil society is constituted. With the expansion of transnational activity not subject to the laws of nations, the responsibility of governments to ensure justice, economic and otherwise and to protect people from policies that threaten their livelihoods or their very lives has taken on new urgency. The strategies that women have used and might use to engage and confront the private sector, state and international organizations are critical for the future.

In this regard, the growing importance of NGOs, acting as representative and in the interests of civil society, was considered throughout the Program of Plenaries. NGOs are viewed as at once promising and suspect. They are appreciated as potential agents of change and vehicles for promoting democratic values, but there is also a wariness about some NGOs whose claims to representativeness are questionable, as is their growing role as surrogates for the state. At a panel specifically on NGO accountability, panelists shared lessons learned from efforts to build accountability in their organizations. They pointed to the important role NGOs can play if they remain independent from governments and donors, as self-sustainable and accountable to their constituents, especially grassroots women, and as pressure groups to make governments accountable

Institutional Transformation

Finally, the need for a politics of transformation is a recurring theme. This includes the struggle for women's equal access to, and representation in, all institutions—educational, professional, governmental and intergovernmental, and others—and at all levels, from the local to the international, through affirmative action and gender-responsive planning. While the call for "mainstreaming" women is not a new one, the emphasis now is not simply on access, but on transforming institutions and through them the structures of inequality and oppression in society at large. The aim of such policies is to see that power ultimately be used for human-centered development that ensures peace and secure livelihoods for all people.

The constitutional, legal, and political strategies used to achieve some of the very real gains made over the past 10 years were presented, as were the shortcomings. The resistance faced by women who have run for political office, who have held political office, or who are working for affirmative-action policies and the integration of gender issues into institutions, along with the endemic problem of institutional marginalization of gender issues, all reflect the very real threat that true integration and mainstreaming constitute for the status quo.

LOOKING FORWARD

It was perhaps in the intergenerational dialogue that the issue of greatest importance for the future of the women's movement was most clearly articulated: that of diversity. The question is how to fashion a future that builds on, and seeks strength in, the differences that exist between generations of women, while at the same time recognizing a commonality of interests.

The need to nourish a new generation, to provide role models, and to pass on the mantle of leadership, is a serious issue facing the movement. Acknowledging their debt to those in the movement who came before, speakers in the plenary pointed to the need for youth to listen to the voices of the elders, but also for the elders to hear the voices of young people, to recognize their issues and accord them their rightful places as an integral part of their communities and of the movement. They spoke of the need to accept and respect the differences among them while moving forward on a common agenda.

This was, however, a conversation about more than generational difference. It was part of the broader discussion, crucial to feminism and the women's movement, of the need to ensure diversity, to gain power to empower others to walk their own paths, as individuals and as members of communities. Only through the broadest possible inclusion and engagement with the realities of other women's lives is it possible to begin to peel away the layers of assumptions, myths, and stereotypes that create barriers not only to understanding others, but to knowing oneself as well.

Given the wide range of circumstances in which women find themselves, only genuine diversity can provide the reality check so necessary to gauge meaning and implication across differences of geography, culture, and class, or the relevance to others of the multitude of particular struggles in which women are engaged around the world. Only by dealing with the specific realities of women's lives and experiences is it possible to avoid the tyranny of the well-intended, yet often tortuous, imposition of ideas and wills on others.

Difference enriches and is responsible for the vitality and creativity that nourish the movement. As these plenaries point out, only inclusiveness can ensure its growth and continuity into the next century for the coming generations. What is at stake here is nothing less than the future of the human community.

PART I

OVERVIEW OF GLOBAL FORCES

I • OPENING PLENARY

Opening remarks

Supatra Masdit
Convenor, NGO Forum for Women '95

Distinguished guests, dear friends, sisters, and brothers:

Today, women from the five regions of the world have gathered here to carry out and continue the shared task we started 20 years ago in Mexico. We are here because we share the same vision — we foresee a new world where women and men live together equally and in harmony. For the next nine days, we will work side by side to move closer to that vision.

For those who are unable to attend the NGO Forum, their thoughts, their hopes and efforts are brought to the Forum by their colleagues, sisters, and brothers. We will ensure that their valuable contributions are woven into our strategies and platforms of action.

Our NGO Forum has three main purposes: first, to set the agenda for the women's movement around the world; second, to network women's organizations, South and North, East and West, and across a wide spectrum of ideas and approaches; and third, to lobby the Fourth World Conference on Women in order to put our agenda and platforms of action into the United Nations documents.

To attain democracy, development and peace, women must recognize the diversity within our movements while standing firm and united in our commitment.

Hence, the key to our focal strategy is women's active participation in decision-making at all levels in our society. How can we achieve all the purposes we have set forth? One essential approach is the empowerment of grassroots women. The NGO Forum hopes to encourage the idea of

women speaking for and among themselves. One such example is the active and meaningful participation of grassroots groups in this NGO Forum. This is the strength of the NGO Forum — its power to inspire women to build equitable and respectful relationships with one another and the world.

Message
(presented on videotape)

Aung San Suu Kyi
Nobel Prize Laureate 1991, Myanmar

It is a wonderful but daunting task that has fallen on me to say a few words by way of opening this Forum, the greatest concourse of women (joined by a few brave men!) that has ever gathered on our planet. I want to try and voice some of the common hopes which firmly unite us in all our splendid diversity.

But first I would like to explain why I cannot be with you in person today. Last month I was released from almost six years of house arrest. The regaining of my freedom has in turn imposed a duty on me to work for the freedom of other women and men in my country who have suffered far more — and who continue to suffer far more — than I have. It is this duty which prevents me from joining you today. Even sending this message to you has not been without difficulties. But the help of those who believe in international cooperation and freedom of expression has enabled me to overcome the obstacles. They made it possible for me to make a small contribution to this great celebration of the struggle of women to mold their own destiny and to influence the fate of our global village.

The opening plenary of this Forum presents an overview of the global forces affecting the quality of life of the human community, the challenges they pose for the global community as a whole and for women in particular as we approach the 21st century. However, with true womanly understanding, the Convener of this Forum suggested that among these global forces and challenges, I might wish to concentrate on those matters which occupy all my waking thoughts these days: peace, security, human rights, and democracy. I would like to discuss these issues particularly in the context of the participation of women in politics and governance.

For millennia, women have dedicated themselves almost exclusively to the task of nurturing, protecting and caring for the young and the old, striving for the conditions of peace that favor life as a whole. To this can be added the fact that, to the best of my knowledge, no war was ever started by women. But it is women and children who have always suffered most in situations of conflict. Now that we are gaining control of the primary historical role imposed on us — of sustaining life in the context of the home and family — it is time to apply in the arena of the world the wisdom and experience thus gained in activities of peace over so many thousands of years. The education and empowerment of women throughout the world cannot fail to result in a more caring, tolerant, just, and peaceful life for all.

If to these universal benefits of the growing emancipation of women can be added the "peace dividend" for human development offered by the end of the cold war, spending less on the war toys of grown men and much more on the urgent needs of humanity as a whole, then truly the next millennia will be an age the like of which has never been seen in human history. But there still remain many obstacles to be overcome before we can achieve this goal. And not least among these obstacles are intolerance and insecurity.

This year is the International Year for Tolerance. The United Nations has recognized that toler-

ance, human rights, democracy, and peace are closely related. Without tolerance, the foundations for democracy and respect for human rights cannot be strengthened, and the achievements of peace will remain elusive. My own experience during the years I have been engaged in the democracy movement in Burma has convinced me of the need to emphasize the positive aspects of tolerance. It is not enough simply to live and let live: genuine tolerance requires an active effort to try to understand the point of view of others; it implies broadmindedness and vision, as well as confidence in one's own ability to meet new challenges without resorting to intransigence or violence. In societies where men are truly confident of their own worth, women are not merely tolerated, they are valued. Their opinions are listened to with respect, they are given their rightful place in shaping the society in which they live.

There is an outmoded Burmese proverb still recited by men who wish to deny that women, too, can play a part in bringing necessary change and progress to their society: "The dawn rises only when the rooster crows." But Burmese people today are well aware of the scientific reason behind the rising of dawn and the falling of dusk. And the intelligent rooster surely realizes that it is because dawn comes that it crows and not the other way round. It crows to welcome the light that has come to relieve the darkness of night. It is not the prerogative of men alone to bring light to this world: Women with their capacity for compassion and self-sacrifice, their courage and perseverance, have done much to dissipate the darkness of intolerance and hate, suffering and despair. Often the other side of the coin of intolerance is insecurity. Insecure people tend to be intolerant, and their intolerance unleashes forces that threaten the security of others. And where there is no security there can be no lasting peace.

In its *Human Development Report* for last year, the UNDP noted that human security is not a concern with weapons, it is a concern with human life and dignity. The struggle for democracy and human rights in Burma is a struggle for life and dignity. It is a struggle that encompasses our political, social and economic aspirations. The people of my country want the two freedoms that spell security: freedom from want and freedom from war. It is want that has driven so many of our young girls across our borders to a life of sexual slavery where they are subject to constant humiliation and ill-treatment. It is fear of persecution for their political beliefs that has made so many of our people feel that even in their own homes they cannot live in dignity and security.

Traditionally the home is the domain of the woman. But there has never been a guarantee that she can live out her life there safe and unmolested. There are countless women who are subjected to severe cruelty within the heart of the family which should be their haven. And in times of crisis, when their menfolk are unable to give them protection, women have to face the harsh challenges of the world outside while continuing to discharge their duties within the home. Many of my male colleagues who have suffered imprisonment for their part in the democracy movement have spoken of the great debt of gratitude they owe their womenfolk, particularly their wives, who stood by them firmly, tender as mothers nursing their newly born, brave as lionesses defending their young. These magnificent human beings who have done so much to aid their men in the struggle for justice and peace — how much more could they not achieve if given the opportunity to work in their own right for the good of their country and of the world?

Our endeavors have also been sustained by the activities of strong and principled women all over the world who have campaigned not only for my own release but, more importantly, for our cause. I cannot let this opportunity pass without speaking of the gratitude we feel toward our sisters everywhere, from heads of governments to busy housewives. Their efforts have been a triumphant demonstration of female solidarity and of the power of an ideal to cross all frontiers.

In my country at present, women have no participation in the higher levels of government and none whatsoever in the judiciary. Even within the democratic movement, only 14 out of the 485 MPs elected in 1990 were women — all from my own party, the National League for Democracy. These 14 women represent less than 3 percent of the total number of successful candidates. They, like their male colleagues, have not been permitted to take office, since the outcome of those elections has been totally ignored. Yet, the very high performance of women in our educational system and in the management of commercial enterprises proves their enormous potential to contribute to the betterment of society in general. Meanwhile, our women have yet to achieve those fundamental rights of free expression, association, and security of life denied also to their menfolk.

The adversities that we have had to face together have taught all of us involved in the struggle to build a truly democratic political system in Burma, that there are no gender barriers that cannot be overcome. The relationship between men and women should, and can, be characterized not by patronizing behavior or exploitation, but by *metta* (that is to say, loving-kindness), partnership, and trust. We need mutual respect and understanding between men and women instead of patriarchal domination and degradation, which are expressions of violence and engender counterviolence. We can learn from each other and help one another to moderate the "gender weaknesses" imposed on us by traditional or biological factors.

There is an age-old prejudice the world over to the effect that women talk too much. But is this really a weakness? Could it not in fact be a strength? Recent scientific research on the human brain has revealed that women are better at verbal skills, while men tend toward physical action. Psychological research has shown, on the other hand, that disinformation engendered by men has far more damaging effect on its victims than feminine gossip. Surely these discoveries indicate that women have a most valuable contribution to make in situations of conflict, by leading the way to solutions based on dialogue rather than on viciousness or violence.

The Buddhist *paravana* ceremony at the end of the rainy-season retreat was instituted by the Lord Buddha, who did not want human beings to live in silence "like dumb animals." This ceremony, during which monks ask mutual forgiveness for any offense given during the retreat, can be said to be a council of truth and reconciliation. It might also be considered a forerunner of that most democratic of institutions, the parliament, a meeting of peoples gathered together to talk over their shared problems. All the world's great religions are dedicated to the generation of happiness and harmony. This demonstrates the fact that together with the combative instincts of man, there coexists a spiritual aspiration for mutual understanding and peace.

This forum of nongovernmental organizations represents belief in the ability of intelligent human beings to resolve conflicting interests through exchange and dialogue. It also represents the conviction that governments alone cannot resolve all the problems of their countries. The watchfulness and active cooperation of organizations outside the spheres of officialdom are necessary to ensure the four essential components of the human development paradigm as identified by the UNDP: productivity, equity, sustainability, and empowerment. The last is particularly relevant. It requires that development must be *by* people, not only *for* them. People must participate fully in the decisions and processes that shape their lives. In other words, people must be allowed to play a significant role in the governance of the country. And "people" include women, who make up at least half of the world's population.

The last six years afforded me much time and food for thought. I came to the conclusion that the human race is not divided into two opposing camps of good and evil. It is made up of those who are capable of learning and those who are incapable of doing so. Here, I am not talking of learning in the narrow sense of acquiring an academic education, but of learning as the process of absorbing those lessons of life that enable us to increase peace and happiness in our world. Women in their roles as mothers have traditionally assumed the responsibility of teaching children values that will guide them throughout their lives. It is time we were given the full opportunity to use our natural teaching skills to contribute toward building a modern world that can withstand the tremendous challenges of the technological revolution, which has in turn brought revolutionary changes in social values.

As we strive to teach others, we must have the humility to acknowledge that we, too, still have much to learn. And we must have the flexibility to adapt to the changing needs of the world around us. Women who have been taught that modesty and pliancy are among the prized virtues of our gender are marvelously equipped for the learning process. But they must be given the opportunity to turn these often merely passive virtues into positive assets for the society in which they live.

These, then, are the common hopes that unite us — that as the shackles of prejudice and intolerance fall from our own limbs, we can together strive to identify and remove the impediments to human development everywhere. The mechanisms by which this great task is to be achieved provide the proper focus of this great Forum. I feel sure that women throughout the world who, like me, cannot be with you, join me now in sending you all our prayers and good wishes for a joyful and productive meeting. I thank you.

Keynote address

Winona LaDuke
Indigenous Women's Network; Seventh Generation Fund, United States

I am from the Mississippi Band of Anishinabeg of the White Earth Reservation in northern Minnesota, one of approximately 250,000 Anishinabeg people who inhabit the Great Lakes region of the North American continent.

Aniin indinawaymuginitok. Megwetch Chi-iwewag. Megwetch Ogitchitaikweway. Nindizhinikaz Beenaysayikwe, Makwa nin dodaem. Megwetch indinawaymugunitok.

I am greeting you in my language and thanking you, my sisters, for the honor of speaking with you today about the challenges facing women as we approach the 21st century.

A primary and central challenge impacting

women will be the distance we collectively as women and societies have artificially placed ourselves from our Mother the Earth, and the inherent environmental, social, health, and psychological consequences of colonialism and the subsequently rapid industrialization of our bodies and our nations. A centerpiece of this problem is the increasing lack of control we have over ourselves and our long-term security. This situation must be rectified through the laws of international institutions such as the United Nations and also through the policies, laws, and practices of our nations, our communities, our states, and ourselves.

The situation of Indigenous women, as a part of Indigenous peoples, we believe, is a magnified version of the critical juncture we find ourselves in as peoples, and the problems facing all women and our future generations as we struggle for a better world. This conflict is manifested in the loss of control over decision-making, loss of human security, militarism, the globalization of the economy, the further marginalization of women, increasing intolerance, and the forced commodification and homogenization of culture through the media.

It is a very great honor as a young mother of two to be invited to speak to you sisters today — women who have great courage and commitment, women who are peers and leaders and who, like myself, are the mothers of our nations.

The Earth is our Mother. From her we get our life and our ability to live. It is our responsibility to care for our Mother, and in caring for our Mother, we care for ourselves. Women, all females, are the manifestation of Mother Earth in human form. We are her daughters, and in my cultural instructions: Minobimaatisiiwin, we are to care for her. I am taught to live in respect for Mother Earth. In Indigenous societies, we are told that Natural Law is the highest law, higher than the laws made by nations, states, municipalities, and the World Bank. We are told that one would do well to live in accordance with Natural Law, with that of our Mother, and in respect for the Mother Earth of our relations — *indinawaymujgunitook.*

One hundred years ago, one of our great leaders, Chief Seattle, stated: "What befalls the Earth befalls the People of the Earth." And that is the reality of today, and the situation of the status of women, and the status of Indigenous women and Indigenous peoples.

While I am from one nation of Indigenous peoples, there are millions of Indigenous peoples worldwide. An estimated 500 million people are Indigenous people — or some 5,000 nations of Indigenous peoples in the world today. We are the Cordillera, the Maori of New Zealand, we are in East Timor, we are the Wara Wara of Australia, the Lakota, the Tibetans, the peoples of Hawaii, New Caledonia, and many other nations. Indigenous peoples: we are not populations, not minority groups; we are peoples, we are nations of peoples. Under international law we meet the criteria of nation states, having a common economic system, language, territory, history, culture, and governing institutions. Despite this fact, Indigenous nations are not allowed to participate in the United Nations.

Nations of Indigenous peoples are not, by and large, represented at the United Nations. Most decisions today are made by the 180 or so member states of the United Nations. Those states, by and large, have been in existence for 200 years or less, while most nations of Indigenous peoples, with few exceptions, have been in existence for thousands of years. Ironically, there would likely be little argument in this room that most decisions made in the world today are actually made by some of the 47 transnational corporations and their international financiers whose annual income is larger than the gross national product of many countries of the world.

This is the centerpiece of the problem. Decision-making is not done by those who are affected by those decisions, people who live on the land, but by corporations with an interest that is entirely different from that of the land, or the people, or the women of the land. This brings forth a fundamental question. What gives these corporations like Conoco, Shell, Exxon, Diashawa, ITT, Rio Tinto Zinc, and the World Bank a right which supersedes or is superior to my human right to live on my land, or that of my family, my community, my nation, our nations, and us as women? What law gives that right to them? Not any law of the

Creator or of Mother Earth. Is that right contained within their wealth, which is historically acquired immorally, unethically, through colonialism, imperialism, and paid for with the lives of millions of people and species of plants and entire ecosystems? They should have no such right. And we clearly, as women and as Indigenous peoples, demand and will recover that right, that right of determining our destiny and the destiny of our future generations.

The origins of this problem lie with the predator-prey relationship that industrial society has developed with the Earth and subsequently the people of the Earth. This same relationship exists vis-a-vis women. We collectively find that we are often in the role of the prey to a predator society, whether for sexual discrimination, exploitation, sterilization, absence of control over our bodies, or being the subjects of repressive laws and legislation in which we have no voice. This occurs on an individual level but, equally and more significantly, on a societal level. It is also critical to point out at this time that most matrilineal societies — societies in which governance and decision-making are largely controlled by women — have been obliterated from the face of the Earth by colonialism and industrialization. The only matrilineal societies that exist in the world today are those of Indigenous nations. We are the remaining matrilineal societies, yet we also face obliteration.

On a worldwide scale and in North America, Indigenous societies historically, and today, remain in a predator-prey relationship with industrial society and earlier to colonialism and imperialism. We are the peoples with the land — the land and the natural resources required for someone else's development program and amassing of wealth. The wealth of the United States, that nation which today determines much of the world's policy, was illegally expropriated from our lands.

Similarly the wealth of Indigenous peoples of South Africa, Central and South America, and Asia was taken for the industrial development of Europe, and later for settler states which came to occupy those lands. That relationship between development and underdevelopment adversely affected the status of our Indigenous societies and the status of Indigenous women.

Eduardo Galeano, the Latin American writer and scholar, has said, "In the colonial-to-neocolonial alchemy, gold changes to scrap metal and food to poison; we have become painfully aware of the morality of wealth which nature bestows and imperialism appropriates." Today, on a worldwide scale, we remain in the same situation as 100 years ago, only with less land and fewer people. Today, on a worldwide scale, 50 million Indigenous people live in the world's rain forests. A million Indigenous people are slated to be relocated for dam projects in the next decade (thanks to the World Bank), from the Narmada Project in India to the Three Gorges Dam Project here in China to the James Bay Hydro Electric Project in northern Canada. Almost all atomic weapons which have been detonated in the world are also detonated on the lands or waters of Indigenous peoples, most clearly evidenced here in China, and in the Pacific with France's obscene proposal to detonate atomic weapons this upcoming month, in Mururoa. What exactly gives France the right to a French Polynesia, I have to ask?

This situation is mimicked in the North American context. Today, over 50 percent of our remaining lands are forested, and both Canada and the United States continue aggressive clear-cutting policies on our land. Over two-thirds of the uranium resources in the United States, and similar figures for Canada, are on Indigenous lands, as is one-third of all low-sulphur coal resources. We have huge oil reserves on our reservations, and the Western Shoshone Nation has the dubious honor of being the most highly bombed nation in the world, with over 650 atomic weapons detonated there.

We also have two separate accelerated proposals to dump nuclear waste in our reservation lands, and similarly over 100 separate proposals to dump toxic waste on our reservation lands. We understand clearly the relationship between development for someone else and our own underdevelopment. We also understand clearly the relationship between the environmental impact of types of development on our lands and the health impact on our bodies as women. That is the crux of the problem.

We also understand clearly that the analysis of North versus South is an erroneous analysis. From our perspective, it is not an issue of the North dictating the economic policies of the South and consuming the South. Instead, it is a problem of the Middle consuming both the North and the South. That is our situation. Let me explain.

The rate of deforestation in the Brazilian Amazon is one acre every nine seconds. (Incidentally, the rate of extinction of Indigenous peoples in the Amazon is one nation of Indigenous people per year.) The rate of deforestation of the boreal forest of Canada is one acre every 12 seconds. Siberia, thanks to American corporations such as Weyerhauser, is not far behind. In all cases, Indigenous peoples are endangered. And there is frankly no difference between the impact in the North and the South.

Uranium mining has devastated a number of Indigenous communities in North America. Uranium mining in northern Canada has left over 120 million tons of radioactive waste. This amount represents enough material to cover the Trans-Canada Highway two meters deep across the country. Present production of uranium waste from Saskatchewan alone occurs at the rate of over one million tons annually. Since 1975, hospitalization for cancer, birth defects, and circulatory illnesses in that area have increased dramatically — between 123 and 600 percent. In other areas impacted by uranium mining, cancers and birth defects have increased to, in some cases, eight times the national average. The subsequent increases in radiation exposure of both the local and the larger North American population are also evidenced in broader incidences of cancer, such as breast cancer in North American women, which is significantly on the rise. There are no differences in the problems caused by radiation, whether it is in the Dene of northern Canada, the Laguna Pueblo people of New Mexico, or the people of Namibia.

The rapid increase in dioxin, organichlorides, PCBs (polychlorinated byphenols), pesticides, and other chemicals in the world as a result of industrialization has a devastating impact on Indigenous peoples, Indigenous women, and other women. Each year the world's paper industry discharges 600 to 3200 grams of dioxin equivalents into water, sludge, and paper products, according to U.S. Environmental Protection Agency statistics. This quantity is equal to the amount that would cause 58,000 to 294,000 cases of cancer every year, based on the Environmental Protections Agency's estimate of dioxin's carcinogenicity.

According to a number of recent studies, this has increased significantly the risk of breast cancer in women. Similarly, heavy metals and PCB contamination of Inuit women of the Hudson Bay region of the Arctic indicates that they have the highest levels of breast milk contamination in the world. In a 1988 study, Inuit women were found to have contamination levels up to 28 times higher than the average woman in Québec and ten times higher than that considered "safe" by the government.

It is also of great concern to our women and our peoples that polar bears in that region of the Arctic have such a high level of contamination from PCBs that they may be facing total sterility and coerced into extinction by early in the next cetury. As peoples who consider the bears to be our relatives, we are concerned also about our own ability to reproduce as a consequence of this level of bio-accumulation of toxics. We find that our communities, like those of our relative the bear, are in fact in danger of extinction. Consequently, it is clear to us that the problems also found in the South — like the export of chemicals and bio-accumulation of toxics — are also very much our problems, emanating from industrial society's mistreatment and disrespect for our Mother Earth, and subsequently are reflected in the devastation of the collective health and well-being of women.

In summary, I have presented these arguments for a purpose: to illustrate that these are very common issues for women, not only for Indigenous women, but for all women. What befalls our Mother Earth befalls her daughters, the women who are the mothers of our nations. Simply stated, if we can no longer nurse our children, if we can no longer bear children, and if our bodies themselves are wracked with poisons, we will have accomplished little in the way of determining our destiny or improving our conditions. And these problems reflected in our health and well-being also inherently result in a decline in the status of women, and are the result of a long set of historical processes that we as women will need to challenge if we are ultimately to be in charge of our own destinies, our own self-determination, and the future of our Earth, our Mother.

The reality is that all of these conditions — those emanating from the military and industrial devastation of our Mother the Earth and our own bodies and the land on which we live — are mimicked in social and development policies which affect all women.

It is our belief at the Indigenous Women's Network that:

• Women should not have to trade the ecosystem for running water, basic housing, health care, and basic human rights.

• Development projects, whether in the North or in the South, whether financed by the World Bank or by the coffers of Rio Tinto Zinc and Exxon, often replicate patriarchy and sexism and, by and large, cause the destruction of matrilineal governance structures and land tenure and cause a decline in the status of women. By denying us the basic land on which to live and the clean food and streams from which to eat, and instead offering us a wage economy in which privilege is often dictated by class, sex, and race, Indigenous women are frequently moved from a central role in their societies to the margins and refugee status of industrial society.

• The intellectual knowledge systems today often negate or deny the existence of and the inherent property rights of Indigenous people; and they negate or deny our cultural and intellectual knowledge by supplanting our knowledge system with industrial knowledge systems, calling us "primitive" while our medical knowledge, plants, and even genetic material are stolen (as in the Human Genome Project) by transnational corporations and international agencies. This situation affects Indigenous women as a part of our communities, but on a larger scale has affected most women.

• Subsequently, our women find that the basic right to control our bodies is impacted by all of the above, through development policies aimed at non-consensual or forced sterilization, medical testing, invasive genetic sampling, and absence of basic facilities and services that would guarantee us the right and ability to control the size of our families safely and willingly. It is also essential to preserve our rights to self-determination, control our bodies, and our own sexual orientation. Unfortunately, these rights remain impacted, and these same development policies often are based on tourism, which commodifies our bodies and cultures (Pacific and Native American as prime examples) and causes the same with women internationally.

Collectively, we must challenge this paradigm and this international arena. I call on you to support the struggle of Indigenous peoples of the world for recognition and to recognize that until all peoples have self-determination, no one will truly be free, free of the predator, and free to control our destiny. I ask you to look in the International Covenant on Civil and Political Rights, Part I, Article I, which provides that "all peoples have the right to self-determination." By virtue of that right, they may freely determine their political status and freely pursue their economic, social, and political development.

All peoples would be construed to mean that Indigenous peoples have the right to self-determination. And by virtue of that right, they may freely determine their political status and freely pursue their economic, social, and political development. Accord us the same rights as all other nations of peoples. And through that process, allow us to protect our ecosystems, their inherent biodiversity, human cultural diversity, and those matriarchal governments which remain in the world. And with the Unrepresented People's Organization (UNPO), we reaffirm that definition of self-determination provided in Article 1 of the International Covenant on Social, Economic, and Cultural Rights, further recognizing that the right to self-determination belongs equally to women and to men.

We believe that the right of all peoples to self-determination cannot be realized while women continue to be marginalized and prevented from becoming full participants in their respective societies. The human rights of women, like the human rights of Indigenous peoples, and our inherent rights to self-determination, are not issues exclusively within the domestic jurisdiction of states.

For further discussion of this, please see the international agreements and accords struck by hundreds of Indigenous nations, such as the Karioka Document and the Matatua Document.

Finally, while we may, here in the commonness of this Forum, speak of the common rights of all women and those fundamental human rights to self-determination, it is incumbent upon me to point out the fundamental inequalities of this situation so long as the predator continues, so long as the middle, the temperate countries of the world, continue to drive an increasing level of consumption and, frankly, continue to export both the technologies and the drive for this level of consumption to other countries of the world.

From the U.S. position, consider the following: The United States is the largest energy market in the world. The average American consumes seven times as many wood products per capita as anywhere else in the industrialized world, and overall that country consumes one-third of the world's natural resources. By comparison, Canada's per capita energy consumption is the highest in the world.

Levels of consumption in the industrial world drive destruction of the world's rain forest and the world's boreal forest, drive production of nuclear wastes and production of PCBs, dioxin, and other lethal chemicals that devastate the body of our Mother Earth and our bodies.

Unless we speak and take meaningful action to address these levels of consumption and the export of these technologies and levels of consumption (like the international market for nuclear reactors), we will never have any security for our individual human rights as Indigenous women and for our security as women.

Frankly, it is not that the women of the dominant society in so-called First World countries should have equal pay and equal status if that pay and status continue to be based on a consumption model which is not only unsustainable but also causes constant violation of the human rights of women and nations elsewhere in the world. It is essential to collectively struggle to recover our status as Daughters of the Earth. In that is our strength, in that is our security and the security of our Mother and our future generations. In that, we can ensure our security as the mothers of our nations.

Megwetch mi su go minuk megwetch.

II • Regional Perspectives

Opening remarks

Irene M. Santiago, Moderator
Executive Director, NGO Forum on Women '95

We felt that if we came here today and really looked at the strategies which have worked and not worked, in order to be able to plan our future actions, we would be more strategic and more focused. That is the reason for the plenaries, and that is the reason we decided to have the plenaries the way they are. It doesn't mean that at the end of this we are going to have a single unified action. I think that we are so diverse as NGOs that we cannot hope to have action agendas that are collective, but at least we will struggle to that end. We will struggle so that our action agendas come from having discussed the issues in a common way and having understood the issues in a common way, so that when we develop our responses we come from a common understanding of what the problems are. The process of decision-making is decentralized, but the process of getting to the action plans is strategic. This is the reason for the plenaries.

The reason for the plenaries is also that at this moment we need to start cutting across issue lines. We have dealt with many of our issues according to health, environment, education, peace, and human rights, but the forces that are coming at us are not categorized that way. The forces coming at need an integrated rather than an issue-by-issue approach.

What is different about our world today? What is different about women? We often read that the world has changed, and yet it has remained the same. We have gains, we have awareness, we have become more efficient agents in putting our issues on the public agenda. For example, ten years ago in Nairobi we were just starting to talk about violence against women. Who would ever have thought that violence against women would now be on the United Nations agenda? Who would ever have thought that we would have advanced so far in the struggle to make women's rights be seen as human rights, something we now take for granted? Who would now dare talk about sexual harassment as a private issue? Who would now dare talk about women as poor credit risks? I think we have come a long way.

But we all know that one of the reasons we are here is that we are in great danger of losing our autonomy. The autonomy we have gained and fought for, we are going to lose if we do not now face up to where we are and how we can respond to the forces that would take that autonomy away.

What remains are two big issues that we have not really dealt with and that we need to work on for the next however many years: poverty and power. These regional perspectives that we are going to hear today will deal with those issues. The plenaries we are going to have during the next two days will look into the changes that have happened over the past ten years — changes in the political, economic, and cultural contexts of the human community. It is very very important that we have the following analysis so that we can get to the root causes of the problems.

I remember that in Nairobi in 1985 it seemed as if the obstacles were very clear. If you want to use the nice word, you call them *obstacles*; if you want to be more realistic, you say *enemies*. We did not fear obstacles or enemies. In Nairobi we used words like *patriarchy, capitalism, imperialism*. Do you remember? Spotting the enemies was very clear.

How is it in 1995? This is why we are here for the plenaries: to hear analyses about these forces so that can we have a better understanding and then name the enemies. It is an important act to name the enemies. After we have gone through the analyses, we will hear about the strategies that women all over the world have used in order to respond to the global forces; that way we can find which strategies have worked, or we can find some new synergy among the earlier strategies that have not worked, and so we can become more effective.

One of the things that is very important at the end of this Forum is a discussion of the institutional mechanisms and international forces that are needed to move us from here today. Two other very important element are the plenaries on responsibility and accountability, systems for national governments and institutions but also for NGOs.

In the end, there are three things we have to remember, three things we want to put on the public agenda and that we have to grapple with in the next decade or so: poverty, power, post-Beijing. If we can get our hands on which strategies can be useful in this task, these plenaries will have really contributed a lot to the advancement of women worldwide.

The forces shaping women's lives

Gita Sen
Development Alternatives with Women for a New
Era (DAWN); Indian Institute of Management,
India

Friends, sisters, brothers, at 9:15 this morning I saw a solid wall of women's bodies, trying to get through to this end of this hall. I realized to myself that women can do anything. Why are we afraid of globalization, fundamentalisms, and patriarchies? When we can handle the situation of having a plenary hall for 36,000 women that can hold only 1,500, we can truly do anything.

I have come to you today to speak from two perspectives: as a member of DAWN, the Southern Women's Network, Development Alternatives

with Women for a New Era, and as someone who lives and works in the Asia-Pacific region to bring a regional perspective to the global issues being discussed here.

Let me first speak from the broader global perspective of DAWN. DAWN began its journey in the search for alternative development around the time of the Nairobi Conference in 1985; at that time, our main agenda was to identify those forces that to us seemed key in shaping the character of women's lives in the world. We identified three.

The first — and to us most important — was the development model, which seemed to place much higher priority on economic growth over human well-being, regardless of the cost and the quality of human lives. Second, we identified what were clearly the growing crises of debt, of food, of fuel and water, and of livelihood that were resulting from that development model. And women — placed on the crossroads between economic activity, production for income, and the care of human beings — inevitably found themselves on the horns of a dilemma caused by that crisis. Third, our purpose and our approach was to determine what kind of vision we could provide. What did we think the future should look like, given this identification of forces?

Our vision was one, not of equality within that government mainstream development paradigm, but of the fundamental need to change the development approach itself so that it would better serve the interests of most women, and of men, especially the poor, the exploited, and the marginalized. The struggle for equality and for gender justice had to be argued then and must indeed be now. So we related to the struggle to transform the dominant paradigm of economic development and of economic growth.

In the ten years since the Nairobi Conference, we know that the forces of globalization have grown, if anything, even stronger and much more cumbersome in our lives. In DAWN, we have recognized that these forces contain old elements as well as new. The old elements include the unabated and seemingly endless crisis of livelihood experienced by poor people and ordinary people everywhere, North and South; of economic and political insecurity; of great and growing impoverishment; of environmental degradation; and of continuing violence based on gender, class, race, and caste for many in the world. We know that what is old and continues includes the growing marginalization and privatization of the basic services essential to enable human beings to reproduce and care for themselves in a dignified and humane manner. We know that these old forces still exist. The reason they are becoming even more powerful is the increasing inequality among peoples, between North and South, within the geographical North, and within the South, which have been growing even more and more rapidly during, and as a consequence of, the processes of globalization that we are now in the middle of.

What is new? — and by the way, when I say "new" I do not mean that these forces have appeared out of nowhere. They are the forces, in fact, of development, but they have been newly co-opted, and we have to come to terms with them much more carefully than we had to, say, ten years ago. Most important, I think, is the speed of the globalization process itself, and its indications, not only for economics, but in the political sphere, in cultural life, and in our personal lives. Technological revolutions in microeconomics and in biotechnology have made it possible for transnational corporations to increase their scope and their range of action and control in a far greater way and to a greater extent than they ever could before. They have led, from women's point of view, to a much more flexible use of women's labor than has ever been the case.

Women are pulled into the labor force, women are thrown out of the labor force, and the use of female labor in this process of globalization has become far more flexible and complex than ever. Women move across borders. Women are drawn into export-processing activities. Women are in agriculture and in electronics workshops. Women are migrants working far away from home for many years at a time. Women are drawn into sex tourism, which is not some underground activity but is promoted by governments for reasons of export earnings. The use of sex and of female labor in this much more complex manner are an integral part of the globalization process.

A second very important part is what is happening in the realms of global trade and finance. The wider reach and the greater instability of global trade and finance have meant that there is far greater pressure on governments to earn foreign exchange and to make sure that they follow all the dictates of international institutions so that they will not fall into financial crisis. The recent case of Mexico has shown us the consequences and how they deprive people's lives.

The third is that this globalization is not an even process; it is a highly *un*even process. It has reshaped and is reshaping traditional economic alignments and group dynamics across the world in very different ways. And one thing of very major concern for us, particularly those of us coming from the South, is the fact that the Third World — as we used to call it in those simple days of Nairobi — now finds itself almost incapable of acting in global economic fora in a concerted manner. The unevenness of this globalization means that parts of the South, such as the region I come from, include some countries that are growing at rates much faster than anyone has historically seen, as well as other countries in which dire poverty and low rates of growth coexist.

What are the consequences for people, for women, in these different situations? They are not the same; we have commonalities, but there are also differences we have to come to terms with because women on the ground have to grapple with those differences in their daily lives.

And the fourth thing is a very important force I have already alluded to: the undermining of the economic role of governments, of states, so that the state is unable anymore to do even the minimal things it used to do, such as providing people with the public services of health, of education, of clean water, and of sanitation. This has been done under the aegis of structural adjustment programs developed by institutions that are the storm troopers of the globalization process, and they have broken the capacity of governments to impact this process. But this undermining of state capacity and state economic growth has not undermined the repressive capacity of the state, which continues to repress its people — particularly when they attack the forces of globalization — and this, as you know, affects our daily lives across the world.

The next force we are seeing is new forms of violence. The cold war has ended, and yet what has this left in its place? Attention has been shifted to the South, and governments that can no longer provide even minimal services of health and education are holding onto and even increasing their military expenditures, because of the tremendous push of global arms industries. Another aspect of this violence is an economy in which there are increasing and alarming proportions of drugs, arms, and money laundering, thus changing the political culture of many countries in very problematic ways. And the third aspect of this violence — which we women know only too well — is the growing incidence of gender violence and the connected violence in communities, on the streets, by the state, and in our homes.

The penultimate force is the resurgence of patriarchal elements and the rise of various fundamentalisms and patriarchal interpretations of religion. Throughout history, men have fought wars through controlling women's bodies, women's rights, and women's lives. Yet we have survived. We are here in Beijing to say to the world that we *will* survive.

The other side of fundamentalism is the global hegemony that controls our media and culture, leading to an objectification of women's bodies, sexuality, and lives. This is the other side of those who would send women back to the dark ages. However, we also know about globalization from our capacity for survival. I am told that somewhere in the town of Huairou is a place you can buy or rent a cellular telephone, which can make it possible — despite the enormous logistical problems — for organizations to communicate with and influence what governments do in Beijing during this Conference. Women can turn globalization to our advantage because of the creativity and flexibility we are all used to using in our lives.

But more important is the fact that we as women are part of building the institutions of civil society that are heard across the world. We have seen the experience, understanding, and capacity of women's organizations, not only at local, community, and national levels but also at the global level. In one UN conference after another, we women have asserted ourselves and our capacity for organization, our capacity for bringing our issues and passion to the center of the world. There is global pressure on states and organizations to become more open, more transparent, and more accountable.

In China, where we are today, we are seeing a country undergoing tremendous economic growth and linking itself to that globalization process, but we are also seeing growing inequality, a growing cost in public services, and growing gender inequality as women become the last hired and the first fired. One of the fastest growing industries in China, I am told, is the cosmetics industry, as Chinese women are made to believe that their color and their faces are not appropriate to the global marketplace. But we know that these extremes and contradictions of globalization are present in Asia in their most intense form, as we see when we look at the extremes within countries or we compare countries in South Asia with those in East and Southeast Asia. Economic growth is to a great extent built upon the unrequited and unrecognized labor of women, if we look at Japan and Korea, if we look at Thailand, if we look at a number of countries in the region.

Finally, let me say what I think are the three crucial aspects of our agenda in the context of globalization. I think we need to continue to challenge capitalism, the major force unleashed by globalization. I think we need to work to transform our governments and our states, not to destroy these institutions but to transform them so that they become more accountable to us. And I think we need to continue to build the institutions of civil society of which we are a part.

I would like to say to governments, to agencies, and to those forces that want to push women back into the dark ages: We are here, we are everywhere, we are watching, and we will not go away.

The regional contribution to the global future: A Latin American and Caribbean perspective

Virginia Vargas
Flora Tristan, Peru

It is not easy to speak of Latin America and the Caribbean; the reality of the region is one of contrast and nuances.

It is not easy to speak of a region at a moment when there is globalization of the economy and of culture, in which every region is part of a larger scenario. Nevertheless, we wish to emphasize the uniqueness of this region and its possible contribution to the construction of new ethical, political, and social frameworks for the coexistence of our citizens. The NGO Forum must try to maintain a balance between the previous decade and looking toward the future; it must discuss and propose strategies which will contribute to the eradication of discrimination, violence, and exclusion. This Forum must also serve to draw up mechanisms to guarantee the strengthening and sustainability of the achievements women have made in the last two decades.

Governance, political participation, and citizenship

The sociopolitical situation and the conditions of governance of the countries of Latin America and the Caribbean have varied considerably in the last few decades. Some countries have emerged from dictatorships and face the difficult task of building democracy in a context where neo-liberal policies are being implemented, aggravating the inequality between men and women.

Other countries are facing processes of modernization characterized by authoritarianism. The increasing complexity of societies and the challenges of building democracy in our countries, a shared objective of our region, demand a rethinking of the relationship between state and society. We must also consider ways of facilitating the creation of vast public spaces in which the various social groups can identify their needs, voice their demands, confront other groups with their proposals, in short, exercise their citizenship.

We need to think about a new state, a new institution, which is more efficient and more transparent, open to all citizens, and more capable of regulation and intervention to ensure equality of opportunity for all. It is equally necessary to generate social conditions in which the different groups can affirm their identity, develop as social and political individuals, and affirm their citizenship.

Our region has suffered long periods of political, social, and economic crisis, periods in which women have played an important role in the survival and maintenance of the social fabric. It was the work and the organization of women that allowed many homes to come out of extreme poverty; the networks generated by women were those that counteracted the tendencies towards social fragmentation.

Moreover, the eruption of the women's movement in the region has been one of the most subversive and creative phenomena of the region in this century. Its creative force has changed the conscience and horizons of society and politics. It has contributed to putting new themes on the public agenda that not only favor women but also contribute to society in general.

These new themes — such as reproductive and sexual rights, domestic violence, the feminization of poverty, the importance of recognizing and respecting diversity, as well as the implementation of mechanisms for positive affirmation of excluded groups — are breaking the rigid division between public and private, between productive and reproductive. They are breaking the abstract universality of the concept of rights, and they are allowing social subjectivity to be seen as a central aspect of the construction of democracy. One of the fundamental achievements is that women have been able to demonstrate that their problems are of general interest and are linked to the aspirations of the progressive forces toward democracy, at the same time that they confront, broaden, and enrich them.

In this decade, some women have gained positions of intermediate power; others have gained personal and collective confidence and assertiveness. All women have become more visible, and this has increased our capacity to intervene at state levels responsible for equal opportunities for men and women.

In this decade, too, we have combined our strategy for the struggle with a minimum threshold for exercising our citizenship and the power of expressing our specific demands; we have gained the right to have rights by forming ourselves into a pressure group which has enriched considerably the concepts of citizenship and democracy.

Nevertheless, we must remember the big differences that exist among the various groups of women from Latin America and the Caribbean because of cultural differences and wide social inequality. If we cannot count on permanent channels of communication among women themselves and among women and public institutions at various levels, we run the risk that the benefits gained will be concentrated among particular groups of women, increasing the inequality among them. At the same time, the lack of channels of communication makes those women in positions of intermediate power more vulnerable to being co-opted by the logic of the existing power structure.

For these reasons, for us the concept of citizenship is not reduced to political participation in the formal sphere. It is a more complex concept, which starts by accepting and developing civil, economic, social, cultural, political, reproductive, and sexual rights. It sees institutional structures and the state as emerging from, and in the service of, civil society.

The tasks that we women face in this scenario can be summarized basically as consolidating our position as social actors; continuing to generate channels of communication and networks among women to avoid isolation; deepening our growing tendency to be a force monitoring the transparency and transformation of the society; and above all, coordinating our efforts not only to intervene in the management of public and state institutions but also to create conditions for the growth, strengthening, and reproduction of a vast number of women capable of placing on the social agenda new themes and problems that society and institutional structures are not yet capable of seeing. For example, related to the global Platform for Action

which comes out of this Conference, we should monitor the fulfillment of what was approved and continue the struggle for what is not approved, creating spaces to identify needs, interests, and new rights, even though they may not necessarily be institutionalized — creating spaces and strength to convert some of our social demands into public demands if we wish or need to.

Peace, human safety, militarization, violence, and poverty

The end of the cold war has not meant greater opportunities for peace nor the resolution of old tensions, as had been expected. New conflicts have emerged, based on underlying tensions of a nationalistic, religious and cultural nature.

Social unrest, internal armed conflicts, wars across frontiers, and continuing measures of economic strangulation that belong to the era of the cold war, as in the case of Cuba, are taking place in a scenario characterized by processes of social, economic, and deep political change.

Expenditure on national defense and internal security in the region has been maintained, and in some countries has increased, to the detriment of investment in human development. The doctrines of national security, militarism, police culture, and violence as a solution to conflicts continue to be strong and restrict democratic initiatives that propose new forms of peaceful, negotiated, and significant solutions of the conflicts spanning the region.

In this case, we cannot refrain from mentioning sexual abuse and violence against women, which is a constant in daily life, aggravated by the tensions of militarization and internal war.

Armed conflicts have brought harm and specific risks to women. Crimes committed have remained unpunished. A majority of displaced people and refugees are mainly indigenous women. The measures adopted by governments and agencies to deal with displacement have not considered the specific situation of women. At the same time, women have been ignored and not considered in the processes of peace negotiations.

The restructuring of the world economy, the important transformations of the productive structure and forms of management of the economy, greater access to information, and the massive globalization of the mass media have not been translated into a greater social distribution of resources or greater levels of social equality.

Our region displays the dramatic record of having one of the worst indices of distribution of wealth maintained in a vast population in a situation of extreme poverty and social vulnerability. Instead of speaking of pockets of poverty in our region, we should speak about pockets of extreme wealth. The degree of social exclusion in this way presents a threat to peace and social stability. The link between poverty and wealth could be social violence and the shadow of internal armed conflicts.

The challenges of technological development and of economic restructuring find us lacking in human capital, which is particularly evident in the case of the development of women's potential. They are mostly absent in economic activities, and they make up the majority of the groups which show the highest incidence of illiteracy. Women's access to the labor market and the way in which they are incorporated into it can be negatively affected.

Finally, in these times, private initiative, the desire to achieve, and personal success are presented as contradictory to the development of solidarity and social networks. This puts at great risk the social activities already under way and the possibilities of counteracting the increasing social fragmentation and weakening of the social units.

The issues of women in economic restructuring can be summarized as:

• creating conditions of equal access to opportunities opened up by economic restructuring, such as knowledge, technology, and the flexibility of human resources;

• preventing women from being located in the most precarious, unstable, and informal sectors of the economy; and

• enhancing the capacity and creation of women's links and networks of solidarity in order to transfer them to the social fabric, so that initiative and economic success should not be contrary to attitudes of solidarity and the creation of communities and spaces for collective interests.

To reinforce this, we women can also be key elements in creating new ways of integrating production and reproduction: for example, creating new ways of using time — that is, how to use time for production, recreation, to take care of ourselves, for pleasure, for personal growth, etc. This is the fundamental contribution of women.

Conservatism

In the face of the secularization and modernization of societies, conservative forces have emerged which are calling for a return to the past, to the system of ascribed roles and status, ignoring the right to development and the personal and collective autonomy of individuals. These forces are resistant to change.

The old order has broken down. The new order is not emerging. There is a breakdown of standards and an urgency to create new and more just forms of social coexistence; and this is creating uncertainty and doubt. We have to insist on the creation of these standards to avoid the temptation of a return to the past in the search for social protection.

Conservatism also confronts the transformative power of the women's movement. Conservative forces try to impose values and define the place of women with arguments claiming that the domestic sphere is the only natural one.

Specifically, sectors of the Catholic church hierarchy are carrying out a series of campaigns and developing strategies to prevent the recognition of the sexual and reproductive rights of women. A culture of guilt, fear, and sin claims to be a possible culture for our people. They are trying to erase the difference between church and state by trying to convert states into confessionals, imprinting public policy with religious dogma.

The intolerance of the conservative forces for diversity shows that it is impossible for them to recognize others as equals and, therefore, as individuals with rights. Women, including indigenous peoples, young women, the disabled, lesbians, and those who are different from the norms, face violent situations and are condemned to exercise their citizenship in an even more restricted way.

Media, culture, and globalization

When a woman from a favela in Rio says, "I would rather have a TV set than a refrigerator; there is always something on TV," or when a Peruvian peasant community decides to purchase a parabolic antenna in order to acquire access to national television, they are simply pointing out the relationship to a means of communication that links them to one of the forms of the global world through a language of images, ideas, and messages and permits them to know what is happening in the world at the same time that a New York businessman does.

To be present by means of a satellite is to be able to communicate with millions of people coming from different walks of life, from different economic conditions, with nothing but a TV set in common.

Monopolized and globalized media such as mass electronic media (computers, videos, radio) create a broad new sphere which can and must be disputed by the new democratic and pluralist social forces globally. This is what we have been doing before and during the Beijing Conference. Undoubtedly, it is impossible to imagine our success without counting on our own electronic media and our impact on and within the monopolized media.

How can we achieve a presence in this space which creates opinion, which orients citizens globally, and which links the local to the global? How can we succeed in stopping the unfavorable image of women projected by the mass media? How can we turn our demands, proposals, and reflections into news? How can we enter an industry which has predetermined models and interests? How can we manage to keep all these questions continuously presently in our daily actions?

We have to comprehend the media. They are not simple tools but spaces within and through which "world visions" are constantly being created, as are our collective self-images, our ideals, dreams, and hopes. We women are no victims of soap operas, wars, and violations: we are able to reprocess them and to use them for our occasionally subversive purposes. Women's movements lack conventional resources, prestige, and power, but reaffirm the development of new self-images, ideals, dreams, and hopes.

We must recognize this new globalized cultural arena as an arena that is more favorable to us, more open than others to debate and new influences. It is through the use of these tools and the appropriation of these spaces that the women's movement will be able to influence the global citizenship.

Global forces and their impact on women: An African perspective

Winnie Byanyima
Women's Caucus, Constituent Assembly, Uganda

It is a great privilege for me to share this platform at the opening plenary session of the NGO Forum on Women, Beijing 1995, with my eminent sisters Gita Sen, Virginia Vargas, Charlotte Bunch, and Irene Santiago. I bring you greetings and very warm wishes from the people of Mbarara town, whom I represent in Uganda's Constituent Assembly.

"As a woman I have no country. As a woman I want no country. As a woman my country is the whole world." These words of Virginia Woolf, from her 1938 work *Three Guineas,* influence my perception of the global trends which are shaping humanity's journey into the new millennium. There is no doubt at all: the world is going through a transformation. We are living in a rapidly changing world order, characterized by political and economic uncertainties. One thing we are becoming certain about, though, is that ecologically and economically we shall swim or sink together. In the interdependent world of the 21st century, neither individuals nor nations will be able to prosper in isolation. We all must work together, or none of us is likely to work at all.

Obstacles to peace and human security

Having been a battleground of the cold war, Africa received the news of its end with a great sigh of relief. During the cold war, the interests of African women and men were submerged by superpower rivalry. From Somalia to Ethiopia, from South Africa to Mozambique, from Namibia to Angola, and all over the continent, it became possible to end superpower wars, and it looked as though we could begin to address African problems. South Africa was liberated, bringing to an end the African struggle against colonialism. We salute Nelson Mandela and the African National Congress! We salute our sister Winnie Mandela for her leadership, courage, and resilience in the struggle for the freedom and dignity of the African people! The people of Mozambique, Angola, Ethiopia, and Eritrea are reconstructing societies which suffered the ravages of superpower conflicts. After 20 years of war and hundreds of thousands of lives lost, Jonas Savimbi has agreed to stop the war in Angola and take a cabinet post. But an Angolan woman somewhere still pays the price when she goes to the field to fetch firewood and gets hit by one of Savimbi's land-mines.

The prospects for peace are real, yet women and men in Africa are still victims of ugly internal armed conflicts. A genocide of unseen brutality wiped out one million people in Rwanda. Women and children continue to live in refugee camps and to suffer the consequences of wars they do not understand and would rather do without. Women and children constitute 80 percent of all refugees worldwide. Despite being the poorest region in the world, sub-Saharan Africa spends $8 billion on armaments, and the children go without food, basic education, health, and clothing. What a shame!

The peace we had hoped for after the cold war was not to be. Suppressed conflicts erupted as soon as it ended. Ethnic nationalism, the quest for national self-determination, competition over scarce natural resources, and lust for power by some men have fueled internal conflicts. It takes two to tango. Wherever there is a war in Africa, there is an arms supplier and an African buyer. Fearing job losses, some industrial countries are encouraging the manufacture and export of weapons to potential trouble spots. It is our duty to press harder for world disarmament, and to focus our attention on the new forms of conflict, which

are mostly within national borders and which occur mainly in the developing countries and have high civilian casualties. Rape is often used as a means of waging these wars. Women must demand full participation in conflict-resolution mechanisms at all levels, including the global level. We must pose these questions: Where is the peace dividend? Why is it not being invested in women's health and children's education? Who is making profits from the manufacture and sale of weapons?

Governance

Democracy, as an ideology and a system of governance, has swept throughout the world, beginning in Latin America in the early 1980s and catching on in Africa from 1989 onward. The transition from one-party states and military dictatorships to democratically elected political systems presents African women with new challenges and opportunities. When the male political elite decide to split one party into several parties and to form a multiparty system, ordinary women and men do not have to get excited. They do not necessarily get democracy. Multiparty democracy can be for rich and powerful men and can operate in much the same way as military juntas and one-party systems — entrenching power and privilege for small cliques, marginalizing the majority of people and excluding them from decision-making. The transition to democracy can be meaningful to women only if it opens up more political space to them so that they, too, can be actors and not mere spectators or victims of decisions made by a few men.

The challenge before us, then, is to extend the call for democracy and accountability to all levels of decision-making and to increase the participation of all people — men and women, rich and poor, urban and rural — in any forum that makes decisions which affect their lives and the environment. The challenge is to extend and entrench the rule of law and respect for human rights by *all* actors, including the state. The challenge is to build and strengthen civil society in Africa so that it balances the power of the state and the free market. What is the use of a free press when only one-half of the people can read and write? Of what use is a ballot paper to a sick and hungry woman?

Can she eat it? Building the capabilities of people, especially the most marginalized, by providing them with basic health and education and by organizing at the grass roots for effective political participation, is and has to remain the focus of our action as we enter the 21st century. We *must* transform the structures and culture of governance. We *must* redefine democracy and claim it for women, for the poor, for the disabled, for all marginalized people.

Across Africa, women in politics are forming cross-party alliances and broad coalitions with women's NGOs — and with the youth, people with disabilities, and other groups — to demand change, to demand that their concerns be put on the political agenda. They are demanding affirmative action to redress historic imbalances and to support women candidates in elections. This dynamic movement is gaining more and more power and influence over governments and international decision-making organs such as the United Nations. The appointment of Dr. Speciosa Wandira Kazibwe to the post of Vice-President of Uganda, the first woman to hold such a senior position in Africa, was a response to the momentum for change. Barriers are being broken. Attitudes about women in leadership are changing.

The democratization process in Africa is fragile. We are emerging from a long history of feudalism, slavery, and colonialism, and have just embraced the idea of democracy. Our attempts to build democracy are frustrated by the limited resources available for experiments and the high price our people pay for failure. The struggle for democracy in Africa should be supported morally and materially, and above all, it should be understood in its historical context.

The rise of conservatism in its various forms

Political parties in Africa have tended to form around identity issues such as ethnicity and religion because of the absence of clear social classes. Ethnicity is eating away at the heart of the young African states and is undermining nation-building efforts. In all this, women are not faring well. Cultural revival is often interpreted to mean reversing the gains women have made in the past by resorting to patriarchal structures in the family and community. Ethnic platforms and traditional values are increasingly being used to gain political office, making the political atmosphere more hostile to women.

Demobilized and disillusioned by one-party and military dictatorships, frustrated by the economic mismanagement of the 1970s and 1980s, some people have made religion their rallying point for political change. Religious fundamentalism is a serious threat to peace on the African continent. Let us, women of the world, stand in solidarity with the women of Algeria who are at the front lines of the struggle against fanaticism. Let us not fear to express our solidarity with all the people of Africa and other regions who are resisting religious bigotry. Fundamentalism in Africa is trying to push us back to forms of autocracy — and as women leaders, pointing the way to the 21st century, we have a duty to exert our collective will and ensure that democracy prevails.

Of course, conservatives are right in observing that the excesses of modern society have brought about a deterioration in spiritual values and the disintegration of the family unit. In Africa we believe in families. The world is in need of a cultural and spiritual renewal, there can be no doubt, but this renewal cannot be found in narrow, rigid interpretations of long-discarded dogmas.

Globalization of the economy and the information and technological revolution

The world is witnessing a rapid expansion of trade in goods and services. National frontiers are becoming less and less important as international linkages in trade and finance intensify, made possible by advances in information and communications technologies. International trade is shifting from primary commodities, the main exports of African countries, in favor of high-technology products and services. Success in the global market is measured by how much a country can attract direct foreign investment. Although developing countries are increasing their share of total foreign direct investments, most of these investments go to ten countries. Africa's share in 1992 was a marginal 6 percent of the total to developing countries. Unlike other regions, Africa's debt burden has been increasing. So cynical and ironical is the debt situation that Africa, the poorest region in the world, pays out more to the World Bank and the International Monetary Fund than it receives. The benefits of a globalized economy have not accrued to African countries — at least not yet. The general picture remains one of stagnation and even regression. All the evidence shows that the gaps between rich and poor are widening. Whichever way you may wish to look at it, Africa is excluded from the global knowledge-based economy. It is those who have (technology, information, and capital) who are getting more. As for those with less, even the little they have is being lost. This is the global free market, and all — weak and strong, old and young — must compete, and moreover, they must compete equally. From a social point of view, protection is usually given to the weak and the young, but that is not the logic of the global free market.

Many studies now confirm what most of us see daily with our eyes. Structural adjustment and economic recovery programs, the prescribed means of entering the global economy, are hurting the lives of poor women and children. They are undermining women's health, cutting children's education, and eroding the incomes of families. The girl child is a victim of adjustment. Hard economic times combine with a culture of discrimination to make her more vulnerable than she already is. Women workers are insecure in the private sector, which is being courted by governments and which prefers to employ men in the traditional industries characteristic of Africa. The questions we must ask are: Who designs adjustment programs? Who is supposed to benefit? How and when? Are free markets really free? Are they free to women and the poor? How global is the global economy? Who is participating in it? We must not be sacrificed; we must strategize to have a say in shaping economic policies for our countries and for the world.

Media, culture, and communication

Technological advancement is most dramatically seen in the means of communication now found in the world. One might call the technologies of communication the technologies of intrusion. CNN brings the world to us even if we do not want to receive it. Some of it is unquestionably good (the art and natural beauty of our lands); some is questionable (the commercialization of everything); and some of it is clearly negative (the vulgar coarseness of much of what Hollywood chooses to call entertainment). There must be a middle position between free access to all, both the coarse and the sublime, and the distortions of government control of the media. Can we penetrate the airwaves and infuse them with feminist values so that they transmit what is good and wholesome? Can we all ride the electronic superhighway?

Conclusion

The world is now convinced, more than ever before, of global interdependence. Environmental threats, such as the emission of greenhouse gases and deforestation, affect climate all over the world. Globalization has increased prosperity for many, but the gaps between the rich and poor within and between nations have widened. Between 1960 and 1991, the richest 20 percent increased their share of global income from 70 percent to 85 percent. During the same period the poorest 20 percent declined from 2.3 percent to a minuscule 1.4 percent. Today more than three-quarters of global income belongs to only one-quarter of the world's population, mostly in the North, according to the UNDP *Human Development Report 1994*. Poverty, pollution, drugs, terrorism, AIDS, and other problems flow across national frontiers, threatening human security everywhere in the world. The emerging world order, therefore, calls for a new system of global governance[1] that is democratic and engendered and that protects the interests of poor people in order to ensure global human security. The global system of governance should be balanced by a global civil society that draws its vision and strength from the grass roots. It should oppose violence as a means of resolving conflict or effecting change. It should seek a feminist transformation of all structures of governance. The women's movement is the nucleus, the heartbeat of a global civil society which can shape and balance a new system of global governance.

Indeed, there is need for balance in seeking global solutions to the global problems. Europe in the last 50 years has graphically demonstrated that the extremes of both left and right do not work. The individual must have the freedom to choose, while collectively we actively seek solutions for all of us. Women and men are not in mortal combat over roles, rights, and resources. Neither should nations be. We need to work together. As an African woman and a woman of the world, I seek the empowerment of women to benefit all members of society, especially the weakest.

We are all here because in one form or another, we are actively involved in the political process. Politics are much discredited in the world today because of corruption, fanaticism, autocracy, and elitism. The challenge before us, on the eve of the 21st century, is to transform the nature of politics, locally and globally, and to challenge the dominant paradigm of development. It is to put people at the centre of politics and development. It is to give all people — women, men, and children — freedom: the freedom to choose, the freedom to participate, and the freedom to live full and happy lives. We have the capacity and the will. We can do it.

Note

1. The Stockholm Initiative on Global Security and Governance. *Common Responsibility in the 1990s.* 22 April 1992.

Through women's eyes: Global forces facing women in the 21st century

Charlotte Bunch
Center for Women's Global Leadership,
Douglass College, United States

This panel has confirmed my sense that we are indeed a global movement, because although we are all supposed to speak from the perspective of our own regions, my co-panelists have already given much of my speech. But I am not going to pass up the opportunity to reinforce what they said and to add how I view this critical juncture from what we used to call the belly of the beast — Europe and North America. This Conference is occurring at a critical juncture in time throughout the world. It is a time of transition, a time when the ways of governing, the ways of living and of doing business, the ways of interacting amongst people and nations are in flux.

In my region, Europe and North America, which has a long history of war and domination that has affected the entire globe, we see this transition in what is called the end of the cold war. We have now what I call the hot peace. Rather than a truly peaceful era, we are seeing a shift in power blocs in which the anticipated peace dividend has turned instead into increased racial, ethnic, religious, and gender-based conflicts and violence. In this escalation, the role of women — and questions of women's human rights and the violation of women as a symbol of their cultures and peoples — has become central.

These global changes offer both opportunity and danger for women, as in any time of crisis. The opportunity is there for women to offer new solutions, to enter the public policy debate in a way that we have never been able to do before. And the danger is that even those advances we have made in this century will be reversed if we are not able to take this opportunity to move forward.

When I talk about women entering the global policy debates and influencing those discussions, I don't see this as totally separate from, but rather building on, the work that women are already doing. Women are usually the leaders at the local community level. Women are the leaders who have held families and communities together in times of crisis. Women have managed budgets that were inadequate to raise children and have managed to keep people together in times of war and other conflicts. And yet, as power moves up the ladder from the local community to national and international policy-making, women's voices and women themselves disappear. It is precisely a movement to change this that women have begun in the last two decades — we have begun to demand a place at the table of global policy-making as well as at the table in the kitchen.

The incredible failures of international policy in this century make it clear that women's expertise and experience must be brought to the global agenda if we are to see change in the 21st century. Let me give one poignant example – Somalia. For many years during the various conflicts there, women preserved the communities and sustained daily life, as they have in many other conflict situations. Yet when efforts were made to seek peace, these women were not given any role. They were not recognized as important to the future. The international community did not bring them into the peacemaking negotiations, did not ask them to participate in the peacekeeping process. I believe that if these women had been legitimized by the United Nations, by my own government, and by other governments in the world, then we would have seen a different resolution to that country's problems. And so too in many other parts of the world.

While there is much talk these days around the United Nations about global governance, there is not yet talk about global governance that includes our half of the population. But in reality, we already have a form of global governance in the world. We have an undeclared, unaccountable governance by the global economy with the IMF and the World Bank and various military alliances making the basic decisions that govern our lives. The other speakers have described the impact this has in the Third World in terms of structural adjustment policies. I would like to add that in the

North we see the dismantling of social welfare, both in formerly socialist countries and in the West, which is structural adjustment in our part of the world. This dismantling of social welfare has the same impact as structural adjustment in that it sacrifices human needs and human rights for economic expediency. And it is women who suffer the most in all of our countries from these policies, because it is women who must make up for the services lost to family and community.

Both economic and cultural life are becoming more global as they are more dominated by global market values. Even in my own lifetime in the United States, a country which probably seems very homogeneous to most of you, I have seen the erasure of distinct geographical diversity and cultural variations in the process of the creation of a common McWorld of consumerist culture that sacrifices difference. And now I see that process being transported throughout the world. Women have to find a better way for the world to have development and find common ground while still retaining cultural and other forms of diversity.

While we have a global economy and a growing global culture, we have no effective global political structures for overseeing these processes. On the contrary, in the world today we are facing two polar opposites: we are told we either have to accept the global economy with its homogenized, consumerist culture, or we have to return to "traditional" cultural patterns and life. I believe that women must devise a third way, a third option.

On the traditional side, we see groups reacting against the global economy and their lack of control over their economic life by clinging to local identities that involve more and more narrow definitions of who they are and what they are about. We see the growth of a narrow, nationalistic ethnic fragmentation into separatist enclaves where all "others" are demonized and seen as less than human. This is obviously expressed in ethnic cleansing in the former Yugoslavia or in the ethnic battles in Rwanda. But it is also present in the neo-fascist, white supremacist forces that are rising in the United States, France, Germany, and many other countries in my region.

Another form of such reaction is the rise of

religious fundamentalist movements that take a narrow patriarchal view of religion, whether Muslim, Christian, Hindu, Jewish, or other. These movements often cross national lines and sometimes become global forces, but they too are based on a narrow call for identity that dehumanizes "the other" — those who are not members of their religious group. And therefore an identity, a commonality is developed in opposition to and seeking domination over others, rather than building a spirit of solidarity, of humanity, and of tolerance for those unlike oneself.

These conservative reactionary forces, whether nationalistic or religious or both, all seek to control women. This control is absolutely central to religious or ethnic or cultural purity and identity. If they cannot control the women, they cannot ensure purity of race and identity, and in that very key point lies the vulnerability and potential strength of women. Women must refuse these narrow definitions and say that there can be diverse cultures and ethnic identities living together, that there can be tolerant religions that don't have to be in opposition to one another, that we can live in solidarity and respect with those who are different. If women do this, we can be the key to denying narrow fundamentalist movements their source of power and of regeneration. In this area, women must speak more forcefully about how we are being manipulated, and we must redefine this debate and create the third force I called for.

Another reason women are key is that many of the fundamentalist forces see the family, women, and culture as areas that they can control even when they can't control global economic forces. This has fueled the conservative backlash against women's autonomy and against all minority "others" who might live differently, such as immigrants, gypsies, lesbian and gay people, etc. This brings us to the question of the very definition of the family.

Feminists have been accused of being anti-family, but the conservative forces have continually narrowed the understanding of what the family really is. Women must point out that we are pro-family, but the families we are pro are democratic, pluralistic, nonviolent, tolerant families that are based on respect for the human rights of everyone in them. Such families do not form the basis for narrow ethnic enclaves that will fight other families and other ethnic groups but instead create the basis for family members to respect minorities and other groups.

The same forces that seek to return women to a narrow definition of our role in the family — solely as reproducers and caretakers of the race — are agitating against the rights of minorities, whether racial, ethnic, or religious groups, gay and lesbian minorities, gypsies, or immigrants. Defining a group as "the other" in your culture is part of the way in which the humanity of all of us is destroyed. If we accept that any group is less than fully human and therefore deserves to have fewer human rights, we have started down the slope of losing human rights for all. And women, especially, should understand this. After all, as women, we still live in a male-defined world where we are still the original "other," and most of the definitions of and approaches to issues in this world still do not fit our experience.

For example, many of us have worked over the last few years to transform the definitions and interpretations of human rights so that they will recognize the reality of the violations that women experience everyday. The original terminology of human rights, as we know it today, came from the experience of the white, propertied European/American male who did not need to worry about violence in the family or poverty because those were not his problems. His human-rights needs, where he felt his humanity was most violated, existed in relation to the state, in terms of matters such as his right to freedom of religion and freedom of speech.

While these issues are also important to women and other groups around the world, we have had to seek a redefinition of human rights which acknowledges that the first and most fundamental of all human rights is the right to exist, the right to life itself. This requires looking at the right to food and the right to freedom from violence, both in the home and in the streets. Of course, women also need the right to freedom from violence from the state. But many women do not even get to the point where the state is the problem, because women are still so oppressed in their homes and by the economy that they are often unable to take political action which might put them into human rights conflict in the political sphere.

This work on human rights is part of the process of redefining what women are doing in relation to all the fundamental questions of our global order: democracy, development, environment, peace, and so on. We must look at these questions from the point of view of women's lives and from the point of view of all those who have been marginalized by the dominant paradigm and definitions of these concepts. In this way we begin to pose alternatives, to move toward a model of society that is not based on domination and alienation and the divisiveness we see in the world today. The challenge in terms of human rights is to find a model that shows one can have and create respect for the common humanity and universality of the human rights of every person, regardless of gender, race, ethnicity, religion, sexual orientation, age, disability, and so forth, while also respecting and creating space for the incredible multicultural diversity that exists among us so that everyone doesn't have to become like the dominant group in order to have rights. Human rights is not static but is an evolving concept that responds to how people see their human needs and dignity over time. Thus, as people exercise their human right to self-determination, there will always be a dynamic process of both expanding the concept and ensuring that the exercise of rights does not allow for domination over others.

Women's involvement in this human rights dialogue is part of the process of breaking away from the polarization that the global economy has brought on between moving back to the past to preserve identity or moving to the future simply by accepting the values and domination of the global economy. Women must become more involved in seeking to develop global democratic structures for global governance and in demanding accountability and respect for human rights from those bodies, such as the United Nations, that are engaged in these conversations.

Because the United Nations itself is the ultimate expression of male domination, it can hardly become the body that will create global governance that respects women's human rights — that is, not unless it, too, changes. So, as we enter into this NGO Forum and send our messages back to Beijing to the government Conference, one of those messages has to be that women in the world are watching the United Nations. We are watching, and the United Nations itself is on trial here. We are watching to see whether it can become the governing body from which we develop global democratic structures of governance that fully include women or whether, indeed, we will have to go elsewhere.

Seeing the importance of the recognition of women's human rights and the need of all these nationalistic and fundamentalist movements to control women's sexuality, reproduction, and labor, helps us understand why this Conference and the Cairo Conference are under so much attack. These events represent women's efforts to move into the global arena, to have a voice, to become a global force that must be reckoned with. When I look at the list of the global forces that we are to speak about today, I realize the one most important to me is the global force of women in movement around the world today. This force has many different names — call it feminist, call it womanist, call it women in development, call it women's rights or women's human rights. Call it many different things because each of us has found different terms that describe best for us that reality of domination and change. Women are the most important new global force on the horizon in the world today, with the potential to create a more humane future and a humane global governance.

For women to be such a force, however, carries great responsibility. We cannot be a movement that thinks and speaks only from our own experiences. We began our movement in these past few decades with the concept that the personal is political and with the need to put women's experiences on the agenda because these were missing. Women's issues, women's perspectives, women's experiences were and still often are left out of policy deliberations. But if we don't want to be simply an added-on dimension, we must also bring in all those whose voices are not heard — all the diverse women and men whose voices have been muted — so that we show it is possible for this world to hear from all its peoples. There will be conflicts, but we must seek nonviolent ways to resolve them that move toward the future and away from the militaristic models of domination from which the world operates today.

This Beijing Conference comes at a critical time in the process of women becoming a global force in the world and has become in many ways a referendum on the role that women will play in the 21st century. In that regard, it is also a referendum on the human rights of women. It is about how far we have come in being recognized as full and equal citizens of the world, with equal human rights and with full responsibility for the future direction of the globe. Whether the issue is poverty, education, health, violence, or some other crucial concern, it involves the question of women's access to full humanity, to full human rights, to the conditions necessary to exercise political rights and to take responsibility for enacting visions of where we want to go in the world. This is what it takes for us to become a global political force involved in shaping the next century.

In this process of empowering women to become greater actors in shaping our societies, women's human rights are key in many different ways. Perhaps the simplest way to put this is, How can leaders talk about creating a democratic, sustainable development or a culture of peace and respect for human rights in public life if there is still pervasive denial of development and violation of the human rights of half of humanity in private life? The violence and domination of women that prevails at the core of society, in the family, undermines any talk of such goals. I believe that it is this connection that women have understood. The public and the private are not separate spheres. As long as we teach violence and domination at the core, in our homes, and allow them to permeate children's lives from the beginning, we are never going to be able to end the militarism and violence that dominate other relations around differences of race or religion or nationality. Children are taught very early to accept domination based on differ-

ences and to see violence as an acceptable solution to conflict and to believe that they have to be either victims or conquerors. To alter such violence in public life requires eliminating it in private life as well.

I want to add, in relation to violence, that I think the United States has a severe problem of cultural tradition. We often refer to cultural traditions as if they existed only in the third world. The cultural tradition of the United States is a tradition of violence. This violence extends from the family to the media to our sport stars to our militarization around the world. And it is this cultural tradition that we must counter in our region, just as women from other regions challenge the domination of women in their cultural traditions. So I ask that we never again make the mistake of talking about culture and tradition as if they did not apply to every country and every region of the world when we speak of the process of changes necessary for the achievement of women's human rights.

Finally, at this Conference, we must take one step further into the global arenas of this decade. I think of UN world conferences as global town meetings. They are opportunities to meet and talk to one another across the lines of nationality, across lines that we don't often have other opportunities to cross. But as global town meetings, they are also occasions for us to show the world our visions.

Looking at the world through women's eyes is an excellent slogan for this Forum because this is the place where we can demonstrate the visions of possibility that come from women. This week at the NGO Forum we must send forward to that UN Conference next week in Beijing the idea that we believe the world can be transformed by our looking at it through women's eyes, and that in so doing, we are ever widening the horizon so that what gets onto the global stage, into the Internet, and onto that CNN television screen reflects more of reality, more of what women believe can be done for change. So we put the United Nations and the governments on trial, not only this week but this year and this decade.

We are participating now, we are watching, we are demanding, and we are here to see if this can become the arena of real participation, where global governance and policies can be created with a human face that is both male and female and where all the diversity of both male and female can emerge. And if this does not prove possible, women must say to the United Nations and to all of our governments: We have a vision for the next century; this is where we are going. We hope they will allow us to participate and to lead, but if they don't, we will take leadership anyway and show that the world can be better for all in the 21st century.

III • Approaches to Governance

Including Questions of Citizenship and Political Participation

Opening remarks

Judy Rebick, Moderator
CBC Newsworld, Canada

Today our topic is approaches to governance, including questions of citizenship and political participation. I think a very good framework was set yesterday by our speakers. What was clear to me from all of the talks was that what we are talking about now is no longer simply getting more women into positions of political power, although we still have to struggle to continue to do that. What we are talking about now is: Once we are there, once we are in positions of influence, what are we going to do with those positions of influence?

In Canada, an aboriginal woman leader said that women who climb the ladder of success and pull the ladder up after them don't do very much good for other women. I think what we are talking about here is how women who have managed to get into positions of influence, whether that's in political society or civil society, use that influence not only to bring other women along with them but also to transform those institutions that were built by men for men, and to transform those institutions to reflect the values of the women's movement, of what I call feminism.

This is an incredibly difficult struggle. We have a tremendously rich experience around the world in this struggle. We have been at it for a long time now. What we know, and I think one of the reasons the topic is what it is, is that simply working inside the traditional political institutions, you cannot achieve everything. It is a combination of women working inside those institutions, the women's movement, and women in other social movements in civil society who can make the kinds of political changes that we see today.

When we in the women's movement talk about politics, electoral politics are only part of what we are talking about. We are talking about the movements of people for social change, and these movements are as important to the process of transformation towards equality and peace as the formal political institutions are.

We have on our panel today three women who have a tremendous variety of experiences on these issues.

Women and decision-making: The need for our own agenda

Hilda Lini
Member of Parliament, Republic of Vanuatu

First of all, I would like to bring greetings from the ancestors and revolutionary leaders of the Pacific region to the revolutionary leaders of China. I believe that China has shown us so much of its vision and its ideology, and that these have shaped China into one of the great countries of the world.

I was asked to give a regional perspective on approaches to governance. The Pacific is made up of about 26 countries, so I will try to do justice to the regional perspective. I come from the Republic of Vanuatu, which to those of you from the older generation was known as the New Hebrides. Vanuatu became an independent nation in 1980. In 1983 it became the first nuclear-free state in the world, followed by New Zealand and others such as Palau, which has a nuclear-free constitution and has been fighting with the United States about this until now.

When you look at the Pacific region, you find it is the most heavily militarized region in the world. It is also the most multicultural region in the world, with over a thousand languages and cultures that still exist, upholding and sustaining our societies against the forces that are trying to destroy them. One of the issues that persists today in the Pacific is colonization — the political status of the countries that are still living under colonialism — and also the matter of citizenship. New Caledonia, French Polynesia, and West Papua are still fighting for political independence to be able to decide their own destinies. The Maoris of New Zealand and the aborigines of Australia are still fighting for sovereignty and recognition, but the colonial powers would rather call it something else.

I was the leader of the women in the liberation movement of Vanuatu. I believe that if women had not taken up the initiative and were not mobilized, Vanuatu would still be a colony today. It was the women's participation that enabled Vanuatu to become an independent nation in 1980.

When you are a small country, when you are an ignorant people, other powerful, industrialized nations want to use you. This is the case in the Pacific region. The cold war is probably over in other parts of the world, but not in the Pacific. We have been struggling; we have been fighting. The cold war is still on for us. This is where nuclear testing has been taking place for ages by the British, the United States, France, and even China, which shoots missiles into the Pacific Ocean.

We have to cope with so many challenges when we look at women's issues. Just coming to China, where there are separate venues, Beijing and Huairou, is so artificial for us in the Pacific, because in the Pacific the cultures work together with the government — the churches and the women and the NGOs. There is no separation. We are one people, working together for a cause. As a region, we stand together against the forces exploiting our countries.

Women may have made very substantial contributions in the past. They still are making very important contributions. Women play essential roles in the Pacific in sustaining family units and the extended family, which is the basis of social security for us. We are very small countries, but we believe that small is beautiful. We also believe that respect is honorable and that peace is powerful. We believe that our traditional sense of community is both wise and practical.

If we have to make changes, we must organize ourselves into communities, especially the global community. As for the industrialized nations who want to dictate to smaller nations what should be done: I believe that the big nations can learn more from the small nations. Our governments in the Pacific are new in terms of political sovereignty. In 1963 the first independent nation was proclaimed in the Pacific region. Now we have 15, and some have associations with their former colonial powers. It is still a problem for us because the colonial powers continue to want to control what our governments do. They want to find a way to come in and control the political decisions.

I believe that the Pacific needs revolution right now. I also believe that the whole world needs a revolution. If we look at the quality of life for the whole world and for different regions of the world, we need a new revolution of mentality. We need to put our resources into the most important needs for human survival. But this is not what is happening today.

The most important areas are mobilizing at the national level and having to include women's perspectives in decision-making, in planning, in monitoring and evaluation, and in reviewing. We need to make sure that we update ourselves about what we feel has been working against us and try to develop new actions and new agendas. We need to put resources where the biggest need is. So many resources today are being used in funding institutions and the military. And all the money we have used in funding the military and institutions — even the United Nations — what good has it done for us, the grass roots?

The global women's movement started in 1975. It's now been 20 years. Have we progressed? Yes, to a certain extent — in our organizations, in our own countries, we can identify areas where we have progressed. But for a whole lot of the population of the world, have we progressed? I don't believe so. The situation has become worse, and we're still having UN meetings to look at this, putting money into meetings and meetings and meetings while people are dying. Who is making the decision to have meetings? Who is making the decisions about where the resources should be allocated? It's the men.

Let's be honest with ourselves. If we are saying that we have progressed on the political level and there are women in decision-making, I would say there aren't *enough* women in decision-making. The number is too small. One of the biggest problems I face as a minister and still as the only woman Member of Parliament is that I don't know whom to discuss things with. I have to have tea with all the men. I have to discuss with all the men, because there are no other women there to share and to brainstorm with when something very important comes up on the floor.

I think the other thing we have to look at is the women's movement making contributions to the decision makers. Some of us believe that women's movements have become fed up with trying and have given up. But I also believe that some governments are ready to listen. Some Members of Parliament are ready to listen. We hear that our women are building networks with all the people in decision-making, but from my own experience, I find that I have been isolated as a decision maker. The women did not tell me what they wanted me to do. I had to decide for myself. I had to scrounge for the information. I had to go and read as much as I could. The women think that as a woman, you should know everything about women and women's issues and community issues, that you don't need to be directed. That is wrong. There are so many women who need to be directed when they get to those positions.

I believe that in order for the United Nations to look seriously at poverty eradication, unemployment, food security, housing, water supply, and providing appropriate education for today and future generations, we have to put women's perspectives into the United Nations and into our own national governments. To do that, we have to change our governments at the national level first, because if governments remain the same, they will not go to the United Nations and make changes for us. They are the ones to decide. We have to work very hard at the national level to make sure that we make those changes.

The male-dominated governments that exist in most of the countries today — who elected them? If 50 percent of the voters are women, then why is it that the women elect men who do not make decisions that are good for us? Where is the accountability that we are supposed to make sure is maintained? Many of us think they know what they should do. We don't even tap their shoulders and say, "Look, you've gone the wrong way; this is where you should be going." I believe that we still have a lot to do as women. We need more women in decision-making bodies, because only then can we discuss, make policies, and formulate laws that we will be able to push through a male-dominated cabinet and a male-dominated government or administration.

As the only woman Member of Parliament and a former minister, my experience, which I'd like to share with you, is this: I believe that information and knowledge are power for women. When you get to those positions, you have to have information at your fingertips as it is needed to challenge the male mentality about women's issues or community issues. If you do not have it there, they think you are ignorant, that you don't know what you're there for, that you don't know anything about community issues. Information is very important and also the skills to organize your statements; this gives people confidence in women. I believe all women are politicians. Some of us are elected to political positions; some of us are not. We are politicians when we are making decisions at home and at work. Politics is all about making decisions and having the right to make those decisions, and we should be able to have that right at national and global levels.

I would like to end by saying that as we all go home from Beijing, we should have a very clear vision of where we want to go in the next five years. We need to develop our ideologies and try to implement those ideologies. Men will not help much. The initiative has to come from us. We must monitor and review. We need women's leadership to take us through, because if we don't have it, we will be loaded down with still more problems, and the situation will get worse and worse as we enter the next century.

In the liberation movement I was told that you had to develop your own agenda and then follow it. Don't listen to anybody else's agenda. That was how we won.

The emerging democracy in South Africa

Cheryl Carolus
African National Congress (ANC), South Africa

Introduction

• I come from a country that has one of the highest levels of representation of women in parliament, just over 30 percent.

• We have one of the most progressive laws dealing with violence in the family. This law even outlaws rape in marriage.

• We have an interim constitution which is one of the most progressive, modern constitutions in the world. Women's rights are firmly situated in the realm of human rights by locating those rights in an equality clause which outlaws any form of discrimination, including on the basis of sexual orientation. Women's reproductive rights are firmly entrenched. The supremacy of the constitution over traditional and customary law is unambiguous. The constitution provides for the establishment of a commission on gender which will be housed in the Office of the President.

• We have an integrated program for development, the Reconstruction and Development Program (RDP), which was unanimously adopted by the Government of National Unity. All major business groupings have come out in support of it.

The RDP was drafted by mass-based organizations and progressive NGOs before the democratic elections. It was the main platform used by progressive organizations to challenge political parties and organizations about their commitment to fundamental change. Both business and our political opponents tried to discredit the program but soon had to give up, because the progressive movements managed to prove convincingly that the RDP was not an additional program but rather a program which advocated a more just and equitable distribution of existing resources as its starting point.

The RDP deals with the tasks of reconstructing our country from the ashes of apartheid and attempts to ensure that the new state which emerges will be a developmental state. One of the key indicators for measuring the success of the RDP is the impact of every government program on the most disadvantaged sectors of our society, i.e., blacks, women, youth, and rural dwellers. The RDP does not have special sections dealing with each of these constituencies. It was felt that the constituencies which the RDP seeks to prioritize are all more than 50 percent of the population. Creating special sections would have reduced the scale of the problem. So in dealing with each section in the RDP, the impact on each of those sectors was evaluated.

Implementation of the RDP is the responsibility of the President's Office, where it is managed by a minister without portfolio. One of the first projects tackled by the RDP office was the drafting of the country report for this Conference.

• There is unanimity amongst all political groups in government that the Convention on the Elimination of All Forms of Discrimination Against Women (CEDAW) must be ratified.

• Children under six years, pregnant women, and breast-feeding women have free access to health care. This should go a long way toward reducing maternal and infant mortality and morbidity.

• A Ministry of Health commission has just submitted recommendations on how to incorporate reproductive health and women's reproductive rights into a primary health care system.

This must sound like every woman's dream come true — a government, a society which is dealing seriously with the rights of women as a fundamental component of building a culture of human rights. Yes, we have come a l-o-n-g way, but there is still much to be done.

Background: Reasons for the progress

• South Africa has a long history of struggle. A very special characteristic has always been the vibrant civil society which was born through that struggle. Ordinary women and men formed a wide range of organizations which opposed one or another aspect of life under apartheid, e.g., civic organizations, youth organizations, religious movements, health organizations, etc. We have one of the strongest, most militant trade unions in the world. Firmly in center stage of the anti-apartheid struggle was always the women's movement. As in the case of many other struggles, women form a large part of the active membership of progressive organizations. Through our victories over the years, women had tasted the power of mass mobilization and organization.

• Political parties and organizations contesting the first democratic elections in South Africa woke up and realized that women held 53 percent of the vote! Women across the political spectrum united around a key set of demands, which were enshrined in the Women's Charter. Political parties were involved in negotiations for an interim constitution that would form the basis for government while a permanent constitution would be negotiated after the elections. Because women were organized and united and because they had a clear set of demands, they were able to establish key criteria for giving their 53 percent of the vote. As a result, all parties took very progressive positions on the issues, which I outlined earlier.

• All parties were represented by two delegates in the negotiations for the interim constitution. The ANC put forward a proposal that all parties be obliged to send at least one woman delegate. There was of course much heated debate about whether this was a quota system that would result in tokenism and therefore inadequate and weak representation. Again, women across the political spectrum rallied together and won. Today many of the men who were involved in the negotiations will concede, even if it is with a nervous titter, that women more than held their own and that they brought a new seriousness and new skills of conflict management which had been absent before. Everybody agrees that the process was expedited by the skills and approaches of the women.

• The next battle was to ensure that women were adequately represented in the first-ever democratic parliament and government. Again there was passionate debate about tokenism, merit, etc. — I'm sure you have heard all the arguments in different forms. However, we managed to get an acceptance that we needed, a mechanism which would ensure that the many competent women in our country would take up their rightful place in the future government and in society.

As a result, one of the electoral requirements was that at least 30 percent of all party candidates had to be women. So we ended up with slightly more than 30 percent of our MPs being women. Again, everyone agrees that those women have more than held their own. In fact, as is often the case, women have had to perform much harder with much less support to get recognition. As a result of this success story, the ANC has decided that at least 50 percent of our candidates for local government elections must be women.

But there are still many problems

On 28 April 1995, the day after the momentous elections, nothing concrete had changed for South Africans. The poor were still poor and still lived in the most appalling racially defined ghettos.

The lives of women have not changed in a meaningful way in South Africa. The women who spent eight hours a day gathering firewood are still doing that; there has not been a substantive number of women who have successfully used the new law on domestic violence; only two cases of rape in marriage have come to court; and working-class black women are still the hardest hit by the spread of AIDS.

We still have only two women ministers and three women deputy ministers. All of them are ANC appointees. None of the other parties were prepared to allocate any of their cabinet positions to women.

Does this mean that we have not achieved anything? Absolutely not! The constitutional and legal frameworks which we have had to fight for and which we have won are prerequisites for establishing a human rights culture that recognizes women's rights as human rights. But on their own they will be meaningless, and in fact dangerous, because they can instill complacency and provide a good smokescreen for suppressing the real goals of our liberation struggle: namely, that *all* should share in the fruits of our society.

The only people who will benefit from this formalization of equality will be mainly middle-class black men and a few middle-class black women.

South Africa: Potential pawn in redefining the cold war

Through its destabilization policies, racist South Africa — aided and abetted by powerful countries such as the United States of America — ruined our region, Southern Africa, and our continent, Africa. Today many destitute refugees flee to South Africa from economic and political hardship in their countries.

We are very mindful of the fact that not too long ago, most of the powerful governments of the world refused to recognize the ANC or any of the progressive organizations. They called Nelson Mandela a terrorist. Together, through our joint grassroots mobilization of the anti-apartheid movements inside those countries and the mass movements inside South Africa, those governments started to put pressure on the apartheid regime.

But we are also seeing continued attempts to manipulate the world in the interests of the power elites in the powerful nations. In many respects, the cold war has in fact been intensified. There are too many attempts to build a unipolar world.

South Africa has become an important pawn in the power games of the supernations. There are attempts to use my country as a regional surrogate force. There are also attempts to abuse our concept of a Government of National Unity (GNU) by imposing this form of governance on countries like Angola and Mozambique, with scant regard for the fact that much pressure was exerted on those countries to hold multiparty elections. When the MPLA and FRELIMO won those elections, the countries which had exerted so much pressure on them to hold elections were not prepared to help the democratically elected governments uphold the election results. Instead, new pressures were exerted

to accommodate the losers. Yet none of those countries accommodates its defeated opponents after an election.

In South Africa, it was *our* choice to opt for GNU.

Low-intensity democracy replacing low-intensity war

Now there are fresh attempts to impose on us a permanent GNU/coalition government. We will not bow to it. If we do so, it will be our choice. What does concern us is that these attempts are symptoms of the new "low-intensity democracy" strategy that has replaced low-intensity war. The objective is to have a popular government but also to embark on a series of activities to ensure that the popular party never becomes too popular or strong. The result is a lame-duck government which cannot govern effectively. Such a government is bound to fail eventually.

And so the dream which the democratic South Africa represents to the rest of the world will have died a natural death.

Freedom must be real

There are so many blatant efforts at hijacking our struggle. It is a very decisive period for our country. In many ways the real struggle for freedom is only just starting. Freedom is not an abstract thing. It must translate into freedom from poverty, freedom from fear, freedom from hunger, and so forth. We have the vehicle to move forward, namely, a democratically elected government which is committed to addressing the needs of the most disadvantaged.

The challenges are to maintain this commitment, to maintain the vision of the Reconstruction and Development Program, and to follow policies which will not enslave us to the International Monetary Fund, the World Bank, or the international finance houses.

Beyond ideological baggage

• *Sound economic policies*

We have been bold (and perhaps a little defiant) in committing ourselves to fiscal discipline. But we have defined fiscal discipline for ourselves. It means not spending money you do not have. It means spending the money you have in a cost-efficient manner. It means intersectoral planning. It means investing money in high-return areas like education, primary health care, water and sanitation, electrification, and housing. It means cutting down on government consumption expenditure — our cabinet ministers have taken a cut in salary. In short, it means building a developmental state.

• *Growth and development*

We are committed not only to sharing the cake more equitably but also to increasing the size of the cake. We are consciously seeking economic growth. We do not believe that growth and development have to be contradictory. We believe that we can have growth *through* development. Our vision for this is through a massive infrastructure provision program.

• *Beyond the market*

We have adopted a mixed-economy policy. (This sometimes means that you get attacked from all sides.) We have decided that markets can play a positive role in the economy, but the market also has many inadequacies. It does not have the capacity to identify or provide for the needs of the most vulnerable, the poor. So we believe that the democratic state also has an important role to play in the economy.

• *Globalization*

Globalization has impacted on our economy in a big way, and we have had to make some difficult decisions — some of them because we had no option. These decisions are made jointly by a tripartite forum consisting of the full spectrum of the trade union movement, business, and the government. A regional, Southern African approach is also crucial.

A new approach to governance

It is neither possible nor desirable for the government to take all responsibility for development. We therefore believe that it is important for us to shift from the concept of "government" toward that of "governance." Fundamental to this is the notion that the smooth running of our society is possible only through partnership and joint responsibility shared by government and a vibrant civil society.

This means moving away from statism. It is based on an assumption that people and communities have great capacity and desire for being active participants in the transformation of their lives. It means consultation, joint decision-making, and joint responsibility for outcomes.

This concept has been formalized through the establishment of the National Economic Development and Labor Council (NEDLAC), which has a number of different chambers where decisions are made jointly between government and the various components of civil society. Decision-making has thus far been on the basis of persuasion and consensus, but it is also accepted that if consensus is not possible, government must make a decision which takes all factors into account and which is in keeping with its mandate from the electorate.

We will continue to need a strong civil society

People often ask why we are so optimistic about the future of our country, despite the difficulties which we ourselves point out. My answer is part lighthearted, part serious — that the people of our country know how to make themselves ungovernable. They are fiercely conscious of their rights and their power. They will use their organizations and their power to assert their rights. Our present government understands and values this.

Democracy is a coin with two sides

But our people also understand that democracy is a coin with two sides: rights and responsibilities. They are actively assuming responsibility for doing what they can to improve their own lives. It is a myth that people are sitting back with inflated expectations of government.

It is true that people have higher expectations. But so they should have. That is why we fought for a change in government. And people do not have unreasonable expectations. Ask any poor person what they expect from Nelson Mandela's government. They will tell you that they want a job, a house, education for their children, a water tap — all the things which many of us take for granted as basics. The job of the government is not to lower these expectations. It has to meet them. We all know that it will take a long time to solve the problems and inequalities created by over 300 years of colonialism and apartheid. The ordinary South African also knows this. All that is needed is active consultation on priorities and visible signs of government commitment.

What they do expect is that government must lead, that it must create an enabling environment for those who can help themselves and must look after those who are most vulnerable.

Strengthening mass-based community organizations

Democratic government must seek to play its part in strengthening democratic formations, including assisting with resources, but we should be cautious to maintain the independence of our organizations. We should also understand that extreme financial dependence (to the extent of whether an organization can survive or not) is very undesirable.

Strengthening women's participation

It is absolutely essential, but not enough, only to increase the numbers of women who participate in governance and public life. It is essential, but not enough, only to have a good constitutional and legislative framework which deals with women's rights as part of a comprehensive package of human rights.

We need to create mechanisms to provide skills. We need to take into account that most women, even the most personally liberated, still live in a society and in relationships which place sole responsibility for child care and housework on her shoulders. This means creating support mechanisms such as child-care facilities. But it also means educating men and educating our society.

Women in power can empower or disempower other women

There is a great deal of pressure on women in power to conform to the norms of power and to behave like men. It is important for women in power to maintain contact with one another and with their grassroots base and values.

Conclusion

I have so much more to share with you about my country — its triumphs and its tears — but time does not allow. I have shared many of the positive aspects. I want to warn you that we are also making mistakes. Only those who do nothing do not make mistakes.

A viewpoint from the Central and Eastern European countries in transition

Marina Beyer
East-West European Women's Network (OWEN), Germany

First of all, I would like to express my sense of honor and excitement to have been invited as a speaker to this great plenary of the NGO Forum. I am here as a representative of an NGO called the East-West European Women's Network, shortened to OWEN in German. When we East Germans founded the network in 1991, we believed that our specific situation placed us in a ideal position to begin to build bridges between East and West. We had been born and raised in the German Democratic Republic, the showpiece of the former Eastern bloc, and we lived in the Federal Republic of Germany, the showpiece of Western-style capitalism and democracy. Our aim was to bring together women who had been isolated from one another for political and ideological reasons.

Thus the thoughts I am going to share with you are based mainly on conclusions I have been able to draw by working in this network for the past four years, including experiences we have had building a partnership with the global grassroots women's network, GROOTS International. Built into my speech as well is my personal view as an East German native who grew up in a family that believed in the ideals of democratic socialism as an alternative social model and that experienced the disappointment of the gap between vision and reality in the GDR.

I have been asked to speak about approaches to governance for women in Central and Eastern Europe after the end of the cold war and about the role of women as citizens sharing in national and global governance. I will be concentrating on a few critical concerns which, in my opinion, are the key issues for the advancement of women: poverty and the political power of women, especially poor women.

Since the end of the cold war and the breakdown of the Eastern bloc four years after the Nairobi Conference in 1985, the world has experienced profound changes that have brought new challenges and opportunities for women. The global situation we are facing today teaches us that neither the model of state socialism nor the model of capitalism and Western civil society have been able to create a framework for human and sustainable development or to move us toward human security for all.

The 20th century socialist model, linked with the totalitarian power of the state and with planned state economies that produce inefficient growth, has collapsed because it ignored people's willingness and capacity to participate as active subjects in society. This model treated people rather as objects of an ideology, and a great chance to create a human-centered society, based on human values and human rights, was wasted.

This Fourth World Conference on Women offers us unique and new opportunities. Now, 50 years after the founding of the United Nations and in the midst of the opening of Central and Eastern European nations to the democratization of their societies, women from the South, the North, and the former Eastern bloc can come together to exchange their experiences of equality and equity within differing political and economic systems. For the first time, we can identify and appreciate the resources for political empowerment that women everywhere possess.

When the third NGO Forum took place ten years ago in Nairobi, only nongovernmental and government representatives who confirmed their countries' socialist politics were given the opportunity to participate. The true mood of the women of those countries could not be expressed authentically. A public discussion about the disadvantages of state socialism was not part of the Conference.

Today, in 1995, we find ourselves in a completely different situation. Nevertheless, few newly founded Central and Eastern European women's groups have the opportunity to take part, as citizens, in national and international governance. Glancing over the list of invited speakers in the plenaries, I find among the 84 women invited only three whose thoughts would be based on experiences with state socialism as well as with current transitional economies. Considering that approximately 370 million people live in the transition countries of the former Eastern bloc, three representatives do not seem proportional. In my opinion, the reason for this lack cannot be explained solely by the recentness of the development of an independent women's movement in those countries. To me it is also a sign that the global importance of the transition of the former Eastern bloc is still very much underestimated by the United Nations.

If the United Nations really feels obliged to foster the participation of women in governance on all levels, it must adjust its agenda, strategies, actions, structures, and working methods according to the specific needs of this group of women who, for numerous reasons, are not yet sufficiently represented on the international level.

IV • Obstacles to Peace and Human Security

Including the Effects of Militarization, Violence, and Poverty

Opening remarks

Edith Ballantyne, Moderator
Women's International League for Peace and
Freedom (WILPF), Switzerland

Human security is an integral part of peace. Without human security there can be no peace. What do we mean by human security? What is it?

There is a rapidly growing realization on the part of people that human security cannot be seen in military terms. On the contrary, modern weaponry and warfare threaten not only our security; they threaten the very survival of the human race. Only a small number of the nuclear weapons in the existing arsenals of the nuclear powers are enough to destroy everything living on this planet. So why do nuclear weapons continue to be developed, built, and deployed? Why are other weapons built and stockpiled — and used — that maim and kill us and destroy our environment? Even if some of these weapons are never used, building and testing them cause illness and death.

Conflicts are part of life and are likely to be always with us. But more efforts at finding peaceful solutions will be made if no weapons are at hand.

Vast natural resources and human labor are spent on the military at a time when more than two-thirds of the world's population cannot have their basic needs satisfied. Unfair economic and social relations within and among nations lead to strife and violence. Conflicts are simmering and erupting on every continent. We are learning that there can be no security for anyone as long as some of us are illiterate, unemployed, hungry, or suffering from lack of education, inadequate shelter, and preventable diseases.

Human security must be sought in reordering global and national priorities and in investing our natural and human resources in socially oriented production. For example, this was the clear message that emerged from the studies and discussions undertaken in preparation for the World Summit for Social Development.

Unfortunately, the solutions proposed by the Summit itself fell far short of the kinds of changes that have to be made in order for economic and social justice — or human security — to be built. The Summit's advocacy for more "free markets," more "privatization" of institutions, more "deregulation" of industry is not the solution. It is the problem. What are *our* answers, *our* proposed solutions? We women have an immense stake in finding answers to these critical issues. Without building human security and peace, the advancement of the great majority of women will move on fragile ground, if it moves at all.

Our speakers in this plenary will touch upon a number of aspects of human security or lack of it. They will challenge us to look at our realities and indicate ways to change them.

Obstacles to peace and human security in the Pacific

Amelia Rokotuivuna
Asian-Pacific Development Centre, Fiji

Introduction

The Pacific region faces obstacles to peace and human security similar to those faced by other regions, but because of political history, geography, and the size of its population, some of the obstacles are exacerbated. The Pacific Ocean is littered with islands, many of which are coral atolls.

In comparison with other regions, the population of the Pacific region is small. Both old and new colonial powers have territories in the region.

In this presentation I will address the following obstacles:

1. The nuclear presence in the Pacific;

2. The violation and denial of the right to self-determination by the colonial powers in the region;

3. The inadequacy of present state political institutions and procedures to deal with pluralism and accountability;

4. The violation and lack of restoration of the rights of indigenous peoples and the lack of respect for their culture;

5. The plunder of resources by the transnational corporations and its impact on governance;

6. The impact of structural adjustment programs (SAPs) in worsening the material living conditions of ordinary people; and

7. The effect of the unjust system of international trade, particularly on the price of primary commodities.

There are other obstacles, but I will restrict myself to the seven I have mentioned.

The nuclear presence in the Pacific

In proportion to its population, the Pacific is a highly militarized part of the world, and militarism is pervasive in the region. The Pacific is home to the world's largest military empire, the US Commander-in-Chief Pacific (CINPAC), located in Hawaii and controlling one-half of the world's surface and 60 percent of its population, from the west coast of the American continent and covering Asia and the Indian Ocean to the east coast of the African continent.

In the post-cold war era, dismantling the nuclear arsenal floating in the Pacific has not yet happened. About one-fifth of the world's strategic nuclear arsenal continuously cruises around the Pacific in eight U.S. Trident missile submarines and 22 Russian ballistic missile submarines. The total count of U.S. warheads on the eight submarines is 1,526, capable of destroying 1,526 cities, while that of Russia is 999 warheads. Important to the efficient functioning and accuracy of the arsenal are communication and spying installations, which crisscross the Pacific.

All the major nuclear powers have tested either their bombs or their missiles in the Pacific region. For the past 50 years, the Pacific has been the location for 310 nuclear bomb tests.

Between 1946 and 1962 the United States of America conducted 106 atmospheric tests in the Pacific, 102 of which took place on four small coral atolls in Micronesia. Johnston Island was the site for 12 tests; Enewetak for 43, Bikini for 23, and Christmas Island for 24. The United States continues to test missiles over the Pacific, with splash-down near Kwajelin Atoll in the Marshall Islands. Between 1952 and 1957 Great Britain tested 12 bombs in the atmosphere on aboriginal lands in Australia. France conducted 177 tests between 1966 and 1990 in Tahiti (French Polynesia), 130 of which were atmospheric and 47 underground. The locations of these tests were Fangataufa and Mururoa atolls. Under the Mitterrand government France suspended its test program, but as soon as Jacques Chirac was elected president early this year, he announced the resumption of testing. This program of eight tests commences next week — done in total defiance of international opinion and overwhelming objections by the inhabitants of the Pacific. We, the people of the region, are outraged by the display of such arrogance and the complete disregard of our voices and livelihoods.

The Pacific is also being used as a nuclear waste dumping ground. Johnston Island is the only active nuclear incinerator of the United States, so it dumps its nuclear waste and surplus weapons there. Even the cold war stockpile from West Germany was carted halfway around the world to be brought to our region.

One may well ask, Who is the enemy on which this arsenal will be used? The simple logic is that if you have such an array of weapons and such a support system, then you will find an enemy.

Violation and denial of the right to self-determination

The process of decolonization in the Pacific has not yet been completed by the United States, France, and Indonesia. Struggles for self-determination and independence are being waged across the Pacific; some are protracted wars, while others are taking place in the arena of legal and political negotiations.

The protracted wars are occurring in East Timor — waged by the Maurable People's Independence Movement — and in West Papua — waged by the Oganisiasi Papua Merdeka (OPM), or Free Papua Movement. Both wars are being fought against the Government of Indonesia.

When the Dutch withdrew from West Papua in 1962, the United Nations, under an agreement, formed a caretaker authority composed of Indonesian and Pakistani army units as well as Papuan police units. Aided by the United States, Indonesia took over the leadership of this authority. The UN agreement also stated that the Papuans were entitled to a free choice of their political status. Indonesia, however, never agreed to an independent West Papua, so in 1963 it seized the administration of the territory and in 1969 staged a bogus "Free Choice" referendum. The majority voted to have West Papua become part of Indonesia. The armed struggle began in the early 1970s.

In East Timor the struggle for independence began in 1965 with a unilateral declaration for an independent East Timor by the Revolutionary Front for an Independent East Timor (Fretilin) in the wake of an Indonesian invasion and massacre of the Timorese. When the Portuguese colonial power collapsed without formally giving independent status to its colony, Indonesia seized the opportunity for territorial expansion by invading East Timor in 1975.

Many East Timorese and West Papuans have been killed in these wars of independence.

Regarding the French presence in the Pacific region, the three French colonies are Kanaky (New Caledonia), Tahiti (French Polynesia), and Wallis and Futuna. The Kanak independence struggle began in 1975 and consolidated in 1984 with the formation of the Kanak Socialist National Liberation Front (FLNKS). A 1988 framework for self-determination, negotiated between FLNKS and the Government of France, agreed to the condition that a referendum on independence be held in 1988. This has not yet occurred, and a substantial number of Kanaks are unhappy about the delay. In addition, because of its nuclear testing program, France is reluctant to enter into negotiations with political parties in Tahiti that are demanding independence.

The United States also presents impediments in the region. It is denying full independence to Belau because the people there are demanding a nuclear-free constitution, which the United States opposes because of its plans to use Belau as a refuelling base for its nuclear warships. Also, in 1988 the voters of Guam expressed a desire for a new political status and asked the United States to begin negotiations for independence.

All three colonial powers are members of the United Nations but pay no heed to their obligation to implement the right to self-determination.

The inadequacy of state political institutions to deal with pluralism and accountability

A number of nations in the Pacific, such as Fiji, Aotearoa-New Zealand, and Australia, are rural societies made up of very divergent ethnic groups. However, the interests of these groups have not been adequately taken into account by the political institutions and processes of the state. The Westminster model of parliamentary democracy does not deal appropriately to diverse cultural groups and therefore has marginalized the Aborigines in Australia and the Maoris in Aotearoa. In Fiji, a military coup was staged ostensibly to protect the interests of the indigenous Fijians.

Political corruption has been increasing in the independent island states of the Pacific. The model of parliamentary democracy inherited from Western colonial powers does not provide for adequate accountability by those in power.

Violation and lack of restoration of the rights of indigenous peoples

Some of the worst instances of genocide against indigenous peoples have been committed in the Pacific region. The Aborigines of Australia were almost completely obliterated during their first contact with Whites in the last century, as were the Maoris of Aotearoa-New Zealand.

In Hawaii, Australia, Aotearoa-New Zealand,

and Guam, the first peoples lost their lands and fishing grounds, and their cultures were decimated. For a long period into the present century the Government of the United States — in the cases of Hawaii and Guam — paid no respect whatsoever to the culture, traditional practices, or languages of the Hawaiians and the Chamorros of Guam. The Governments of both New Zealand and Australia marginalized the indigenous people of their countries. Efforts of the indigenous people to regain their culture and repossess their land and fishing grounds have now had some effect, however, and the Governments of Aotearoa and Australia have tried to set up institutions and processes through which they could work to restore the rights of the indigenous people. Unfortunately, there are serious flaws, the first being great doubt on the part of the indigenous people that the intentions of the government are genuine.

The plunder of resources by transnational corporations and its impact on governments

Transnational corporations are plundering the forests, the seas, and the mineral resources of Pacific island nations, and governments have proved to be willing accomplices to these operations. A case in point is copper mining on Bouganville in Papua New Guinea.

In 1988 landowners protested against the multinational that was mining the copper at Paguna in Bouganville. Their demand for compensation for environmental damage was led by the Bouganville Revolutionary Army (BRA). The multinational closed the mines because it felt that the landowners were making unrealistic demands. The corporation was concerned that its profit margins would be reduced, while the Government of Papua New Guinea was concerned that it would lose a substantial portion of the income of the national budget.

In response to the impasse, the BRA unilaterally declared an independent republic of Bouganville in May 1990. The Government immediately imposed an economic and medical blockade, and today the war is continuing, affecting also the relationship between Papua New Guinea and the Solomon Islands.

The impact of structural adjustment programs (SAPs) on the living conditions of ordinary people

Several Pacific island nations have tax-free zones. As is quite well known, wages in these zones are set by employers and are not negotiable. Workers are not allowed to organize, and working conditions are fairly stringent. Most of the tax-free zones in the Pacific are host to garment industries whose labor force is predominantly women. In Fiji in particular, the garment workers are amongst the lowest paid and work under intolerable conditions.

Fiji in the past practiced tripartite bargaining as a method of settling disputes between employers and employees. With the advent of SAPs the Government has abandoned the practice of tripartite bargaining and in its place passed draconian labor legislation with no room for wage negotiations, improvement of safety standards, or improvement of working conditions. This of course has worsened the condition of workers in Fiji. Whereas before there was a legislated minimum wage for the manufacturing sector, now there is nothing.

Effects of an unjust system of international trade

Many countries of the Pacific have one major primary-commodity export, such as sugar, copra, or seafood. The prices of these commodities fluctuate drastically, depending on whether there is an oversupply or an undersupply. In the past there have been international agreements, such as the Lome Convention, offering price stabilization and subsidies. With the demands of an open-market economy, championed by GATT and the World Trade Organization and calling for the removal of this preferential treatment, earnings from the primary commodities of the Pacific island states will be subject to greater fluctuation and run the risk of losing much of their value.

Aid to the Pacific is increasing. One of the major sources of development financing is earnings from exports, but if the market pays its prices and price-setting is unpredictable, there will be little hope of respectable earnings from these commodities.

General questions

What mechanisms do we need to prevent any further increase in the world's nuclear arsenal? What arrangements should we have for the disposal of the accumulated nuclear waste and nuclear arsenal? The control of nuclear armaments and the proper disposal of nuclear wastes can be monitored properly only at the international level, with proper international standards and procedures.

How can the United Nations be strengthened to monitor properly the implementation of international instruments of human rights? How can we make the member states respect international standards and norms and behave accordingly, particularly toward their own people?

There is a need for a system of governance, at both international and national levels, that provides transparency and accountability. Accountability is a facet of participation that, when properly instituted, will make for effective democracy.

Transnational corporations that control the capital flow of the world need to be regulated and monitored. Nation states do not have the capacity to monitor the activities of these corporations unless there is an international framework to provide the standard. Therefore a call to implement a code of conduct for the transnational corporations is appropriate.

The only effective engine for sustainable development is a just and fair international system. No amount of aid will help the countries of the South out of their misery unless they are given the chance to make an honest living.

Peace and security of the person

Françoise Kaudjhis-Offoumou
International Association for Democracy in Africa
(AID-Afrique), Côte d'Ivoire

It is a privilege for me, both as an African and an Ivoirian and in my capacity as president of the International Association for Democracy in Africa (AID-Afrique), to speak in this august forum where the most distinguished female personalities from all over the world are meeting.

AID-Afrique is a mixed NGO created by Africans in 1993 in the city of Atlanta in the United States. Its headquarters are in Niger, and the chairperson is an Advocate at the Bar of Côte d'Ivoire. Its purpose is the defence and promotion of democracy and human rights in society, good governance, and sustainable development. It has branches in Côte d'Ivoire, Gabon, Guinea, Mali, Niger, and Senegal. Among its activities are those geared toward the promotion of peace and the security of the human being — in particular, its declarations on Rwanda and Burundi; its declaration on the devaluation of the CFA franc; a September 1995 communication in Cairo on democracy and population, addressing demographic explosion and its consequences; and various conferences.

The theme "peace and security of the person" provides us at this fourth meeting of women with the opportunity to determine the context and concepts; to discuss obstacles to peace and security and to find solutions to these obstacles; and to establish worldwide strategies and the means of adapting them to every country.

THE CONTEXT

Conflicts worldwide, and particularly in Africa, are sources of misery and underdevelopment. They bring about the destruction of human resources and are a hindrance to the edification of a prosperous nation. For example, we can refer to the catastrophic happenings in Rwanda, Burundi, Liberia, Somalia, Angola, the Middle East, Algeria, the Gambia, Haiti, Mozambique, and Zaire, and to the Toureg problem.

Africa and the rest of the world are aware that women and children are the greatest victims of these conflicts, victims of all forms of violence and insecurity. Indeed, since 1990 there have been 82 conflicts, of which about 70 are national. Eighty percent of the world's 18 million refugees — corresponding to 14.4 million people — are African. Seventy percent of the world's refugees, or

12.6 million people, are women and children. Forty percent of countries worldwide have at least five ethnic populations, whereas half of these countries have experienced ethnic struggles. In Angola three children out of ten die before the age of five.

Indicators of the absence of security in a given society can include the following: cases of extra-judiciary executions, torture, and arbitrary arrest and detention; the absence of well-being due to insufficient training, education, health care, freedom of political participation, and freedom of speech and association, as well as discrimination regarding women's rights, cultural rights, and economic rights; and the acceptance into a country of another country's toxic wastes. These indicators should be considered in the light of the Universal Declaration of Human Rights, the International Agreement on Civil and Political Rights, the International Agreement on Economic, Social, and Cultural Rights, and in accordance with the Convention on the Elimination of All Forms of Discrimination Against Women.

In the four months between April and July 1994, half of Rwanda's population — 3.5 million people — were killed or compelled to flee their homes and country because of tribal conflicts. As of 31 December 1993, the Liberian refugees in Côte d'Ivoire numbered 250,863, with women and children representing 90 percent of this population.

At the beginning of this century, 90 percent of civil war victims were soldiers. Today 90 percent of such victims are civilians, including children and women apart from those who have lost family and home. Only 5 percent of the victims of World War I were civilians. During World War II this figure rose to 50 percent.

Nonetheless, the annual military spending of developed countries is equal to the total income of two billion of the poorest people of the earth, and World Health Organization expenditures on health are well below this figure. Spending on military programs accounts for more than $800 million per annum — equal to the income of about one-half of the world's population. According to the report of UN Secretary-General Boutros Boutros Ghali, presented at the World Summit on Social Development, a child falls ill and dies every second of the day; one million persons are without basic health care; one adult in four is illiterate; and one-fifth of the world's population is undernourished.

DEFINITION OF THE CONCEPTS

The concept of security of the person

In the above-mentioned context, the security of the person should not be confused with human development. Security enables the individual to choose freely without any fear of danger, whereas human development is a process leading to the enlargement of the choices and opportunities available to each individual. Progress made in the development process of the individual strengthens the security of the individual, and the absence of human development leads to insecurity.

Whether we live in a rich country or a poor country, we are all concerned with the problem of the security of persons. This security has a number of components: economic security; food security; health and social security; environmental security; the security of the community and society; job security; and political, legal, and communications security for the individual. At the national level, this concept (in a restricted sense) could imply the security of national borders and military security, including that of nuclear, chemical, biological, and tactical arms.

The concept of peace

Peace is a state of harmony among individuals and implies harmonious relationships propitious to the prevention of the use of threats, force, civil and military aggression, and oppression, and of nonrespect for fundamental human rights. Peace is not only the absence of war. It is the lack of violence, the respect for social and economic justice, and equality for all. Thus the conquest of public liberties constitutes a search for peace.

A true promotion of women's rights can be obtained only in an atmosphere of peace and security for the family, for the nation, and for the world. For this reason, the meeting of the Commission on the Status of Women, held from February 25 to March 5, 1980, decided to elaborate a draft declaration on women's participation in the struggle for the enhancement of peace and international security. This question, raised at the 39th session of the UN General Assembly and at the Nairobi conference in 1985, is still topical. Most recently, it was brought forward by the national preparatory committees for the Fourth World Conference on Women in Beijing; at the regional conferences, in particular at the November 1994 conference in Dakar; at the March 1995 NGO consultations in New York; and at the 39th session of the Commission on the Status of Women, held in New York during March-April 1995.

Women should show more interest in matters of peace and the security of the person. These are prerequisites to achieving the objectives of this decade, inasmuch as the notion of women's participation in the security of the person and in the strengthening of peace is founded on the idea that those who participate in the decision-making process benefit, as a priority, from the decisions taken and the programs implemented. It is therefore necessary to determine the obstacles that hinder women's participation in the peace process and in the movement toward the security of the person and to elaborate strategies for women's full participation in these arenas.

THE OBSTACLES

Obstacles to peace

War hangs over every country like the sword of Damocles. A page has been turned in the history of apartheid in South Africa by that country's democratic government, led by President Nelson Mandela, and in the plight of Palestinian women and children by the Gaza-Jericho accord. Yet current happenings in Rwanda, Liberia, Somalia, Algeria, Angola, and elsewhere suggest that war and insecurity threaten every human being.

The involvement of women such as Winnie Mandela of South Africa; Heila Chahed, the PLO representative in Paris who condemned the removal of Palestine from the face of the earth; and Israeli prime minister Golda Meir, who refused to accept the existence of the peoples of Palestine, was a strong factor in mobilizing the international community toward resolving these conflicts. What, then, prevents women from becoming more involved in present-day conflicts?

We are all aware that illegal arms sales to African countries have been intensified and that 86 percent of arms supplying is done by the five permanent members of the Security Council. Hindering women's mobilization for peace may constitute a form of violence against women, whatever their origin.

The absence of information and political education; the absence of a civil democratic culture, social behavior, and the norms that foster self-government; and the absence of a culture of human rights contribute both to preventing women from perceiving their role in the peace process in Africa and to a misunderstanding of the importance of and the interest in women's participation in the peace process.

There are many obstacles to peace: sexual discrimination; religious fundamentalism, which considers women to be inferior beings; nepotism, which hinders the expression of women's competence; women victimized by violence; ignorance; fear; genocide; armed conflicts; overpopulation, with its accompanying disease, poverty, unemployment, misery, famine, and poor housing; lack of respect for cultures and traditions; class struggle; increased criminality; intergenerational conflict; the low level of women's participation in decision-making on peace; violations of the UN Charter. In addition, family conflicts, tensions, and divorce foster certain mental diseases, and the psychological shocks endured by children influence their relationships with their families and their behavior as citizens in society and participants in political life.

By contrast, women — considered as the custodians of the human race — are greatly concerned by matters of peace.

Obstacles to the security of the individual

All people, whatever their country or economic situation, are concerned with the security of the person. The world shall never live in peace if every individual does not enjoy the security necessary to daily life. Insecurity may be caused by famine, the rending of the social fabric, pollution, drugs, ethnic conflicts, living conditions, and so on. Threats to security in this century have been raised, not due to outside aggression, but to demographic explosion and the mismanagement of our cities resulting from high birth rates and immigration.

Indeed, rapid population growth is likely to aggravate living conditions in most African countries, where urban areas are overpopulated and experiencing unemployment. In sub-Saharan Africa the average unemployment rate in towns is about 20 percent of the labor force. The informal sector accounts for about 60 percent in urban areas. In rural areas more than one-half of the labor force is unemployed. In North Africa and the Middle East the rate of unemployment varies between 10 and 20 percent, the youths being the most affected.[1]

An increasing labor force necessarily results in the reduction of arable land, which leads to the creation of slums. A high population density leads to alcoholism, drugs, insecurity, delinquency, poor health conditions, environmental degradation in the form of air and water pollution, the destruction of forests, high-level migration, disease, and hunger. These in turn affect the quality of life, terrorism, fundamentalism, and slavery.

Human insecurity is a universal problem. If poor countries are more concerned by famine, disease, fundamentalism, and slavery, rich countries must face delinquency, drugs, and a very high level of urbanization. States should therefore pay more attention to funding for the protection of their borders and the protection of the individuals inside those borders.

STRATEGIES

The strategies aimed at lifting obstacles to peace and security and enabling the participation of women in the peace process should consider the effective application of the 1993 Kampala Plan of Action on Women and Peace and the 1995 Plan of Action adopted by the World Summit for Social Development in Copenhagen.

At the family level

Wars are created by men. And it is in the spirit of men that peace should be created and preserved,

as is stated in the Declaration on the Preparation of Societies to Live in Peace, adopted by the UN General Assembly on December 15, 1978.

The family has a primal role in building up a propitious environment for peace by teaching the child the qualities of tolerance, friendliness, and amity in his or her relations with others, which must be devoid of aggression and the desire to dominate. Education should be received in a spirit of peace. Parents should avoid offering their children games or allowing them to see films or read books that kindle a liking for war, aggression, cruelty, an excessive desire to gain power, or other forms of violence. Appropriate measures should be taken to prevent and resolve family feuds.

More especially, constitutions and civil institutions and laws should strengthen family protections, an area in which experts and specialists in infant and family matters could make a contribution. Preparation for family and marital life could be fostered by instituting premarital schools or consultation centers.

There should be mandatory medical treatment for all alcohol and drug addicts as well as social welfare assistance to alcoholics and drug addicts who agree to undergo treatment. Where such preventive and curative measures fail, penal law should be accepted as the ultimate solution to all abuse of the rights of the family. Centers must be established to receive and care for battered women.

At the national level

It is essential to educate our youth for peace. Educating for universal peace should be founded on the notion of peace within each individual and each country. As with all concepts, peace can be taught and developed. Its principal aspects are respect, tolerance, and mutual understanding, with a view to achieving national and international concord.

This type of education should be implemented as governmental policy, and each country's constitution should guarantee religious tolerance and respect for differing religious beliefs. National educational policy should instill in the minds of youth ideas of peace and their personal responsibility in the maintenance of peace. Moreover, national and international affairs should be seen as maintaining peace.

Education should enable youth to acquire an objective perspective of the world. In order to obtain international peace, future generations should be taught notions of national peace. In this regard, it is desirable to develop linguistic exchanges and "town twinning," or sister cities, to institute a national Day of the Child, to maintain international relations with the Scouts movement, and to establish international student exchanges involving both schoolchildren and students pursuing an advanced education.

At the state level

The state is called upon to maintain a constant atmosphere of peace. This should take due notice of constitutional rights and of the role of the family and relevant institutions and organizations in order to ensure that the means used to guarantee peace and security — including educational practices and the mass media — are compatible with the task of preparing the society, particularly younger generations, to live in peace. There should be diverse fora and international conferences organized to promote bilateral and multilateral cooperation, for and by both international government and nongovernmental organizations, with a view to better prepare society to live in peace and security and to exchange experiences undertaken in this direction.

To do this, it would be necessary to determine to what extent the state cares for the individual, through the abrogation of all discriminatory provisions in national laws, inasmuch as true peace depends on the extent to which people's real interests and rights and the guarantees of these rights are reflected in the laws of the land.

The international status of the state influences the living conditions of its citizens. Hence the state should develop a pacified economy, with the possibility of using the fruits of citizens' labor for their immediate interests. It should also reduce military spending in order to increase the material gains of one and all, making it possible to safeguard peace and security. At the state level, increases in military spending are made to the detriment of education, health, culture, and other necessities of life, thereby producing a threat to peace and security.

National development must enable women to participate actively in society. The equality of citizens' rights, in their political and social contexts, should be ensured without distinction of race, sex, or creed, thereby preventing national discord and guaranteeing peace and security.

Peace and security within one country contribute to universal peace and security. The limitation of sovereign rights is therefore necessary in order to establish the mutual defense of peace and security. Actions likely to destroy the living conditions of people constitute preparations for war, which are illegal and should be suppressed.

The individual's right to work should be guaranteed by the state. Each individual should also respect national sovereignty and strive to strengthen amity among nations. Good neighborliness, mutual understanding, and cooperation should be integrated into the teachings of peace, security, democracy, and human rights.

A women's march for peace — including meetings, conferences, demonstrations, and collections of signatures supporting the promotion of peace — should be organized. A peace day should be instituted in every country.

All international instruments for the protection of human rights — in particular, the Convention on the Elimination of All Forms of Discrimination Against Women and the Guarantee of the Fundamental Rights of Women and Children in Situations of Conflict — should be ratified.

At the international level

It is impossible for a single state or people to resolve the problems of peace and security. It is therefore essential to banish suspicion, confrontation, and isolation, and to make every possible effort to establish human solidarity in the event of a civil war or during political and armed conflicts.

Measures should be taken to provide education and protection for repatriated or displaced refugees, who should by no means disturb the peace and tranquility of the local populations. In this regard, women — the essential link between peace and security and vocational education — should play their role as artisans of peace.

To achieve this, the arms race must be stopped. Military spending should be reduced so as to benefit the security of individuals. The following goals should be stressed: well-being, education, health and development, respect for the rights of citizens over the intrigues of the state, the effective application of the UN Charter, the creation of a buffer force, state commitment to arbitration or conciliation, establishment of an African court of human rights to settle all differences in cases of violation of the principles of peace. These are preferable to the creation of a multitude of tribunals or to members of the Security Council refusing to subsidize exports in order further to enhance security and development. Women should be nominated to posts of responsibility, and in the diplomatic field women's presence at negotiating tables and their access to political power and decision-making centers should be implemented.

At the NGO level

Women can contribute to the establishment of peace and international security through information and the development of a culture of peace, civil democracy, and human rights. Such a culture would make it possible to accept the right to difference. It would promote mutual understanding and the recognition of human dignity; freedom of thought, speech, and association; the right of access to political power and centers of decision-making; and effective participation in the international campaign for disarmament. Artists, writers, and journalists should become more involved in the peace process by publishing works, plays, and songs for peace and, financed by the state, should participate effectively in the search for peace.

NGOs and governments should publish existing treaties and agreements in order to slow down the arms race. The year 1986 was declared the International Year for Peace, and NGOs should mobilize civil society to participate in annual celebrations of this event.

NGOs should act as mediators in ongoing conflicts. They should act as pressure groups to compel states to cease discriminatory practices involving women and cause states to provide equal access to women in the diplomatic field, setting up institutional measures to facilitate women's participation in the peace process. NGOs should help ensure a judicious distribution of resources, thereby eliminating injustice and inequality. They should develop women's aptitude to fend for themselves and should cultivate effective solidarity among women.

NGOs should undertake firm actions to enhance traditional peacekeeping bodies and create the necessary conditions for promoting women's awareness of important problems in international relations, such as the need for a fair trial for political prisoners and guarantees of the fundamental rights of citizens.

CONCLUSION

The concepts of peace and security should be seen by the Fourth World Conference on Women as a major challenge to be met in this century. More importance should be laid on prevention through substantial economic and social investments and reforms and through long-term sustainable development.

Peace and security, seen in the light of global commitment and cooperation, should be founded on the interests of rich and poor countries alike and not on a beggar-giver relationship. This concept should be reviewed from the perspective of protecting the national potential of future generations through the preservation of natural systems.

Poor countries are struggling against contagious diseases and drugs in order to contribute to environmental protection. Both poor and rich countries can also provide mediation as their contribution to world peace. Furthermore, if the World Summit on Social Development has raised questions of poverty, unemployment, pollution, drugs, migration, social exclusion, and so on — which compromise the security of the individual — an institutional mechanism defining the indicators and the threshold of tolerability of insecurity are still to be created.

Therefore we should start reflecting on the creation of this institutional framework. With respect to peace, the rights of women should be guaranteed through effective protection against physical, sexual, and psychological assaults. Armed conflicts, political conflicts, and civil wars in Africa bring about untold destruction of human resources and hinder all economic and social development. Peace is a prerequisite to the achievement of equality and development in both the public and private lives of women. Full integration of women, the victims of the consequences of conflicts and wars, is indispensable to implementing proposed strategies for the year 2000 and beyond.

Women, the artisans of peace, should be the ferment of the culture of peace. In this regard, they should work tirelessly toward the promotion of justice, which alone can guarantee a better and more peaceful world for all in the process of sustainable development.

Note

1. The World Summit for Social Development—Report of the Secretary-General. A/CONF/166/PC/6, 4 January 1994.

Never again a war: women's bodies are battlefields

Vesna Kesić
Be Active, Be Emancipated (B.a.B.e.); Croatia

Socialism was not a system that implemented gender equality. Women in Croatia and the whole of former Yugoslavia, like women elsewhere in Eastern Europe — once called the countries "behind the Iron Curtain" — participated in the democratization processes with enthusiasm and confidence. Women started to raise their voices in politics as well as in public life. Women's groups and their networks in the former Yugoslavia were the first sign of civil society and the first fighters for independent political status since the late 1970s. We were the first who wanted to organize autonomously and to get out of the frozen bureaucratic system of state socialism and a society controlled by the rule of one party. The fight was not easy, given the patriarchal, hierarchical environment in which male dominance was hidden by formal equality and deeply rooted in tradition and the political system. In the 1980s, we had a feeling that we had started to succeed. At least women's voices became louder.

Today we read the news about former socialist countries' "further successes" to be "included in the world system of the free market, individual freedoms, and Western-style democracy." The extreme exceptions are the countries of the former Yugoslavia and the former USSR. These two countries were rather different in terms of their political systems and economic life. Now war makes them more alike than ever before. In the former USSR, war is still occurring on the margins of the former empire. The war in the former Yugoslavia is reaching its culmination with four million displaced people and 16,000 children killed or dead. Reliable statistics are unavailable, but international humanitarian groups estimate that around 80 percent of the dead are civilians. About 20,000 to 30,000 women (or even more) have been raped as part of the war strategy and ethnic cleansing. I agree with those who claim that ethnic cleansing is at the root of this latest Balkan war — not a mere consequence. Women's bodies once again are the battlefield for big ideas and huge historical fights; they provide the ultimate proof of male dominance over his male enemy and the enemy's property.

In that sense, the difference between the former Yugoslavia and other ex-socialist countries-in-transformation is enormous. Nevertheless, there are some structural similarities. The most visible is the deterioration of women's social and economic status. As Upendra Baxi has said, "The Berlin Wall fell on the bodies of women." Women are the losers: They disappear from paid labor; violence against women is increasing; they lost such previously granted rights as the right to freely choose legal and safe abortion and the right to free health care and social security for themselves and their children; they are not involved in decision-making processes; they have lost their previous right to guaranteed (at least legally and formally) equal wages; they are not significantly present in the emerging class of owners. The bureaucratic oppression and exclusion of women in patriarchal and hierarchical socialism has been replaced with the free-enterprise spirit of competition, conflict, commercialism, and insecurity. The new entrepreneurs greedily run after their first million dollars, and in exactly the same way, new would-be democratic leaders greedily run after power. As my friend Zorica Mrsevic, a feminist from Belgrade, says, "State socialism is replaced with predatory capitalism."

The question I pose is: When the powerful men of the world — politicians, bankers, advisors, newspaper editors — talk about the "successful privatization, democratization, transformation, etc.," in Eastern Europe and Third World countries, what are they talking about? Who is the subject of their analysis? What sort of peace and human security is it if we agree that social insecurity, poverty, lack of dignity, and gender oppression are just as much a threat in everyday life as war, even if the consequences are not so visibly cruel? Once again, this is talk about big history and mainstream politics in which women and less powerful men are predestined losers.

War is, no doubt, the first and biggest obstacle to peace and human security. It is the ultimate violation of all human rights in that the right to life is endangered. Wars do not just happen. They do not appear from nowhere or from a deep, dark reservoir of human nature. That is the lesson I learned during the development of the war in the former Yugoslavia. Once upon a time, I believed that the scene in an old Hollywood movie, showing riots starting when a man slipped on a banana peel and unwillingly hit another man, was realistic. I also believed that conflicts and wars could be prevented by the rational involvement of people and wise politicians. I believed that people have a will to prevent armed conflicts. In good old Europe, we talked about 50 years of rational politics. We remembered the lessons of the Second World War, and we said: Never again a war, never again a holocaust! Yet it is happening all over again. This time it has an appropriate new name invented just for the occasion: ethnic cleansing. It is exercised by all sides in this war.

Now I know better. I am not a follower of some obscure theory of conspiracy, but I observed the whole course of the war: how the war was produced and heated; how people and whole nations and ethnic groups were forced against each other by warmongering manipulations, media propaganda, seductive political speeches, historical reductionism, blindness created by hatred, and — what is most important — in the interests of somebody. The international community has not been willing to do anything serious to prevent that war.

Being myself deeply involved in humanitarian and human rights activism, I often remember a fact I heard at one conference: The United Nations spends on war prevention only 2 percent of the money it spends on resolving the consequences of the wars. Would this be true if wars were not in someone's interest? Humanitarian aid, refugee protection and assistance, development investments, peacekeeping or peace-protecting forces, negotiating teams, education and training of people in the so-called new democracies or postwar societies and the countries of the Third World can also be big business — regardless of the good will and best intentions of the organizations and people involved in those support systems.

I want to repeat: Wars — there are some 150 going on all the time around the globe — are in somebody's interest. Perhaps it would be better to say: in the interest of something. Real socialism was a cruel and unbearable form of society for people to live in. It was definitely not the world of human rights and freedom. After its collapse, it is hard to say that modern wars, with all the technology and sophisticated weapons that they involve, are only the tip of the iceberg of global capitalism. Global capitalism includes the notion of global economy, global markets, global TV networks, global hamburgers and colas, global enterprises, conflicts, supremacy, technological and nuclear competition, global ecological disasters, global governance.

Women have entered this global world with the intention of changing it. Women bring the ideas of new leadership, new psychology, new ways of communicating and negotiating, new approaches to power and governance, new forms of feminist communities, new and better relationships between genders and among all people.

But we shall not be successful if we cease to criticize the existing world and if we don't develop visions of the new one. To do this, we must seek the answers to the following questions, among others: Who is selling arms to whom? Whose national income depends on producing and transferring technologies and whose on rice and silk shirts? Those should be the most important issues of conferences like this one. Militarization, violence (including that against women in war), and poverty are not just the consequences or the effects of something unknown. They are not the consequences of wars themselves. They are not mere obstacles to peace and human security that appear regardless of global and structural processes. Militarization, violence, and poverty are intrinsic parts of the world that — although called global — really has only one thing in common: the global market and the interests of global capital. In such a world, the goods and well-being of people are unequally divided, and they are not universal. Militarization, violence, and poverty belong to one part of that world, and that is its larger part — the South, the Third World, the underdeveloped, the women, name it as you wish.

This is the world in which women can be a metaphor for the global South, as my Indian friend Corinne Kumar would say. Since recently, most of the former socialist countries belong to that metaphor, although the whole process of democratization and freedom started with the invitation to, and people's enthusiasm for, Western democracy and global free enterprise. The war in the former Yugoslavia and other emerging wars — besides all the other complicated causes — have their origin in the mermaid's call of the global West that was not thoughtfully reconsidered. The women of the world should be aware of the seductive calls of shopping malls if they want to change the world.

How the military impacts our lives

Rosalie Bertell
Voice of Women, Canada

We can consider military impacts on women by referring to three levels of military visibility: first and most obvious, the violence of war itself; second, the socioeconomic impact of war and preparations for war; and third, the more hidden impact on the human habitat and life-support system of modern technological warfare and megadeath production. No one of us escapes injury on at least one of these levels.

The violence of war

Boot camp is a concentrated effort to erase all of the gentle upbringing of a young man or woman. "Any woman's son will do" is an old saying. However, few of us realize the depth of the brutalization process designed to make the combatant "comfortable" with killing. The sex or age of the "enemy" makes no difference. Any child or elderly woman can be carrying a hand grenade. Using antipersonnel weapons "shortens the war." Rape of women is their "just desert"; it both humiliates the "enemy" and prevents the comfort he obtains from "his woman"!

We are all, unfortunately, familiar with the brutality of war, with its pillaging and slaughter. However, we seldom stop to think that it is really unnatural for humans to kill; otherwise it would not require so many external forces to keep the killing activity in place: special uniforms (to keep them from running away), better food than civilians and various other bribes, camaraderie, close living quarters where one can be watched. In an extreme, for example in the Falklands/Malvinas war, men were shot in the foot so that they could not run away. Deserters are severely punished, even killed. There are elaborate social pressures, especially on young men, to fight for the glory of Country, Motherhood, and the Flag. If war were natural, these measures would not be necessary.

The myth of war being a part of human nature

needs to be exposed as a lie. Along with this myth there are myths that men go to war for women; hence women must satisfy their sexual desires as "payment." Even UN peacekeepers believe that they are entitled to rape women in return for their "sacrifice." Indeed, it must be women's concern to erase these destructive myths and behaviors from civil society.

Violence never ends a dispute or conflict; it only biases the dialogue which must take place at the end. Biased dialogue forced by the more powerful opponent is never just, and the loser always waits for the next opportunity to renew the conflict in the hopes of "winning" and dictating the "peace." War begets nothing but more war. It is uncivilized, brutish, and unjust. It is behavior which needs to be renounced, just as civilized people renounce slavery and cannibalism.

The socioeconomic impact of war and preparation for war

War and the preparation for war depletes society of needed money and resources. The strategy of the West in the cold war was to so push the nuclear and space race that they broke the economy of the Soviet Union. It was a reckless gamble that economic strain would not break the Western economies first or cause the Soviet Union to launch a nuclear war rather than admit defeat. Even as the Soviet Union collapsed, so did the West sink into depressed economies from which it has not yet emerged. The German and Japanese economies, those of the two countries forbidden to build up their militaries after World War II, were of course the exception. They had not participated in the "race," and therefore they could put their human and natural resources to civilian tasks.

In order to maintain the cold war, both the West and the Soviet Union resorted to surrogate wars in which they could try out their weapons systems and through which they could sell some of their surplus military production. Stockpiling all the military production would quickly lead to bankruptcy. The wars in the economically developing world were fed through this rivalry, bringing unspeakable physical, emotional, and economic harm to most of the world's people. The so-called low-intensity wars left countries devastated and impoverished, caused millions of refugees, and led to slaughter, maiming, and dislocation of countless numbers of innocent people.

Another aspect of war preparation in the high-technology world is the brain drain. Young, intelligent students are picked up by the military as they complete their education, and they are captured for the secret military projects into which money and resources are poured. The nations undertaking such practices want to "harness technology" in the cause of world domination. This brain drain has the effect of harming all civilian enterprises, including medical and educational services. It is difficult to obtain funding unless projects are related to some area in which there is military interest. It biases the economy and the intellectual efforts of society toward military priorities. I remember being outraged when I visited a U.S. university in the 1970s and found that freshman university students were torturing large animals under a research project testing nerve gas for the army. Video games are designed to prepare young people for technological warfare. Nuclear power reactors were a highly dangerous method of boiling water to produce electricity, but they were needed by the military to gain civilian support for their industrial needs.

The impact of war on the human habitat and life-support system

There is a more dangerous and subtle level of military impact on women and children and on the survival of the human race. This impact is like a cancer in society. It begins quietly, becomes part of the living organism, and gradually saps away all of the life force. A good example of this is what I like to call the "peaceful chlorine program." In World War I, military scientists separated chlorine gas for the first time in large enough quantities to become one of the poison gases used in warfare. Chlorine does not exist as a gas naturally in this biosphere we call home.

After the war scientists tried to find uses for this gas, as if it were a new and wonderful toy. Some scientists became chlorine chemists, who systematically built up chlorinated molecules and then tried to find uses for the new products. Some of the early ones were carbon tetrachloride, the cleaning fluid which we now know is carcinogenic. Another was chloroform, once used as an anaesthetic but now not used because of dangerous side-effects. Eventually chlorine chemistry produced the herbicides, pesticides, and defoliants which were used to kill the jungle in the Vietnam War. These chemicals were devastating to plants, animals, and humans, causing skin eruptions, reproductive abnormalities, malformed children, and cancer. They were watered down for civilian use, causing many farm-related illnesses and fatalities, loss of prime farmland, and general dependence on chemical farming.

Although chlorine was used to kill bacteria in drinking water, thus reducing many water-borne diseases, it also was transformed in the environment into organochlorines, which we now recognize as copycat hormones. These man-made chemicals are able to replace normal estrogen in the body and are likely implicated in a number of reproductive organ anomalies, such as reduced sperm counts, undescended testes in newborn males, and cancers. In the Great Lakes region of North America organochlorines have been implicated in sex reversals (de-masculinization and de-feminization) of birds, fish, and animals in the wild. Studies of the implications for human sexuality and reproduction have just begun. However, we cannot claim to be immune to these ubiquitous chemicals.

Today there are over 11,000 different chlorine chemicals in large quantities in our land, water, and air. None of these occurred in any significant way in our environment prior to World War I. I call it the "peaceful chlorine" program because of the similarity in development to the "peaceful atom" program after World War II. Like chlorine, nuclear radiation products are becoming embedded in our civilian economy, being used for farming, mining, medical tracers, smoke alarms, research, food irradiation, sterilization of medical instruments, generation of electricity, etc. Again, there was no question about using this death technology broadly and exposing men, women, and children of all ages and states of health while we learned the consequences of exposure. Our warriors like to learn

through large-scale human experimentation. Their death-dealing discoveries are presumed "innocent" until proven "guilty" beyond any reasonable doubt through tragic human experiences.

Looking to the future

We are here in Beijing, women acutely aware of the physical, social, and economic violence of our masculine-dominated society, aware that physical or technological power assures the nation and the individual of the right of dominance. We realize that our human relationships — marriage, family life, community, and nations — are threatened by this cancerlike poison. Even more frightening is the realization that the slow poisoning of our land, water, air, and food by the spin-offs of a military death culture are gradually attacking the integrity of the gene pool — source of all future life on the planet — and making the earth habitat unlivable. This is a death process for the human species. We are producing offspring less able to cope and giving them a world more hazardous to cope with.

While we are here looking back on the mistakes of the past, the warriors among us are out creating even more spectacular and lethal technologies. I will just mention one which may be new to you. The U.S. government, through its U.S. Defense Advanced Research Project Agency, is building and testing in Alaska a High Frequency Active Auroral Research Project (HAARP). This appears to be a model of the "full global shield" designed by Bernard J. Eastland — capable of destroying satellites and missiles and of totally disrupting all radio communications around the globe. The HAARP design calls for powerful blasts of electromagnetic energy, causing a heating of the earth's protective ionosphere and creating artificial magnetic lines around the globe. These magnetic lines can eventually direct massive energy (more than an atomic bomb can deliver) to pinpointed locations on the planet.

The HAARP experiment is predicted to be able to cause the earth to wobble on its axis, which may cause a see-saw motion. Some see this motion as capable of causing the planet to move further away from the sun. Others speculate that the energy experiments will cause an implosion reaction, causing the earth to move toward the sun. The HAARP technology could be used to change climate and weather patterns, and is likely to change the chemistry of the ionosphere in ways which are difficult to predict. Life on earth depends on the delicate balance of oxygen, nitrogen, and water in the atmosphere. The prototype HAARP facility is now operating, and construction on the second and larger antenna array was begun early in 1995. It is expected to be operative in late 1997. An ARCO company, ARCO Power Technologies Inc., has the bid for construction. There was no competition for the contract, and the total cost of the project far exceeds the yearly budget of the small company. It is thought that ARCO patents for this experimental technology are being used, although the military denies this. The site of this military facility is Gakona, Alaska, on the north slope.

According to the U.S. Office of Naval Research, November 4, 1993:

Similar [to HAARP], though less capable, research facilities exist today at many locations throughout the world and are operated routinely for the purpose of scientific investigation of the ionosphere. In the U.S. such systems are located in Arecibo, Puerto Rico, and Fairbanks, Alaska. Other installations are at Tromso, Norway; Moscow, Nizhny Novgorod, and Apatity, Russia; Karkov, Ukraine; and Dushanbe, Tadzikistan. None of these existing systems, however, has the combination of frequency capability and beam-steering agility required to perform the experiments planned for HAARP.

The power to deliver immense pulses of destructive energy anywhere in the world; the power to change weather, modify climate, and disrupt all radio communication on the globe; the power to cause the earth to wobble on its axis and change its position relative to the sun; the ability to destroy satellites, missiles, and planes! — this hardly constitutes providing for the national security.

This small and fragile earth-home is a place for us to live, breathe the air, enjoy the sunshine, and bask in the brilliant diversity of life. No nation has a right to destroy this in the name of military power. This addiction with violence, this military cancer on civil society, has reached the point where either we destroy it and renounce war forever, or it will destroy us. There is no human security in the face of military excesses. National defense produces nothing but insecurity. It is time that we took our stand for life, for justice, for sharing, and for conflict resolution. War and militarism must go the way of the dinosaurs, or we are the last generation to enjoy a still-intact planet.

Women must take the leadership in restoring true security based on justice, sharing, and cooperation. We must demand that international recognition go not to bully nations but to those who demonstrate honesty, compassion, and right living. We need to recognize and honor nations for their intelligence and diligence in solving human problems and improving the quality of human life. Violence and threats of violence will never hold together the global village. It will fail just as it fails to hold together a marriage or a family or a community.

Like other aberrant behavior, violence is similar to a communal addiction. It must be confronted. It must be destroyed by our noncooperation with it. This is our home planet, to be cared for and lived in and passed on to our children. It is not a place to be experimented with or a place for achieving new and better ways to use efficient killing technologies. This dark part of our societies needs to receive women's light, scrutiny, and healing.

V • Challenges Posed by the Globalization of the Economy

Including the Impact of the Technological Revolution on Work

Opening remarks

Yoko Kitazawa, Moderator
Pacific/Asia Resource Center (PARC-AMPO), Japan

I belong to the NGO called Pacific/Asia Resource Center, which is based in Tokyo, Japan. This organization has been working for the last 20 years making critical analyses of global forces such as transnational corporations, the Japanese government, the IMF, and the World Bank. We focus on the impact of these forces on the people, particularly on women. We have been proposing reforms of the IMF and World Bank and also a code of conduct for transnational corporations.

The task given to this session is to deal with the globalization of the economy, which is a critically important issue. We have four panelists who are experts and activists on this theme, and each one is representing a region.

Let me briefly state the common understanding of our theme. What is the globalization of the economy? Globalization is promoted by global forces. What are the global forces? Who are the actors that make the economy globalized? They are the transnational corporations, the IMF, the World Bank, GATT, and even the United Nations. Who are the beneficiaries of this globalization? Certainly not the people. The beneficiaries are the minority, the rich people. Who are the victims? Who sacrifices? The answer is the vast majority of the people, particularly women in both North and South.

We now have four panelists who are going to speak on the globalization of the economy, not only as victims but as challengers to the global forces.

Women: A powerful motive force for the development of the global economy

Duan Cunhua
Sumstar Group Corporation, China

Recent years have witnessed a rapid growth of the world economy, spurred by two upsurges: globalization of the economy and regional economic integration. In this worldwide drive for development, the economic rise in developing countries is particularly eye-catching. This global economic development, viewed from an overall perspective, has the following salient features:

• There has been an unprecedented increase in trade, flow of funds, and exchange of technologies and personnel among countries.

• Finance, insurance, real-estate development, service, and other new industries are experiencing new growth and expansion.

• When breakthroughs have been made in the technological field, the world economy increasingly integrates these new achievements. Indeed, the progress of science and technology has boosted productivity and in turn given rise to a wide range of new technologies, products, and industries, bringing about profound changes to modes of social production and lifestyles.

• Because of this economic growth, it is now possible to make education available to everybody while improving its quality. Education in itself is thus able to supply society with workers of better quality and to constantly change people's thinking.

In short, the world economy is undergoing a period of great development, readjustment, opening, integration, and competition. With each passing day there is a growing trend toward reciprocal dependence and interpenetration of different national economies. Meanwhile, a global market economy is in the making, which, made up by national markets, will be diversified and pluralistic.

To women, this new period means ever-expanding scope and a better material basis for their development. Nevertheless, there exist two diametrically opposed views in modern society with regard to women's role in economic development. One holds that women, as a group bound to be sifted out in the wake of this rapid economic growth, should go back to the kitchen. The other, however, describes women as a major force in economic development and insists that any idea, as long as it underestimates women's contribution to economic development, is utterly wrong. For a consensus of opinion, let's consider the following facts.

The situation in China

China has made great achievements through its reforms. The rapid development and sustained growth of its economy have provided women with an opportunity to prove their own worth. As a matter of fact, women have become an important force that promotes China's economic development.

The country has greatly enhanced its overall economic strength in the course of striving to shift from a planned economy to a market economy and to make its national economy conform to international standards. Since the policy of reform and opening to the world began 16 years ago, the country's GNP has grown at annual rates averaging 9.4 percent. China is now reputed to be one of the countries experiencing a development that is vigorous and rapid, not just in the Asia-Pacific region but throughout the world.

While the national economy is growing rapidly and in a sustained manner, the labor market has grown in volume and so has the demand for female workers. In 1990 women accounted for 45 percent of China's working population, up 1.3 percent from 1982. During the period of 1982-1990, 63 million women came into the workforce, among whom urban working women increased 23 million, representing 36.7 percent of the total urban em-

ployment growth, while rural women laborers showed a 40 million rise, making up 54 percent of the increase. Throughout the 1979-1988 period the growth rate of urban female employment, which averaged 5 percent annually, was higher than that of urban male employment and 1.27 percent higher than the national average. According to rough estimates, employed women furnish half of China's GNP and tax revenue every year. Moreover, 50 to 60 percent of China's gross agricultural output is generated by rural women. Women account for one-third of the 14 million rural workers in individual and privately owned enterprises and 40 percent of those employed by township-run enterprises. With a per capita income 3.5 times as great as the average for the entire rural population, these women, while standing on their own financially, help improve the conditions of their families. Women working with township enterprises earn 2.5 times as much as the national rural average.

To Chinese women, the great changes in China's economy mean an improved employment structure and more jobs of higher caliber. Seen from a horizontal perspective, female employment is expanding from the textile industry and handicrafts, the traditional fields of occupation for women, into electronics, machinery, and other technology-intensive undertakings as well as post and telecommunications, communications, commerce, catering, trade, and tourism. The number of women employed in new industries such as finance and insurance has doubled and redoubled. Seen from a vertical perspective, a growing number of women have proved themselves to be outstanding in economic activities and become reputed as business managers, factory directors, scientists, technical experts, and skilled workers. For example, nearly 2,000 women have become directors and managers in township enterprises in Guangdong Province, while in Fujian Province the number is 3,000. With their contributions to the development of China's national economy, Chinese women are showing the world a strength which nobody can make light of.

Chinese women have significantly improved their own cultural attitudes, and great changes have taken place in their mental outlook. In 1993,

852,000 women received higher education. They accounted for 33.6 percent of the total enrollment, up 9.4 percent from 1979. The Chinese women have freed themselves from traditional ideas of male superiority and female obedience under whatever circumstances. These ideas, a legacy of China's feudal society, bound them hand and foot for thousands of years. While tapping their own potential in contributing to China's economic development, and along with the improvement of their status in society and in the family, Chinese women have acquired a better understanding of their own talents and capabilities. Testifying to this is a 1990 sample investigation into women's social status, conducted in a certain place in China. Only 15 percent of the rural women covered by the investigation agreed to the assertion that "by nature, men are superior to women." Among those young and middle-aged women questioned, only 6 percent agreed that "women should not try to gain a higher position in society than their husbands." In contrast, 53 percent of the women expressed hope to "exceed men of the same caliber in personal achievements." Besides, 39 percent of the women were confident in their ability to "hold still higher positions."

This mental liberation achieved by women means that they will be able to make even greater contributions to China's economic development.

The international situation

Economic cooperation is gaining momentum in the Asia-Pacific region, and significant changes have taken place in the social status of women and in their contributions to the region's economic development. The Asia-Pacific region, particularly Southeast Asia, has been the scene of exceptionally rapid economic growth over the past decade, with annual rates averaging 8 percent.

This has been accompanied by a significant improvement in female employment in both quantity and quality, which in turn exhibits women's growing contributions to the economy. In Malaysia the employment rate of women rose from 37 percent in 1970 to 47 percent in 1990, a steady increase that is obviously higher than the rise in men's employment rate. In Bangladesh the rate of female

employment has reached 41 percent. In Singapore 51 percent of able-bodied women had jobs in 1994, and 45 percent of married women continued working, up 15 percent from 1991. Indonesian women have a higher rate of increase in employment than their male compatriots. In Laos female employment rose from 35 percent in 1985 to 49 percent in 1992. In the Maldives it increased from 25 percent in 1985 to 31 percent in 1991.

Equally significant is the improvement of the quality of female employment. In 1970 women accounted for only 4.3 percent of those working in high-tech fields in Southeast Asia. The figure rose to 27.1 percent in 1980 and by 1990 had reached 35.9 percent. In Hong Kong this qualitative improvement manifests itself in the fact that senior and managerial posts taken by women are increasing. In 1961, 2,500 Hong Kong women took managerial posts, representing a ratio of 1:12.4 relative to men of the same caliber. By 1991 the number of female managers there had grown to 50,000 and the ratio had changed to 1:3.9.

The same changes are found in the highly developed United States, where the number of enterprises started and managed by women has increased from 2.5 million in the 1980s to 7.7 million today. It is estimated that over one-third of the small enterprises in the United States are owned by women. Moreover, large numbers of American women have come to be employed in service industries. As a matter of fact, women now outnumber men in banking, accounting, retail sales, insurance, and consultancy businesses.

Main conclusions

• Women are a powerful motive force for global economic development. Their involvement generates new managerial concepts and helps diversify management forms. With natural endowments characteristic of their sex, they are actually unique in themselves. Their experiences, the role they play, and their talents and capabilities are of unique value to sustained environmental and economic development. Low efficiency in economic operations has nothing to do with women, nor have women been a "burden" that hampers economic development and social progress. Involving women in global economic issues is an inevitable choice by the international community. For women, this constitutes a historic mission of epoch-making significance.

• The level of development of productive forces does not correspond in a linear way to the number of people employed. It is true that the level of development of productive forces determines the number of jobs available in society at large and to women in particular. Nevertheless, this is a rule only in a very broad sense, its upper and lower limits being variables governed by the competence of each social group. Social standards, rather than standards in favor of men, should be applied to ensure fair competition for employment. Persons meeting the same social standards should be treated as equals, regardless of the sex of the individual.

• The scientific and technological progress brought about by the globalization of the economy is not a factor that restricts women's involvement in economic development. On the contrary, women are able to take part in a broader range of economic activities precisely because of this progress.

• Women throughout the world, especially those in developing countries like ours, should have a clear understanding that improvement of their own qualifications and their initiative in participating in economic development decide to what extent they get involved in economic development and to what extent women's liberation can be attained. They should constantly influence and improve the social and community conditions for their participation in economic development.

• Women's involvement is as badly needed as men's in global economic development. It can definitely be said that economic development will be greatly restricted without the participation of women, who make up one-half of the world's population. This involvement is not a favor bestowed upon women by men or governments, but is something demanded by economic development. I believe that at the next World Conference on Women, more examples will be cited to prove this truth. But we still have a long way to go, and we still face problems and barriers.

Problems

Women are facing a host of new problems while helping advance economic development globally. Many countries are restructuring their industrial set-up and reorganizing the various factors of production as globalization of the economy and regional economic integration proceed. This is giving rise to new requirements and challenges for women.

Women are facing a host of common problems also because changes in traditional ideas, religious cultures, and social awareness often fail to keep pace with economic development.

• Female employment remains limited to relatively few fields and relatively low jobs. Employed women are working mostly in service trades. The rate of female employment is low in some countries and regions — for example, 21 percent in North Africa and 23 percent in Western Asia.

• Only a tiny percentage of women have taken the leading posts. According to U.S. estimates, it is as low as 5 percent. Statistics in this regard are commonly lacking in most countries, which has greatly prevented public support and promotion of women entering high-level management. It is therefore essential that statistics bureaus in all countries make further efforts to collect such gender-specific data and record such achievements made by women.

• In many countries and regions, women to varying degrees are the victims of unequal pay for equal work and have to bear greater risks of unemployment than men . The principle of equal pay for equal work is far from being a reality, although since the 1960s or even the 1950s it has already been included in the national laws of many countries. To this day women have mostly remained in relatively low-paid jobs, and within a given profession women often are in a lower position than men. In Japan women earn only 41 percent of the wages earned by men.

• In some countries women have relatively limited access to training and education. This hampers the efforts of women to improve themselves, which in turn holds back economic development and social progress.

• Labor protection and working conditions need to be improved; this seems especially urgent with regard to women in developing countries.

Our appeals

• Sisters the world over, we are a vital new force in world economic development. The 21st century is waving to us; let us act immediately so that our wisdom and talent will shine brightly on the world economic stage. May the next World Conference on Women be honored by the presence of still more female entrepreneurs and female owners of multinationals.

• We appeal to the UN women's organizations to list the question of women and global economic development as a major subject for study and to give, in a way still more positive and effective, all-out support and encouragement to women's involvement in economic development.

• We appeal to national governments to pay still closer attention to the question of women and development; render women still greater and more practical legal and financial assistance in their effort to participate in economic development; provide more care and assistance to women in underdeveloped regions — in rural areas, for example; and give them more opportunities for education and training, so that they can bring their wisdom and capabilities into full play.

• Gentlemen throughout the world, look at your wives, mothers, sisters, and daughters to see what a big role they are playing in the family, the society, and economic development. They are promoting world progress, making history, and building up civilization. Lend them a helping hand, and they will be able to display their wisdom and capabilities in the vast social-economic arena and prove their worth. This will be an honor and at the same time an unshirkable obligation and responsibility of yours. Women have over the past decade made great contributions to the promotion of "equality, development, and peace." You should be proud of them for these great achievements. And from a longer perspective, you have every reason to be even more proud of their future.

Global economic development is gaining momentum, and history is going through a period of great development and competition. It is a great challenge that our time is posing for us, and it is a grand stage that the world is setting for our own development.

Let us unite and work together to create a still more beautiful future. We are convinced that with our surpassing contributions, we will win, beyond controversy, the Nobel Prize for economic development.

The impact of economic globalization on women

Marcia Rivera
Latin American Council of Social Sciences
(CLACSO); Development Alternatives with
Women for a New Era (DAWN), Argentina

Good morning friends, colleagues, sisters, and all the women of the world who acompany us on this historic journey. Special greetings to the thousands of Chinese workers who have made the organization of this Conference possible, and to the members of the working committees from New York and the five regions who have dedicated months of intense labor to make this Conference a reality.

Greetings also to the hundreds of journalists who are covering the Forum and who will carry our concerns to the millions of women who could not join us. Those women are mindful of our discussions as they are confident that the results of this Conference might impact their quality of life.

Today I want to discuss the processes of globalization — processes that from the start are contradictory. For example, these forces have facilitated our meeting here today — facilitating our ability to communicate easily with one another, giving us the opportunity to share experiences and to develop a common consciousness regarding the problems of inequality and subordination of women, and to develop concerted strategies for achieving equality.

Nonetheless, in many ways, the processes of economic globalization are unleashing forces that contribute to a greater division between nations and to wider social polarizations within those nations. These processes are having profoundly divergent effects on men and women and it is extremely important for us to understand the tendencies of these processes so that we may shape our collective actions today and in the future.

Elements which have contributed to the acceleration of globalization

I would like to begin by examining the elements that have contributed to the acceleration of globalization within the last decade — a decade of upheaval, in which we witnessed the deepening of war, conflicts based on issues of ethnic or racial identity, the spread of epidemics such as AIDS threatening the fate of the majority of the earth's population, and the worsening of hunger and misery in many countries within the African continent.

But it has also been a decade of important achievements: significant advances in the areas of health and education, impressive successes in the sciences and in technology, the launching of democracy-building efforts in many countries, the end of military dictatorships in South America, and important progress in the discussion of issues affecting women's development.

The technological revolution

Perhaps the greatest factor in the acceleration of globalization has been the technological revolution of the last decades. Many levels of this process are clearly visible. But so many more levels escape us, and these processes are present in our daily lives. They are constantly modifying and will ultimately change the world and people's lives in unexpected ways.

Experiments on conductivity at high temperatures, the creation of new materials that nature never imagined, the use of fiber optics in communication systems, and the search for artificial intelligence are among the advancements that will soon change the forms of production, the products on the market, and the relations that human beings have with one another and with nature. We are rapidly moving toward complexity and toward the integration of technologies and systems of production and distribution. From that integration will come the greatest advances and changes we have ever known.

Of all the technological changes contributing to the acceleration of globalization, there are four which I would like to highlight today: computer technology, the new forms of communication, the design of new machinery and forms of production, and genetic engineering.

In many parts of the world the development of personal computers has radically transformed the ways in which people work, study, shop, and entertain themselves. In the industrialized nations the computer has become a household appliance, offering multiple daily uses. Children are using computers in elementary schools, and already, the core of the academic curriculum relies on the computer as its central tool.

In less than five years, the market will see one of the principal results of artificial-intelligence research: the intelligent, human-voice-activated computer, capable of understanding the questions we ask and able to deliver coherent answers to the demands of information research. This reality coexists with another equally shocking fact: many African schools still do not have books, pencils or paper, the basic instruments of education, not of the present day but of the last century.

Communication systems have also experienced unlikely changes. Giant supersonic airplanes can cross entire continents in hours — travel which before could only be achieved with much difficulty. How could we have organized this meeting without fax machines? In less than ten years, saying that someone lives in a remote place will be outdated once cellular telephones become available in all the corners of the world.

But even more significant is how computer and communication technology have been integrated to produce new developments in electronic communication. Computer science will provide the greatest changes in our daily uses of technology. Soon in most countries, the information highway will allow the interconnection of channels of information and communication, bringing the capacities of television, the telephone, and the computer together in one device. Certainly the lifestyles of the wealthier classes of the world will benefit from these advances. But what will happen to the rest of the world? Will they have access to these developments or will they face new forms of exclusion?

The use of robots and the development of new synthetic materials are rapidly changing the design and organization of production processes. The materials and the modes of production for cars, homes, clothing, and equipment are significantly different than those of twenty years ago. In laboratories, technology is succeeding in decoding many of nature's secrets, imitating its abilities and adapting it to current needs, and often jeopardizing the future through the inadequate disposal of waste materials and the inappropriate use of unrenewable resources.

On the other hand, genetic engineering has unleashed impressive discoveries and debates that we cannot ignore. The identification of destructive genes has made possible significant advances in the control of diseases such as cancer. The manipulation of DNA has allowed for the chemical reproduction of vital human substances such as insulin and growth hormones. Genetic engineering has also served to fortify varieties of agricultural products, making them more resistant to disease and more abundant, changes which could lead to important improvements in nutrition levels of the world's population. New ethical questions have also emerged in this field: to what extent, for how long, how, who, to what end, does one use this genetic technology to alter the capacity of human procreation? This emerging debate directly concerns women.

I want to emphasize a point essential to the discussion of technological transformation: technology seeks to feed itself in a cyclical manner: the developments in one field induce rapid changes in another, which in turn contribute to the redefinition of the former. The integration of the four systems I have described has had the following impact:

• *Increased acceleration of technological change.* For example, the first personal computers became available thirty years after the existence of large computer systems; but now, every two years we are seeing new models which represent revolutionary advances over the first personal computers.

• *Dispersal of production.* Businesses can decide when and where to produce at their own convenience; mobility can be virtual reality.

• *Substitution of primary materials.* The traditional role of countries that provide these materials is being redefined. It is no longer necessary to have or not have aluminum, copper, or cotton as the base of production.

• *Remote supervision.* Computer technology allows for the supervision of production from any place via electronic communication. There are video conferences, telecommuting, and many other ways to track production from a distance.

Unification of structural adjustment policies and liberalization of markets

Another element that has strongly influenced the acceleration of economic globalization has been the trend toward standardizing state policies of reform and market liberalization. During the course of the last decade, the majority of the world's nations turned toward a neo-liberal economic model that calls for the downscaling of the state aparatus and the deregulation of the state's fiscal activity, evidenced for example in the opening of markets. What does this mean? In reality, every day the state is exerting less influence and the economic power structure is determining more of the decisions that impact the lives of all humans.

The state reform process has had two fundamental components: on the one hand, the implementation of "structural adjustment" policies designed to achieve fiscal balance and to control inflation; and on the other hand, "privatization," which seeks to strip the state of all those activities that are not considered fundamental, according to the terms of this model.

It is widely documented that all aspects of these policies have contributed to the growth of poverty and social polarization. And above all, they have contributed to the acute impoverishment of women. Despite the corrective measures instituted in recent years, women represent 70 percent of the 1.3 billion people who actually live in poverty.

The liberalization of markets, amid deregulation mechanisms and the elimination of tariffs, has also brought contradictory consequences. On the one hand, it is true that doors have been opened, allowing the exchange of products from the poorer nations to wealthier nations; but even though the doors stand open, the competition is so fierce and the disparity of the conditions for competition is so vast that, in fact, in this past decade many of the poorer nations lost a great deal of property in the international market. The majority of the poor nations opened their markets, eliminating import barriers and lowering tariffs to stimulate free trade, the cornerstone of the new model for global economy. Nonetheless, a look at recent data shows that for the developing nations this process resulted in the loss of economic opportunities at the level of $500 billion a year — a figure ten times greater than the amounts those nations received in foreign aid.

The immediate significance of this is that as a result of free markets, the wealthier nations became wealthier. Today 20 percent of the world's population receives an income at least 150 times greater than that of the bottom 20 percent. It is clear that the opening of the markets has only benefited those who were already in a position to compete and export. In Latin America, for example, liberalization resulted in a deteriorization of the commercial balance. For the first time in ten years, the commercial balance showed a negative balance, with a deficit greater than $10 billion for the entire region. This figure would have been greater if Brazil had not had a surplus of $1.57 billion.

At the global level, Latin America's participation in total exports fell to 3.6 percent, the lowest level recorded in this century. In almost all the nations there is a significant drop in export capacity, as well as an increase of imports, which indicates still greater pressures for national producers and significant changes in the population's spending patterns.

The end of protectionism has brought greater power to transnational corporations, in clear detriment to the small and medium-sized national firms. The transnational corporation is not limited to the field of production; rather, it quickly extends to commercialization and services, including traditional items such as food. The competition created for medium-sized and small producers by this expansion of transnationals is immoral, but nothing has been done to address these inequities because the "neo-liberal model demands it to be so." Meanwhile, every day, nations are seeing the closing of local businesses and the growth of unemployment.

Many governments in South America are caught up in the attraction of transnational corporations and foreign capital because these are associated with the idea of modernity. Unfortunately, more effort is being given to attracting foreign capital — which is often flighty — than to stimulating national production, a fact which leaves nations in conditions of greater vulnerability.

In summary, we can affirm that the programs of adjustment and the liberalization of markets have contributed to the economic globalization via the following processes:

• Growth in the sphere of influence of transnational corporations.

• Diminished national economic sovereignty.

• Greater interference by international financial instiututions — today the IMF and the World Bank set the guidelines for economic policies.

• Growth of the financial speculation market — 95 percent of all financial transactions made in the world correspond to speculation and not to transactions of purchases and sales of goods and services. This generates great vulnerability for nations, as was clearly illustrated in the case of Mexico.

• Weakening of the state aparatus and reduction of its services.

• Feminization of poverty and growth of unemployment.

• Increased social polarization and tension within and among nations.

Changes in the organization and legislation of labor

The third element which has strongly influenced the rapid growth of globalization is the change in the organization and legislation of labor. As we have seen, the technological changes of the last decade have contributed to the redefinition of modes of production. To confront the challenges presented by these, there is a need for new skills, attitudes, and approaches to organizing production. As a result, employers everywhere have called for or are calling for changes to expand the "relaxation" of labor legislation. But in reality, what we are seeing is an erosion of rights previously acquired in the areas of safety and employment, compensations, social security, and overtime pay, among others. Relaxation has benefited only employers; it has yet to benefit workers, especially women, who have been calling for flexibility in terms of work schedules.

The policies of relaxation have accentuated a mode of recruitment for part-time work or contract work. Every day more workers are recruited in this manner, allowing employers to evade compensations that traditionally have been paid to full-time workers. This mode of recruitment is common in jobs that rely mostly on women, for example, in the clothing industry and in sales in large department stores. The exploitation of women workers has taken on new, or not so new, forms which resemble those of early capitalism. The maquiladoras, the industrial zones, and the workshops employing undocumented migrants are examples of how the global economy mocks the labor legislation that took so long to achieve in the history of humanity.

These changes in labor legislation were achieved because they coincided with a period of increased unemployment in all nations and the reduced power of unions. As a result there are few places in the world where there remains the necessary collective power to negotiate agreements, defend workers' rights, and to represent workers in litigations or protests, especially when production is lagging due to fragmentation, segmentation, and capital that flows from multiple origins, all elements which define globalization.

The logic of global economy, as I warned in the beginning, is profoundly contradictory. It is based on speed, risk, creativity, but also, now that there no longer are mechanisms to regulate the collective interests of humanity, on the impunity of the international order. But above all, this logic is built upon people's insecurities, especially those living in the poorer nations. Production is transferred from countries with high earnings to those with low earnings, financial speculation is carried out without any consideration of the consequences (except for the proper capital), cultural and spending patterns are disarranged, and irreversible ecological damage is inflicted upon the earth, without concern for future generations.

Globalization has constantly and increasingly contributed to social exclusion and polarization, undermining the foundations of a harmonious and peaceful coexistence. Not to mention that increasing alongside globalization are forces that lay claim to local space and restricted identities, such as the emergence of dangerous xenophobic nationalisms and religious intolerance, which threaten peace.

In summary, the most important consequences of economic globalization we must keep in mind as we develop our strategies appear to be:

• The redefinition of the concepts of nation and state.

• Increased tensions surrounding questions of identity (national, ethnic, racial, cultural, etc.).

• Fierce competition in production and distribution of goods and services.

• Consumer globalization.

• Rapid decision-making in all sectors (political and economic).

• Formation of regional economic blocks.

• Large concentration of economic power and its increased influence in policy-making, a power from which women are almost entirely excluded.

The challenges of this Conference are enormous. We are the women who have taken up the question of the actual economic model of globalization, and we have confronted the task of proposing alternatives for development based on the needs of people, the respect for natural resources, and the practice of equity in all its dimensions and capability of long-term self-sustainment. For this, we need to completely understand the processes facing us, agree on strategies, and act efficiently.

From this Forum should emerge concrete and consensual proposals to promote a new framework that will guide the development process, with clear and essential goals. Humane development is possible; the world has witnessed significant advances in the areas of education, health, technological progress — but in unequal ways. We must create the foundations for equal opportunities for all. To do so, it is essential that we achieve new social pacts within each nation, as well as new international social accords that will drive a new world order and redirect cooperation toward development and not toward bureaucratic welfare. Let us work arduously toward this end as we step forward on this journey.

Since there will be a plenary that will discuss strategies confronting globalization, I take this opportunity to present to the Forum the following suggestions for action:

• We need to concert our efforts to open the global debate on development models, taking on a gender perspective and insisting on the need to move toward a development strategy which positions people at its center.

• We need to call for discussions and actions at the parliamentary level to revise and institute legislation that is anti-monopolitical and anti-oligopolitical, in order to limit the power of transnational capital.

• We must demand the institution of a tax on financial speculation transactions and on games of chance, and ask that those resources be turned over to social programs addressing gender inequalities.

• We should concert our actions with labor organizations to avoid the continued erosion of workers' rights. Perhaps the moment has arrived for us to rethink and restructure union organizations with respect to women's actions — now that in the majority of nations the unions, historically dominated by men, have lost power and legitimacy.

• We need to create working groups in each nation that can monitor and document ethical violations and inappropriate uses of technology. Committees like those for human rights should be created to monitor issues such as genetic manipulation or the use of ultrasound equipment to verify the sex of fetuses, among others.

• We must set forth strategies to reform the political terrain and to increase opportunities for women, who are conscious of the limitations of the prevailing economic model, to accede to power.

Poverty in Africa: The impact on women

Esther Ocloo
Sustainable End of Hunger Foundation, Ghana

I am very happy that training and its impact on women is being given attention at this Forum, because it is a very serious issue for women. An overview, an analysis of global forces shows that poverty in Africa is on the increase, partly because of the following factors:

• a global economic recession — resulting in loss of livelihood and economic restructuring processes such as structural adjustment programs (SAPs);

• an increase in natural disasters, civil wars, and political conflict — with the worst victims being women;

• a debt crisis — as Africa is swallowed in debt, there is enormous, pathetic impact on women.

SAPs have come with trade liberalization, job cuts, and increases in the cost of living. Women suffer most because they have to manage household consumption and production under very challenging conditions. In the area of agriculture, for example, women have to contend with the high cost of inputs because of the removal of subsidies. Due to job cutbacks in both the private and public sectors, a great number of people, the majority of whom are men, have moved into the informal sector. As a result, women, who form the majority of this sector, are gradually being forced out because they cannot compete.

In regard to political participation in countries where democratization is taking place, it has been observed that very few women can stand for election, primarily due to poverty and lack of sound education. Many women cannot afford to fund election campaigns. But I would like to assure you that African women in various countries are organizing and pressing for a membership quota in Parliament, and in Ghana we had a meeting in support of voting for all women, no matter what their party.

When we talk about obstacles to peace and human security in Africa, I would say that political and ethnic conflict have been rampant. Women and children are the ones who suffer most. Due to the increase in unemployment, there have been increases in crime rates, prostitution, and abandonment of children by mothers who cannot afford to look after them.

Media, culture, and communication pose both adverse and positive challenges. Although information is one of the strongest tools for empowerment, women's access to and control over the media and other channels of communication and information is limited, partly because of constraints. The infrastructures do not exist in most rural areas; where they do exist, women cannot afford to purchase the television sets, radios, telephones, etc. The poor in African countries who have access to radios cannot even afford to buy batteries for them. In the urban areas, where facilities do exist, many parents are gradually losing control over their children because of the children's exposure to alien cultures and to the violence found in Western films. This is becoming very serious. Formerly, we did not have the sorts of crime we now see in Africa, but because of the coming of CNN and all the foreign films and video, African culture is being affected adversely.

As for the impact of the technological revolution, even though technological advancement has great benefits, some of the technologies introduced have deprived women from earning an income. In agriculture, for example, the use of machinery has displaced women. The need to use modern technology to improve production cannot be overemphasized if you want to compete on the world market. But the issue which needs to be addressed is how we can achieve this without displacing women.

The introduction of medium-level technologies that still utilize some amount of manual labor might deal with this problem.

Africa is starting to face real challenges, and the contribution of African women in agriculture and industry is great. Without their economic contribution, Africa would be in a far worse crisis. What we want to do at this congress is to appeal to all of you to see how funds can be made available, say, to UNIFEM, to other funding agencies, and to our NGOs who are helping women to cope with the global economic crisis we are now facing in Africa.

The impact of global trends on women has been adverse. There is a need to provide adequate safety nets and strategies and basic support systems to help women understand what is going on and what can be done. When it comes to training, I was listening to a lady speak about how they used radios to train women in the villages. In our situation this is not possible, and this is why we are calling for the strengthening of state-based and community-based support. I hope you will tell your governments to channel their support to the United Nations Development Programme so that our NGOs who are working day and night can help these women stand up to the challenges.

The global economy: Its history and future challenges

Helen O'Connell
Women in Development Europe (WIDE), United Kingdom

This plenary is on the globalization of the economy and is separate from other plenaries on such issues as the obstacles to peace and human security, including the effects of militarization, violence, and poverty, and the plenary on approaches to governance. However, all these issues are very closely linked to the subject of this plenary. The globalization of the economy is an intensely political issue.

The term "globalization of the economy" is new. But in my view, the trend towards globalization has been evident for many decades, if not centuries. The globalization process is now more rapid and sophisticated.

One could argue that colonization, from the 15th century to the present, is part of this trend. More recently, since the end of the Second World War in the post-colonial period, the driving force of the aid and development business has been economic — to open up markets and gain access to resources along with the political objective of exerting influence. This is true for much of the aid and development from North America, Western Europe, Japan, and the former Soviet Union to the countries of Africa, Asia, Latin and Central America, and the Caribbean.

In this period, too, we saw dramatic changes, with the development of new technology and telecommunications. Companies from North America or Europe, keen to avoid the high wages demanded at home that are linked to high employment — greatly assisted by development aid and loans and enticed by financial incentives, cheaper labor, few regulations, and nonunion agreements in the countries of Asia, Latin America and elsewhere — relocated the labor-intensive parts of their production. Some relocated for production for local consumption; most relocated to produce cheaply for export.

The debt crisis that began in 1982 and the measures promoted by the international financial institutions and the G7 governments to deal with it — namely structural adjustment programs — signaled the next phase in the globalization of the economy. Under structural adjustment, the governments of indebted countries liberalized, deregulated, and privatized their economies. They were encouraged to export more, to roll back government involvement in managing economic affairs — in essence, to become further incorporated into the global economy and, of course, to repay the outstanding debts. In the 1980s, too, most Northern countries were embarking on a process of economic liberal-

ization, deregulation, and privatization that is still in full swing today.

The end of the cold war opened another phase in the great economic globalization project. The commercial objectives of aid and development could become openly the top priority — above strategic or foreign policy objectives. And a new political objective, political liberalization, emerged on the international agenda, and in some cases was linked to new loans and aid.

The North expressed great interest in multiparty elections in the South and extolled the virtues of good governance and democratization. The European Union is particularly keen on this political agenda, but to date it fails to examine the contradictions between its actual commitment to economic liberalization and its professed commitment to democratization. Democracy is not for one day only, it is not only a matter of elections; it is for every day.

The final stage in the sophistication of the globalization process was the end of the Uruguay Round of the General Agreement on Tariffs and Trade (GATT) and the establishment of the World Trade Organization. This completed the picture. Now transnational corporations and international finance companies run the global economy; they control global trade, global finance and credit, global production, and intellectual property. International finance moves US$1 trillion dollars each day without regulation or taxation. The world has been made safe for advanced capitalism.

Now the stated objective of the development cooperation programs of the European Union and others is poverty reduction. The main strategy for achieving this is by "integrating developing country economies into the global economy" — a global economy characterized by widening inequality and poverty.

What does all this mean?

It means that women workers in the United Kingdom and in the Philippines or India work for the same companies but for different wages. One recent study showed that women data processors in the Philippines earned 12 times less than women doing the same work in the UK.

It means that middle- and high-income consumers in Europe can purchase fruits or vegetables from Colombia or Guatemala or Thailand every day.

It means that farmers in those countries have increasingly no option but to produce what the rich North wishes to consume.

It means that I can communicate instantly by telephone or fax or e-mail with someone in South Africa, Mexico, Peru — if they have the technology.

It means that we have global mass communications; the same soap operas can be seen all over the world. The 1994 World Cup was seen live on television in every country. It would be nice to think the Fourth World Conference on Women was also seen live in every country.

We have seen fantastic changes in the last 50 years. However, not everyone is benefiting from this globalization of the economy, and very many are in a worse position economically, socially, and politically than before.

These changes in the economy have not in any significant way improved the economic or social position of the majority of women. In fact, the technological changes have repeated and replicated the same hierarchies.

Shortcomings

The shortcomings of the global economy as it is currently structured are many. I would like to draw attention here to three.

First, countries in Latin America, Africa, Asia, the Caribbean, the Pacific, and now in Eastern and Central Europe are not free to choose their path to development — or even decide what development means. This is especially the case for countries that have large external debts. We have one dominant model.

Second, the whole ethos of the global economy is to maximize and accumulate wealth, not to distribute wealth. The ethos is short-term. We have an unprecedented mobility of capital, which can move finance within seconds, and can avoid economies with good labor or environmental codes. The arms trade is enormous and critically important to the economies of the North. This poses a fundamental problem. How can we work for peace when our economies are based on war?

We are witnessing a massive monopolization of resources, wealth, and technology, and the commodification of everything — including ourselves and every aspect of our lives. We see the emergence of powerful trading blocs, such as the North America Free Trade Agreement and the European Union.

Third, poverty is increasing. At least one billion women, men, and children do not have enough to live on each day. The way in which the global economy is structured entrenches and reinforces inequalities within countries and between countries on the basis of gender, race, and social group. This is not to deny that many people have achieved great improvement in their lives in the last decades. However, very many have not.

The informal economy is growing everywhere. Unemployment is rising. It is estimated that by the end of 1995, there will be 20 million women and men without waged work in the European Union. We have the phenomenon of jobless growth: we are told that the only way companies can increase productivity is to introduce more technology and cut jobs. We are seeing a mushrooming of casual and part-time employment and of homeworking. And, of course, many of these casual, part-time, and homeworking jobs are low paid. We see manufacturing and data processing jobs relocating weekly to countries which offer better opportunities to corporations. We are told we must be flexible to survive. At the local level, small-scale enterprises are squeezed out or forced into the global economy. They are dependent on inputs — whether technology, consumer goods, or raw materials — the source of which is increasingly within the dominion of large corporations.

Parallel to these changes are others: the privatization of public services and the cuts in public spending. In Western Europe, there is a challenge to the very concept of mutual solidarity which underpins our social security systems.

Challenges

We face two main challenges, both urgent: one immediate and one more long-term.

First, how to reduce poverty, how to redistribute wealth and resources so that those living in extreme poverty get their fair share, so that those dependent on social welfare can live with dignity, so that those living on low wages get a better deal. Immediate urgent action is needed, and it is action which is well within the means and capacities of the global economy.

Second, how do we democratize the global economy? How do we manage the international financial institutions, the transnational corporations, international finance? How do we expand and deepen the political agenda? We need to say what we understand by democratization, by accountability, by development. How do we transform the relationship between economic affairs and social and cultural affairs?

The international women's movement, alongside other progressive movements, must continue to organize and build alliances at every level, and we must continue to educate ourselves and others. We have to be both original and pragmatic in our thinking and actions.

VI • The Rise of Conservatism in Its Various Forms

Religious, Nationalist, Racial/Ethnic, and Homophobic

Opening remarks

Ramabai Espinet, Moderator
Ontario Society for Services to Indo-Caribbean
Canadians (OSICC) Women's Collective;
Seneca College, Canada

I live now in Canada, having grown up in Trinidad. One hundred fifty-seven years ago, my ancestors left India. As redemption, they were to work in the sugarcane fields of the Caribbean, after the emancipation of Africa, with others of the South Asian diaspora, including the populations of Fiji, Mauritius, and South Africa. I make my living as an academic, teaching postcolonial literature. However, in my real life, I am an activist, poet, writer, feminist, and the mother of two children.

I am most honored to be with you today as the moderator of the plenary on the rise of conservatism, and I thank the NGO Forum for having invited me to do so. This second plenary of the morning will focus on the global force of the rise of conservatism in various forms and, most particularly, on the interconnectedness of these forms. Our speakers will look at the impact of the rise of conservatism at the local and global levels and will frame key questions which impact upon women's struggles for equality and social justice.

There are fundamental issues facing us in this post-cold war age. Perhaps one of the most fundamental questions from the South is obvious: How can the rise of conservatism be ended? And for whom might it be ended, and where have other wars, hot or cold, begun?

What are the other fundamental questions? What about the very visible resurgence of conservatism as a global force, particularly with respect to race, ethnicity, nationalism, religion, and homophobia? What is the relationship between economic restruc-turing and the rise of conservatism? What are the implications for family, for ideals of family structure? What are the implications for our children, particularly our girl children? What are the specific challenges that face us in our different regions? How can we build strategies, in spite of these setbacks, for change and for advancement for women? How can the global movement of women form allegiances to work across the barriers that divide us?

Make no mistake about it. We need to form these allegiances; we need to work across these barriers. Now more than ever, we need the space to express and negotiate our differences while building common ground for action.

Finally, how do we begin to look within ourselves and our organizations for the ways in which we have internalized the very structures that allow and even promote the rise of conservatism, the ways in which we reproduce relations of domination, of divide-and-conquer political organizing, and all the other myriad ways in which we as women work against one another?

The conservative mind is the mind that has stopped thinking. The conservative mind is locked into reproducing the known, the tried and tested. Conservatism to the conservative mind is comfortable. How can we afford to be comfortable in times like these?

In these plenaries, part of our purpose is to dislodge what is comfortable, to rethink all our ways of seeing and thinking, to effect the shift from complacency to creative action, to help each other envision a new reality. Our speakers this morning have the task of assisting us in this endeavor.

Conservatism's dangerous appeal to identity

Nighat Said Khan
ASR Resource Center, Pakistan

In many ways, perhaps I am not the best person to be speaking on the rise of conservatism, since I am not only perplexed and disoriented by this phenomenon but also often find myself bordering on despair. I am a socialist and a feminist. Increasingly, I feel like a dinosaur. I look back on Nairobi with wonder and nostalgia: look back at the time when one could talk and struggle for socialism without being snickered at; when one could dream dreams without being told to be practical; when women were called women and men were called men; when patriarchy was not mystified under the concept of gender; when history — and indeed ideology — had not been declared dead by a few while the majority still yearned to make history; when postmodernism had not validated every expression, every specificity, no matter how reactionary and regressive and amoral; when heightened individualism did not prevent people from coming together into a movement; when the women's movement itself was more a spontaneous political struggle and not a collection of activities and projects and action plans.

As I engage in and grapple with the issue of identity as expressed in religion, nationalism, racism, ethnicity, and homophobia, I find it difficult to disengage the many strands of this problematique, indeed, even in myself. Certainly, it is far easier to take a stand on the other areas of globalization, since we are able — however incorrectly — to locate the problem outside ourselves. The issue of identity, however, does not give us this luxury because each of us has multiple identities within us — all of which carry the seeds of conservatism. We are the present of our own history; and there is a part of each of us that consciously or unconsciously wants to, or needs to, conserve the secure, the familiar, the known, the fixed. That is what makes conservatism even more frightening. There is an inherent danger that conservatism can tamper with a core even in the most radical of us, and subvert that radicalism for its own purpose. This is the reason for my despair, and this is the focus of my presentation.

Those of you who have been attending these plenaries — and those of you who have been working on the issues and living and experiencing globalization — would be familiar with the collusion of political, economic, ideological, and military forces that are drawing the world into their own orbit. It is a new imperialism in the guise of nationalism that purports to be inclusive, as the world trade order or the World Bank or the International Monetary Fund or the United Nations or regional cooperation or development assistance or the free market, when, in fact, these are articulations and institutions that seek to centralize the world and to conserve it to their own ends. They give the freedom to be, the freedom to compete, the freedom for the free market in an unequal situation where the die has already been cast and the rules have already been set.

What is sinister about this new world order and the new conservatism is that they work in insidious ways, not with the crudity of conquering armies. They hide behind the masks of freedom, democracy, human rights, workers' rights, women's rights, minority rights, sexual rights, racial integration, environmental protection, faceless capitalism, liberalism. This conservatism is politically correct.

The danger then is that each one of us can be extensions of this conservatism, since we can get lulled into negotiating space within the system rather than challenging the system. I think that, by way of example, what is dynamic about capitalism is that it has been able to co-opt the trappings of people's movements. It did take on workers' rights issues such as the daily wage, minimum wage, and some demands of the workers. It did take on some of the environmental issues and human rights issues and women's rights. But within that, it is defining a space, co-opting us, so that we are lulled into thinking we are doing something and finally getting ourselves onto the agenda when, in fact, it is negating a struggle against the system itself.

This is not to suggest that the crude does not

exist. Indeed, the crude is all around us, in religious fundamentalism, racism, violent nationalism, ethnic superiority, sexual oppression, and the repression and exploitation of women.

While the new world order subsumes all diversity, we see a world pitted against itself with innumerable local wars and conflict situations resolved almost invariably through violence. Women are the target of the violence. They are the target as a symbol of the honor of the other, as an extension of male honor and a means to humiliate the other. The North has been involved in these processes, sometimes very obviously, sometimes in a more covert way.

The experience of Pakistan and our neighbor Afghanistan highlights much of what this world order is saying, and how it changes its face and changes itself so much that our governments are left reeling. In 1977, the military took over in Pakistan and actively promoted the process of what is called Islamization, moving the state toward being an Islamic state. This was supported by the North, particularly by the United States. The aid Pakistan received at the time was $6 billion. That $6 billion was used essentially to support a regime that was not just dictatorial but also essentially negated the rights of women and minorities.

Today that same United States talks about women's rights. It is the same North that tells us that aid will be linked to whether a country gives women rights and whether it includes women in development. It has also been very supportive of dictators, oppressors, religious fundamentalists, national struggles, racism, and the oppression of women — not just in an instrumental way but in terms of its ideology. Today, if there is a different position, it is only because it suits capitalism. While these countries have been buttressed and supported by the North, particularly the United States, there has also been a tremendous undermining by international institutions and by national governments in the North, undermining the nation-states in the South.

The result is more than has already been stated: that the state is withdrawing from its responsibilities to its citizens, all of which affects women and minorities much more. It has also kept the state alive as well.

On one side, we have the advocacy and the space, but the state itself has not been allowed to wither. The state has been reinforced by a continuing reinforcement of the class structure, reinforcement of ideology — including popular religion as a means of control — and by strengthening the institution of the family. Although in our region we haven't quite got the type of homophobia that is being experienced in the West, it is precisely because of the articulation of rights by the gay movement that an insecurity has been created that this might be a challenge to the institution of the family. Capitalism and imperialism and the new world order cannot take the disintegration of the family, because it is the only institution through which it now articulates itself in a very concrete way. It has put us all in front of television sets within the home. Within the home, it can control. That is why Reagan was particularly perturbed that the United States was disintegrating, because the family was disintegrating. So nationhood and family have been interconnected. This creates an area within civil society itself that becomes homophobic as it becomes insecure that the nation is somehow at risk, even of being destroyed.

This is all possible primarily because all of us have multiple identities. Identity does not stem only from being women. Identity, ideology, and religious expression are constructed and informed by several objective and subjective realities, including the state, race, class, sex, ethnicity, and culture. It is often difficult to disengage these. Yet the women's movement needs to understand that the identity of women will surface as the central identity within the women's movement when there are so many other identities playing for expression. All women do have multiple identities.

The question then for the women's movement is: Under what circumstances does one particular identity emerge? In particular, when is it that we become women and identify ourselves as women, and when do we articulate our other identities? This is extremely important because it is this particular interplay that makes for the divisiveness within the women's movement. The issue of which particular identity will prevail at a particular moment is important.

But it is also important for us to work toward an understanding of how identity is constructed. It is not constructed in isolation. It invariably depends on another. In other words, identity is always relational, because one inevitably constructs oneself in relationship to another in the process of differentiation. One's identity also gets constructed by the other when the other seeks differentiation. The articulation of identity is therefore dependent on location and specificity. I am sure all of us have experienced that certain identities will emerge at certain times. I know, in my own case, I am least a Muslim when I am in Pakistan. But when I am confronted with a situation or with a stereotype or a political situation, this identity tends to emerge and locate me either by identifying with the Muslim world or by reacting to other forces that might be struggling against it. I think it is a complexity we need to look at.

The women's movement has done a lot in the last ten years and certainly made a lot of gains. What is disturbing is that it has taken on a lot of the conservatism; it has become a part of the system of the dominant culture. I do not just refer to the ethnic, racial, and national identities. What is disturbing to my mind is the religious identity that women are assuming — not just the women in religious fundamentalist groups, but in the women's movement itself. To me it is disturbing that there is a sense of reinterpreting, of revivalism, of assuming an identity, of reinforcing that. However empowering that may be, it will eventually be that core that the fundamentalists of your faith can actually tap.

The agendas that we have worked out have been co-opted by capitalism. The fact that we are here today, the fact that the United Nations has given us this space, the fact that our governments have brought national delegations, the fact that many of us are allowed to lobby in the United Nations gives legitimacy to us, but also makes us a part of that establishment. The problem is then that we tend to respond as the establishment. We tend to become located in it without realizing that this space has been defined so as to confine the

movement and not to let it challenge those very structures.

I personally am also perturbed by the concept of gender. Apart from everything else it is a very profound notion, but it has been made utterly simplistic and has utterly trivialized the issue of patriarchy. It has been successful and has been used by the World Bank, the UN, and others to neutralize, to demystify, and to take away the political edge, to take away what they call the confrontation. To that extent, it has succeeded, although in many cases what it means is women. Many times we use gender when we are talking about women. Our programs and projects are very much geared to simply changing the word rather than the concept. We've also been getting into this postmodern notion of understanding everything, taking it as given, as though there were some moral in that. We tend to hide behind false notions of feminism.

The year 1995 could be a watershed for the women's movement. I believe that history is not dead. I believe the biggest challenge is to take energy from our gains, to be proud of these gains without stagnation, without becoming part of the establishment, without becoming the establishment, and to try to bring the dynamics and the politics back into the movement; to bring perhaps even some of those earlier messages and principles on which we founded ourselves: the personal is political, the speaking out, the personal support, the consciousness-raising — all of these indeed become extremely important. It is very strange that we have even gotten the United Nations to accept that the public and the private should not be a false dichotomy, yet even in most women's groups we have fragmented ourselves. We also must not hide behind the issue of "one world." If it remains merely a slogan, we must confront our identities, hierarchies, maleness. We need to identify the enemy; we need to name it. I think this is a difficult process of looking at ourselves and challenging ourselves. We do need to move towards this; we do need to bring back the courage to dream, to be free, to change, and to make history.

The rise of race-based conservatism in the North

Linda Burnham
Women of Color Resource Center, United States

A conservative tide has risen in the countries of the North that threatens the democratic and human rights of us all. As my sisters on this panel have noted, this conservatism takes many forms and mobilizes around a range of issues. Some of the most powerful levers used to mobilize the right are deeply entrenched racism and white ethnic chauvinism.

We women, who are here participating in this historic Fourth World Conference on Women and who have come to Huairou to do some intensive strategizing about how to improve the condition of women worldwide, have no choice but to be deeply concerned about the increasingly vigorous articulation of racist ideology and the promotion and passage of racially and ethnically discriminatory legislation. And we have no choice but to incorporate into our programs and our organizing strategies an explicit and consistent anti-racist content, because the rise of conservatism mobilized on the basis of racial supremacy is a threat not only to communities of color in the North — a serious enough concern in itself — but also to the peace and security of all of humanity, insofar as resurgent racism and white ethnic chauvinism nurture the seeds of fascism.

What we are witnessing today is the concerted attempt to roll back the gains made on racial and ethnic justice issues in the years following World War II. The anti-colonial struggles of the postwar period had, obviously, a substantial and vigorously asserted anti-racist content. As the peoples of Africa, Latin America, Asia, and the Pacific asserted their right to political independence and self-determination, they also toppled an old racial order that presumed the inherent superiority of the peoples and nations of Europe.

In North America, the two decades immediately following the war saw the rise of movements for civil rights, black power, self-determination, and sovereignty that fundamentally challenged the economic, political, and social domination of white elites. These movements were, of course, of great consequence to the rise of the women's movement — both because of the millions of women of color who were brought into political and social struggle and because they served as an organizing model and inspiration to second-wave feminism.

It is the concrete and very precious gains of these movements — gains that were won through tremendous sacrifice — that are mortally threatened by the rise of the right. I want to focus on three issues around which the racist right has mobilized — affirmative action, immigration, and the rights of the poor to social support.

First, on affirmative action or positive discrimination: The legislation and regulations that require universities, government agencies, and private businesses to take steps to reverse past patterns of discrimination by hiring and promoting and admitting to universities qualified minorities in substantial numbers are some of the most important practical gains of the civil rights movement. They represent the recognition that promises to end discrimination are not enough. Preventing a reversion to deeply entrenched patterns of racism absolutely requires monitoring and oversight. This recognition pushed open a door through which many white women walked, along with people of color.

I want to tell you a story. A few months ago my organization received a visitor from a black women's organization in São Paulo, Brazil. She talked about the very impressive work of her organization on issues of women's health, and working with youth to create positive, anti-sexist cultural messages, and investigating complaints of racial discrimination. She explained to us that the black community in Brazil had struggled for years to raise consciousness about racism and discrimination and that they looked to the U.S. affirmative action legislation as a model for the implementation of legislation in Brazil. She was appalled at the turn things have taken, which brought home an important lesson: that we focus, and quite correctly so, on the negative values exported from North to South and sometimes forget that the fruits of our struggles are also exported and shared in ways that we do not even know.

Today the received wisdom is that discrimination is a problem of the past, that it has been substantially resolved, and that the only criteria for hiring and university admittance must be individual merit. The largest university system in the United States has just recently eliminated affirmative action in admissions and there is no doubt that it will be followed by other universities and by a full-scale assault at the national level. Frightening levels of racial hostility have been unleashed in the course of the attempt to undermine affirmative action.

Though both minorities and women have benefited from these policies, the racial motivation behind the right's mobilization on this issue is front and center. The anxieties of working-class and middle-class whites about their declining economic prospects crystallize around the supposed privileges being accorded to racial minorities at their expense, rather than around the corporate and government policies that are at the root of their economic insecurities.

Though the assault on affirmative action is primarily racially motivated, we may be sure that if it is qualitatively undermined, the gains that white women have made will be in jeopardy. And I imagine that we will revisit in the strategy session here the question of how the cooperative efforts and coalitions that theoretically make perfect sense — between the anti-racist and anti-sexist movements — can in practice be launched and sustained.

I turn now to another element of the right's mobilization on the basis of race and ethnicity — the anti-immigrant sentiment and policy that has taken hold in the countries of the North. It was never intended that the former colonial subjects of the South would appear and demand their rights in the former imperialist nations of the North — and appear in massive numbers. In the expanding economies of the postwar years, there was active recruitment of labor from, for example, the Caribbean, Mexico, and North America to North America and Europe. But after a period of relatively liberal immigration policies, protecting the national borders from being overrun by the colored hordes has become a major rallying cry of the right.

The unexpected and undesired mobility of former colonial subjects has created racially heterogeneous societies in Europe and posed a very complex challenge to the coincidence of national identity with white racial identity. In North America, the dynamics are slightly different. There, the settler colonies of Canada and the United States forged their national identities in the course of the brutal subjugation of the indigenous peoples and, in the United States, the enslavement of African peoples. These societies have been racially and ethnically heterogeneous from the very beginnings of the colonial era, but laying full claim to the national identity has been a privilege reserved for whites. And so, while the low-wage sectors of the economies of the North — garment manufacturing, agricultural labor, and service work, for example — are fully dependent on immigrant labor, and while second- and third-generation immigrants have been incorporated into a broader range of economic strata, the relationship between national identity and racial or ethnic identity remains profoundly conflicted and subject to dangerous manipulation by conservative and neo-fascist forces.

In Europe, this has taken the form of the coalescence of the right around a virulently anti-immigrant platform and physical attacks on immigrant communities and individuals perceived to be immigrants from the South. In Canada, government policy has shifted to cut back on immigration from the South and encourage immigration from Europe. And in the United States a major effort is under way to deny immigrants — both undocumented and legal — access to social services.

I should also note here a very dangerous linkage that has been made between conservatives in the environmental and population-control movements and anti-immigrant forces. It is argued that immigrants, with their higher birth rates and higher level of dependence on social services, are overburdening the environmental carrying capacity of the societies to which they have migrated. It is a very short step from this argument to not only restricting entry at the borders, but also advocacy of coercive and eugenicist birth-control policies.

The impact on women of the conservative anti-immigrant campaign is manifest. With primary responsibility for their family's health, nutrition, and childhood education, the denial of access to social services places an intolerable burden on immigrant women. Because of the fear of having their undocumented status exposed, diseases go untreated, and family violence, sexual harassment, and extremely exploitative working conditions go unreported. As we move into the strategy section of this plenary process, I'm sure we will want to discuss how central to the global women's agenda is the struggle to resist and roll back racialized anti-immigrant campaigns in the countries of the North.

Another plank of the conservatives' racial platform is the demonization and criminalization of the poor. As another speaker already noted in an earlier plenary, one of the most conspicuous forms of global restructuring in the North is the radical disinvestment in social services in the interest of ensuring an increased and unceasing flow of social wealth to the top. This disinvestment is accompanied by and accomplished through a propaganda campaign that casts the poor as lazy, criminally inclined, overly sexualized, and generally unworthy of any form of social support. In societies in which the poorest sectors are disproportionately or even overwhelmingly composed of racial and ethnic minorities, the attack on the poor is intended as an attack on people of color and a reassertion of white racial supremacy. The conservative solutions of choice to the deepening problems of poverty in the North have been uniformly punitive, coercive, and repressive. In the United States, one of the fastest growing industries is the prison industry. Whole communities, many of them rural and remote from urban centers, base their economies on the continually rising incarceration rates of a prison population both male and female that is disproportionately African-American, Latino, and Native American.

I am here in Huairou with a group of women who are focused on the issue of women and homelessness. In the ten years since the Nairobi conference, conservative policies of social disinvestment have meant that women and their children have been made homeless in ever increasing numbers and compose an ever larger portion of the homeless population. Here again, racial and ethnic minority women are heavily overrepresented.

We women are used to tending many fires. As we move to the strategy sections of these plenary sessions, let us focus intently on how anti-racism can be brought — finally and fundamentally — to the core of women's agenda.

The impact of conservatism on women's lives

Marta Benavides
Ecumenical Ministries for Development and Peace
(MEDEPAZ); International Institute for
Cooperation Amongst Peoples, El Salvador

Buenos dias, hermanas y hermanos de todo el mundo. I am a Salvadoran by birth, a citizen of the world, part of the energy of the universe. I am. I celebrate this, and I celebrate that you also are. This is a magic time, a time which we have forged in many ways and for a long time: to be together to celebrate our dreams, our lives, our being. This 21st century is already here, and it is us! There is no way back, no matter what. Because in spite of all kinds of forces which forcibly try to negate us, we without doubt can proclaim: We are!

Reflection is a sacred time. It allows us to look at the conditions we face, the various forces giving shape to the world and the societies in which we live; and to determine where we are going, what we want to be, what are the possibilities, and how to work with them.

About 500 years ago, what is now the Western world was going through great turmoil. There were witch hunts and burnings. The Jews and the Moors were being killed and kicked out of the Iberian Peninsula (what is now Spain). In the whole of Europe, there was great poverty, and there were religious upheavals related to class and nationality.

People were persecuted, jailed, killed, uprooted from their homes. At that time, the people, the Christian church, and institutions of knowledge swore that the earth was flat and that the sun turned around it, creating day and night. They also knew that women were only like children. So women could not own property or make decisions, and for sure they could not vote!

At the same time, Galileo continued to believe that the earth moved around the sun. The Christian church blessed his punishment and death. Five hundred years later, it acknowledged that he was right. Meanwhile, Christopher Columbus concluded that he could safely risk sailing around the globe in search of new and more profitable world trade routes to Asia (India and China), which Spain needed badly for its empire. Thus, in spite of the millions of peoples living in Abya Yala, the newcomers claimed that they discovered it and baptized it America, in honor of their geographer. They also thought they had reached the western part of India; thus they called the islands of the Caribbean the West Indies. Imagine getting so lost. This is conservatism!

Modern times were inaugurated by this. Under such conditions of retrenchment and misunderstanding, the Europeans started to "colonize" and "civilize" the whole world. It was claimed that we were being civilized because, regardless of our rich, diverse civilizations and cultures, the Europeans could not recognize anything as good enough for them. They could not understand the traditions, the relationship of humans with nature, and least of all that nobody had titles to land or water passages. These native people did not seem to know the value of land and mines; worst of all, they did not know about market value. They did not even want to sell. How to understand that the peoples around the world, no matter how imperfect, saw that their relationship was with nature and the land?

Who were these newcomers who put a price on their mother, the earth, and could own and possess her and do with her as they saw fit? The relationship of the people with land and nature, with the universe, and amongst themselves, reflected a spiritual way which could not be understood. It was unrecognized, negated. It was superstition, not

good enough. The newcomers could not understand the infinite manifestations, the diversity of that Spirit which is God. So, in the name of God, they proceeded to give us one language and killed ours, to exploit and dominate and subdue the earth and all that was creation, as they understood the Bible to have said. They built a civilization with a culture of use and exploitation, which they saw as progress. And for that our culture had to be destroyed, because this civilization knew how to make things better and obtain profit from it.

One of our great Latin American novelists has written *One Hundred Years of Solitude*. This is just a nice way of talking about these five hundred years of the same. Each nation of Latin America and the Caribbean has been living this imposed reality. The "colonization and civilizing" process has never ended for us. Whole nations of indigenous people were made to disappear from the face of the earth forever; for some they live in the culture and blood of the Garifunas, but the diversity of one and many cultures has disappeared. The slave trade of Africans and others spread worldwide. Hundreds of animal and plant species also disappeared with them, as well as the knowledge of their special properties. The new world order of global markets and profits had been established — the result of conservatism and the destruction of diversity.

Yet the peoples continue to dream. This life, which is the call and power to be, pushes forth this dream. Thus you see constant insurrections, revolutions, marches, street and official building takeovers, demanding justice, tortillas, beans, medicine, pencils, books, the roof, the park, clean water, responsibility, punishment for those who kill. We see it in El Salvador, in Guatemala, in the Philippines, in India, in Mexico, in Haiti, in Nicaragua, in Peru, in South Africa — everywhere.

We know conservatism. It has always been there. We see it when we look at the drug wars in our region, at the various "civil conflicts," as the bloody wars are called, at the invasion of Panama, at the recent collapse of the Mexican economy after Mexico entered into the North American Free Trade Agreement. We see "new democracies" — the new, elected, nonmilitary governments — complying with the budget balancing imposed by the World

Bank and the International Monetary Fund through structural adjustment programs. These governments do not cut military expenditures, but they do privatize all public, basic, and supportive services; and they open our economies to private investments to industrialize and to export to keep within the global economy. More of our peoples had to join the most formal "informal" economy, especially women, children, and youth.

Education funds are cut to include only those who will help to bring about the export economy that we must now have, as part of the globalization of "free trade" within the recently agreed pact for a free trade zone of the Americas. While these cuts are being carried out, the Pan-American Highway is being widened at a very high social, environmental, and financial cost. We do not know what the debt will amount to, but we have gone from unemployment and underemployment (that is, barely having an income), to marginalization and extreme misery, which those who want to govern our lands promise to combat. Many of our nations suffer social and environmental degradation; there is no unpolluted water, no clean air anymore. But now we have environmental commissions, offices for the rights of women, even though the people in power would want to hide this. There are similar ones for the rights of children, and for indigenous peoples too, though they are told that rights to land are not something the people in power are in a position to support. Conservatism is there.

The churches have been involved mostly in charity work, in projects that fund their existence; and more and more those in the leadership are elected abroad and promise not to mention human rights, or any type of rights. New churches are springing up like mushrooms, and their members are given a series of don'ts, as if to take them out of this world. Conservatism is there. But the people are seeking; that is why they join; and nothing stays the same. They learn to be different, to break away, to face up to authority, to find new ways. The military are strong, and they want to continue to be the only real power in nations. Nevertheless, they have had to negotiate, they have had to take off their uniforms. Many have had to leave. Yet there is no justice, and people are not happy.

We are still behind in bringing about relations of equality and justice in the family, amongst peoples, between people and government, between nations, between people and the environment. As our friend the writer says, "Love exists even in the time of cholera." We still have not surpassed that stage. Yet it is this same love for life that pushes us not to accept life as it is being forced on us. People participate, and we transform what we touch, no matter what we have to face, because that is the law: Nothing is static. The interaction of peoples always affects existing reality. We have to recognize this power, affirm it, know that it is a matter of using effectively our life-given abilities. We must work at unity and cooperation, share dreams, and figure out common strategies which effectively will use each person's power for the purposes of equality, justice, and peace.

We must learn and practice governance, by the way we live locally and in our organizations. Then we will become a power that can have an impact on government, and thus in the international arena. We must seek clarity of purpose, not for the takeover of power, but for the wisdom of knowing how to reach our goal and maintain it. If we want peace, justice, and equality in the 21st century, we must start living them now. Consistent practice, not political parties or politicians, will illuminate our path. We must recognize and affirm our power to be. Peace, justice, and equality are not elusive. We must choose to live them every day in all our ways and for all our needs. This is freedom.

Dangerously rising conservatism in the United States: Racism, sexism, and homophobia

Mab Segrest
U.S. Urban-Rural Mission, United States

I am honored and humbled to be speaking to this global body of women. I am speaking to you as a lesbian, which might accomplish the "dislodging of the comfortable" that our moderator has suggested is part of combating conservatism. In any case, I ask of you a sisterly listening.

The "rise of conservatism" from my perspective in the United States is too much of an understatement of what we are facing after 15 years of ascendant conservatism: the rise of fascism.

My grounding is from within the United States, but our experience in the U.S. both creates and echoes similar phenomena in Canada and Europe. Reagan, Gingrich, Thatcher, Mulroney, Berlusconi, Helmut Kohl — whatever the names, the themes are the same: the dismantling of the "welfare state" (which means the protection of the vulnerable, especially women and children) in the name of an unbridled "free market." We should be clear that this market may be free to goods and capital, but it comes at great cost to many humans and to the natural world. In the Atlantic alliance, there is a common fortress mentality, an ironic and compensatory drawing of racial/national identities at the moment in which multinationals have decided that the nation-state no longer serves its interests. The failures of this "freedom" of the market are obscured by deep racism, deep xenophobia, deep homophobia and deep sexism. In a world of corporate homogenization — of Ronald McDonald and Coca-Cola — and rapid cultural flux, religious fundamentalism is on the rise as people look for security in ancient patriarchal texts, usually the narrowest interpretations of the texts most constrictive of women's possibilities and of human sexuality.[1] From my own Christian tradition, for example, there are plenty of passages about love, but fundamentalists go for the ones about abomination

every time, and it makes me crazy.

My country in 1995 is a country both propelled forward and rushing backwards. Like countries all over the world, we are on the cusp of a new era of capitalism. Electronics and computers are restructuring the global assembly line. Now the "comparative advantage" of countries of the South is not only raw materials, as it was during the first stages of colonialism, but also cheap labor. With the tremendous mobility of capital that comes when money is transferred electronically, jobs flee South and people flood North. For example, take the Rio Grande River; jobs on the U.S. side pay $4 an hour, jobs on the Mexican side $4 a day. And workers on either side feel lucky to be paid even that, as Mexican workers in El Paso or Asian workers in Oakland or New York work long hours in sweatshop conditions for wages that are often promised but never paid.[2]

Elites move forward with their own agenda, sometimes conserving power in some places, expanding it in others, and always retaking and expanding it wherever they can. Within the United States over the past 20 years, this "conservatism" has worked as backlash to various people's advances. Its roots are in the not-so-ancient regime of colonizers who fought genocidal wars against indigenous people in order to claim ownership of land which they would then work with African slave labor. These practices required a range of justifications that shape us still: white supremacy, manifest destiny, class inflected by race inflected by gender. The greatest early victory against these forces in U.S. history was the abolition of slavery. The 13th, 14th, and 15th Amendments to the U.S. Constitution erected a legal wall abolishing slavery; prohibiting denial of the vote due to race, creed, or previous condition of servitude; and ensuring due process of law, equal protection, and a definition of citizenship that included all people born or naturalized within the United States.

The late 19th and early 20th centuries brought a labor movement that improved wages and working conditions, although disproportionately for white men. In 1919, the Russian Revolution brought a counterforce to capitalism that helped to seed local and national uprisings in the United States during the Great Depression of the 1930s, resulting in a "New Deal" of social welfare programs that provided U.S. workers some safety net in exchange for their continued participation in the capitalist system.

In the 1950s and 1960s, a mass movement of African Americans in the southern U.S. overturned racial segregation and voter disenfranchisement, policies that had been put in place to reinstitute white supremacy after the abolition of slavery. These advances were consolidated in two Civil Rights Acts, which also gave protection to women and put in place "affirmative action" hiring programs to begin to address past economic injustices which the Bill of Rights and the U.S. Constitution had not touched. People of color and many young white people in the United States, inspired by national liberation and anti-imperialist movements in Third World countries, increasingly challenged our economic and political system. Third World countries at the same time had begun to build their economies through direct intervention of the state, at times moving to protect national industries from foreign investment, competition, and control, and forming a "nonaligned pact."[3] In the United States, movements of women, lesbians and gay men, and the disabled broadened this impetus for justice.

At this moment of burgeoning liberation, the "New Right" in the United States was born. After a devastating electoral defeat in 1964, the Old Right elites saw they needed a populist base and a new facade, which resentments to liberation movements of the 1960s could provide. Conservative business nationalists such as Joseph Coors and Nelson Hunt donated millions to fund a conservative infrastructure to devise ideologies and strategies to mobilize a mass base. Hunt, for example, donated $10 million to Pat Robertson's Christian Broadcast Network in 1970, politicizing Robertson and other evangelical TV ministers with issues of abortion, homosexuality, and prayer in the schools.[4] Today Christian broadcast networks are the single most listened-to broadcast media in the world.[5]

At this moment when the Old Right moved to defend itself against new challenges, corporate officials also made their decisions to deindustrialize the United States. Faced with growing foreign competition, they knew we could either increase productivity and improve our products, or cut labor costs. They went after labor, moving plants overseas or to Mexico, where they could save $20,000 per worker per year, resulting in the loss of 1.8 million manufacturing jobs between 1981 and 1991.[6] Automation is perhaps an even greater threat to the status of the American worker. "More than 75 percent of the labor force in most industrial nations engages in work that is little more than simple repetitive tasks," Jeremy Rifkin writes. In the United States, that means that more than 90 million of a 124 million-person labor force can potentially be replaced by machines. Given both plant relocation and automation, corporate reengineering could eliminate 1 to 2.5 million jobs a year "for the foreseeable future," according to the *Wall Street Journal*. Two-thirds of the new jobs created are at the bottom of the wage pyramid.[7]

The U.S. electorate remains dangerously uninformed of these developments. Their main tools to grasp the rapidly changing world in which they find themselves are chiefly the scapegoating ideologies hatched and promoted by conservative intellectuals and strategists and propagated through corporate-controlled media and massively funded electoral campaigns. When the World Bank or the IMF in the 1970s began forcing developing countries to refinance their debt and impose "structural adjustment policies,"[8] people in those countries more clearly saw the foreign control and the collusion of their governing elites. In the U.S., the policies are often the same: slashing social programs, reducing wages, privatizing government functions, deregulating capital, increasing the police state. But historically racism, sexism, and more recently, homophobia have kept most people profoundly confused about the class system and very vulnerable to ideological narratives that "blame the victim" and point away from corporate decision makers as originators of these policies.

The core of these scapegoating narratives is racist: the concept of "reverse discrimination." This story persuades people of European descent — who are still a significant though falling majority in the United States — that the two civil rights laws of the 1960s achieved an "even playing field" in a society that is now "color blind." Attempts to redress centuries of inequity by affirmative action programs are "reverse discrimination," and the most oppressed group in the United States is now white men. When white people lose their jobs, they often believe it is the fault of "poorly qualified" people of color hired through affirmative action, not multinationals that are eliminating two million jobs a year.

If working people have less real wages, propaganda tells them that the problem is not a lowering of the wage structure but that they are paying too much in taxes for the bloated bureaucracy required to run a welfare state. The solution they propose is the elimination of taxation, especially taxing the rich and businesses. So there has been a massive transfer of wealth, once again, from the poor and middle class to the very rich. The result in the United States, in the words of a recent article in *Harper's* magazine, is an "enclave class" and the beginnings of a "new feudalism."[9] In Third World countries, structural adjustment programs achieved a similar "astounding net transfer of $178 billion from the Third World to commercial banks" between 1984 and 1990 through loan repayments. "Not since the conquistadors plundered Latin America has the world experienced a flow in the direction we see today," commented a former executive director of the World Bank.[10]

Militarism was a key factor in running up the U.S. debt. With the cold war as justification, massive military spending, first under Carter but hugely under Reagan and Bush, ran up the national debt to $2.4 trillion. Now the re-slashing of social programs decimated in the Reagan years and the elimination of government services — privatization — is carried out by Republicans under the banner of "reducing the deficit" that they themselves ran up!

We are facing a society in which 75 percent of the jobs will be lost to automation. Yet many Americans have been persuaded to believe that poverty is created by a failure of personal responsibility and that the main drain on the economy is payments to welfare mothers — who are imagined as exclusively women of color, although 38 percent are white women.[11] One centerpiece of the Republican "Contract with America," which has been rapidly instituted since the 1994 elections, is called the Personal Responsibility Act, which slashes $29 billion in welfare payments, including $11 billion in nutrition programs for women and children.[12] In some states, thousands of women and their children are cut from the welfare roles and end up on the streets, where homeless organizers say they have six months to get to them before life on the streets makes them crazy.[13]

Conservative propaganda convinces voting majorities that the economic crises in states such as New York and California are due to immigrants draining the states' economy through the welfare system. Proposition 187, which denies welfare payments to "illegal" immigrants, was approved by popular ballot in California.

Civil and human rights, conservatives persuade people, are not God-given but are endowed by the majority to reward "good behavior," i.e., heterosexuality normalized by Christian marriage.[14] The Christian Right has anti-gay ballot initiatives in over 17 states and cities that deny lesbians and gay men protection from discrimination and from even petitioning the government to change anti-gay practices and laws. The AIDS epidemic is viewed as a disease caused by homosexuals, not by a virus, and everywhere research and treatment is impeded by homophobia and a reticence to deal with issues of sexuality. Republicans in my home state of North Carolina recently debated instituting the death penalty for sodomy[15] — and I don't think they were worried about the sheep.

In the midst of social confusion and deterioration, law and order, like welfare, is coded by race and gender. In racist ideology, women of color are promiscuous; men of color are innately criminal. One of the few places where government is spending more in the United States is in building prisons. The "criminal-industrial complex"[16] is rapidly taking the place of the "military-industrial complex" as depressed communities compete for prisons. When neo-Nazi David Duke came close to winning the Louisiana governor's race, his program was welfare and crime. Democratic "centrist" Bill Clinton ran for the presidency on a program of health insurance, welfare, and crime, and he could not move the national health insurance. His Omnibus Crime Bill added the death penalty for 50 new crimes and a "three-strikes-you're-out" provision that mandates lifetime imprisonment after a person is convicted of three felonies.[17] In the United States, 25 percent of African-American males are expected to be in prison at some point during their lives, and prison policy is increasingly punitive. In Alabama, my state of birth, prison officials have reinstituted the chain gang, and prisoners are sentenced to the hard labor of breaking up large rocks with sledge hammers, producing gravel for which there is no use. In other places, industries are moving inside prisons. But we do not call these *gulags*.

How far backward could all this go? One of the targets of these assaults is the 14th Amendment to the Constitution, with its provisions of due process, equal protection, and citizenship as the birthright of people born in the United States. We have to ask ourselves quite seriously what it means that this range of right-wing forces has targeted the barrier erected between us and chattel slavery. All across the United States, right-wing militias have armed themselves to take back their government and assert the rights of "organic" citizens (not "citizens of the 14th Amendment"). Men from one such cell are charged with launching a terrorist attack on the Federal Building in Oklahoma City last spring, killing over 250 women, men, and children.

These policies and practices have their equivalents in Canada and in Europe. In Canada, five years before NAFTA, a Free Trade Act decimated Canadian industry and their proud tradition of national health insurance. A rise in French nationalism in Québec has precipitated a constitutional crisis. In Europe the influx of immigrants from former colonies after World War II has brought a pluralized and racialized population, with the move to deny citizenship to the children of immigrants born in European countries (a step ahead of California's Proposition 187). The year 1994 brought the electoral victory of Italy's fascist party, and in Germany Helmut Kohl won by incorporating nationalist, anti-welfare, and anti-immigrant sentiments.

Skinheads are the street soldiers of grassroots fascist movements, attacking Jews and immigrants. The demise of Soviet control in Eastern Europe has brought an upsurge of ethnic and national strife and "ethnic cleansing" policies against Muslims in Bosnia.

As a lesbian, it is clear to me that what is happening within the United States and internationally is not only the masculinization of the state, not only its racialization, but also its heterosexualization — its attempt to reassert itself as normatively, supremely heterosexual. One example recently was the codification of sexuality in Trinidad and Tobago (in 1986) and the Bahamas (in 1989). My friend Jacqui Alexander, a Trinidadian lesbian, has brilliantly analyzed these laws, which in the Bahamas in 1989 imposed up to 20 years in prison for lesbian sexuality at the same time that rape within marriage was criminalized. "The state has eroticized the dissolution of the nation, producing apocalyptic (mythic) visions of dread and destruction . . . brought on by prostitution and the practices of lesbian and gay sex. Yet it simultaneously enacts the dissolution of the nation" through the introduction of multinational capital and tourism, which appear as integral to the "natural order" as heterosexuality. This involves, among other things, the "symbolic triumph of the nuclear family over the extended and other family forms." A masculinity wounded by racism and colonialism seeks to reconstitute the nation to redeem itself.[18]

These Caribbean policies echo developments in the United States, where the Personal Responsibility Act would require that mothers up to 20 years old must live at home or marry to receive Aid to Families of Dependent Children — with the money saved to be directed, among other things, into orphanages for confiscated "illegitimate" children of poor women. And how many of the world's children are born outside of heterosexual legal marriage? Are they all being abandoned as well in the heterosexualization of the state?

The bracketing of large portions of the document for this Conference have made clear that homophobia and heterosexism have profound consequences to all of the world's women. They can bracket the whole question of gender in the UN document because, among other things, it is considered a code for lesbianism. It represents a broader attempt to bar attention from gender as a category constructed by such social forces as Catholicism or Islamic fundamentalism. All the women at this Conference have already been branded as anti-family lesbians, so you — we — might as well learn to defend ourselves by actively opposing homophobia. At stake is the bodily integrity of women and our access to the full range of nonexploitative sexual and emotional expression — our rights to love and pleasure — however those express themselves within the liberative elements of our cultures.

Lesbian and gay movements in the United States — deeply divided by race, class, and gender — would have much to learn in a global movement that does not replicate our own narrowly nationalist version of ourselves as "queer." We should rather all be, in a South African term, *ubuntu*, i.e., born to belonging. Either we are all *ubuntu*, "born to belong," or some of us are born to privilege. I don't think we can have it both ways.

In a world order that increasingly seeks to set nation against nation, race against race, man against woman, young against old, faith against faith, heterosexual brother against lesbian sister, rich against poor, it is this sense of human community on which we must all build. It is the sense of global community with one another as humans — and with our brothers and sisters, the animals and plants and rocks and stars — that we seek to reenact together as women here in China, and to take home with us when we leave, to live and to die by in the years and decades ahead.

Notes

1. See the World Council of Churches' current study process on "Gospel and Cultures" for a fuller discussion of the occasions for which the Christian tradition has arrived as "good news" and when it has arrived as "bad news" for particular cultures.
2. Asian Immigrant Women Advocates in Oakland, California, is waging a campaign against McClintock on behalf of garment workers denied back wages, to make the industry accountable to its workers. AIWA can be reached at 310 8th Street, Suite 301, Oakland, CA 94607.
3. Walden Bello and Shea Cunningham, "Reign of Error? The World Bank's Wrongs," *dollars and sense*, Sept/Oct 1994, p. 10.
4. Matthew Lyons, "Business Conflict and the Right in the United States," paper prepared for the Blue Mountain Working Group, 1994, p. 13.
5. Scot Nakagawa, National Gay & Lesbian Task Force.
6. Jeremy Rifkin, "The End of Work: The Decline of Mass Labor in the Production of Goods and Services," The Foundation on Economic Trends, 1130 17th Street, Suite 630, Washington, DC 20036. 202-466-2823.
7. Rifkin.
8. See Pam Starr, "What is Structural Adjustment?" in *Mortgaging Women's Lives: Feminist Critiques of Structural Adjustment*, ed. Pamela Sparr (Atlantic Highlands, New York: Zed Books, 1994).
9. Michael Lind, "To Have and Have Not: Notes on the progress of the American class war," *Harper's* Magazine, June 1995, pp. 35–47.
10. Bello and Cunningham, p. 11.
11. "Break the Contract on America: Stand up for your rights!" Center for Constitutional Rights, 666 Broadway, 7th floor, New York, NY 10012.
12. *House Republican Conference Legislative Digest*, 27 September 1995, p. 19.
13. Conversation with organizers from the Kensington Welfare Rights Union in Philadelphia, part of the National Welfare Rights Union, and the National Union for the Homeless, October 1994.
14. Conversations with Suzanne Pharr of the Women's Project. See their newsletter, *Transformation*, 2224 Main Street, Little Rock, Arkansas 72206.
15. Monitoring by the North Carolina Coalition for Gay and Lesbian Equality, conversation with Kenda Kirby.
16. This phrase is from the Rev. Sam Mann of St. Marks Church in Kansas City, Missouri.
17. *Legislative Digest*, p. 7.
18. Jacqui Alexander, "Not Just (Any) Body Can Be a Citizen: The Politics of Law, Sexuality and Post-Coloniality in Trinidad and Tobago and the Bahamas," *Feminist Review* #48 (Autumn 1994), pp. 5–23.

Religious fundamentalism

Toujan Faisal
Member of Parliament, Jordan

I will start by clarifying one point. Some of you know about my dilemma with the fundamentalists. Today I am speaking about conservatism with a special focus on religious fundamentalism. I am not bringing with me a personal vendetta. I am a politician; I cannot afford to be personal. So if through my speech, some think I condone or condemn fundamentalism, it might not be the right judgment.

What I am trying to do is analyze and understand. I think it was Socrates who said, "To understand all is to forgive all." I don't claim to be that forgiving, but I want to understand, because I want to make a change. If you understand my speech within this context, I don't think anyone will feel that I am aligning with one side rather than the other.

The topic of our lecture is the revival of conservativism. Revival means that we are talking about the old patterns through which social and political entities were divided. The smallest is the ethnic, starting with the tribe. Then we have area-wide groups that create nations and then become religions. The religion starts with the ethnic and with the national.

When a prophet starts a message, he starts it with his own people; it spreads, and it becomes identified with ethnic or national identity (as Islam is mixed with Arabism and Christianity was mixed with the Roman Empire). Actually, after some time, with all the religions that spread all over the globe, religion cuts across nationalities and ethnic groups. In a way, this is an issue that is similar to women's issues. Women's issues are now one force that is cutting across different nationalities and even different religions.

The idea of citizenship, on the other hand, is a modern one. So all we're talking about is the old model of classifying and dividing political and social entities. The modern one is citizenship; that is, when these entities were defined, they were defined not by natural boundaries creating isolated groups with specific characteristics, but with artificial political and military borders: within this line you're a citizen of this state and not that one.

Now we are talking about the revival of this kind of conservatism: racial, ethnic, and religious. The urge behind it is an urge for identification and sovereignty. In this context, women should be the most capable of understanding these issues, because women see them — identification and sovereignty — as the ability to make the basic decisions in their lives. But if we look at what survives of all these conservative systems, it is not the matriarchal. We had matriarchal religions, we had matriarchal ethnic groups, we had matriarchal races, but these are bygone now. Very few of them exist, and they operate on the social level but not as political powers.

What we have now, we should admit, is all patriarchal. In this context, women are among the victims of these conservative systems. When women join the general national force or the religious advocates and preachers, what we do is serve some sort of democracy — like the Greek democracy — in which there is a cause. But of the people who are supposed to be the leaders of this cause, half of them do not have the same right. It is like the Greek democracy that we still uphold as the first example of democracy: women and slaves did not have any rights. So with this urge for identification and sovereignty in which women also participate, the slaves are almost abolished, but the women remain, and they don't get a share of that cake.

We talk about global change; we talk about the opening of culture, one trade, mass communication. At the same time, we see a contradiction: the international village on the one hand and on the other, the rise of ethnicity, racial conflicts, and religious fundamentalism. To look at it, to understand why we have these two contradictory things going on at the same time, we should look at the political aspects of this change.

There is a global change going on. It is a historical fact. We should not mix it up with the political decisions or the political manipulations of this kind of change. We do have culture transferred from one area to another. We have mass communication; we have the common interests of many groups scattered all over the world which unify them. The fact that we can sit here, women from all over the world, and communicate easily and feel that we know each other is an outcome of this globalization in which the other is no longer an alien, but another human being with the same feelings and aspirations, and we don't see the surface cultural differences as basic differences. We see each other as human beings. There are aspects in globalization that are positive, and we should not mix them up with the negative, political ones.

Women interested in women's issues cannot be separated from the aspirations which motivate nations to claim their national identity or religious identity, because women's issues are part of a whole society's issues. You cannot separate them. If the society progresses, women's status progresses. If there is unemployment, women are going to be most affected. So this is one reason why, when we talk about women's issues, we cannot but talk about political change.

There is another reason for that, which is that women do care and care more, because they do not work just for themselves: they work for the rights of their children, for the next generation, regardless of whether this generation is male or female. Every woman loves her son the way she loves her daughter. In this context, women are involved — whether they want to be or not — in the whole state of the nation. We cannot separate them from the issue.

In my part of the world, political issues are very, very hot. The area has spent over 100 years under Western colonization. Prior to that, we had all kinds of colonizations during the Mongols. So ours was always an area in which people were trying to fight and invade us. It has created political problems.

The last issue in Western colonization was the creation of the state of Israel. This created the Israeli-Arab conflict and affected not only the lives of the Palestinians, but the lives of everyone in the whole area. It was actually a conflict between Arabs and Israelis. In this context, we do have a nation called Palestine. We are all Arabs, but the Palestinians are the ones who lost their identity.

So it is unquestionable that they would keep striving to get a space that is called Palestine.

So even though we are all Arabs, this problem has created an internal problem within the Arab world, because the Palestinians are scattered all over the Arab world. They are Arabs, but they are not nationals in these countries. Those who are under occupation are suffering a lot. Within this context, the area is very hot politically. Women are involved in this struggle as well as men. They cannot separate themselves from what goes on.

During the fights against colonialism — and we could start with a very vivid example like Algeria — when Algeria fell to occupation by the French, it was not a fundamentalist country, not Islamic in that sense. It was just tribal. Coming from that area, I know how much the tribal sometimes contradicts religion — takes over even. That is, the tribal custom sometimes comes prior to religious preaching. The area was just like another area. But when they had to fight and occupy, usually to gather people around this struggle, they had to find some sort of an identity. The religious identity is the strongest, because you are asking people to die for the cause. That's why there was, through the liberation movements, a revival of the Islamic sentiment.

What happened is that that war went on too long; they fought for 100 years, and they paid the price of a million martyrs. One million might not sound like a big number, with the mass destruction weapons that are now used in conflicts. But at that time it was a really big number, which stunned us when we were in our early childhood.

Then comes the second element. Those who succeeded, by paying a high price in liberating these countries — sometimes they came as groups of liberators, as in Algeria; sometimes they came as reformers who took over the regime in a coup saying they would reform the misdoings of the previous regime. What happened is that they stayed too long, and the corruption of the state caused poverty and injustice. Whenever poverty and injustice increase, fundamentalism finds good soil, because when your problems in this world are not being solved, you wish at least to be rewarded somewhere else.

There is another element besides the corruption of the leadership. There is also the fact that the Israeli state is a declared Jewish state. The other side, to help its own cause in the fight against the invader of its lands, stresses the same kind of identity — that of religion. The religious state of Israel encouraged the surrounding countries to market fundamentalism.

In this sense, these revivals of traditional, conservative political systems — whether they are ethnic, national, or religious — in the beginning none of them were bad. They started with good intentions: the right of this group of people to be sovereign and to have self-determination. When most good intentions are carried too far, then they become wrong; this is the real story of fundamentalism. If we don't understand it, we are not going to be able to tackle the issue.

Now we come to what we should do about this. Jordan has fundamentalism, just like Egypt or Algeria. But what happened is that in a very critical moment, we shifted to a sort of democracy. I didn't say a full democracy. But at least these people were pushed to act on the ground. Much of the halo around them collapsed with practice. People had the chance to test them. We had the chance to answer back. They did not control all the platforms. This minimized the role and the effect of fundamentalism. In elections, they were successful in 1989. But in the second election in 1993, they got only half the seats. Their power was cut down by at least half.

One answer is democracy. But it is not just local democracy. What we need is international democracy. My colleague spoke about the imperial practices of the West. The next step is not only to call for democracies within these states, but to call for international democracy.

These days we are celebrating the 50th anniversary of the United Nations. This is the best time to look again into the charter and laws of the UN to ensure that this is a democratic structure. What we want is justice, and justice not just as a slogan — justice as real practice, by modifying and amending the laws. If we just keep repeating the slogans, if we just talk about peace without solving the real conflicts that cause war, we will end up with only short intervals of peace — in preparation for other wars.

There is another thing we could do for justice, that is, literally take the aggressors to court. The international courts are there, but they are limited in their power and their roles. The way they are run is not perfectly democratic. What we need is to expand their authority and to create new international courts. One of them has been suggested by different women's groups — I expect to hear support for it here — which is a court to look at human rights aggression during wars, especially aggression and violence against women. These are forms of international courts which, if we support them, will make the heads of state, the militia, the aggressors, the occupiers hesitate before they confiscate the human rights of the people they are fighting against, or ruling, or occupying. These courts should become as common as other courts, and every individual should have the right to reach them and sue whoever has done wrong regardless of his position. It is not a hard thing to achieve if we join hands.

I end by saying that I have stressed women's issues for some time in my life, but I never gave them supremacy or priority. Because I come from a very hot political area, I learned that I cannot solve women's problems if I do not work to solve the source of the problem itself. Some women have refused to spend any time or effort on their own issues while the whole nation suffers from the same injustice. How could we speak about the rights of women, knowing that these women belong to societies in which even men don't enjoy basic human rights?

In this context, I think we should all become political. If we don't become political, we don't have a cause; we will never win. That is why I have chosen politics as a profession. I don't believe there is a politics of men and a politics of women. There are wrong politics and right politics. It is the same in medicine, where there is a bad doctor or a good doctor, regardless of sex or gender. In this context, all women's movements should be involved in politics and should be politically oriented, or else we will not make the big decisions and we won't have a comprehensive solution.

VII • Media, Culture, and Communication

Challenges and Opportunities

Opening remarks

Zenebeworke Tadesse, Moderator
Council for the Development of Social Sciences
in Africa (CODESRIA), Ethiopia

Remember when we first got together at the UN world conferences, we used to have a very ambiguous relationship with the media — with how the media conceptualize women, how women are left out of the media? We appealed to the media to address women's concerns and also represent women as the force we really are. I think we have come a long way. In this Conference, what is different from the other world conferences is that women are no longer asking to be included in anything, but are asserting their presence in terms of how they can shape these global forces and the impact of these forces on their lives in the coming century.

Today I am very honored to present to you a panel of speakers on every aspect of the media. I am sure they will address questions we have started to touch on since the first day of the plenaries. One of the questions we will be concerned with is what the media as a global force has meant in our lives.

Culture is the major responsibility of women, whether we want it to be or not. Some of our speakers will address the issue of how the homogenization that comes through the media — particularly the global media — shapes our lives and how women can have an impact in maintaining our diversity. From the first plenary, we have been talking about how we have to celebrate, respect, and maintain the diversity that women and other peoples of the world represent, and that we should not be homogenized as if our diversity was not the very essence of our existence.

The panelists will also address the roles women play in the media and what roles we can play as we move on to another century.

Challenging corporate society: Media domination and press control from a woman's perspective

Yayori Matsui
Asia-Japan Women's Resource Center; Asian
Women's Association (AWA), Japan

It is my great pleasure to be given such a precious opportunity to speak to you, sisters from all over the world, about the newspaper media from a national, Asian regional, and global perspective, since the voices of women from East Asian countries are hardly heard at international conferences — including women's conferences — due to the language barrier. Language is the means of global domination; in reality, English is the only dominant international language, illustrating the globalization of communication and culture, which benefits only those who are privileged to speak that language.

WORKING IN THE MALE-DOMINATED MEDIA IN JAPAN

Japan is a country of newspapers

I want you to be able to share my own experience of working in mainstream media for more than thirty years, until my retirement last year, specifically for the *Asahi Shimbun*, the second-largest newspaper in Japan, with a circulation of more than eight million.

In Japan there are nearly 100 daily newspapers; among them are five major national newspapers with a circulation of several million. The total circulation amounts to 52 million, and the percentage of readers in the population is the highest in the world.

Japanese newspapers claim to be independent, neutral, and objective because they pledged right after World War II never to repeat the history of severe suppression of press freedom that was instituted by the militarist government. This is true: the Japanese media does not experience direct state control or censorship, and Japan is one of the few countries in Asia with freedom of the press, freedom of speech, and freedom of expression.

Only 5 percent of newspaper reporters in Japan are female

Despite these freedoms, I had to face a different kind of constraint every day of my work life. I suffered from gender discrimination from the first day on, because I was the only woman to pass the *Asahi Shimbun* entrance examination in 1961. I was angered by the chief editor's rude comments that a female reporter couldn't be as capable as a male reporter. I felt isolated in the big editorial office, surrounded only by male colleagues.

For 20 years after the start of my career, the number of women reporters in the entire nation remained at little more than 100, and only since the 1980s, perhaps under the influence of the UN Decade for Women, has this number gradually increased. It is still only 5 to 6 percent.

During three decades of working as a journalist, I had to struggle day to day. I made every effort to have my stories published. My last articles before retirement were, for example, on child prostitution in Asia, the trial of a teacher arrested because of his support of illegal migrant workers, and the plight of Taiwan's aboriginal people, to mention a few.

I was persecuted not only for being a woman but also because I used a woman's point of view to challenge the Japanese model of economic development based on competition, efficiency, and discipline; because I questioned consumerism, which commercializes and commodifies everything, including women's sexuality, for profit; because I criticized the conformism of Japanese society, which discriminates against minorities such as Korean residents, Ainu indigenous people, and foreign migrant workers; because I condemned the economic and sexual exploitation of other Asian women. In other words, I confronted sexism and racism in Japanese society through my reporting because I shared the pain and humiliation of those who were victimized by the Japanese system.

Reporting on Minamata and the women's environmental movement

The most serious problem caused by overly rapid economic growth was industrial pollution. Minamata disease was most tragic. Since the late 1950s hundreds were killed, thousands paralyzed, and many babies were born severely handicapped due to mercury poisoning discharged by the Chisso Chemical Company in the city of Minamata in the southwestern part of Japan. I wrote about the mothers in poor fishing villages who suffered most and fought back most courageously.

It was also women who took the lead in the nationwide anti-pollution struggles of the early 1970s. I highlighted women's decisive role in environmental protection. Food safety, pesticides, medicine, and consumer product safety were also issues that male colleagues didn't want to take up. I made a scoop that cow's milk had been seriously contaminated by BHC, the most widely used chemical for rice cultivation, and forced the government to ban it totally. The dairy industry, damaged by the sharp decrease in milk sales, called me a witch. Editors and colleagues at the newspaper labeled me anti-corporate.

Nowadays environment, ecology, a green philosophy, and corporate responsibility are authorized and fashionable themes for any journalist, but in those days, male colleagues were rarely interested in such subjects. Editors were afraid of hurting corporations and only reluctantly agreed to publish my stories.

A TRANSBORDER APPROACH TO ENVIRONMENTAL ISSUES AND SEXUAL EXPLOITATION

The export of pollution to Asia and tropical rain forests

The strong environmental movement had certain results. New pollution-control laws were put into effect, court cases brought victory to victims, and public opinion toward corporations turned more and more severe. The response of many companies to this situation was to relocate their polluting plants to neighbouring Asian countries. Since the mid-1970s I have visited the affected areas, tracing these plants and reporting on the export of pollution.

In 1986 I travelled deep into the rain forests in Sarawak in eastern Malaysia to see the ravaged forests and the indigenous people's suffering, which was caused by wealthy Japan, the largest importer of tropical timber, more than half of which comes from Sarawak. I believed it was the responsibility of journalists to let Japanese people know what was going on in Asia. In order to motivate the public to organize in support of the local struggle for survival, I exposed how the indigenous men, women, and children of Sarawak were fighting back by blockading the logging roads.

Sex tourism and trafficking in women

Another issue that made me aware of Japanese-Asian and North-South relations was the sex tours taken by Japanese men in the early 1970s. A small demonstration at the Seoul airport by young Korean women opened my eyes to a problem Japanese women knew nothing about in those days. Many hundreds of Japanese men were travelling to Korea in groups for sex. I investigated and wrote an article about it, but the editors didn't like the article, and after several days only the lead section — some 20 lines — was published. Furthermore, I had to face the hostility and anger of male colleagues; some of them even openly accused me of being a naive moralist or a man-hater.

To my encouragement, however, I received more and more support from outside the company, especially among women readers. My friends and I decided to form a small women's group, the Asian Women's Association (AWA), and to make an appeal concerning the sex tour issue by publishing a newsletter. A mere 2,000 copies of the AWA newsletter became a powerful and effective tool to mobilize women, not only in Japan but also in other Asian countries, to protest sexual aggression by Japanese men. Meanwhile, newspapers with eight million readers neglected the issue.

Since the early 1980s, several thousand Asian women have been sent into the expanding Japanese sex industry each year. Trafficking in Thai women is now an especially serious human rights issue in Japan. They are treated as sex slaves, confined, beaten up, threatened, and forced into prostitution. Some have been killed by customers, and some have murdered their exploiters in an attempt to escape and are now in prison. It can be said that they have been abused and exploited as contemporary "comfort women" for company warriors, half a century after the exploitation of comfort women for the benefit of the Imperial Army.

Various forms of sexual exploitation, such as sex tours and trafficking in women, are spreading all over Asia. The phenomenon is growing into a huge multinational sex industry that brings enormous profits and wealth to its organizers. It is a system that dehumanizes women, who are lured due not only to sheer poverty but also by the consumerism promoted by the free-market economy.

THE ROLE OF THE WESTERN MEDIA IN PROMOTING A MARKET ECONOMY AND CONSUMERISM

The stereotype of Asian women as sex object or subservient wife

It is not only Japanese men who are sex tourists in internationally known pleasure zones in Asia. In the sex districts of Bangkok, Pattaya, Manila, Cebu, and even Phnom Penh, it is common to see large white men accompanying small young girls. Furthermore, recently more and more Korean and overseas Chinese men can be seen in these places. They are mainly from the newly industrialized countries (NICs); the more economically developed the country, the more the men go abroad for sexual adventure.

What are the factors behind the aggravation of global sexual exploitation of women on such an unprecedented scale? The Western media plays an important role in promoting sex tourism and trafficking in women, describing Asian women as sex objects with such common terms as "Oriental charm," "Asian beauty," "sexy little girls," etc. The other prevalent stereotype of the Asian woman is the docile, subservient, sexy wife. The number of Filipina and other Asian women marrying foreign men is increasing, either through mail-order bride agents or as a result of the women's going abroad as entertainers.

However, the problem is not only such direct sexist and racist descriptions of Asian women. It is more important to realize how the global media are disseminating consumerist values all over the world to put people under psychological pressure to buy more, consume more, and waste more products made by global factories. Sex becomes one of the cheap, disposable commodities. Poor people in the South are also attracted by Western media fantasies that make them forget about daily misery. It isn't easy to resist the market power propagated by the media, and the poor are discouraged from organizing collective actions to change present conditions.

Globalization of media and the Gulf War

The media that influence people's lives have become globalized. This means that Western media dominate the world, because all competing media empires are based in the United States or Europe and form a powerful oligopoly equipped with all available communications technology. Now people of the non-Western world are mere receivers of news reported by Western media. Some sources estimate that 80 percent of the world's information is provided by the Western media. According to a 1986 survey done in England, 77 percent of the news on CNN International was about the United States and 21 percent of the news on the BBC World News was about England. This shows how the news circulated by two television news systems is biased toward national interests.

This situation was exemplified by the Gulf War in 1991. I was attending a women's meeting in Malaysia when the first bombing of Baghdad was reported. Television was showing U.S. soldiers coming back from bombing raids looking happy and making comments such as, "It was successful," "Baghdad was in flames," "It looked just like Christmas trees." Women from many Asian countries were watching TV and looking angry and sad. They were thinking of the Iraqi women and children who might have been killed or hurt. It was an unforgettable contrast between celebration of victory and resentment toward the killing of innocent Iraqi people. At the market in Kuala Lumpur, I saw a candy box with a photo of President Saddam Hussein. I noticed that I was in a country with a Muslim majority that sympathized with the fight against the West.

After the end of the Gulf War, I was horrified to see on CNN a scene of all the U.S. congressmen and congresswomen giving an endless standing ovation to President George Bush for the victory over "Saddam." It looked like wartime in Japan, when there was almost unanimous public support for the militarist government, and anyone who was critical of it was condemned as a betrayer.

During the Gulf War I felt embarrassed and disappointed to see CNN news, which described American women being so dedicated to supporting their government's war policy against Iraq and which glorified women in the army fighting together with male soldiers. Do we want such equality and participation, where women join the army to fight together with men and kill innocent women and children? No, we want the equality that comes from changing men so that women and men can work together for peace and human rights.

Persecution of Vietnam and Cambodia by the Western media

In the early 1980s I was based in Singapore as Asia correspondent for *Asahi Shimbun*, the only permanent female correspondent from a Japanese newspaper in those days. During the four years of my assignment, I concentrated on reporting the situation of grassroots people, especially women in Asian countries, because Japanese people were poorly informed about their Asian neighbours due to their Western-biased media and education. I had sort of a sense of mission about being a pioneer in Asian reporting, even though I knew how difficult it was going to be for my stories to be accepted by editors. And it was really difficult. I always had to wage battle with the editors in the Tokyo office.

One of my most unforgettable experiences was my first visit to Cambodia in 1982. I wanted to see the situation inside the country with my own eyes, because it was little known, overwhelmed by Western coverage of the situation of Cambodian refugees near the Thai border. For three weeks I traveled across the killing field of this devastated, ruined country. I saw thousands of skulls and bones just piled up or scattered everywhere, and I met hundreds of widows, orphans, and handicapped people trying to rebuild their country, which had been destroyed by U.S. war and the Pol Pot regime. Visiting village after village, I shared tears with many women who had lost their families.

I made three trips to Cambodia from Singapore. I was really disappointed in and angered by the Western media, which just ignored the suffering of the Cambodian people or attacked and denied the Heng Samrin government that was backed by Vietnam. The media was tolerant of the genocidal former regime continuing its guerrilla war, supported by Chinese military assistance, while the media always portrayed Vietnam as the bad guy. Consequently it was Pol Pot's group that was favoured. It was never prosecuted internationally for butchering millions of its people; furthermore, it even got a seat at the United Nations. Because of the cold war mentality, the Western media is responsible for the prolonged suffering of Cambodia.

I also visited Vietnam to report on victims of Agent Orange, the chemical defoliant that contained poisonous dioxin and was sprayed by the U.S. Army during the Vietnam War. Agent Orange not only destroyed and contaminated vast areas of farmland and forest but also damaged the lives and health of millions of Vietnamese people.

The most horrifying effect of this chemical warfare was the birth or early death of thousands of malformed babies. I was really shocked to see how women suffer from giving birth to severely handicapped babies.

I will never forget the scene in Tu Du Hospital in Ho Chi Minh City, full of such babies and children and crying mothers. In many poor villages I saw mothers with victimized children who got no assistance from anywhere.

The United States has never apologized to or compensated the Vietnamese people; on the contrary, the United States forced economic sanctions against Vietnam for many years. U.S. mainstream media didn't question such government policies; it even supported them, just as it justified the atomic bombing of Hiroshima.

THE STRUGGLE FOR FREEDOM OF THE PRESS AND WOMEN'S HUMAN RIGHTS IN ASIA

Government control of press freedom and women

How, then, to confront the global domination of the Western media? During the 1970s the South advocated a New World Information Order (NWIO) to get the right to choose news coverage and interpretation, but it failed. However, was it really the demand of the people of the South to put media under government control? Wasn't it the intention of governments of the South, which were afraid of press freedom for their own people?

Actually, there are still many countries in Asia that suppress freedom of expression. I experienced this in Singapore. Many journalists are detained; some are even killed. Here in China, a woman journalist named Gao Yu is still in jail 80 kilometers from Beijing, according to Amnesty International.

Criticism against the Western media shouldn't be used as an excuse for violating human rights — of which freedom of the press is a part — by any government, North or South. All this affects women's rights.

For example, former comfort women who were forcibly taken to be sex slaves for the Japanese army during World War II had to keep silent until a few years ago, partly because the dictatorial governments of victimized countries in Asia wanted to have good relations with the Japanese government and didn't want these women to speak up or take action to demand Japanese government compensation.

In the case of South Korea, the women's movement was too occupied with resistance against their repressive regime to deal with the issue of comfort women, and without the support of the women's movement, former comfort women couldn't come forward. Even today some governments, such as Malaysia, don't want them to speak out.

In China four comfort women recently and courageously broke their silence. They were about to speak at a press conference in Beijing last month, because they had been prevented from visiting Japan to file suit in Tokyo. However, the press conference was disrupted and banned by Chinese authorities, and several of the women were taken into custody. They aren't allowed to attend this NGO Forum, but I appeal to you to think of them.

At this moment, I am thinking also of Taiwanese women who were denied visas to come here, because I have written many articles about their committed activities, not only for women's equality but also on behalf of the aboriginal women who are being sacrificed by economic development.

Democratization is the key test

I firmly believe that human rights should be universal and indivisible. No woman of any country, North or South, East or West, should be deprived of her democratic rights. It should not be the state or the global, multinational media that should have access to and control of the media — it should be the people.

We need now to make concerted efforts and launch a transborder women's movement to take back the media for ourselves. It is a struggle for democracy at the local, national, and global levels. We should have more women journalists in all types of media who are willing to play a decisive role in this challenging struggle, hand in hand with women in all sectors of society.

Linking UN conferences from 1990 to 1995: Engendering communications

Maria Suárez Toro
Feminist International Radio Program (FIRE),
Costa Rica

Allow me to take you on a trip to all the UN conferences held in this past decade, to share with you the symbolic images that we have used in the Feminist International Radio Program (FIRE). The trip includes scenes of what we believe have been the barriers to the efforts of the women's movement and the political officials of the UN conferences, specifically the State members.

My first international conference was the World Congress of Women for a Healthier Planet in 1992, held just before the UN Conference on Environment and Development, or the Earth Summit. The event brought together 1,500 women from across the world. They were convened by the Women's Environment and Development Organization (WEDO) to draft an agenda for the Earth Summit.

Since then, as FIRE's producer, I have covered each and every conference. Through images that did not appear in the mainstream media's coverage of the summits, we, along with those whose voices are unheard, have brought forward one of the key issues that confront women who seek to influence the international agendas: the invisible forces that do not have a "vote" in the UN conferences, but who nonetheless have more influence on them, more than those who have votes or those movements that exert pressure to get their issues of interest onto the international agendas.

Let me take you back to the past conferences, showing them to you through the images that we have used on our radio:

Image one

Rio de Janeiro, 1992, site of the UN Conference on the Environment and Development (UNCED), also known as the Earth Summit. In that conference the women's tent at the NGO Forum was separated from the official reunion by a distance of 40 kilometers. It so happens that the conference was on the environment and development.

Stories told by Brazilian women revealed that all of Rio de Janeiro was once an enormous swamp, now drained in the name of development for the benefit of the large tourist industry. Forty kilometers of earth that had been subjected to forced sterilization separated the women's movement from the political officials in said Conference.

Halfway along that 40-kilometer route stands Favela Rosiña, known in Latin American and Caribbean oral history as the largest slum in the continent. Favela Rosiña is a very big hill, with very poor people, located in a remote area that in reality looks like a piece of cake that starving people have nibbled at, bit by bit, later settling themselves in its remains, placing pieces of cardboard over the deserted ground to have a roof over their heads.

During the fifteen days of the UNCED reunion, the main public road at the bottom of the hill where the favela ends was lined with military tanks that held their machine guns permanently aimed at the favela. "So that we won't go down to the conference," a woman resident told us.

I thought if Rosiña could not go to the conference, then I would go to visit her. "No way," said the same woman. "The drug dealers have made it clear that no journalists are allowed to enter during the conference, and if they do, they won't come out alive."

Five kilometers from Rosiña stands Villa del Parque on the small lake of Tijuca. From our hostess, Sueli García, we learned of the decade-long struggle that brave men and women had waged in defense of their property and of the only piece of swampland that remained in all of Rio. The swampland was threatened by a large industry that wanted to drain it and convert it into a shopping mall. Already two residents had been mysteriously murdered.

When I sat down to observe the official Summit, not even the transnationals of the tourist industry or the military or the drug dealers were present.

Image two

Vienna, 1993, site of the UN's second World Conference on Human Rights.

At this conference there was no land separating the Site for Women's Rights and the official Conference. Both events took place in the United Nations building, with one floor separating them. On one floor (the top one, of course) was the UN Conference. And on the lower floor, the NGO Forum.

But the vertical hierarchy wasn't what separated the two meetings. There were security doors that one had to pass through every day in order to move from one conference to the other. Security doors. Selective control of people at a conference on human rights!

"Security" to decide who could sit and listen, and who could not. "Security" to decide when the NGOs could enter and supervise the States, and when they could not.

In fact, the "security" was selective in that it only offered protection to the official Conference. Let me give you an example. Emma Hilario, a Peruvian woman and one of 33 women who testified before the World Tribunal on Human Rights Abuses Against Women, told her story as a survivor of a death threat from Peru's terrorist organization The Shining Path. A few hours later, while she was walking in the same UN building where the conference and the forum were taking place, Hilario was followed by members of that same terrorist group. While we walked to the hotel, Hilario was verbally threatened by seven terrorists present at the NGO Forum.

There was no security for her. The women who were with her had to guard her and rescue her from that situation. Finally, under pressure from the women, the Austrian authorities assigned bodyguards to Emma. The United Nations kept its security guard at the entrance to the official meeting.

The security officials, nonetheless, came once to "visit" the Site for Women's Rights. "We have been informed that there is an illegal radio station installed here and that is not allowed," one of them told a woman activist who was there when the security police entered.

The "illegal" radio was nothing other than a

control board, a telephone, microphones, and a telephone exchange with which we were transmitting live to FIRE via a simple telephone line from the UN building. The guards looked at it and decided there was nothing illegal about it. But security had come because it was necessary to control.

At that official reunion, I also did not see that the security had seats in the UN meeting.

Image three

PrepCom III, International Conference on Population and Development.

No land in between, no intermediate floors. This reunion was held in the same building, at the UN headquarters in New York, and on the same floor.

The women's movement and the State delegates, together at last! Guess what came between us and the States? The Vatican! In the name of religion, fundamentalist politicians came between us and those who make the decisions.

I won't tell you the story. You already know the story because the other force that came between us and the political officials was the media. The media have told the story throughout the world, but it has been told from the Vatican's perspective. In our region, Latin America and the Caribbean, the only story told of the Cairo Conference was the one of the Vatican's opposition to the draft agenda. The media did not give a voice to the women, not even to their issues as they appeared in the Cairo agenda, or to the States that supported the draft for the agenda.

The Vatican and other reactionary religious fundamentalists were the ones who received wide media coverage. Along with the media, they were the ones who intervened between us and the decision makers.

The same thing happened in Cairo during the Conference. While we were covering the activities for FIRE and pressuring the media to recognize women's voices, we discovered that the media's message was beginning to take on a slight variation.

Once the Vatican and the Islamic fundamentalists assumed obstructionary positions, having decided that the Plan of Action approved in Cairo re-flected a philosophy and a series of actions that went beyond family planning as a form of population control and that held human rights, women's participation, broader definitions of reproductive and sexual health, the need for education, women's equality, and advocacy as official objectives, then the media proceded to distort the objectives of the women's caucus at the Conference.

Nonetheless, at the UN headquarters, the Islamic fundamentalists sat in their States' seats. The Vatican supposedly observes, and the media cover the proceedings.

Image four

New York, PrepCom II toward the Summit on Social Development.

I want to share with you one of the first images I saw and a gut feeling I had on the first day of the PrepCom last August, the last PrepCom before Copenhagen.

While Peggy Antrobus, representative for the organization Development Alternatives with Women for a New Era (DAWN), was making a presentation in our name to the plenary of the official meeting, I glanced at the seats for the representatives of the International Monetary Fund and the World Bank, placed side by side.

There they were. Seats for observers, voice, but no vote in a conference on social development.

So I thought they were listening to the women while Peggy talked. Soon I discovered that I was mistaken. They had been sitting there waiting for their turn to speak. A few minutes after Peggy's presentation had ended, they took the floor. They spoke, but immediately after speaking, they left the meeting. During the rest of the meeting, their seats remained empty. They came only to speak, not to listen. And we already know the results of the summit in that regard. The Bank and the IMF were not restrained, not even subjected to the governing and control of the UN's economic and social council. The invisible forces of the conference: the true decision makers, even at the Conference, without having a vote!

There are three elements to the relationship between these stories and women's media groups:

First, due to our position in society, we are the

ones who have nothing to lose in identifying them by name, in rendering them visible so that women and others can design effective strategies to fight those invisible superpowers and justly present our struggle to the United Nations.

Second, we are the ones who are identifying them as the obstacles who come between us and the political officials because we have not been blinded by having high representation in the governments.

Third, at the conferences, women's media groups are primarily responsible for observing the armed forces, large industries, drug mafias, selective security, fundamentalist forces, the mainstream media, the IMF, and the World Bank. Because when the media is in our hands, we do not enter into the negotiations or use the media as an intervening force.

But this also holds implications for the women's movement in the mapping of oppositional strategies. I would like to close with a saying we have in Latin America and the Caribbean: "You can't put all your eggs in one basket." In effect, we have to appeal to the States at the UN headquarters to take responsibility for what they have initiated: to launch platforms and action plans that are responsive to our needs. But our primary struggle continues to take place on the streets confronting the transnationals, in schools and in hospitals, in front of military bases and in our homes, on the plantations and in the rural outskirts. We have to maintain our struggle everywhere using all the methods we have learned to rely on.

The first time I spoke of the invisible powers that manifest themselves at these various conferences, I said that at the World Conference on Women and at the NGO Forum we would present a stronger articulation of those forces. Today we find ourselves in Beijing, just days away from the opening of the meeting of States, and we can affirm that yes, they have been more clearly articulated.

Nonetheless, the mainstream media have tried once again to alienate the realities that we are living. I ask you, if it is not true that those problems which have been labeled "logistical" and "bureaucratic" in the two years of organizing this For-

um and this Conference are not substantial. It is, in my opinion, the lack of power for women.

And I also ask you, if behind the explicit agendas of the Conference and the NGO Forum, what we are experiencing here and the information that is being sent back to our countries, is not also an agenda — of those invisible powers, including the mainstream media — to obscure those agendas with a geo-political agenda? We have to exercise and articulate our feminist power so as not to become trapped here during these three weeks that will undoubtedly affect the path of progress in the next decade.

I invite you to consider these reflections as part of the analysis that is being elaborated during these days in the tents, panels, workshops, plenaries, hotel lobbies, radio shows, videos, and women's press — and to prepare ourselves to decide in the policy-making and strategy-building plenaries if we are going to make Huairou a turning point, or if we are going to keep dancing the dance of the disempowered. We have the voice. This Forum must be ours! Thank you.

The impact of technology

Robin Abrams
Apple Computer, Inc., Hong Kong

My role on this panel is to provide a perspective on the impact of technology on media, culture, and communication, and to discuss the particular challenges and opportunities for women in this area.

Computing technologies, in the form of digital communications via the Internet and multimedia integration, have already had a great role by:

• Creating open and immediate access to information and dialogue;

• Providing a "meeting place" for people of like minds;

• Broadening discussions to allow global, multiple viewpoints;

• Expanding expressive capabilities through a variety of digital media; and

• Increasing impact via pervasive, immediate, interactive communication capabilities.

Digital communications via the rapid expansion of the Internet are breaking down the barriers of traditional "one-way" media such as magazines, newspapers, radio, and television.

A few years ago, the "buzz" about the media was the immediacy of television coverage of world events, and we could watch graphic images of human dramas taking place on the other side of the earth unfold in our homes in real time.

Today the focus is on digital technologies offering multimedia capabilities and ubiquitous communication via the Internet, which are not only immediate and can present vivid images, but are interactive as well.

These technologies can give women immediate access to information and avenues for expression and also allow us to participate in discussion and influence policy in very tangible ways. But only if we use them.

The fundamental first step is opening up access to technology to women and girls, because access to technology equals information and influence.

Men and women tend to view technology differently, and women are often discouraged from participating in the male-dominated "cult" of technology.

We've seen that men tend to view technology as a way to "conquer the universe," while women are more likely to see technology as a means to an end, as a way to "meet people's needs." Women are less likely to be intrigued by the machines themselves, but rather what they can accomplish with them.

In addition, technology businesses, professions, and usage are largely "boys' clubs," and computers themselves have been put forth as mysterious and confounding machines.

For a variety of reasons — whether social, political, or economic — women generally have greater angst about, and less access to, computers and other technology tools than men.

Our challenges are to eradicate gender-based stereotypes, overcome the "fear factor," and provide access to the world of technology for more and more women. If we do so, we can use the power of technology to become full participants in the making and reporting of news, to make sure that our experiences and perspectives are understood and preserved, and to create communities of interest with real influence and power.

The overall goal is to provide women and girls equal access to information, because information is power; and at its best, it is not power that "conforms," but power that "re-forms." And that is one of the primary reasons we are all gathered here.

Gaining access to technology tools and stature within the scientific community is the first step. Once we have opened that door, we will see multiple avenues of expression opened to women and men around the world.

Multimedia technologies such as graphics, video, sound, storage, and distribution mediums such as CD-ROM, optical disks, and Web pages can help us preserve and promote our cultural diversity and illuminate the unique experiences of women throughout the world.

This is particularly important, as our perspectives, histories, accomplishments, and opinions are vastly underrepresented in the global community.

The challenge is to create technology that doesn't force people to give up their individuality, but rather enhances it, because individual expression equals preserving and promoting cultural diversity.

That's another reason we think that Apple Computer was asked to participate in this Conference. Our computers have some unique technologies which enable people to work easily and express themselves in their preferred languages — in fact, in 44 different languages.

Multimedia capabilities, in addition to words and language, enable people to use graphics, animation, video, and sound to create vivid representations of their ideas. At its best, this adds up to an experience which is easy and intuitive, so much so that the computer itself "disappears," and what remains is the expression.

There are many stunning examples at this Conference. A visit to the "Exploring Your Potentials" area, the conference Business and Press centers, as well as the "Once and Future Pavilion," will give you an idea of what I'm talking about.

There are workshops, performances, training seminars, collaborative projects, and other exhibits which clearly show the expressive potential of technology and celebrate the diversity and creativity of women's lives.

For example, you can see easy-to-use video editing technology, send e-mail via the Internet, learn how to create a Web page, see cultural traditions which are being preserved on CD-ROM, create animations, publish newspapers . . . just an extraordinary variety of media for creative expression.

Another extremely important element is the communications and networking capability that technology can bring to women.

Clearly it has played a major role in this Forum. A year ago, Apple equipment was donated to help NGO organizations and the Chinese Organizing Committee to communicate easily, no matter where they were located in the world.

Here in Huairou, an infrastructure for electronic lobbying has been set up so NGOs can give their input to the Platform for Action via e-mail to the caucuses at the UN Conference in Beijing.

In addition, using e-mail, Forum participants are holding global town hall meetings to share information and maintain dialogues with women in other parts of the world who were unable to attend.

Apple technology is especially well suited for this, as studies have shown that our users are almost three times more likely to use their computers to access information via the Internet and to participate in online discussion than users of other systems.

The time has come to embrace technology to make our vision a reality: as women, as policy makers, as artists, as historians, as thinkers, as educators, as students, and as creative individuals. Technology is playing, and will continue to play, an increasingly greater role in improving the status of women, but we must be committed to action.

We must ensure that computing technologies are made available to an ever-increasing number of individuals around the world, and that these computers are made increasingly easy to use. This was the founding philosophy of Apple Computer; it continues to be our passion, and it is one of the primary reasons we are participating in this Conference.

We have to make sure that application software is developed that focuses on the special needs of women, truly helps people challenge the way they think, work and communicate, and aids them in achieving tangible results.

As a group, we must be dedicated to improving the status of women and helping women advance to the highest levels of responsibility in technology professions.

Individually, we must be committed to growth and self-improvement. We can and must share the richness of our diverse perspectives, nurture our communities of interest, and communicate with our hearts as well as our minds.

We must believe we can contribute to solving world problems and making things better in very small and very big ways. Because we can . . . and we do.

Challenging the conventional wisdom of the media

Judy Rebick
CBC Newsworld, Canada

It is an honor to be invited here to speak, but a strange topic for me. It is true that I now work in the media. It is also true that I spent a lot of time in the past 15 years trying to get media coverage for feminist issues and struggles. But like most of you, I have not really viewed the media as a political issue.

I am struck by how few workshops there are on the media in the program, how little comment by plenary speakers there has been on the media. We all recognize the vast importance of the media in creating and reinforcing images of women, imposing and accelerating the imposition of Western culture and values, and imposing what Noam Chomsky has called the manufacturing of consent and what I would go further and call the construction of reality.

The women's movement has focused on four areas in dealing with the media:
- participation of women as journalists;
- sexual stereotyping and violence;
- getting coverage with women's issues; and
- developing alternate feminist media.

On Friday, Media Watch, a Canadian women's group, released a report on women's participation in the news. The report was the result of a global media project in which women in 71 countries monitored newspapers, radio and TV. The results were striking. Forty-three percent of journalists are women. This demonstrates remarkable progress, but has it changed the way the news is framed? The same report shows that only 17 percent of those interviewed by the media are women. Moreover, there is no correlation between the proportion of women journalists and the number of women interviewed. In fact, India has the highest number of women journalists, 71 percent, and the lowest number of women interviewees, 10 percent.

These statistics reinforce my personal experience. Women journalists are trained to see news in the same way as men. Once they are on the job, they feel pressure not to fight for a more feminist perspective on the news. While there are many strong feminist journalists around the world who continue to push coverage of women's issues and women's concerns, they are few and far between, especially in the current right-wing climate in much of the North.

My own personal experience with my TV show indicates how difficult it is to change things. Of course, it is a very high priority for me to get women and minorities to participate in the debates on our show. Almost everyone involved with the show sees representation as important to what we

are doing. But we are a daily show and always under deadline pressures. When we call an organization, most of the time they will give us a male spokesperson. Even if we ask for a woman, they will usually insist that the man is the best one. And, here, I am talking about progressive organizations, since our show usually has someone on the left and someone on the right. Then when we call a woman, she will often say she is not expert enough on that topic to come on the show. Men almost never decline an invitation on that basis. Believe me, you don't have to be that much of an expert to be on TV.

In 1989 FAIR, an American media watch group, found that ABC *Nightline* and the *MacNeil/Lehrer News Hour* had 90 percent white expert guests and almost 90 percent males. Canadian TV does much better than that, but still the proportion of women interviewed on TV is less than one third. In Canada, too, people of color — and in particular women of color — are seriously underrepresented on television. In another study by Media Watch, they found that CBC had the highest proportion of people of color on air, 7 percent, but only 1 percent women of color. CTV, our private network, had only 2.1 percent people of color.

As in politics, getting more women into positions in the media is only part of the problem. Women, people of color, poor people and other marginalized people are marginalized in the media because of the very definition of what news is.

News is power and conflict. Let's use this Conference as an example. There is one sure way to get the media to stop talking about visas, mud, bad rooms and tents collapsing. Start a fight. A big bloody fight on the floor of this plenary will no doubt shift the focus of the news: "Women's Movement Divided"; "Internal Divisions Prevent Coherent Action."

Why don't we see headlines or stories on the remarkable common analysis presented here and on how that analysis is the reverse image of what is presented as fact by most politicians and mainstream press? How come we don't see these headlines or sound bites: "Vibrant Women's Movement Meets in Beijing"; "Women's Movement Alive and Growing"; "Spectacular City of Women Fights for Equality, Justice and Peace"?

The media is always ready at a moment's notice to declare feminism dead. They do it every four or five years in North America. So why isn't it news then, when almost 40,000 women gather together to discuss the way forward in the struggle for women's liberation?

Much has been written about the corporate concentration of the media. In Canada, two corporations control 59 percent of newspaper circulation. One cable company controls access to 39 percent of all households. This corporate control of the media works in subtle and not-so-subtle ways. The corporate view of the world, particularly on economic issues, imposes a virtual consensus in the mainstream press supporting trade liberalization, deregulation, privatization, and massive cutbacks in social programs to reduce the deficit. Alternate voices are either ignored or trivialized. These economic policies are not even presented as the best alternative; they are often presented as the only alternative. One columnist in our national corporate newspaper, the *Globe and Mail*, said that debate over the need for cuts in government spending to reduce the deficit was like debating if the world is flat.

I'll give you another example of what I mean. A few years ago in Toronto, there was a demonstration of 1,500 businessmen who got on the subway at Bay Street, where they work, to demonstrate at Queen's Park, the seat of a newly elected provincial social democratic government. This demonstration was front page news and the lead story on most national TV newscasts. Several months later, about 100,000 workers, women and others demonstrated on Parliament Hill in Ottawa against the economic and social policies of a conservative government. They traveled from all over the country to get there, and it was the biggest demonstration since the 1970s. But it got much less coverage than the 1,500 businessmen. When I challenged this news call, I was told that workers demonstrating against the Tories was not news, but businessmen hardly ever demonstrate, so that was news. Of course, they hardly ever need to demonstrate, which was really the news.

How transparent is this explanation when business think tanks put out report after report calling for yet further cuts in government spending, and they are almost always on the front page. Why are they news?

Many years ago the women's movement recognized that formal equality was not the same as substantive equality. Simply having laws on the books that outlaw discrimination doesn't bring equality. We need positive action.

Similarly, freedom from state censorship does not really guarantee freedom of the press. As long as we have a corporate media that marginalizes dissent and constructs the news to focus on people in power and conflict primarily, and as long as people challenging the status quo have to struggle ten time harder than those defending the status quo to gain access to the media, then we don't have real freedom of the press.

The women's movement has to turn our considerable analytic and organizing power to the task of transforming the media to make it more democratic and accountable — to transforming the media so that women and other marginalized groups matter.

This session is not on strategy, but I want to put out a few ideas: We have to become more media savvy. It is harder for women's groups to get media coverage, but it can be done, and we all have to learn how to do it. This is the easy part. We should encourage feminists in the media to organize. There are very few women's caucuses on newspapers, radio, or TV. If you identify as a feminist, you are seen as biased. But most other women professionals have organized and fought to change their profession, such as women lawyers, and so should journalists.

Women outside the media should support women and men in the media who are trying to make changes. Yayori Matsui tells us that the only reason she could survive in an extremely male-dominated Japanese newspaper, exposing issues like the sex tourism of Japanese men, is because of the support that she got from the women's movement. We have to make our media more accountable. In each country, this will mean different things: from national content regulations to research reports on media bias or exclusion to consumer pressure. We can find creative ways to challenge the mainstream media without challenging freedom of the press. The media is too important to remain unchallenged. I know a lot of people who are so angry with the media, they won't talk to them at all for fear of being stereotyped and misrepresented. Others are afraid to criticize at all for fear of being shut out. What we have to do is find effective ways to challenge the conventional wisdom of mainstream media and to fight for a more democratic, accessible, and accountable media.

Accomplishing by doing

Sally Field
Save the Children Federation, United States

I am from the United States of America, and I have been a professional actor for almost 31 years. I have three sons, who range in age from 25 to 23 to 7. I'm representative of my generation of women. Only one of my sons is here with me: my 23-year-old.

I am here representing a remarkable organization, Save the Children. Save the Children has a commitment to making lasting improvements in the lives of children and their families. Through the International Save the Children Alliance, a group of independent organizations, Save the Children is particularly focusing on the girl child, here at this Conference and in their programs in more than 100 countries.

They asked me to speak about empowering women through the arts, and herein lies the problem. When I was asked by Save the Children to represent them, I thought, well, this is very exciting. I will get to go to China. I will get to speak to women from all over the world. I will talk about the arts and women's involvement in the arts as I know it. Surely I can do that.

And then Save the Children asked me if I would visit Nepal first. I'd already been there. They wanted me to see firsthand the work they do. And I thought, sure, that would be great. Eli, my 23-year-old son, was going to join me — fabulous. And I must say that it's been one of the most moving and profound experiences of my life. I find it very hard to now stand up here and simply talk about the arts. It's difficult for me to put these things together, but somehow I will.

I sat on grass mats on a muddy hillside with a small group of village women and their children. They told me how they had formed a group and that it had made them stronger. They helped each other. They could talk. They were less afraid.

They had planted some trees. The trees will be individually harvested. And they were so proud. They had planted these trees in a very small section of land near their village. The Save the Children people had helped them register this land in the group's name. And the men led us, Eli and me, up the mountain to these trees that the women had planted. And how proud the men were of their women.

I went to a midnight literacy class in a small hut that the women had made. It had a red mud floor, and there were little frogs jumping around all over the place. The babies were in there with the women in the hut, and the hut was surrounded by children who were waiting for their mothers to come out. Many of the women had walked an hour to get there and would walk an hour to get home. I asked them what time their day would begin the next morning. One of them said 3:30.

I asked another why she was doing this, and she said, "I want to read. There is nothing too hard that they could put in front of me that would keep me from this."

So I asked what they wanted to do with this education. They said, "I want to read the letters from my children if they leave the village. I want to read signs. I want to teach my children. I want to be equal."

How do I talk about the arts when I've learned that of the 1.3 million who are not educated, two-thirds of them are girls?

I went to a clinic where babies were being vaccinated and women and girls were being taught about various forms of contraception. Most of the women I talked to had between five and eight children. They had all started in their teens. I learned that most of them thought they really would have opted to have only three babies if they had thought these babies would live.

How can I talk about women in film now? How can I possibly try? I couldn't. And I feel very concerned about these issues.

I could talk about the fact that in the United States, 40 percent of theatrical film roles go to men under the age of 40. Men 40 and over get 25 percent. Women under the age of 40 get 25 percent. Women 40 and over get 8 percent. This is a significant piece of information. I care about this piece of information. I care about the inequality of it; I worry about the implications and how we go about changing the image and impact of women on the screen and therefore all over the world.

I know there are more and more women working as producers and directors these days, but I can barely hear the distinction of their voices. And these successful women must make films that work on every level, including commercially. My theory is that there are unique female sensibilities that are being shaken, camouflaged, and simply lost in an environment dominated by male visions and fantasies. But there is so little tradition for women to follow in film.

When Jane Austen wrote, she sat in the family parlor and felt compelled to hide her work when someone came into the room.

But will the little girls in the village in Nepal ever even have the chance to read literature? What does it matter? How can it possibly apply?

There's a recent survey indicating that statistically there are 100 million females missing.

What? Where are they?

Females are not profitable to a family. Get rid of them. Don't spend money or time on their education or their health.

But where women remain illiterate, democratic institutions are more fragile, and the environment is less well managed. It's being proven that investing in girls' education goes hand in hand with economic opportunity. And where women are em-

powered, they not only invest in their own lives but in the lives of their families and communities.

But I have to talk about the arts. That's what I know about. That's where I have any expertise at all. It seems like such a great luxury to me to be able to talk about the arts.

I learned of some areas where women are thought of as dirty while giving birth, and they're forced to give birth in the barn with the livestock. They're young and left alone. They have no idea what's happening to their bodies. Is it a wonder that so many die in childbirth, not to mention their babies?

I do know this: Complaining will not really accomplish anything. It may be a first step. But it does not accomplish anything. It's the doing that accomplishes things. In Nepal I met women who are producing a safe home-birthing kit that contains a string, a razor blade, and a plastic sheet. Many times, the death of an infant is caused because the tradition is to cut the umbilical cord on a coin or a betel nut, so there's also a sterile coin inside the kit, a plastic coin. Over 100,000 of these have been sold.

Change happens by doing. That's what I saw in Nepal. Little by little, person by person, village by village.

The mother in me will never forget the sight of my 23-year-old son sitting with a group of young women from the Untouchable caste who had gone as far as they could with their education. They asked him, "What now?" There was no more for them.

He sat in the hot sun and talked with them for two hours. He told them that they may never see the change they were causing but that they were causing change and that their children would feel it. He told them he admired them. And if you could have seen their faces when this young man told these young women that *he* admired *them!*

Has there ever been a society that properly appreciated and applauded women for all their achievements and their complexities? Is there anywhere today where they adequately utilize their unique capabilities? Would it make any difference if film were able to reveal them more thoroughly: multilayered, complex women in all the stages of their lives? And not just the heroes but ordinary people, the kind of people others can identify with — women young and old, strong and weak.

When society accepts a larger and more diverse vision of women, it will trickle down and eventually affect every little girl in every little village in every single corner of the world.

But as I've learned in Nepal, it doesn't happen by yelling. It happens by doing, it happens by hard work. It happens by walking a mile to a literacy class. It happens through excellence. It changes little by little, film by film, fight by fight, class by class, conference by conference, woman by woman. It changes.

PART II

STRATEGIES AND MECHANISMS

VIII • Governance, Citizenship, and Political Participation — *Strategies*

Opening remarks

Rounaq Jahan, Moderator
Columbia University, United States

The main purpose of the strategy plenaries is to assess how we have worked in the past two decades and draw some lessons for the future. Before I introduce the key questions and the plenary speakers, perhaps I should introduce myself.

I am a citizen of Bangladesh, but like many of you, I have lived and worked in different countries. In the 1970s, when I first got involved in the international women's movement, I used to teach political science at Dhaka University, and I founded the first women's research and study group in my country. In the 1980s, I was misguided enough to think that I would be able to reform the system by working from within, so I joined the United Nations. I directed first a regional and then a global women's program of the United Nations.

I must admit I cannot claim much success in changing the agencies for which I worked. And since I did not want to change myself, I am again back to academia, teaching at Columbia University in New York and enjoying the freedom and autonomy of being a nongovernment person. I considered it a great privilege to participate in all three previous World Women's Conferences — Mexico in 1975, Copenhagen in 1980, Nairobi in 1985 — and now the Fourth World Conference in Beijing.

From Mexico to Beijing, it has been a long road of political struggle. We have achieved significant progress in a number of areas. But we all recognize that in the last 20 years, we have made little or no progress in one arena: governance. Though we are more than half of the world's citizens and nearly 40 percent of the paid labor force, globally only 6 percent of cabinet ministers, 10 percent of parliamentarians, and 14 percent of ad-

ministrators and managers are women. Even more alarming, in the last seven years there has been a 25 percent decline in the number of women parliamentarians, due largely to the collapse of the socialist systems of the Eastern bloc countries.

We need to ask ourselves why our record of progress in gaining decision-making positions has been so dismal. Did we not prioritize it enough in our struggle? Or did we adopt wrong strategies?

In the last several days and indeed in many other forums in the last 20 years, we have repeatedly said that our struggle is not simply to increase our numbers in decision-making positions, that our struggle is for moving our agenda forward and for changing politics and governance as we know them today. But what strategies have we followed to bring about this transformation? Have we worked out consistent strategies to achieve our triple goals of increasing numbers, transforming politics and moving our agenda forward? Have we put too much emphasis on increasing our numbers through affirmative action strategies and not enough in challenging the rules of the game — the influence of money, violence, intrigue, and manipulation that dominate our political life and are the real obstacles to women's gaining entry into leadership positions? And now that the affirmative action strategies are themselves being questioned by the rising conservative forces in the dominant paradigm, that is, in the United States, what strategies have we thought about to counter this emerging threat?

In the last few days we have also talked about how the so-called globalization of the economy and technology have in fact meant domination by a few who control capital, technology, and information — how despite all the rhetoric about democratization and human rights, global governance in the new unipolar world is, in fact, neither transparent nor accountable. What strategies could we pursue to make those invisible global governors accountable to the ordinary women and men of the world? In the last few days, we have also talked about our strength, our power, our contributions, our leadership, and our solutions to this planet's problems. We are fortunate that we have amongst us five speakers who represent the kind of power and courage we have talked about. They are all political activists who have long been involved in the struggle for transforming governments.

Women in the political arena: A challenge to social and cultural values

Ung Yok Khoan
Amara Network, Cambodia

It is a great honor for me to share with you Cambodian women's experience and our strategies toward governance with equal participation and recognition of women and men.

After two decades of war and genocide, Cambodia found a new beginning with the signing of peace accords among the parties in conflict, which led to a general election held in May 1993. Hungry for peace, Cambodian women and men went to the polls despite an atmosphere of political violence and fear. Of the 95 percent of the voters who turned out, 55 percent were women. Cambodia now has a legitimate government, a National Assembly and a Constitution. However, women in Cambodia have gained very little, as their representation at decision-making levels is very limited. Of the 120 MPs, only seven are women, and there is no woman minister or vice-minister.

As we are preparing for the elections in 1998, Cambodian women's NGOs see the need to develop strategies to ensure the following:
• that there be an election in 1998;
• that there be no political intimidation and threat;

• that women are free to make their own choices;
• that there be at least 30 percent women candidates; and
• that women vote for women candidates.

In the past two years, educated women from the city have taken up the challenge of founding and leading their own organizations and associations. We have formed a coalition of Cambodian NGOs advocating for democracy and respect for human rights, women's rights, children's rights, and the rights of indigenous peoples. In the process of preparing for the NGO Forum on Women and the Fourth World Conference on Women, the coalition has broadened its vision to emphasize the development of a national women's movement.

The strategies for our women's movement are:
• to identify and support women leaders in each community;
• to train women in leadership;
• to put women in charge of development programs; and
• to provide opportunities for women to network among themselves and with other movements in the Asia-Pacific region.

The women's network must play a very important role in determining the platform for action in the next election. Women can determine the agenda for the electoral campaign; it should not be set by the political parties.

The women's coalition sees the need to work closely with our present women MPs to support them and to provide them with political training. To increase the numbers in the future, we are identifying and encouraging women to be candidates in the next election. For the electorate, we will develop a strong mass education campaign to raise women's awareness about issues concerning women, children, environment and democracy.

The government is new and fragile. There is the continued threat of a return to violence and armed conflict. The steps toward governance and people's participation are constantly challenged by new legislation which takes away the freedom of the people.

Cambodian women have no other choice but to challenge cultural and social values, and they are doing so by preparing to enter the political arena. The year 1998 is not far away. The World Conference on Women and NGO Forum on Women could not have come at a better time for Cambodian women. Our NGO delegation has 85 women, 17 of whom are grassroots leaders. We hope to learn much from our sisters and friends from all regions. We feel empowered by being here.

Using power to transform

Jacqueline Pitanguy
Citizenship, Studies, Information, and Action
(CEPIA), Brazil

At this moment, when we are here discussing strategies, building alliances, and dealing with the tensions that are part of any process of empowerment, there come to my mind the words of a poet who said, *Caminante no hay camino, se hace camino al caminar* ("Walker, there's not a path; you build the road while you walk"). Building strategies for governance means building paths, opening avenues, and constructing bridges — with different degrees of difficulty according to national and international considerations; according to the economic, social, and political characteristics of each of our countries; and according to our strength and ability to build alliances and to define the frontiers of non-negotiable issues.

Access to governance means access to power, and power in itself is an institution, with its rhythms and rituals, its demands and impositions. Three questions may be posed: how to have access to power, how to use power, and, most important, for what purpose?

The major purpose of all of us gathered here is to influence both our national governments and international forces. The major question we must ask is how to build strategies to accede to power and how to use power, to share power, to wield power not as an instrument of dominance and exclusion — as has been done so far — but as an instrument of liberation and equality. This is a major challenge for women, because throughout this century and in different civilizations, power has been used basically as an instrument of nations dominating nations and of creating hierarchies within nations.

Exclusions based on social class, gender, ethnicity, race, sexual orientation, and age have characterized the social structures of our countries. These exclusions have been aggravated by the increasing impoverishment of Southern nations due to structural arrangements imposed by market-oriented and profit-oriented economies and by the enormous social inequalities which characterize most of the Southern countries, certainly Brazil.

Given the framework of rapid modernization and globalization that characterizes the present moment, let us not forget that poverty creates islands of isolation inside these global processes, that poverty is growing at an extraordinary pace, and that we women are the poorest among the poor in every nation. Let us also not forget the significant disparities among ourselves, due to criteria such as race, ethnicity, poverty, and nationality, and that some of us are more excluded than others, more powerless than others. Let us thus start building strategies for governance, recognizing our diversity, recognizing the inequalities among ourselves, and placing ourselves as political actors who, building a road toward equality, still to some degree carry inside ourselves some characteristics of our oppressor. As Frantz Fanon said, referring to the struggle against colonialism, "We have to take away from inside ourselves what remains of the colonizer." Let us not only accede to power, but most of all, let us share it and change it, reminding ourselves that the struggle against oppression and authoritarianism is never ending.

Building strategies for governance varies from country to country, from moment to moment, from region to region. As a Brazilian, I have greatest experience with the processes of Brazil and Latin America. Let me try to answer within this context the questions I formulated at the beginning: how to accede to and to share power and how to use power to transform.

I believe that one has access to power in many different ways, since the definition of power is dynamic and flexible. Certainly the classical way to accede to power is to hold positions in the institutional channels of power, such as the executive, legislative, and judiciary systems of a society, or analogous positions in societies with other kinds of systems. Yet the statistics show very clearly that, with the recent exception of some Scandinavian countries, we have been historically excluded from such positions. This situation is beginning to change, yet the exclusion reflects only the tip of the iceberg.

What I want to call attention to is that in this process of acceding to and transforming power, we women have been trying to deal with the base, not the tip, of the iceberg. We are building a road to the top by working with the roots, which lie in exclusion. We have been bringing to the public arena such issues as lack of access to formal education, political empowerment, equal wages in the labor market, equal laws within the family, freedom from domestic violence and religious fundamentalism, access to health, reproductive and sexual rights, and the need for a public image of women as full human beings, entitled to rights and capable of taking responsibilities. In this sense, we have been involved in a much slower but deeper process, that of reshaping power.

Thus we are building strategies, not of conquest and dominance, but of change and transformation. We want to use power to help certain issues and values — such as education, peace, social justice, equality, and health — become dominant topics on the political agenda. We accede to power not only by encouraging women to take leadership in existing instruments of power, but also, and mainly, trying to transform those instruments. Yes, we want to make women's voices heard, but most of all we want to break the ghetto and bring the gender perspective to all social, political, and economic issues, to all voices.

In Latin America and in Brazil, feminism emerged as a political factor during the second half of the 1970s, at a time when most of our countries were experiencing military/political dictatorships, state violence, suppression of civil rights, and fear.

But, as is often the case, this was also a time of resistance, of building solidarity among the different sectors of civil society involved in the struggle for democracy. The social movements that became new political actors in the public arena changed the political agenda. The women's movement was part of the struggle against dictatorship, but at the same time, this movement had new visions of a genuinely democratic society. Thus, women denounced state violence but also brought domestic violence to the political agenda, enlarging the concept of peace and denouncing the unseen war that takes place in violent homes. Women denounced social inequalities and the injustice of the social class structure but also denounced other inequalities resulting from gender, race, and sexual orientation. They enlarged the concept of rights, placing social rights in the center and also bringing up health, reproductive, and sexual rights as key elements of women's citizenship rights.

What I want to point out is that besides direct access to institutional power, changing the political agenda has been and still is one of the most powerful strategies used by women to influence the political sphere. I would say that from the 1970s to the 1980s in Brazil, the main strategy of the women's movement was to give visibility to issues that had been considered nonexistent, unimportant, or even ridiculous by the establishment — and forcing these issues onto political platforms and into executive organs.

Since the 1980s we have gone through a time of forging public policies. With the democratization process, we have tried to create spaces inside the state apparatus, at the municipal, state, and federal levels — such as councils of women's rights and special police stations to attend to women victims of domestic violence. We have tried to influence health programs and to influence the media. As president of the National Council of Women's Rights, a federal governmental organ, I worked for four years on the path of enlarging women's rights by using the possibilities of government and trying to work through its limits.

Those of us who worked from inside government were quite successful, considering the historical limits of this approach. We knew that ours was a political time; that our clock ran according to the larger political conjunctions and our ability to use the instruments of power; and, most of all, that we had to expand the alliances and bridges between state and civil society and, in our case, between those of us in the women's movement who were outside these institutions and those of us who were inside. I won't go into the details of our political action. I just want to say that one of our major strategies was to influence our new constitution and that we were very successful in doing so — and that in the dynamics of power, following the dismantling of the National Council due to a change in government, we remained visible in civil society through networks and state councils.

For what purpose should we use power? That was my third question. I believe that we must use it to change and transform — to transform relations in society, to transform the idea of democracy. But there is so much to be done in this permanent building and rebuilding that sometimes we have to run and run just to remain in the same place. Here, in this Conference, we are running to avoid a backlash in relation to the gains made in Rio, Vienna, and Cairo. But we are also running to make ourselves visible and to have the power of this NGO Forum recognized.

There are immense difficulties. Huairou is far away and isolated, and we have come here after long pilgrimages from Mexico to Copenhagen to Nairobi; from Rio to Vienna to Cairo. Some of us managed to arrive here. Others are with us because the echoes of their powerful voices in those other meetings can be heard here. We will not let our voices, our political importance, or our visibility disappear in the tension of diplomatic questions of foreign policy between countries. Writing a Platform for Action must be a joint strategy of NGOs and governments. We are far away from Beijing, but Huairou exists and there are women gathered here. A powerful discourse is being built here. There is no way an agenda for women can be put together with only governmental decisions made in a governmental conference.

Strategies for increasing women's political participation

Miria R.K. Matembe
Constituent Assembly, Uganda

INTRODUCTION

Many conferences — national, regional, and international — have been held. Many instruments — agreements, charters, conventions, declarations, and resolutions — have been made. And yet, apart from the Nordic experience, everywhere women's participation in politics remains limited.

The African experience is complex. In a few countries where democratic processes have been taking place, some attempts have been made to include women in the decision-making machinery. This change in political participation has, however, been limited to increasing the number of women entering the system. It has not yet affected the political agenda or begun to reflect the broad concerns of women. The dominant agenda is still favorable to men.

But Africa is also a place of internal conflict and civil strife, conditions that make it difficult for women to participate in politics. Under such circumstances, women's issues are relegated to the back of the political agenda. Instead, human survival becomes the primary goal. Because of the violence that characterizes African politics, women have also tended to shy away because politics has been looked at as a dirty game.

OBSTACLES LIMITING WOMEN'S POLITICAL PARTICIPATION

There are several obstacles limiting women's participation in politics. These include:
• oppressive and exploitative structures and systems
• poverty among women
• high levels of illiteracy and ignorance
• discriminatory and inadequate laws
• unjust and unfair cultural practices
• women's heavy workload

STRATEGIES TO INCREASE POLITICAL PARTICIPATION OF WOMEN

A number of strategies have been adopted worldwide and also in Uganda to increase women's participation in politics.

National government machineries

In many countries national machineries have been established for the advancement of women. In Uganda a Ministry for Gender and Community Development has been created; its responsibility is to mainstream women's concerns in national planning and development.

In addition to the Ministry, women and youth councils have been established, right from the grassroots to the national level, to organize and mobilize women and youth to participate effectively in the development of the country.

The weakness with such national machineries is that they are marginalized and usually poorly financed and staffed. To be effective, such machineries should concern themselves with coordinating and mainstreaming women's concerns rather than handling implementation of programs and activities.

Affirmative action

This strategy has also been implemented in several countries. Despite some criticism, in Uganda it has made a significant contribution in two areas, education and politics.

• *Education*

For the past five to seven years, to increase the number of women entering university, women entrants to the national university were awarded an extra 1.5 points. In the process, a few other women who otherwise would not have entered university were admitted. This has obviously increased the number of women ready to enter public life and high-level decision-making processes.

The extra points awarded to women entering university, however, do not address the larger issues of women's education in general or the restructuring of the educational system. There is a need to restructure the system in order to empower women with the capacity, knowledge, and skills necessary to challenge oppressive laws and customs. The old adage "To educate a woman is to educate a nation" is a significant challenge for the educational system in Uganda today and for women's education in particular.

• *Politics*

Uganda has a political system which promotes the people's participation in their own governance through resistance councils and committees, with special emphasis placed on women's participation through a mandatory portfolio of the Secretary for Women's Affairs and the district woman representative in parliament. This mandatory position has ensured the participation of women at all levels of decision-making, from grassroots to national. It has also increased the number of women parliamentarians from one in 1985 to 46 in 1995.

Women's participation in the Constituent Assembly was boosted by the presence of 39 specially elected district women delegates in addition to the nine directly elected women delegates and four others representing special interests. This result has yielded tremendous success for women as far as constitutional reform is concerned.

The representation of women in decision-making positions has also been enhanced by the Government's deliberate policy of appointing women to top political, administrative, and judicial positions in parastatal and other constitutional bodies.

Even so, the process of appointing women to high positions remains inadequate. These appointments are not carried out after extensive consultations. Therefore the women who are appointed could be the "good girls," not the troublemakers.

The system of women's representation, in my view, should bring into public life women who are familiar with women's issues and are concerned and able to participate effectively and influence the agenda and decisions of fora wherever they are. My suggestion, therefore, is that it would be useful for women to have a say in the appointment of other women to political and public positions.

Is affirmative action fair?

Women who criticize affirmative action are mainly the very educated women, who argue that it means accepting inferior positions as well as women's intellectual weaknesses. Some women in extremely privileged positions argue that if they have "made it" without affirmative action, why not others? Many of these women have failed to perceive and internalize the woman question in its proper perspective and have failed to appreciate the historical injustices and imbalances perpetuated against women.

My own concern with the strategy of affirmative action is that it is usually based on the will of a favorable political environment and a leadership committed to the advancement of women, rather than being a result of internal processes and struggles by women. Uganda is a good example.

Constitutional and legal reform

This is a necessary strategy to eliminate discriminatory laws and to enact laws aimed at removing customary and cultural practices which promote injustices against women. In Uganda the current constitutional law-reform exercise has yielded good results for women's emancipation. The new constitution of Uganda has entrenched the principle of equality between women and men; it has entrenched affirmative action and contains comprehensive provisions for guaranteeing, promoting, and protecting women's rights. It provides for an equal opportunities commission. Whether these provisions become organic will depend on the ability of the next parliament to enact relevant statutes so that law can be brought into conformity with the new constitution.

Alliances between women and other disadvantaged groups

Women's concerns can be better advanced if they are linked with the interests of other disadvantaged groups in society. This calls for alliances between women and those groups so they can struggle on a common platform. These groups include marginalized youth, people with disabilities, workers, children, the elderly, and so on. Second, and much more important, women need to form and belong to their own groups and organizations, which should be responsible for confidence-building, skills development, and promoting effective participation and advocacy by women.

The women's caucus in the Constituent Assembly in Uganda developed a strategy of forming alliances with youth, workers, and people with disabilities to enshrine achievements in the constitution. Within the caucus we were able to debate and sharpen our arguments with not only factual but also logical presentations and to convince the others that our cause was also a national cause that needed to be addressed constitutionally.

Gender sensitization and awareness creation

This continues to be an important strategy that must be strengthened and intensified.

THE FUTURE OF WOMEN'S EMPOWERMENT

The empowerment of women and their future political participation are linked to the transformation of the existing political structures and systems to make them responsive to women's agenda. Entrance by women into the existing structures and systems cannot yield beneficial results so long as the present agenda remains untouched. This will require that we transform the systems and structures by empowering women's organizations, groups, and individuals to pursue issues of governance, citizenship, and political participation. We need to understand the social and political structures that form obstacles to women's emancipation. This calls for a qualitative leadership with the capacity to transform quantitative potential into a viable political force. Only then can we talk of empowerment and the emancipation of women in a meaningful way.

THE CHALLENGE TO WOMEN

With what qualities are women entering the political arena and public life in a world where politics have been characterized by ills such as corruption, nepotism, dishonesty, and sectarianism? Are women coming in to endorse and fit into the system, or are we coming in with human qualities such as kindness, love, sympathy, peace, and reconciliation, which have been lacking all this time, especially in Africa? Only when politics are played differently shall we show that society has been missing women's participation all along. Women should come into politics and public office to clean them up, to bring light into those otherwise dark fora. Women's entry into politics and public life should bring a ray of hope to the people. Otherwise, our entry will have been in vain.

My experience of an election

Raufa Hassan
NGO Network of Women, Yemen

When I started to work as a broadcaster in Yemen, I brought shame on my family's name. In this Muslim and Arab country, broadcast was shameful, and thus I was damaging my family's name through my occupation. This is how I came to choose my own name. I thought, if their name will be shamed, let me create a new one. And so, confusingly enough, now I have a pseudonym which is better known than my own family name. I consider choosing a pseudonym to be one of my earliest strategies.

I am going to talk about my experience in an election — my failure to be elected but my success at being a candidate. That is another thing which is very important. I am a Yemeni. Yemen is a very good example of Islamic and Arabic countries nowadays, in this new system of international order. Yemen was divided into two countries. One of them was supposed to be pro-socialist; the other one was supposed to be pro-capitalist. Both of them were unified in 1990. When they unified, they made it a democracy. Democracy was a first; it was a must. For that reason, women's role also changed.

Let me tell you a little bit about what it was like in both countries after unification. In one of them women enjoyed a position under the law that was more progressive. Southern Yemen, which was called the Democratic Republic of Yemen, had a family law which was very advanced and progres-

sive in the Arab world, as did Tunisia, which also had a progressive law. The northern part, where I came from, had the worst personal law for women ever created. When both of them unified, it was expected that the position of women in the North would become better. The men of our northern country and the men of our southern country, all of them decided they could take some of the best laws from both countries — but not the personal law. So they took the law of the North, which was not the progressive one. We, the women of the North, thanked God and said, "Better than nothing. Now we have a case to fight for. We will have women around the world lobby with us for that old family law." In fact, women in Yemen didn't benefit much, because they didn't know how beautiful the old family law was. They didn't take advantage of what they had.

At the same time, they allowed us to be in the election. Our constitution also guaranteed equal rights to men and women. In 1988, when the election came up in the northern part of Yemen, we were denied the right to be a candidate. In 1993, after unification, being a candidate in itself was an achievement.

Here is where I found myself.

I wanted to run for election for four reasons. The first reason was that I wanted to be a candidate, which in itself was a step. The second was that I wanted also to provide an example to my colleagues, who were afraid to go into the election, and also to create some sort of tradition of a democracy where women participate. I actually ran in the most conservative constituency in the whole country. The people there do not even accept women working outside of the house. I was representing them. They were not just conservative, but also the three main political parties were using religion to get elected.

I was among 21 candidates, and I was independent. This is one of the things I learned a woman should not do. If you want to go into an election, you had better have a political party to support you, or you will be very much alone. The fight used everything, including religion. I thought, Why not, let's use it. If they are using it, let's use it too.

In 1988 when they prevented us from being candidates, they used the Islamic code, which said that women could not run for election. In 1993 when I ran, I went to the *mufti* of the Republic and asked him a nice question. I said, "I am trying to run, and I have a team. Every time my team tries to work, men and women around us tell us that this is not Islamic and that I have no right to run. What is your opinion, religiously speaking?" He said, "Nothing in the Quran or in the Prophet's sayings prevents women from running in the election or from winning — especially if they are people like Raufa, whom I myself am going to vote for."

I have tried to learn from this. I didn't win; I came in sixth place after the five political parties. The three biggest ones used religion against me. We were on the same level from this point of view. We were not on the same level in terms of funding, because the one who won spent 6 million in Yemeni money, while I spent 100,000. You see the difference.

From that I learned that without establishing a fund for women in elections, there is no way for us to win. Second, I learned that women themselves were used against me. In fact, 700,000 women in Yemen went to vote for the *muftis* rather than for women. They said, "We should not encourage women to be mixed up in this. They are not set up for that kind of dirty politics. We don't want to put them there. You don't need to make it difficult for other colleagues, so better to choose men." A few of them — 200,000 — chose me, some of them because of relatives, some because they found me nice, a few because they really found they had a cause.

Of 52 women who ran in 1993, only two won. Both of them were supported by political parties. This is not only the case in Yemen; it is the same throughout the Arab world. In every parliament you will have only the decoration of democracy. Wonderful women — they sit in the seat well. They never talk, but they are there for the decoration. This is what we should really change.

When I ran in the election, I found nothing written about the experience of women in politics in the Arab world to help me to run my campaign. Whoever is here — academics, militants, whoever is in politics — write down your experiences and help others read about them. That is one of the important things.

I think three things must be done: fund women in elections, help them with materials, and raise the awareness of other women that when they are voting for women, they are voting for themselves. When they are voting for men, they are continually losing.

Strategies toward equal political participation

Anita Amlen
NGO Forum Office, Sweden

I would like to talk about strategies. Equal opportunity in Sweden means:

1. An equal distribution of power and influence between men and women;

2. The same possibility for women and men to achieve economic independence;

3. Care for children and home;

4. Equal access for girls and boys, women and men, to education, including the same opportunities to develop personal ambitions, interests, and talents; and

5. Freedom from gender-specific violence.

Equality refers to the belief that all individuals and groups in society are of equal value, regardless of sex, race, religion, ethnic origin, or social class.

One of the cornerstones of equality is equal opportunity. The quantitative aspect of this implies an equal distribution of women and men in all areas of society. The definition of quantity is that neither sex should have less than 40 percent representation.

Today women's political organizations in Sweden think it should be fifty-fifty. Since women are half the population, we should also have half the power. Equality is an important part of democracy.

Women's economic independence has been one

of the overall political goals for Swedish women's political organizations.

In Sweden, our former minister of equality passed a bill stating that one month of parental leave is compulsory for men. That month cannot be transferred or used by the mother. This is to support the men when they are planning parental leave. Too many men who didn't take the chance to be with their children when they were small regret it later on in life. This reform is to support men's participation in family life and in the household.

The qualitative aspect of equality implies that the knowledge, experience, and values of both women and men are given equal weight. I don't understand how any society can afford not to ask for, or even scream for, women's experience, which is different from men's.

In the samples to which I have referred, most of the issues are about attitudes. You cannot change people's attitudes by passing a bill in Parliament. To change attitudes is long-term work. But you can pass a bill on concrete issues to start pushing the process of changing attitudes.

In Sweden, we had elections last year in September. We now have a Social Democratic government, and 50 percent of the ministers are women. The spokesperson of the parliament is a woman. The vice-prime minister also holds the portfolio for equality issues. She is a young person who stresses that she is a woman, a wife, and a mother. She is the head of the delegation for Beijing and will come to the NGO Forum on Women.

In Parliament today, there is 41 percent women's representation. In county councils, 48 percent are women. On local councils, 41 percent are women.

A few years back, the political women's organizations had a campaign before an election to promote and nominate women to different offices. We cooperated under an overall theme: each second one should be a woman. That definitely didn't mean that women should be the second name on the list.

We also investigated what the representation actually looked like within our own political parties. And the result wasn't too good. Even if we know

by feeling, it's very important to visualize reality with figures in black and white. If the representation is there, show it in numbers. As a result of several investigations with the same result, Parliament adopted a three-year program to increase female representation in decision-making bodies in public administration. The program was approved by Parliament. The strategy employed, which is still in force, can be summarized in three steps:

1. Make the shortage of women visible by presenting annual statistics to Parliament that can be followed up every year;

2. Establish concrete time-specific targets for increasing the proportion of women; and

3. Pursue measures that help to achieve these goals.

The government decided that statistics on women and men in public administration and public committees of inquiry should be presented to Parliament each year. It then set up the following specific targets:

• By 1992, women's representation on boards and committees should increase to 30 percent.

• By 1995, it should increase to 40 percent.

The final goal is for the government-authorities boards, as well as the official committees of inquiry, to have equal representation. According to the government, this should be possible by 1998.

What we have learned is that on the lists shown to the voters, there are more women. But in all important positions on different boards, committees, and so on, where the lists are not shown to the public, there is a big difference in women's representation. That is why there should always be a woman and a man nominated when important positions are to be seated.

Coming from Sweden, I am not satisfied with the situation. Today women are 29 percent of under-secretaries of state and other top politicians. Women hold 17 percent of the top administrative positions.

I can't stress enough the importance of having women in top positions in politics, administration, and any kind of leadership. It is important because we need these women as role models.

To achieve shared power and shared responsibility toward the year 2000 we must:

1. Stop sex-segregated educational choices;

2. Stop sex-segregated occupational and professional choices;

3. Improve women's terms and influence at work;

4. Have equal pay for work of equal value;

5. Guarantee freedom from sex-related violence; and

6. Increase the percentage of women holding management and other positions of leadership.

These are just a few of the issues we have to continue to work on. We also have to continue to discuss the issue of equality, to keep the debate alive; otherwise we will easily have a backlash. We also have to continue to discuss the issue of equality as an issue for both women and men.

IX • Challenges Posed by the Globalization of the Economy — *Strategies*

Opening remarks

Pamela Sparr, Moderator
Women's Division, United Methodist Church
General Board of Global Ministries, United States

Welcome to the second plenary on the globalization of the economy. Yesterday we analyzed trends and emerging issues. Today we focus on innovative organizing strategies. Effective organizing is the key to changing the balance of power in our communities, our nations, and the world, and thus, to bring about the transformations we seek.

I work as an economist in the Women's Division of the United Methodist Church. I help educate and mobilize more than one million women in the church on issues of economic and environmental justice. We work collaboratively with women's organizations outside the church in the United States and around the world. I am also a member of the Alternative Women-in-Development Group which tries to make educational and organizing links between women of the South and North, working on poverty and livelihood issues. It is a great honor and pleasure to serve as the moderator of this panel.

The terms "globalization" and "economic restructuring" are widely used here at the Forum, yet I am not sure we are all working with the same understanding about what these terms mean. To set the context for our speakers, I would like to briefly explain how I use these terms, so that we can begin our discussion at a common starting point.

Globalization

This is a process by which systems and institutions expand their operation around the world. Economic systems, governance, media, culture and communications are rapidly moving toward international integration and coordination. We see

McDonald's arches above Tiananmen Square, we watch CNN on our hotel TVs here, we ride in Mitsubishi buses. While this process began hundreds of years ago, the organizing challenge for us is the scope and pace of the process and its implications for our daily lives at home, at work, and in our communities.

The globalization process essentially is being driven by the actions of transnational corporations (TNCs), which increasingly find national boundaries and allegiances irrelevant and unhelpful. What does this mean for organizing strategies?

1. Now there is a need to organize across borders (as workers, farmers, consumers, communities), because companies can play one community or nation against another in a global chess game of foreign investments, production, and trade.

2. This signals for a need to develop democratic international institutions to set global rules of the game and enforce them.

3. We need to learn the positive potential of global media and communications systems (computers) to more easily learn from one another, share strategies, plan jointly, organize, and mobilize effectively.

Economic restructuring

This term can apply to both companies and countries. When companies do it, they are changing how they operate. For example, "downsizing" is to fire or lay off people in order to have a smaller workforce or to decentralize operations. The major change we will hear about today is the dramatic move to change the conditions so that companies are less responsible for the well-being of workers. We see this, for example, in the rise of home-based production, temporary workers, and contract workers.

When a government engages in economic restructuring, it attempts to alter dramatically what the national economy looks like. It changes the basic "rules of the game," such as the tax code and regulations on business. It also tries to change who the major actors are, for example, by privatizing public companies, or opening the country up to foreign investors, or by establishing a stock market. National economic restructuring comes in many forms and is known by many names: structural adjustment programs, economic reform, "Thatcherism," "Reaganomics," etc. However, the direction is all the same: away from state intervention and toward more free-market capitalist economies.

What does this mean for organizing? We see growing inequality among nations and within individual nations. We see increasing poverty of women. We feel less able to control our own lives. It is more difficult to organize our communities at work in rural areas, etc. We see a decrease or abandonment of public services. We see people pitted against one another: "foreigners," immigrants, racial-ethnic minorities are made the scapegoats for our economic problems, with a resulting increase in tensions, violence, and animosity.

Homework in the global economy

Annie Delaney
Textile, Clothing and Footwear Union, Australia

Today I would like to address the issues of garment workers and, in particular, homeworkers in today's global economy. My contribution is to outline strategies we have used in Australia to assist home-based workers in the informal sector of the garment and textile industry.

In 1908, women garment workers in New York went on strike for 13 weeks. They demanded an end to sweatshop conditions, the right to vote, to organize unions, equal pay, and child care for working mothers. Their strike led to a demonstration on March 8, 1909 — the first internationally recognized women's day — a celebration to commemorate the struggles of working women.

In the last decade we have witnessed the creation and return to sweatshop conditions worse than those of the early 1900s. Once again we demand an end to sweatshop conditions. Globalization is the buzzword of the 1990s. While it is a process that has been occurring for over 20 years, it has taken on new and more serious dimensions in the last decade. Globalization is characterized by the expansion of international trade, investment, production and financial flow, and the growing significance of regional trading blocs and trade agreements such as APEC, NAFTA, and GATT. Other features include the increased influential roles for international financial institutions such as the IMF, the World Bank, and transnational corporations (TNCs).

The price of globalization

Production conditions in the textile, clothing, and footwear (TCF) sectors typify the effects of globalization for manufacturing workers: wages have fallen, working conditions have deteriorated, job security has declined, child labor is on the increase, and health and safety standards are dropping.

Transnational and national corporations have been implementing strategies designed to strengthen profits through attacking trade unions, deregulating wages and conditions, and introducing labor-reducing technology. Globalization and all it means has impacted on production bases in the industrialized and newly industrialized countries in similar ways. Corporations are continually in search of new production bases to produce as cheaply as possible. Worldwide, the garment industry remains labor intensive and reliant on mainly women workers for its production. In most countries women make up from 70 percent to 90 percent of the textile and garment workforce.

One of the most significant factors that has impacted on the TCF industries and others is the decentralization of the production process and subcontracting. Not so long ago, most retailers and label owners had their own factories. Over the last decade, companies have either relocated to an offshore venture based in an economic processing zone (EPZ) and/or contracted their production to a web of subcontractors. These subcontractors may be local or based in another country. What is important is that they deliver the goods at a certain time for a certain price.

A race to the bottom

At the same time, more countries have become producers of textile, clothing and footwear, competing for a share of a world market that has not expanded. Today, more than 130 countries are involved in the production of garments, mainly for export to the markets of only 30-odd countries. As competition between countries increases, the overall economic benefits are reduced. The effect is an overall decline in benefits and workers' conditions.

This process becomes a race to the bottom. Fierce competition between countries has emerged to keep existing foreign investment from relocating. The effect is a greater cost to the host country and exploitation of the workers.

In underdeveloped countries, the establishment of EPZs has provided a model for attracting foreign investors. These investments produce export earnings and create jobs. The rate of foreign investment is high, and the clothing and electronics industries are the main suppliers of jobs in these zones. International investors are lured by incentives of free rent, aid for equipment and subsidized infrastructure. Conditions for workers in the EPZs are harsh, child labor is common, unions are banned, and any attempt by workers to organize or improve conditions is met with immediate sacking and often physical violence. Over the last five years in many countries, the employment rate in these zones has doubled. The workforce is mainly composed of women aged 18-25.

In most industrialized countries where wages are relatively higher, many manufacturers have as a consequence chosen between relocation to a less-developed country or outsourcing to the informal sector, where labor is underpaid and usually performed by women in private homes. The effect is that the industry can operate a dual workforce. One is a core group that is factory-based, and on the periphery it hires workers who constitute a labor reserve. This allows industry to use pick-up labor according to

market demands, without incurring the costs and overhead of a permanent workforce. Women make up this pool of marginalized workers. They work on contract, part-time or from home.

Homework: A key component of the global economy

Homework has emerged as a major feature of the global economy. The International Labor Organization (ILO) has documented home-based work in Australia, Europe, North and South America, New Zealand, Canada, Africa, Indonesia, India, the Philippines, and many other Asian countries. The majority of homeworkers are women — often the main income earner of the family. They are a captive, often invisible and vulnerable workforce. They make up a significant part of the informal global economy based on gender and racial discrimination. Homeworking exploits people who have difficulties working in the open labor market.

The sweatshops have taken on new dimensions. They have entered the domestic sphere — an ideal combination where women can cook, clean, care for children or elderly relatives, and manufacture, all from home.

Homework, therefore, has become a cheap option for industrialized countries because of a compliant, nonunionized workforce. This has intensified as foreign competition increases, trade barriers are lifted, and transnational and national monopolies increase their market share.

I would like to talk about the emergence and effects of homeworking in Australia. The practice of outsourcing and home-based work have long been associated with the textile and garment industry. Contributing factors to the increase in homework include tariff reductions since 1989, which have intensified the effects of foreign competition. Australia has one of the highest levels of retail monopolization in the world. Retailers can set a wholesale price based on prices they are getting, for example, in Indonesia and can expect contractors in Australia to match them.

Australia is an immigrant country. Since the 1950s, immigration policies have generated a labor supply to develop industry and increase productivity. In the 1990s, it is the recent-arrival communities — Vietnamese, Chinese, Central American, and Middle Eastern — who are the laborers of the garment and other manufacturing industries in Australia.

Refugee and immigrant intakes provide a pool of ready, exploitable labor, and make up the majority of women homeworkers. Many have poor English, the dominant language in Australia, and work for as little as 50 cents an hour. The average rate is about $2 an hour, and it is common not to be paid for work completed. Homeworkers are often forced to work 18-hour days, seven days a week, for as little as 50 cents to $2 an hour. Compare that to a legal rate of $10 per hour for a 38-hour week. Conditions are worse than those experienced by garments workers 100 years ago.

In the 1990s, the daily reality for most homeworkers is reported violence and sexual harassment, not being paid for the work they do, working long hours, suffering from work-related overuse injuries, and working to tight deadlines, which force women to involve their children in the production process.

This plenary is about strategies: I would like to outline the activities the Textile, Clothing & Footwear Union of Australia (TCFUA) has been involved in together with a broad range of community-based organizations.

In 1987 the union was successful in getting the labor laws changed. This meant that home-based workers in the garment industry had the same protection as workers in factories. The union had the expectation that home-based workers would become unionized. This wasn't the case, and the union left the issue of home-based work and the informal sector in the too-hard basket.

New challenges have emerged since that time. Tariff barriers have been removed at an accelerated pace; many factories have closed, and unionized workers have lost their jobs. Production has moved to Asian production centers, mainly based in EPZs. Within Australia there has been a huge increase in the use of of subcontractors who pass on work to home-based workers.

Every year for the last 10 years the number of home-based workers in the clothing industry alone has doubled. Ten years ago, the estimated figure was 30,000 nationally. We now have a figure of 330,000. This means that for every worker in a factory, there are now 15 home-based workers. This figure is overwhelming when we consider that the current chances of a homeworker receiving lawful wages and conditions is less than 1 percent.

These factors combined have all contributed to a new union-driven response, combined with a range of new strategies. A national information campaign was developed to address the issue of homework and make the union relevant to this large invisible group of workers.

The main objectives of the national information campaign included the following:
• To provide information in 12 community languages to homeworkers and employers of homeworkers of their rights and legal entitlements;
• To conduct a national multilingual media campaign and a phone-in to respond to workers' queries and better understand their work conditions and the problems they are currently experiencing;
• To liaise and develop an ongoing relationship with communities where homeworkers are from and with community organizations to assist in reaching homeworkers;
• To place homework on the agenda for industry, media, government, and the general community; and
• To identify the structural issues that prevent homeworkers entering the formal economy.

A large number of homeworkers were contacted over an eight-month period. The campaign has received a great amount of national media coverage and extensive community response. A report titled "The Hidden Cost of Fashion" was launched in March 1995 by the TCF union. This report is the first time that detailed information has been collated about the number of homeworkers and the true extent of the use of home-based work in the manufacturing industry in Australia. Documenting the extent of homework and conditions of homeworkers, together with lobbying government, has been successful in securing funding to conduct the campaign over the next two years.

Future strategies

Four key strategies we intend to focus on as the campaign continues into the next two years can be summarized as follows:

• Negotiating contracts with retailers that will flow down the contracting chain and result in protection for home-based workers. The focus is to make retailers responsible for where and how their clothes are made and to facilitate a process of self regulation within the industry.

• Conducting a consumer-awareness campaign to maintain pressure on retailers, liaise with community groups, and link up with campaigns within Australia and internationally. Develop effective media strategies to maintain a high profile on the issue. Work with government departments to implement relevant policies and structural changes to assist home-based workers to increase their access to the labor market and other training options.

• Informing homeworkers of their rights and the role of the union, and building strong links with community organizations to assist in reaching homeworkers.

• Developing organizing models to reach homeworkers and be responsive to their particular needs, and to allow them to participate in the struggle to improve their conditions.

A key aspect of the campaign is to see this as a community problem, not just an industrial one. The approach the union has taken to this campaign can be best described as top down and bottom up.

Top down: An ethical sourcing contract for principal companies

This part has involved reporting the most well-known labels being sewn by homeworkers to the media and through the Australian parliament. The next stage was to develop a model contract to present to retailers and manufacturers. This contract has been developed as a commercial common-law deed.

The TCFUA recently signed the first agreement with one of the largest budget department stores in Australia. This agreement subjects the company and its suppliers to monitoring and ensuring that all their garments are made by workers who receive their lawful pay and entitlements. Alongside this ethical sourcing contract we will be developing a best-practice organization register.

Bottom up: Building a consumer awareness campaign and informing and organizing homeworkers

The information campaign is twofold: to inform consumers about where their clothes are made and by whom, and to connect with national and international campaigns. The desired long-term outcome of this campaign is a fair-trade label that will indicate if a garment has been manufactured under equitable conditions for employees. We believe there is potential for this to develop into an international fair-trade labeling system. Clearly, a key strategy in Australia is to educate workers and consumers about where the exploitation begins. Without a working partnership among unions, community organizations, workers, and consumers we cannot succeed.

The second part of this strategy is to develop flexible and creative ways of reaching and informing home-based workers. Our goal is for homeworkers to have an input and participate in strategies to improve their working lives and become an organized, visible part of the workforce.

We intend to develop key regional bases around urban and rural areas, these centres will become the nucleus for workers to meet, get support from, and have contact with the union. This includes developing services these workers need, for example English classes, skills recognition, information about training, and social welfare programs.

Alongside these strategies we are lobbying our government to support the International Labor Organization (ILO) international convention and recommendations on homework. We intend to develop national laws around the contents of such a convention.

Global solidarity movements

Women workers throughout the world, together with union and social movements, must develop international strategies to confront repressive governments and transnational corporations in a collective struggle for social justice. Global solidarity links are the most important strategy we can develop to meet the global challenge. Many trade union activists have been killed or remain in prison for fighting for the right to form unions, to gain higher wages and better working conditions, and to form independent unions.

Unions are relevant because unionized workers earn more and are protected, and because unions provide the opportunity for collective bargaining to further improve conditions. The way to ensure the effectiveness of unions is through the involvement of their membership. NGOs have an important role to play to support trade unions to assist women workers and to work with trade unions to influence the way women workers can participate.

We are now at a point when many hard-won gains for basic working conditions are under threat. Working conditions in the industrialized North and the newly industrialized and underdeveloped countries of the South are being eroded as TNCs move in search of cheaper labor sites.

Workers in EPZs or working from home for rates below those in factories are not our enemies. We have nothing to achieve out of an increase in nationalism or racism, except trade wars and reduced conditions.

Global organizing

This year a network of organizations around the world was established to develop links and solidarity around the issues for homeworkers internationally. A campaign called Clean Clothes appeals to consumers to be more aware of the origins of the clothes they buy. It places the responsibility on retailers for the conditions in which their garments are produced. These, together with other strategies, can be linked so that women do set the agenda and let the transnational corporations know what we will and will not buy.

In 1996 the ILO will meet in Geneva to decide if there will be an international convention on homework. Women's organizations can lobby in your respective countries for your government to support this. Keep in mind that having the laws is only the beginning. One thing we have learned in Australia is that we must organize and create a groundswell of awareness among unions, workers, consumers, and the media for the laws to become enforceable and relevant to women workers.

Ethical consumerism is about encouraging constructive responses from companies and increasing awareness in our organizations and communities about exploited labor. It is not about stopping the livelihood of workers in any countries.

Yesterday garment-worker advocates discussed the issue of boycotts. While there were no conclusions drawn, there is agreement that they are effective and necessary at particular times. Our strategy has been to name and publicize the companies that are doing the right thing. The implication is that the other companies are not. Clothing is one of the most common consumer goods in the world today. I urge you all to place garment workers and, in particular, homeworkers in your respective countries on the agenda. You may not be aware of it, but they are there. Most likely they are working hard for very little, producing the fashion label and other clothes you could be wearing today.

I hope women here can raise ideas of how struggles in their country can be linked to our global struggles. We have spent a lot of time identifying the problems, we now need solutions. Using the media to publicize our struggles is crucial. To do this we need ongoing national and international networks which are dependent upon low-cost and effective ways of communicating.

There are two concrete things that can be done before we leave this NGO Forum. One is to support a petition initiated by the Organization for the Awakening of Women in India. It demands a unilateral cancellation of all Third World debt. The second is to return the label from the NGO cloth bags to the Esprit headquarters in your country, with a request that they ensure fair wages for all garment workers sewing their products around the world.

Globalization is not just a process of finance, trade, and markets blurring into a monocultural, nationless conglomeration to suit the interests of transnational corporations. It is about people and movements across the globe working and struggling for a 21st century for working people and ensuring that women get a fair deal.

To end I would like to quote two lines sung on the New York garment workers' picket line in 1909:

We showed the world that women could fight
And rose and won with women's might.

Women's demands and strategies: Women workers in the context of economic globalization

Swasti Mitter
United Nations University (UNU/INTECH),
The Netherlands

A decade has passed between Nairobi and Huairou, and we have moved away from the concerns of women in the global economy to those of women and globalization. It is important to highlight this shift in order to appreciate the strategies of empowerment that women need to augment their economic position. In the 1980s in the global economy, jobs were relocated from the First World to export-oriented enclaves of the Third World. Women were the major beneficiaries of these jobs. They were not the best jobs, but for many, they represented new opportunities, and for the first time, they gave women visibility as a major industrial workforce.

In the current period of globalization, women's position, especially as an industrial workforce, has changed somehow. With the opening up of economies, the pressure of modernization is now being felt, not only in export-oriented production but also in all spheres of production. The nation states themselves have become export-processing zones. Only the companies that introduce new technologies now have the chance of survival and expansion. New technologies, especially information technologies, have become the major tool for achieving the competitiveness of nations.

It is not only in the rich world, but also in the poorer parts of the world that the spread of information technology has altered the employment prospects of women and men. The results of automation, robotization, and foreign imports have meant a massive loss of jobs for blue-collar workers. In contrast, information-processing activities have created jobs in the services sector. The impact of globalization and technological changes has by no means been uniform, either on the lives of women or on those of men. In blue-collar jobs, women generally have borne the major brunt. In China, when laying off surplus workers, some factories have been reported to show a preference for "ladies first." In Vietnam during the reorganization, many employees were laid off, more than 60 percent of them women.

By contrast, women have become the major beneficiaries of the new technological-processing white-collar jobs. In the last two decades, the Indian banking industry has experienced nearly 300 percent growth in employment. Women have gained a major share. Women have fared particularly well in the foreign banks, a phenomenon of globalization. In Citibank Bombay, less than 5 percent of the workers were women in the 1970s. Currently, they account for more than 70 percent of the total employment. Women's entry into managerial and technical positions has been minimal. However, some women have made meteoric progress even in that sphere.

It thus no longer makes sense to talk about women as an undifferentiated category. Yet, because of their reproductive role, women all over the world, irrespective of their class, face certain challenges in the workplace that do not affect men. Moreover, the attitude toward women in most societies makes it difficult for them to have access to relevant vocational training and technological education. It is not surprising, therefore, that women are affected differently from men by globalization and technological change.

Strategies of empowerment, in this context, entail a formulation of demands highlighting the challenges that women workers face as workers and as women. The new situation makes it necessary to evaluate the structure of workers' organizations and to identify ways of negotiating with the governmental bodies and the employers. Committed researchers from different parts of the world undertook such an exercise at UNU/INTECH between 1992-1994. The results of the work have now been published in an anthology, *Women Encounter Technology: Changing Patterns of Employment in the Third World.*

With this conviction, we have initiated a novel project at UNU/INTECH: to bring together women workers' organizations and the governmental bodies of eight Asian countries in order to start policy dialogues. The process is not complete, but the learning experience has been immensely rewarding so far. In Kuala Lumpur, Malaysia, in September 1994, the women worker organizations articulated the demands they wanted to place before the policy makers. These are the demands that get missed in the mainstream labor movement and trade unions. They are:

1. Provisions such as maternity leave or child care;

2. Training and education for a sustainable and lifelong career;

3. Flexible forms of employment to enable women to combine their working and family lives;

4. Knowledge regarding the health and safety aspects of high-tech forms of production.

INTECH organized a similar meeting of senior civil servants from the above Asian countries in New Delhi in March 1995 in order to place women's concerns with relevant policy makers. Next April in Bangkok, as a logical follow-up, a joint meeting has been planned for the policy makers and the women workers' organizations to promote women-specific demands in the national industrialization plans.

The initiative represents a shift in strategies from the politics of confrontation to those of negotiation. It may or may not work, but it is worth a try. The process itself is empowering, as women's organizations become aware of the changing international perspective and establish links with similar organizations across the nation. The process contributes to their advocacy and negotiation skills, skills that women and men need in order to change the current state of affairs.

We have been helped immensely in this venture by UNIFEM, as well as by the Ministry of Foreign Affairs in the Netherlands. Given the limitation of time, energy, and resources, we could at this stage focus only on Asia, which contains the fastest-growing economies in the world. The learning experience, however, has relevance for other regions as well.

In developing strategies, however, it is important to take note of the differences as well as the commonalities among regions. The successful strategies for Asia, for example, could have relevance in Africa, but only with due modification. The whole of sub-Saharan Africa has fewer telephones than Tokyo alone. Africa's connection to the Internet, likewise, is extremely small. It is in this context that one should be extremely careful not to stress the politics of gender to the exclusion of others. One's position in the world market depends not only on one's sex, but also on one's class and geographical location. In order to change the world, we need to be strategic and to steer away from unnecessary confrontation.

It is strategic and not necessarily reformist to foster a spirit of dialogue with state power.

In the privatized, deregulated national economies, it is neither feasible nor reasonable to expect the employers to meet all the demands. The demand for maternity leave, for example, can lead to corporate-employer preference for male workers. For unions and for the women workers' movement outside the unions, it will be increasingly necessary to lobby for a different yet more proactive role for the national governments. It is at this point, I must confess, I agree neither with Marx nor with the World Bank.

The withering away of the state power or of the public sector is by no means compatible with the long-term welfare of the workers in the globalized economic order. In the coming millennium, women workers of the Third World will thus demand a new role for the state, for themselves, and for their men.

Food security and sustainable development: An African perspective

Reine-Brigitte Agbassy-Boni
African Women Leaders in Agriculture and the
Environment (AWLAE), Winrock International
Institute, Côte d'Ivoire

ECONOMIC CONTEXT

At the time of independence, Africa nourished great expectations for rapid development. There were many who encouraged Africans to prove their daring, asserting that the continent could find shortcuts in the road toward development. Financial institutions were also very optimistic and furnished resources accordingly. African leaders adopted economic strategies based on the economic theories of the time. In this era, industrialization was considered the driving force of economic growth and the key to the transformation of traditional economies, which exported raw materials while importing finished goods. Agriculture was relegated to a secondary position, behind furnishing raw materials and sources for financing the development of other sectors. For nearly a decade, sub-Saharan Africa has been witnessing a decrease in per-capita revenue, a worsening of food shortages, and accelerated degradation of the environment.

This crisis is the outcome of the accumulation of certain crucial factors, such as persistent drought, accelerated desertification, low agricultural productivity, a decrease in the price of exports, political instability, and rapid demographic growth.

Despite 30 years of aid, these trends — far from being reversed — have become more pronounced, which explains the profound reconsideration of development programs and policies. A sustainable political solution cannot be reached without mobilizing all the energies and researching the opinions of the entire African population: women and men, peasants and experts, heads of enterprises and decision makers. Therefore it is necessary to encourage the emergence of creative, committed African leaders to galvanize the immense potential of Africa's human resources and to find solutions to the problems of hunger, poverty, and environmental degradation.

However, half of the people who could help find these solutions are in fact underrepresented. In Africa women produce up to 80 percent of the basic food commodities. They process, store, and sell a considerable portion of their production. In addition, their activities directly affect the environment, given that women have traditionally been responsible for bringing water and wood to the household. Finally, women have sole responsibility for the health and nutrition of their families.

Despite their important role, rural women traditionally have low representation in institutions that service the agricultural sector. Only 4 percent of trainees are women. This proportion is even lower in decision-making positions in educational institutions, agronomical research, and the agricultural ministries that determine the overall research orientation, financing, and politics. Women are also more or less absent from businesses and private foundations.

This presentation proposes to examine the problems concerning women's role in agriculture and consider the experience of the African Women Leaders in Agriculture and the Environment program in mitigating problems through innovative strategies. The following chart gives an overview of the situation in sub-Saharan Africa.

Demographic and Economic Indicators in Sub-Saharan Africa (1992–1993)

Population (in millions):...............................527
Rate of population growth (% per year):............3.10
Food insecurity (% of population 1980):..............28
Affected population (in millions):....................180
Minimum needs met (% 1988): 87
Rate of growth in agricultural production
(% per year):.......…..................................…2.50
Per capita annual consumption of cereal grains
(kg): ....…...............................122
Annual importation of cereal grains
(millions of tons): 11
Average per-capita income (US$):...................350

FOOD SECURITY AND SUSTAINABLE DEVELOPMENT

Food security problems in sub-Saharan Africa

• *A definition of food security:* "access by all persons at all times to sufficient food for an active life and normal health" or "a guarantee of the availability of sufficient food and access to that food, even for the poor";

• *Agricultural productivity:* a growth in agriculture (2.5 percent) and a decrease in production; questions of subsistence crops and export crops;

• *Population growth:* a demographic growth (3 percent) larger than the agricultural growth (2.5 percent);

• *Supply and demand of food:* demand increasing faster than production, which is decreasing; and

• *Food imports:* 11 million tons of cereals imported per year, which by the year 2000 will reach 20 million tons; questions of external assistance, food aid, and bilateral cooperation.

A view of women's role in food security in Africa

Food security — that is, universal and constant access to sufficient food to enable an active life and normal health — is a concept created during the 1970s in reaction to the setting up of projects related exclusively to production (the means of production, credit, storage, and marketing). Subsistence agriculture remains the essential link in the food security of Africa, and here women play a preponderant role.

In Africa women are the major food producers. According to the Food and Agriculture Organization (FAO), women constitute three-quarters of the workforce involved in food production in Africa. They represent approximately 90 percent of the workforce involved in food processing and in bringing water and wood to the household. They do 80 percent of the work of storing and transporting the harvest from farm to village; 90 percent of the labor in the fields; and 60 percent of the work of harvesting and marketing. Generally, African grassroots women work about 16 hours per day.

In African countries where the demand for food increases at a rate parallel to that of the demographic growth — which is very high, in the range of 3.1 percent — women obviously play a preeminent role on the socioeconomic stage. This role is of prime importance because food security is a factor on which social peace depends and because governments attach a high priority to it.

What is women's contribution to agricultural production? In general, they participate in such production in a variety of ways:

• Women cultivate their own patch of land, if they have one;

• Women help cultivate the communal household fields, either those of the concession or of the family;

• Women help cultivate — often by obligation — the personal fields of their spouses; and

• Women cultivate the collective farms.

Agriculture represents about 30 percent of African countries' gross domestic product (GDP), whereas its importance is preponderant in the economy of sub-Saharan Africa and in the role of women. The figures below illustrate women's contribution to agricultural production in Africa.

Participation of women in agricultural production in several countries of sub-Saharan Africa and the importance of agriculture in their economies:

	Per-Capita GNP in US$ (1991)	Agriculture as % of GDP (1991)	% of women in total agricult. workforce
Burkina Faso	290	44	>50
Gambia	390	23	30-50
Mali	280	44	—
Mauritania	510	22	—
Senegal	720	20	>50
Sub-Saharan Africa	350	31	75-80

Sources: World Bank, *WID Assessment and Strategy*, 1992; World Bank, *Report on World Development 1993*, 1993.

Women's role in agriculture corresponds to diverse activities. Studies done in different sub-Saharan African countries have proven that the role of women in agriculture and other rural sectors is greatly diversified. They are active in agricultural production, livestock farming, picking, processing, and marketing, and this diversification is linked to ethnic groups or to systems of production in different agro-ecological zones.

Women's constraints in food security

Women's constraints in the agricultural sector in Africa limit the efficacy of their activities in the struggle against food insecurity. The major obstacles they face are notably:

• access to land;

• access to decision-making power — the influence of women in the decision-making process is almost nonexistent compared to that of men;

• restrictions imposed by African society and culture on their access to resources, facilities, and to the use of the fruits of their labor;

• limited access to the educational system — there is a low rate of enrollment for girls;

• access to agricultural formation;

• nonaccessibility of markets for the commercialization of their production and the absence of information concerning pricing and markets (media, radio);

• the work overload — domestic tasks plus agricultural work occupy 16 hours per day of the woman's time;

• access to technology;

• access to the results of research;

• access to credit — women's access to credit in rural environments is made difficult by multiple constraints, such as low level of training, the weight of responsibilities, social burdens, and the difficulty of entering production activities;

• demographic growth — African women, who are at the center of growth, lack of information and training in family planning, and certain taboos or religions do not favor birth control.

A large part of the African population who lack food security are small peasants, often women, who live in isolated regions where transportation is expensive, and they have little or no access to mar-

kets. In most cases, intensifying agricultural production and improving the stability of the food supply are undoubtedly the only ways of assuring food security. If one analyzes the demand side of food security, one sees the need to eliminate discrimination against women in regard to access to credit, popularization, and research and development. Like other development partners for the continent, Winrock International Institute recognizes the necessity of increasing food security and the role of women.

AWLAE PROGRAM EXPERIENCES

Faced with food security problems in Africa, several development aid programs initiated by financial institutions, NGOs, and other organizations have decided to commit themselves to improving the food security situation and to sustainable and equitable development in Africa. This is the case with Winrock International Institute within the framework of the AWLAE program.

Winrock is an NGO that originated in the United States and that works to reduce hunger and poverty in the world through the promotion of sustainable development. Its projects and programs to foster increased agricultural productivity fall into four categories:

• developing human resources in the agricultural and rural sectors;

• reinforcing institutions devoted to research, education, and popularization of information;

• creating lasting agricultural systems and strategies; and

• improving the politics of agricultural and rural development.

Analyzing the food situation in Africa and taking into account the preponderant role of women, who produce up to 80 percent of basic food commodities, and their underrepresentation in African societies, Winrock International Institute proposed to begin the African Women Leaders in Agriculture and Environment program in Africa, using the following strategy: Winrock, in collaboration with other international agencies, would attempt to displace the framework and center of development efforts that for a long time had ignored the real and potential impact of women as well as grassroots women who stood at the core of decisions. Working alongside African collaborators, AWLAE serves as a catalyst to reverse years of agricultural and environmental decline throughout Africa by shaping professionals and helping them to reach grassroots women.

Objectives and strategy of the program

This program proposes to assist numerous African professionals and expert technicians who have university degrees and leadership talent, and gives support for long-term professional development in the area of the environment with access to work, promotion, and influence in the agricultural and environmental sectors.

This program, established in Africa in 1990, is being carried out in six countries — Ivory Coast, Kenya, Mali, Senegal, Tanzania, and Uganda — the main objective being to face problems of food security and protection of the environment in Africa and to promote a critical mass of women who are highly specialized, confident, and sensitized to the notion of gender. The principal components of the AWLAE program are:

• the preparation of women leaders by providing access of women leaders to higher education, short training courses, professional expertise, and a guiding role for the younger generations;

• the creation of a favorable environment in which women can have access to positions, promotions, and decision-making;

• the institutionalization of the program by means of strategies and long-term structural development.

This program has evolved unique characteristics that aspire to train women in leadership:

• the pan-African orientation extending over a decade;

• the relationship between professional and grassroots women;

• the creation of networks at every level;

• the commitment of all participants and the involvement of key men;

• the reinforcement of the university program through fostering leadership; and

• the creation of a favorable environment.

Program realization

Thus far, at the level of setting up the AWLAE program, the following should be noted:

• *The creation of women leaders*

There is now a nucleus of women agricultural and agricultural specialists at the Master's and Ph.D. levels in both foreign and African universities. These women were recipients of scholarships and travel stipends under the Winrock-AWLAE program. Sixty-four scholarships have been given to women professionals from 11 countries: Benin, Cameroon, Ivory Coast, Ghana, Kenya, Mali, Niger, Nigeria, Senegal, Sierra Leone, and Tanzania. Among the recipients, six have completed their academic studies and are returning to their respective countries.

The example of the returning Tanzanian recipient illustrates the strategy recommended by Winrock. She presently plays an important role in strengthening and energizing Winrock's national action committee's program in Tanzania. The recipients take part in leadership workshops to reinforce their aptitudes and self-discipline, to prepare individual leadership strategies, and to acquire competence in gender analysis tools for all aspects of their work. Their research, individual projects, and theses correspond to specific needs and to the lives and productivity of grassroots women. Many workshops and training seminars have been organized by the AWLAE program on various themes of women's leadership: food security and the participation of African women, technology, support for rural women in the energy economy, project elaboration, and communication. Approximately 200 professional women have taken part in them.

• *The creation of a favorable environment*

The AWLAE program seeks to develop collaborations and partnerships with institutions based in Africa to furnish scholarship recipients with professional training and experience in the form of fellowships, internships, and research opportunities. The program was developed through sensitization of participants at meetings, roundtables, and conferences held with national and international associations and institutions. National consultative committees were formed in order to allow professional women to become acquainted with one another and to gain the participation of men in the activities of AWLAE. Examples of partnership with institutions include the Centre Ivoirien des Recherches Economiques et Sociales (CIRES) in the Ivory Coast for the creation of a center of excellence; Egerton University in Kenya; and l'Institut d'Economie Rurale (IER) in Mali for the establishment of a center of excellence. Partnerships have been established between AWLAE and 16 different institutions in eight countries.

• *Institutionalization— the creation of sustainable mechanisms*

This program has created national action committees in six major countries. These committees are composed of women and men who work for the improvement of the lives of grassroots women and for the promotion of professional women. AWLAE women have created and stimulated six professional associations that are on their way to being certified as NGOs in Ivory Coast, Kenya, Mali, Tanzania, Uganda, and Senegal. In addition, centers of excellence consisting of libraries, research facilities on the activities of women professionals, and computer data have been set up in both East and West Africa. These centers have been established in the Ivory Coast (CIRES), Kenya (Egerton University), Mali (IER), and Uganda (Makere University).

The program is managed from the Winrock International Institute offices in Washington, DC, in the United States. The activities based in Africa are coordinated via two regional offices, one in Abidjan, Ivory Coast, for West Africa, and the other in Nairobi, Kenya, for East Africa. It is planned to open another office in South Africa.

Impact of the program on institutions, recipient countries, and the general population

The impact of AWLAE in general concerns attitudinal changes at the policy level and their implementation; dissemination of research and development; and young female students and women leaders.

• *Impact on governments and leaders* (ministries, research institutions, universities) — training workshops; changing attitudes of decision makers; particular interest in women's organizations; financing research for projects with a gender component; support for ministries on the status of women;

• *Impact on the dissemination of agricultural research* — development and creation of rural animators; interest from young women in agriculture and the environment; increased likelihood of improvement in subsistence crops and food security; and

• *Impact on women* — increased confidence among women themselves, their families, and the community of women leaders; the mobilization of women and the creation of women's organizations (NGOs, cooperatives) directed and managed by professional women; training women leaders in business skills such as management and accounting.

Perspectives of the program

Progress has been realized during the first phase of the program through changes in attitude and thinking within both institutions and the general population. The second phase (1995–1998) will permit these gains to be consolidated and, as scholarship recipients return to their respective countries, a critical mass of women leaders will be capable of being mobilized. Future activities in this second phase are under discussion.

CONCLUSION

Food insecurity is an African reality. Environmental degradation and increased demographic growth demand innovative strategies. There is no longer a need to demonstrate women's role in agriculture. However, so long as disequilibrium persists in training, in the consideration of women's specific technological needs, and in the dissemination of technology, and so long as this disequilibrium is not corrected, African agriculture cannot realize its full potential for food production. The experience of Winrock's AWLAE program shows it to be, despite its youth, a promising road in the search for solutions to the problems of Africa, notably those of food security.

References
Food and Agriculture Organization (FAO). Technical report. 1992.
International Seminar on Women and Rural

Development. Vienna, May 1989.

USDA-ERS. International Agriculture and Trade Reports: Africa and the Middle East. July 1994.

Winrock International. Activity Reports — Regional Missions in Africa. AWLAE 6, 1995.

"Women in Africa's Agriculture: Policy and Realities." Presentation at ATLAS Regional Conference. July 1993.

World Bank. Review of the Agricultural Sector. October 1994.

World Bank. *Synthesis Studies on Five Countries of the Sahel: Rural Women of the Sahel and Their Access to Agricultural Dissemination.* AF5AG. 19 September 1994.

World Bank. *1993 World Development Report.* 1993.

World Bank. *Sub-Saharan Africa: From Crisis to Sustainable Growth.* 1989.

The impact of regional integration on women: The case of Mexico

Estela Suárez Aguilar
Association Mutual Siglo XXI, Argentina

Introduction

The North American Free Trade Agreement between Canada, the United States, and Mexico (known as TLC in Mexico and as NAFTA in English) went into effect January 1, 1994, but it did not initiate a totally new process in Mexican history.

Mexico, by reason of its geographical location and its most important international economic relations, is within the United States' sphere of influence. NAFTA is a further step in a long history between the two countries that includes three elements: (1) major trading links (four-fifths of Mexico's foreign trade is with the U.S.); (2) financial relations (U.S. capital accounts for the greater part of foreign investment in Mexico, the U.S. is the main creditor of Mexico's external debt, and the "flight" of capital from Mexico is toward the U.S.); and (3) strong migratory, social, and cultural links as a result of the longstanding and constant flow of Mexican workers to the U.S. To these have been added in the past 30 years new joint industrial production relations, under the international subcontracting arrangement known in Mexico as "in-bond garment assembly for export."

Thus, long before the draft of NAFTA even existed, Mexico was experiencing a process of silent integration with the U.S., governed by no explicit rules. NAFTA regulates a part of the process, particularly trade and finance, or in other words, the flow of goods and capital. It leaves out, however, the most contentious aspects of the integration, namely, the problem of free movement of the Mexican labor force, the rights of migrants in the U.S., and the systematic repression to which they are subjected by U.S. authorities. What is new is not the greater closeness to the U.S. that NAFTA entails, but the fact that this takes place in the context of far-reaching changes, still under way, in the Mexican reality.

Can the impact of NAFTA on women be measured? Only one reply occurs to me; that is, the question is not a valid one if it implies that within the complex process of change Mexico is going through — with advances and reverses since the 1982 crisis — it is possible to isolate the impact of NAFTA on Mexican society and, in particular, on women as a social group.

The major changes in Mexico are in response to a demand for development of its internal dynamics within the international context of growing globalization — a process as yet incomplete, and one that entails great risks and uncertainties. NAFTA is a further step, although an important one — as shown by the latest Mexican crisis at the end of 1994 — within a much broader and more extensive process of transformation. Changes as important as these undoubtedly affect the whole of Mexican society, within which women are 50.4 percent of the total population.

In addition, in recent decades significant changes have taken place within the female population. Access to various levels of education has increased.

Women's participation in labor markets has significantly expanded. The homes in which women live and the types of families they are part of have also changed. To this dynamic process must be added the impact of the economic crisis of the 1980s and the economic transformations that followed it. Given the scope and complexity of the topic, this analysis will be confined to considering the most important aspects of the situation of women in the labor markets, as the most significant indicator of their social status.

On the basis of the foregoing, I shall divide this presentation into four sections which seem to me to be important:

• The process of international globalization, to situate Mexico in the context of changes taking place worldwide;

• The transformation under way in Mexico, and in women in the labor markets, to highlight the most important aspects of the changes in Mexico before NAFTA;

• The North American Free Trade Agreement and the first crisis of the 21st century, distinguishing two phases in the short time during which NAFTA has been in force, to bring out the significance of the current economic crisis;

• The role of NAFTA in the current economic situation and the new challenges faced by women.

International globalization

The current process of globalization, which has been taking place since the 1980s, is in part a continuation of the so-called internationalization of capital and of the new international division of labor, accompanied by the development of transnational corporations. It also, however, involves the incorporation of three new processes.

First, the objective material basis for these changes is a far-reaching technological revolution which began in the data-processing sector and is increasingly expanding to the whole range of economic activity, although at different rates of intensity.

Heading this process, which has been termed the third industrial revolution, are the most developed countries, among which three major centers of technological development have emerged that in turn constitute three important financial centers — Western Europe, the United States, and Japan. Generated and directed by the capitalist world, this process is promoting the expansion of mercantile and capitalistic relations worldwide, and was a vital factor in the dismemberment of the "real socialism" of the late 1980s, which proved incapable of incorporating current technological progress without restructuring itself into open markets, the political forms of which still remain to be defined. The process of transformation of communist China is governed by the same factor, but to date has been following a different political course.

Second, and closely linked to the above, is the capitalist restructuring, which could be termed "neo-liberal and post-Fordist" to indicate the elements in it that relate to liberalization of markets, promotion of private initiative, and reform of the State, and those that relate to the incorporation of the new technologies and the changes in the organization of production.

This transforming impulse also extends to major countries in what is known as the Third World. Among them, the most dynamic have previously experienced the collapse of corporate nationalism engendered by linked processes of liberalization of trade and finance, negotiated emergence from the debt crisis, monetary stabilization, and mass privatization of state enterprises.

The third process to be highlighted is the trend towards unification of the world market. In place of what were previously termed the First, Second, and Third Worlds is a tendency to move toward an international economy structured around a single world capitalist market.

The unification of the world market is still under way, and its progress depends on the elimination of barriers that enclosed the three worlds: the fall of the second world and the opening up of the third to worldwide trade, with some score of countries known as "emerging" markets/countries/capitalisms — Mexico among them — occupying a prominent place.

By the end of the 1980s, the economic restructuring of the major Latin American countries was drawing to a close, the debt crisis was being overcome, and these countries were again recognized as creditworthy subjects at the international level. This situation gave rise to a reorientation of trade and of capital.

The 1990s are marked by the increasing importance of the emerging countries as the most dynamic focus of international trade and capital investment. The countries of eastern Asia, headed by China, are in the forefront of this process. Prominent in eastern Europe are Poland, the Czech Republic, and Hungary. Until the Mexican crisis at the end of 1994, Latin American countries were playing a role as important as that of the Asian countries, and still more so as recipients of foreign portfolio investment. Mexico was the main recipient of portfolio investment and ranked second, after China, in direct investment.

In the emerging countries, direct foreign investment rose from less than 15 percent in 1989 to 37 percent in 1993, and stock-market investment from an insignificant level to 12 percent of the world total. Over the same period, foreign trade between Latin American countries grew by 30 percent. They are countries which are not only exporting more, but also importing more. In other words, they are becoming more integrated into the world market.[1] This integration is the outcome not only of institutional reforms, but also of the degree of maturity of capitalism in these countries, and the emergence, in the course of the restructuring during the 1980s, of major corporations with the capacity to export. The same process, in turn, gives rise to greater import capacity.

Although the changes described are still under way, today's world is radically different from that of 20 years ago in at least three main respects:

• There is a trend away from the previous three worlds and towards the emergence of an international economy structured around a single world capitalist market;

• Regionalization into three major blocs (North America, Western Europe, and Eastern Asia) is a complementary phenomenon within the globalization of the world economic space;

• The tendency towards a new polarization between, on the one hand, semi-industrial countries with a high level of dynamism and growing weight in the world economy[2]; and on the other hand, the pre-industrial countries, marginalized from world trade circuits, which depend for their subsistence on world food aid.

Globalization, in the stage it has currently reached, still has a long way to go, especially where new regulatory institutions and/or bodies at the world level are concerned. There is a need for new international agreements and monitoring agencies to limit the risks and uncertainties inherent in open markets. An important step in this direction was the replacement of the former GATT by the World Trade Organization (WTO), established at the end of 1993.

But the current process of globalization, although its starting point is economic, is a much broader phenomenon, tending to include also the most important social, cultural, environmental, and political relations in the modern world. Prominent among these are international migrations and travel, the increase in telephone traffic, the impressive size of mass-communication networks, the proliferation of international meetings of various kinds, the multiplicity of state relations and organizations, and the growing networks of nongovernmental organizations (feminist, women's, human rights, environmental, indigenous, pacifist, humanitarian). Behind this brief listing of world links in various fields of human activity is the development of new types of relationships among different peoples and cultures in the hope of building a better world.

As in the case of any profound historical change, the new capitalist restructuring of the world brings with it not only new fields of conflict and new forms of exploitation and repression, but also new arenas for the development of social struggles and new potentials for expansion and triumph. The new achievements will be associated with a world citizenship still being created.

The transformation under way in Mexico and women in the labor markets

Mexico's transformations are taking place in this international context. They are at three levels: liberalization of trade, the reform of the State, and the change in the political system, which for more than 60 years was based on a single party regime, with the Institutional Revolutionary Party (PRI) in power.

It is important to indicate the most significant aspects of this complex process of change, to place in context the current regional integration and the situation of the female labor force as the sector most relevant for an analysis of the social situation of women.

Starting with the economic crisis in 1982, rapid economic restructuring and reform of the State were initiated in Mexico, involving the transition from a phase of closed growth, with protectionist policies and large State subsidies, to a new phase of opening up the domestic market, restructuring public finance, privatizing public enterprises, and promoting competitiveness at the international level.

In 1985 Mexico acceded to GATT, initiating an opening up of trade. This was intensified in 1988 through the elimination of import permits and the establishment of a maximum tariff rate of 20 percent.

As one of the responses to the crisis, the opening up to the world market was a prerequisite for achieving domestic economic restructuring, in that it compelled Mexican capitalists to modify their production and trading practices in order to compete in cost, quality, and price on the levels required by the international market. The aim was not only to increase exports, but to promote the play of external economic forces in accelerating what was officially termed the "modernization" of the economy.

Around the beginning of 1994, there were three problems in connection with this orientation of the Mexican transformation:

• The priority assigned to economic over political modernization;

• Placing anti-inflation measures and financial stability on a higher level than economic development and social modernization; and

• The priority assigned to monetary stability and support for large financial and business groups, to the detriment of small- and medium-sized businesses, thus affecting sources of employment.

Economic modernization was dome-shaped, favoring a powerful minority and marginalizing broad sectors of society. One of the most signifi-

cant problems is that it gave rise to a fissioning of Mexico's production apparatus into two sectors. One sector consists of large economic groupings financed with dollars from abroad and taking advantage of the relatively low international interest rates (8 to 9 percent) and the overvaluation of the Mexican peso.[3] The other sector consists of the remainder of Mexican businesses, able to secure financing only on the domestic capital market and paying high interest rates of close to 30 percent.

The far-reaching changes in Mexico from the beginning of the 1980s to the end of 1993 already had a high social cost. The gap between the richest and poorest sectors of the population had widened, and unemployment and underemployment had begun to cause increasing concern.

Between 1984 and 1992, the proportion of national income appropriated by the richest 10 percent of Mexican households rose drastically, from 32.4 percent in 1984 to 38.1 percent in 1992. In contrast, the share in income of the poorest 80 percent fell from 50.5 percent to 45.6 percent.[4]

While the economically active population (EAP)[5] has grown by about 15 million people in the past 15 years, over the same period there was an estimated increase of 3.4 million in the number of paid jobs involving normal working hours, 1.6 million of which were created between 1988 and 1994. The number of paid jobs is much lower than the number of people constituting the EAP, because when someone does not find work involving regular hours (more than 40 hours a week) and a minimal level of remuneration (using the minimum wage as an indicator), he or she seeks some other form of activity for a few hours a week, or a job involving more than 40 hours work at a wage below the minimum level, or engages in unremunerated family activities. Accordingly, the open unemployment rate in Mexico is very low, at only 3 percent, despite the fact that the EAP is far higher (at approximately 15 million) than the increase in the number of paid jobs involving a normal 40-hour working week (3.4 million). By 1993, 35.1 percent of the EAP were working less than 40 hours a week, 9 percent of the EAP were employed for more than 40 hours a week at wages lower than the minimum, and some 5 percent were working the same number of hours without pay. On the basis of these indicators, the unemployment and underemployment rate is estimated at ranging between 30.3 percent and 44.2 percent.[6]

In this context, the female labor force exhibits a significantly dynamic trend, of which it is of interest to single out the most important aspects. In recent decades, the incorporation of women in labor markets has increased, and in 1993 they accounted for approximately 33 percent of the economically active population (EAP). The number of women in the EAP has increased more rapidly than that of men. Between 1970 and 1990, according to census information, the male EAP grew by 70.5 percent and the female EAP by 123 percent.[7]

Over that period, the expansion of the female sector had two important elements: a significant increase in the rate of participation by women of reproductive age (between 20 and 49)[8]; and an increase in the female EAP not only in the less skilled jobs but also in skilled posts, especially professional and technical positions. In this category, the participation of women increased by 331.4 percent between 1970 and 1990, whereas the increase in male participation over the same period was significantly lower, at 184.3 percent.[9] This implies that while the increase in women's participation in the labor force is brought about primarily by the greater need for income for survival, accentuated by the economic crisis and its depressive effects on the low wages of the working class, there is also an evident effort by women to advance in the working world.

In rural areas as well, the female labor force has been relatively dynamic since the 1970s. While the economically active population in agriculture is decreasing, the female labor force has begun to grow. This increase is brought about by two factors: the development of commercial agriculture, largely for the export of fruit, vegetables, and flowers; and the increase in male migration, which is leading to a shortage of male agricultural workers.

Traditionally, the primary activities in Mexico have been the province of men, while women, together with children and the elderly, made up the "marginal" labor force,[10] engaged predominantly in equally essential tasks of reproducing the family,

but also engaging in production activities in the primary sector. In addition, both men and women in rural families were diversifying their economic activity through other self-employed activities — crafts, sale of harvested products, small-scale trade. The rural environment in Mexico was characterized by the employment of a predominantly male paid labor force, but towards the end of the 1970s labor markets began to open up in the production of horticultural crops and fruits in which the child and female labor force is more readily accepted.[11] These expanded in the 1980s with the growth of agricultural areas devoted to the export of market-garden crops, fruit and flowers, along with the emergence of a new wage-earning female agricultural proletariat in some regions of the country.[12] By the beginning of 1991, according to the National Employment Survey,[13] women accounted for only 12 percent of the population employed in the agriculture and livestock farming sector, and of this 12 percent, only 27 percent were wage earners. Twenty percent were self-employed workers, and the remaining 53 percent were unpaid family workers. These percentages need to be looked at in a broader context. While no comparable statistical sources are available for an analysis of the evolution of the female economically active population in the agriculture and livestock farming sector over the long term, traditionally, poor women in rural areas migrated to the cities and into domestic service. The high population pressure on the land and the strongly patriarchal structure of the rural family restricted access by women to land ownership and to wage-earning activities in the fields. The development of export production has, according to the case studies cited, been creating a new female proletariat in agriculture, and in some areas the wages being paid to women agricultural workers amounted to two or more times the minimum wage.[14]

The dynamism of the women's sector in labor markets is accompanied by significant advances in the educational field. In recent decades in Mexico, there has been a more rapid rise in the educational level of women as compared with men. While women's illiteracy remains systematically higher than men's illiteracy for all age groups, between

1970 and 1992 the female illiteracy rate fell by 55.6 percent. Compared with their male counterparts, the rates of female illiteracy are tending towards the same level. While in 1970 the gap between literacy for men and women was 7.8 percentage points, by 1992 this had decreased to 3.5 points, a decrease of 69 percent. Moreover, the differences are concentrated in relatively less developed areas such as Chiapas, Guerrero, and Oaxaca.[15]

In preschool, primary, and secondary education, the attendance rates for girls and boys are similar. At the university level, women account for 40 percent of all registered students. While careers such as education, nursing, and social work continue to be the province of women, there is a significantly more egalitarian presence of men and women in careers and professions that are in great demand, such as law, administration, accounting, medicine, and computer science.

For a better appraisal of the impact of these advances by women in education and employment, the differences in financial compensation for men and women need to be considered.

Comparisons of equal working time in similar occupations show that until 1993 men systematically earned more than women. However, these divergences were different for various job categories. Taking the average incomes of men and women for a full workweek (between 35 and 48 hours a week) — where the income differences by sex are lower than those recorded among the population working more than 48 hours a week — the incomes of men in the "professional" category are 34 percent higher than those of women, and in the "officials and administrators" category, 43.2 percent higher than those of women. The greatest differences, however, are between those engaged directly in production processes and in the sales staff and shop assistant group, where men receive respectively 67 percent and 74 percent more than women.[16]

Although this has not been sufficiently studied in Mexico, it can reasonably be concluded on the basis of the data presented that, on the one hand, the efforts women are making in education, qualifications, and commitment to enter more skilled employment are having greater effect — in terms of narrowing the wage gap between the sexes — in the more skilled than the less skilled occupations; but on the other hand, despite their efforts, qualified women are suffering from wage discrimination compared with men in similar occupational categories.

With respect to the greater wage differences in less skilled occupations, the sexual division of social work probably has a stronger impact in this sphere. According to the last population census, women occupy only 19.4 percent of civil service and managerial posts. In contrast, the census shows that 96.6 percent of domestic workers are women. This implies that as the end of the present century approaches there still persists, alongside the greater access of women to skilled jobs, a strong compartmentalization of men's and women's occupations, the latter being concentrated in less skilled positions with lower wages and lower social prestige.

Despite the significant differences described above in terms of women's participation in labor markets, the quantitative and qualitative advances by the women's labor force constitute an important factor in overcoming their historical situation of social marginalization, in the light of the high social costs associated with the current capitalist restructuring in Mexico.

The North American Free Trade Agreement and the first crisis of the 21st century

The Free Trade Agreement Mexico signed with Canada and the United States at the end of 1993, which took effect at the beginning of 1994, must be situated in this international context and in this situation of national transformation, with its inherent high social costs that have already been referred to.

In the short period during which the NAFTA has currently been in effect, the dynamics of Mexico's domestic problems make it necessary to distinguish two clearly differentiated phases.

In the first, from January 1994 through December 1995, there were indeed major unresolved economic problems, but the most significant factor was the deepening crisis in the Mexican political system.

In the second, which began in December 1994 and is of indeterminate duration,[17] a new financial crisis erupted in Mexico, caused largely by the political crisis and the new financial problems of a world economy not yet able to regulate the powerful forces generated by the growing process of globalization.

The first phase of NAFTA

By the beginning of 1994, the policies of Salinas (1988-1994) had achieved significant advances. In the domestic sphere, these included a decrease in inflation, renegotiation of the external debt, restructuring of public finance, and the beginnings of a recovery of social expenditure (on education and health).

Externally, they included new trading links favorable to Mexican capital, such as the entry as the 25th member into the Organization for Economic Cooperation and Development (OECD), centered around the major European countries; the entry into ASEAN, composed of the most dynamic countries in the Pacific basin; the free trade agreement with Chile and the trade negotiations aimed at a liberalization of trade with Central America from 1996 onwards; as well as long-term trade agreements with Venezuela and Colombia in what is known as the Group of Three (G-3). This active foreign trade policy was addressed both to the areas of the main industrialized countries and to countries less developed than Mexico.

In foreign trade, there was a substantial increase in exports, but also a growing trade deficit as a result of a larger rise in imports. Nevertheless, the increase in exports of approximately 20 percent in 1994 indicated two important factors: a substantial level of modernization of production plant, in that exports were growing despite the overvaluation of the national currency; and the impact of the NAFTA agreement with the U.S. and Canada as a factor in the expansion of Mexican exports.

However, these objective achievements rested on a very vulnerable basis.

The political difficulties — among them the armed uprising in Chiapas of January 1, 1994, and the internal problems of the ruling party, PRI,

which led to the murder of high-level political figures (Colosio, the PRI presidential candidate, in March 1994, and Ruiz Massieu in September 1994) — led to a loss of trust and to increasing doubts as to the government's capacity to handle the situation.

In February 1994 an increasing outflow of capital began, and in response the government took two steps to combat this trend: a devaluation of the peso by approximately 12 percent to establish a flotation range of 3.1 to 3.5 new pesos to the dollar; and the establishment of a new financing mechanism: treasury bonds, payable in dollar equivalent, to attract "highly volatile," or short-term speculative, capital.

Mexico had been able to attract some 100 billion dollars of portfolio investment, and its reserves amounted to only 27 or 28 billion dollars. This was undoubtedly a high-risk situation. At the beginning of 1994 with the armed conflict in Chiapas, the withdrawal of investment began, and was accentuated as the political crimes were committed and signs of a crisis in the Mexican political system became more acute. The country's financial fragility was made apparent.

The average profit rate for foreign investors in Mexico was 20 percent, the highest in the world, but starting in 1994 it fell to around 12 percent as a result of the devaluation of the peso in real terms.[18] This had two consequences: some of the capital went abroad, and the remainder was concentrated in treasury bonds.

The government obscured the seriousness of the situation, perhaps because of, among other reasons, the August 1994 presidential elections. Once the elections — conducted for the first time with the presence of international observers — were over, despite the victory of the former ruling party, the political crisis continued its upward course with the murder of Ruiz Massieu, the new President of PRI, in September 1995, a crime for which responsibility was attributed to members of the ruling party. The outflow of dollars was increasing, the problems of liquidity had become more acute, the overdue portfolio of the banks was increasing, and in December 1994 the government was compelled to devalue and establish a floating exchange rate, given the shortage of dollars to back it. A spectacular financial crisis had exploded which officials of international agencies and economic analysts described as "the first crisis of the 21st century" and/or "the first crisis of globalization," in that it affected not only Mexico but also many of the newly emerging countries in Latin America, such as Argentina and Brazil, through the so-called tequila effect.

The second phase of NAFTA

With the crisis in late 1994, the second phase in the short existence of NAFTA began. Within the space of a few months, Mexico was transformed into the weakest link in the international credit system, whereas previously it had been a model to be followed, recommended by the International Monetary Fund and the World Bank.

However, Mexico's current financial crisis cannot be understood unless it is related to the country's incorporation into the international capital market and to the transformation of that market.

First, as was pointed out above, Mexico was the main recipient of portfolio investment among the so-called emerging countries of the former third world. The progress made on structural reform, the deregulation of the financial market, the existence of large consolidated corporations, and the trade integration with North America made it an important player at the international level.

Second, the structure of international private credit has undergone major changes since the second half of the 1980s. The loans which previously were made by banks have been replaced by the issue of bonds, shares and commercial papers (debt bonds, forms of portfolio investment characterized by the fact that they are all tradeable bonds, which can be bought and sold in the stock exchanges). In other words, bank credit is losing ground, and non-bank portfolio investment is gaining ground. As a result, the stock exchanges have acquired an important role at the international level. The new financing is provided by pension funds, mutual funds, protection funds, and security companies. People are already placing their savings not in banks, but in mutual funds, which charge a commission on the transaction and put together the most attractive possible investment packages. The major corporations are doing the same.

The result of this process is that the competition to earn profits leads them to place funds in the emerging countries because: they pay higher dividends than those paid in the industrialized countries; they can raise a large amount of capital on the stock exchanges; and the national currencies of these countries are tending to be revalued as a result of their dynamic processes of restructuring and raising productivity.

These new funds are not subject to the regulatory standards that apply to the activities of banks, and are characterized by placement as short-term investments in the search for higher profits. This is a highly volatile form of investment which is not regulated at the international level. The movement of this speculative capital is capable of affecting the world's economies and peoples within a short space of time, with a marked negative impact on the economy itself.

At the international level, the Mexican crisis and its rapid expansion highlighted the enormous and unregulated power of speculative investment of highly volatile capital, and this is why it was termed the first crisis of the 21st century. This shows the importance of making much more rapid progress in the process of world globalization, regulating short-term investment institutionally through international agreements such as the one which brought into existence the World Trade Organization (WTO).

In domestic terms, the crisis unleashed in December 1994 is intensifying the trend toward social polarization which has characterized the ongoing restructuring process.[19]

The expectation for 1995 is a drop of 5.5 percent in gross domestic product (GDP) and an inflation of approximately 50 percent, while the accumulated drop in average wage per hour worked amounted to 20 percent for the first six months of the year.[20] The decrease in production is eliminating jobs, and to this must be added the number of people entering the labor market for the first time, estimated at 948,000 for 1995. An increase in underemployment is foreseeable; in other words, an increase in the number of people working involuntarily for less than a normal working week, or at a wage lower than the minimum level, and engaging in activities of uncertain productivity — and there is also room for doubt as to whether the informal sector still possesses the capacity to absorb them, as it has done in the recent past.

In the formal sector, according to the register maintained by the Mexican Social Security Institute, from November 1994, when the highest figure was recorded, to July 1995, the number of persons insured decreased by 1.05 million. Of these, 99 percent are part of the urban population, and 44.8 percent of the total are in the construction industry, which employs predominantly men.[21]

The unemployment rate for women in urban areas is higher than that for men. The average unemployment rate for men in Mexico's 39 major cities in the first five months of 1995 was 5.6 percent of the economically active population (EAP), while women's unemployment was 5.84 percent.[22] On the other hand, nevertheless, in the export garment assembly industry, which predominantly employs women, employment rose by 9 percent in the first eight months of the year.[23] In the first quarter, the number of jobs rose by 33,000, and an increase of a further 20,000 in the course of the second quarter is expected.[24]

Two factors are affecting the behavior of industries of this kind: a devaluation of the peso of approximately 50 percent, resulting in a marked drop of 30 percent in costs in dollars, which is the operating currency of the in-bond garment assembly industry[25]; and the surplus labor supply, especially in nonfrontier areas, because they prefer hiring more staff to paying more overtime.[26]

For the first half of 1995, the estimated drop in GDP is 10.5 percent as compared with the same period in 1994, a decrease which exceeds the most unfavorable expectations. With the exception of the in-bond garment assembly industry, the basic metallurgical industries (where production rose by 10.6 percent), paper, printing and publishing (a 5.1 percent increase), and electricity and water (with a 4.8 percent increase), there have been major cutbacks in the remaining production sectors. Expectations with regard to employment are extremely pessimistic.

The role of NAFTA in the current economic situation and the new challenges faced by women

Initially the crisis affected big financial capital in Mexico, especially banking capital, and savers in or pensioners from the U.S., threatening to trigger a new international crisis.

The new commercial links with the U.S. agreed to under NAFTA constituted a positive factor in this situation. Mexico, with the support of the U.S. government, received financial backing amounting to approximately $50 billion to meet its liabilities to its creditors. In addition, the favorable development of its exports in 1994 is increasing still further in 1995 as a result of the positive impact of NAFTA.

The current crisis is accelerating the process of economic restructuring in Mexico. The dynamic impact of the internationalization coefficient, characterized by an increase in industry-based trade, is really important. The ratio of foreign trade (imports plus exports) to GDP in dollars was 30 percent during the 1980s. Before the latest devaluation, it amounted to 45 percent, and a projection of the estimates indicates an internationalization coefficient of 66 percent for the end of 1995.

A prominent feature of this process is the increase in nonbonded garment assembly manufacturing exports, the share of which in total exports has risen from 39.5 percent in 1994 (first quarter) to 43.05 percent in 1995, rising by 44 percent in the first five months of this year.[27] Over the same period, imports have stagnated as a result of the devaluation and the recession. Last year's balance of trade deficit (for the same period) has become a surplus in the case of the United States, Belgium-Luxembourg, Hong Kong, Peru, Chile, Puerto Rico, Uruguay, Bolivia, Haiti, and Norway. In the first two months of the year, there was an increase of more than 100 percent in exports to 25 countries, the major ones being Brazil, Cuba, Hong Kong, Switzerland, and Belgium-Luxembourg.

This dynamism came as a surprise to the authorities and to analysts. The fact that, unlike the two most recent ones in 1982 and 1986, this recession took place in the context of an open economy meant that the extent of the restructuring achieved by the manufacturing export sectors was underestimated, and consequently, so was their capacity to derive advantages from the devaluation of the Mexican peso. The current thinking is that the export sector will contribute significantly to an earlier recovery than in the case of the previous recessions, and more important, will to a large extent consolidate and promote the further advancement of the levels of capitalist restructuring already achieved. In other words, the current economic crisis is accelerating the economic restructuring which Mexico launched at the beginning of the 1980s.

Looking at the political variables, this does not appear to pose any obstacle to the trend described above; on the contrary, the overall direction is an object of substantial consensus among the electorate, notwithstanding its high social cost and despite the increasingly acute crisis in the Mexican political system and the ruling party.

The election results in Jalisco, Yucatan, Guanajuato, and Durango, even if the accusations of fraud in the cases of Yucatan and Tabasco are accepted, do not pose any real threat of a change in the current economic policy. The crisis in the Institutional Revolutionary Party (PRI) does not imply a strengthening of the most radical opposition expressed through the Democratic Revolutionary Party (PRD), but rather a strengthening of the National Action Party (PAN). The latter may briefly be defined as a party of the political center, and in this capacity it is playing an extremely important role in the effort to democratize the country and decentralize the State. It is liberal in its economics, in line with the essential features of the direction taken by the current capitalist restructuring initiated by the ruling party, PRI, in the 1980s; it is confessional, religious, and pro-life in terms of ideology.

Just as in antiquity Greek democracy was only for free men, with no rights accorded to the slaves, the PAN concept of democracy does not recognize the rights of women, nor those of homosexuals and lesbians. Its sexist concept of democracy makes it a threat to the advancement of the rights of women that has been achieved to date.

One example of this was the attempts by PAN deputies, when PAN won the elections in Chihuahua in 1993, to overturn the legislation that, by way of exception, decriminalizes abortion in cases of rape and endangerment of the mother's life. Given the right of women to interrupt pregnancy enjoyed without restriction by 38 percent of the world's population, Mexican legislation is a part of the legislative provisions applicable to 43 percent of the world's population which penalize abortion on principle, while providing for specific exceptions which in the case of Mexico are three in number: when the woman becomes pregnant as the result of rape; when the pregnancy entails a risk of death; and when the abortion takes place through negligence or accident. Only 9 percent of the world's population lives in countries where abortion is prohibited without exception, and no information is available on the remaining 10 percent.[28] In this context, the PAN legislators in Chihuahua are taking the same stand as the fundamentalist Muslim countries that form part of the regions where women experience the worst conditions of subordination and marginalization.

It is important to reiterate that the process in Mexico is still in a transitional phase, with the development of a more equitable society increasingly dependent on the demands for a far-reaching democratic transformation that transcends the economic, social, and political levels of the current reality in Mexico. The new trade agreements that situate the current trends in Mexico's relations in the context of globalization, and particularly of its trading partners in NAFTA, constitute an important external factor in promoting the democratic transformation in Mexico.

At the national level, there is increasing awareness that the complexity of the changes in the world — the new problems arising as a result of Mexico's growing integration into an increasingly globalized world economy, the rising inequity of income distribution, the unjust marginalization of ethnic minorities, and the fight against poverty — call for a process of decentralization of presidential power, full independence of the judiciary, the elimination of impunity and corruption in all areas of authority, and the establishment and strengthening of autonomous institutions that are highly specialized in their technical area of competence, with attributable responsibilities and clearly defined functions, and that will constitute a new structure of modern government, more institutionalized and balanced than that which exists under the current presidential system. In the electoral sphere, the complete elimination of all types of electoral fraud is not sufficient; there is also a need for electoral legislation to guarantee a transparent exercise of power by the parties, agreed upon by the main political forces in the country, as well as for the development of a new culture of citizenship that will eliminate corporate patronage and will call for the political parties to learn to win and lose.

In the face of the new challenges, there is a vital need for participation by citizens, and for the extension of their rights without the discrimination that constitutes a throwback to the past. In this process, women committed to the building of an integrated and pluralistic society in which the rights not only of the majorities but also of the minorities are important have made significant progress, and have much more to contribute.

Access to higher levels of education is undoubtedly a factor in the empowerment of women, and one of the important ways of exercising an impact on the processes of transformation and development, as well as of gaining access to decision-making power. The increasing participation of women, on the basis of the new status afforded them by their dynamic integration into the production of the country's wealth through their work, will undoubtedly contribute to ensuring that the democratic transition currently under way takes the form of a pluralistic, integrative, participatory and multi-ethnic democracy of the kind the Mexican people, composed of men and women, needs and deserves.

Notes

1. Dabat, A., "Los capitalismos emergentes" (The Emerging Capitalisms), *Revista de Comercio Exterior*, Mexico D.F., November 1994.
2. Countries in this situation are, for example, China, Korea, Taiwan, Singapore, Malaysia, Thailand, India, Pakistan, and Turkey in Asia, and Brazil, Chile, Colombia, Mexico, and Argentina in Latin America.
3. In 1993, as is common knowledge, a major increase in the overvaluation of the peso began. While inflation is at 15 percent, the exchange rate is being maintained at an almost fixed level.
4. Fijii, Gerardo G., and Aguilar, Genaro G., "La distribucion del ingreso en Mexico, 1984-1992: Un estudio de componentes" (Income distribution in Mexico 1984-1992: A study of components), in *Revista de Comercio Exterior*, Mexico, August 1995, p. 610.
5. Persons aged over 12 engaging in productive activity or, if unemployed, actively seeking work.
6. Banamex, "Examen de la situación economica de Mexico" (Review of the economic situation in Mexico), Mexico, July 1995, p. 331.
7. Suárez Aguilar, Estela, "El trabajo y el genero: Designualdades entre el varon y la mujer" (Work and gender: Inequalities between men and women), in *Demos* 5, National Autonomous University of Mexico (UNAM), 1992.
8. Suárez Aguilar, Estela, "El trabajo . . .," *op. cit.*
9. Suárez Aguilar, Estela, "El trabajo . . .," *op. cit.* See also INEGI and UNIFEM, "La mujer mexicana: Un balance estadistico al fin del siglo XX" (Mexican women: A statistical balance at the end of the 20th century), Mexico, August 1995, p. 70.
10. Tepechit, *Marxisme et agriculture: Le paysan polonais* (Marxism and agriculture: Polish agricultural workers), Colin, Paris, 1973, quoted in Pedrero, Mercedes, et. al., "Desigualdad en el acceso a oportunidades de empleo y segregación ocupacional por genero: Situación actual en Mexico y propuestas" (Inequality in access to job opportunities and occupational segregation by gender. The current situation in Mexico and proposals), United Nations Development Fund for Women (UNIFEM), 1994.
11. Roldán, Marta, "Subordinación generica y proletarización rural: Un estudio de caso en el noroeste mexicano" (Gender subordination and rural proletarization: A case study in northeast Mexico) in Leon, Magdalena (compiler), *Debate sobre la mujer en America Latina y el Caribe* (Debate on women in Latin America and the Caribbean), Vol. 2, Bogota, ACEP, 1982.
12. Arizpe, L, and Aranda, J., "Women workers in the strawberry agribusiness in Mexico," in Leacock, Eleanor, and Safia, H. (compilers), *Women's Work*, South Badley, Bergin & Garvey, 1986. Barron, Antonieto, Mercados de trabajos rurales: El case de las hortalizas en Mexico (Rural labor markets: The case of market gardening in Mexico), doctorate thesis, Faculty of Economics, UNAM, 1993.
13. Pedrero, M. et. al., *op. cit.*, pp. 7–8. It should also be borne in mind that the number of women working in agriculture is greater than that reflected in the source under consideration, not only be-

cause of traditional problems of underrecording, which are referred to in all studies of the subject (especially in relation to unpaid family work), but also because of the marked seasonality of agricultural activity, as the authors cited point out, and because the date on which the survey was conducted was not the period of most intensive agricultural activity. According to this study, for this latter reason the last national population and housing census, conducted in 1990, also underestimated the economically active female population in agriculture and livestock farming activities.

14. Barron, A., *op. cit.*
15. INEGI and UNIFEM, "La mujer mexicana . . .," *op. cit.*, pp. 87-90.
16. INEGI and UNIFEM, "La mujer mexicana . . .," *op. cit.*, p. 78.
17. As an analysis of Mexico's current situation by the Organization for Economic Cooperation and Development, OECD Economic Surveys, Mexico, July 1995, states, "How long the adjustment will take is an open question."
18. Nominal devaluation together with inflation.
19. The accentuation of inequitable income distribution is one of the effects of the economic transformations that various economies in the world have experienced since the 1980s. This is apparent both in developed economies and in those at an intermediate level of development. In the United States, for example, from 1980 to 1992, the share of the 25 percent wealthiest families in national income rose from 48.2 to 51.3 percent, while that of the remaining three quartiles fell. See Fijii, Gerardo G., and Aguilar, Genaro G., "La distribución del ingreso en Mexico, 1984-1992: Un estudio de componentes," in *Foreign Trade Journal*, Mexico, August 1995, p. 609.
20. Banamex, "Examen . . .," *op. cit.*, p. 367.
21. Banamex, "Examen . . .," *op. cit.*, September 1995, p. 331.
22. Sarabia, Ernesto, "Las mujeres, las mas afectadas por el desempleo" (Women are most affected by unemployment), in *El Economista*, Mexico, July 18, 1995.
23. "El valor agregado de la maquila crecio 14.5 percent en ocho meses" (Added value of in-bond garment assembly rose by 14.5 percent in eight months), in *Excelsior*, Mexico, November 4, 1995.
24. Banamex, "Examen . . .," September 1995, p. 337.
25. The reference point is June 1995 as compared with the same month in 1994. Banamex, "Examen . . .," *op. cit.*, Mexico, September 1995, p. 333.
26. Banamex, "Examen . . .," *op. cit.*, Mexico, July 1995, p. 242.
27. Banamex, "Examen . . .," *op. cit.*, May 1995, p. 167.
28. Suárez Aguilar, Estela, "Mujer y marginalidad" (Women and marginality), in Bejar N., Raul and Hernandez B., Hector, *Población y desigualdad social* (Population and social inequality), CRIM-UNAN*, Mexico, 1993, Chapter XIII, pp. 372 et seq., and "Mujer y marginalidad" (Women and marginality) in *Debate Feminista*, Year 5, Vol. 9, March 1994, pp. 390 et seq.

X • The Rise of Conservatism in Its Various Forms — *Strategies*

Opening remarks

Sunera Thobani, Moderator
National Action Committee on the Status of
Women, Canada

In the last decade, the world has witnessed two very significant phenomena. The first of these is the rise of conservatism, in all its various forms. In some countries this has taken the form of religious fundamentalism; in others, we have seen the rise of fascist movements; and in others, we have seen the rise of the nonreligious right based on economic and social conservatism. The second phenomenon is the rise of the women's movement, at a national level in most parts of the world, and also as an organized political force at the international level.

These two phenomena are absolutely tied to each other; they are interrelated. As conservatism has grown, the women's movement has understood that this poses the greatest threat to women's liberation today. Our movements have correspondingly become more militant and radical, challenging this attack on our rights.

In Canada, which is the experience I will be speaking of this morning, the rise of conservatism is not explicitly tied to the religious right. Rather, it is in the form of the rise of economic conservatism. Governments at various levels have run huge deficits through a combination of massive tax breaks to corporations and the rich, and pursuing high interest rate policies which primarily benefit moneylenders. The relatively high levels of unemployment have also eroded the tax base, along with increasing demands on social spending as jobs have been destroyed.

Governments are now using this deficit as the rationale to destroy our social programs, and in the process, are destroying the gains women have made in the last two decades. Economic conservatism has launched the most serious attack on women's rights we have experienced since the end of the Second World War.

In Canada, the support for the rise of conservatism has also been mobilized through racism, by attacking the rights of people of color, and of immigrants and refugees. The scapegoating of immigrants and refugees by blaming them for the economic and political ills in the country, and the moves to destroy affirmative action programs and employment equity initiatives, have brought together different groups within Canadian society on a common platform, allowing conservatism a measure of support it would not otherwise enjoy.

So, for example, we have right-wing white-supremacist hate groups who organize against people of color and call for an end to immigration. We have a right-wing party, the Reform Party, which calls for drastic cuts to immigration levels, which has more support than the hate groups. We then have the media, which sensationalize and perpetuate stereotypes of immigrants and refugees as engaged in widespread fraud in the immigration system and in the social security system, and, in particular, perpetuate stereotypes of black men as criminals. The media are able to fashion a public response and pressure which reaches all sectors of Canadian society, and the outcome is that the Liberal government responds to this pressure by cutting back immigration and refugee intakes. Racism exists on a continuum, permeating all sectors of society, and liberal forces end up acting on a white-supremacist fascist agenda with massive public support. The alliance of these otherwise differing players is no more exceptional than, for example, the international alliances created as the Vatican comes together with Islamic fundamentalists to destroy the rights of women.

Whether the right today mobilizes to stop

women's access to abortion and to deny women sexual autonomy and control over our bodies, or whether the right mobilizes in the name of "family values" to fuel the homophobic attacks on the rights of lesbians and gays, or whether the right mobilizes in the name of "deficit reduction" to destroy women's access to housing, education, health care, and employment, it is the most serious threat today to democracy, peace, and development.

Whether it is in the name of religion, or culture, or, as in our case, the deficit, conservatism is committed to maintaining and strengthening patriarchal relations, as well as race- and class-based divisions.

The current phase of globalization is increasing economic inequalities, within our countries and also internationally between countries. The right's response to the social disintegration, as poverty and unemployment increase, is a tough "law and order" agenda. The people most hurt by these growing inequalities are scapegoated and criminalized. And so, in addition to privatization, the right calls for more prisons and tougher sentencing. Strengthening the repressive powers of the state becomes the order of the day.

And as the women's movement has fought back against these various forms of increasing oppression, we have become stronger, more radical. We are the most powerful force today for countering the rise of fundamentalism and fascism. In our countries, cities, and communities, it is the women's movement which is fighting against conservatism and for our rights.

Women have worked for increased control over our reproductive and sexual rights. In Canada, we have fought back against the increasing violence around abortion clinics, against homophobic attacks on lesbians and gays, and against other forms of both misogynist and racist violence. We are working to increase women's access to housing, education, health care, and employment.

As our governments are moving to the right, it is the women's movement which represents one of the most powerful, dynamic movements for social change and democracy today.

The presenters for this morning's panel will all address the strategies they have developed in their work to counter the rise of conservatism, and I welcome all three of them this morning.

Are women and men equal before Allah? The issue of gender justice in Islam

Riffat Hassan
University of Louisville, Kentucky, United States

Women such as Khadijah and 'A'ishah (wives of the Prophet Muhammad) and Rabi'a al-Basri (the outstanding woman Sufi) figure significantly in early Islam. Nonetheless, the Islamic tradition has by and large remained strongly patriarchal till today. This means, amongst other things, that the sources on which the Islamic tradition is based — mainly the Qur'an (which Muslims believe to be God's Word transmitted through the Angel Gabriel to the Prophet Muhammad), *Sunnah* (the practice of the Prophet Muhammad, *Hadith* (the oral traditions attributed to the Prophet Muhammad), and *Fiqh* (jurisprudence) — have been interpreted only by Muslim men, who have arrogated to themselves the task of defining the ontological, theological, sociological, and eschatological status of Muslim women. It is hardly surprising that up till now the majority of Muslim women, who have been kept for centuries in physical, mental, and emotional bondage, have accepted this situation passively. Here it needs to be mentioned that while the rate of literacy is low in many Muslim countries, the rate of literacy of Muslim women, especially those who live in rural areas, where most of the population lives, is amongst the lowest in the entire world.

In recent years, largely due to the pressure of the anti-women laws that have been promulgated under the cover of "Islamization" in some parts of the Muslim world, women with some degree of education and awareness are beginning to realize that religion is being used as an instrument of oppression rather than as a means of liberation. To understand the powerful impetus to Islamize Muslim societies, especially with regard to women-related norms and values, it is necessary to know that of all the challenges confronting the Muslim world, perhaps the greatest is that of modernity. Muslims in general tend to think of "modernity" in two ways: (a) as modernization, which is associated with science, technology, and material progress, and (b) as Westernization, which is associated with promiscuity and all kinds of social problems ranging from latch-key kids to drug and alcohol abuse. While "modernization" is considered highly desirable, "Westernization" is considered equally undesirable.

What is of importance to note here is that an emancipated Muslim woman is seen by many Muslims as a symbol, not of modernization, but of Westernization. This is so because she appears to be in violation of what traditional societies consider to be a necessary barrier between "private space," where women belong, and "public space," which belongs to men. The presence of women in men's space is considered to be highly dangerous, for, as a popular *hadith* states, whenever a man and a woman are alone, *ash-Shaitan* ("the Satan") is bound to be there. In today's Muslim world, due to the pressure of political and socioeconomic realities, a significant number of women may be seen in public space. Caretakers of Muslim traditionalism feel gravely threatened by this phenomenon, which they consider to be an onslaught of Westernization under the guise of modernization. They believe that it is necessary to put women back in their "space" (which also designates their "place") if "the integrity of the Islamic way of life" is to be preserved.

Though I began my study of theological issues pertaining to women in the Islamic tradition in 1974, it was not until 1983-84, when I spent almost two years in Pakistan, that my career as an activist began. The enactment of the *Hadud* Ordinance of 1979, according to which women's testimony was declared to be inadmissible in *Hadd* crimes, including the crime of rape, was accompanied by a wave of violence toward women and a deluge of anti-women literature that swept across the country. Many women in Pakistan were jolted out

of a dogmatic slumber by the Islamization of the legal system, which, through the promulgation of laws such as the *Hadud* Ordinance and the Law of Evidence of 1984 as well as the threat of other discriminatory legislation (such as the Law of *Qisas* and *Diyat*, or "blood money"), reduced their status systematically, virtually mathematically, to less than that of men. It soon became apparent that forces of religious conservatism were determined to cut women down to one-half or less of men, and that this attitude stemmed from a deep-rooted desire to keep women in their place, which means secondary, subordinate, and inferior to men.

Reflecting upon the scene I witnessed with increasing alarm and anxiety, I asked myself how it was possible for manifestly unjust laws to be implemented in a country which professed a passionate commitment to both Islam and modernity. The answer to my question was so obvious that I was startled that it had not struck me before. Pakistani society (or other Muslim societies) could enact or accept laws which specified that women were less than men in fundamental ways because Muslims, in general, consider it a self-evident truth that women are not equal to men. Among the "arguments" used to overwhelm any proponent of gender equality, the following are perhaps the most popular: that according to the Qur'an, men are *qawwamun* (generally translated as "rulers" or "managers") in relation to women[1]; that according to the Qur'an, a man's share in inheritance is twice that of a woman[2]; that according to the Qur'an, the witness of one man is equal to that of two women[3]; and that according to the Prophet, women are deficient both in prayer (due to menstruation) and in intellect (due to their witness counting for less than a man's).[4]

Since in all probability I was the only Muslim woman in the country who had been engaged in a study of women's issues from a nonpatriarchal, theological perspective, I was approached numerous times by women leaders (including the members of the Pakistan Commission on the Status of Women, before whom I gave my testimony in May 1984) to state what my findings were and whether they could be used to improve the situation of Pakistani women. I was urged by women activists, who were mobilizing and leading women's protests in a country under martial law, to help them refute the arguments which were being used against them, on a case-by-case or a point-by-point basis. Though I felt eager to help, I was not sure if the best strategy was simply to respond to each argument being used to deprive women of their human (as well as their Islamic) rights. What had to be done, first and foremost, in my opinion, was to examine the theological ground in which all the anti-women arguments were rooted to see if indeed a case could be made for asserting that from the point of view of normative Islam, men and women were *essentially* equal, despite biological and other differences.

As a result of further study and reflection, I came to perceive that in the Islamic, as well as in the Jewish and Christian, tradition, there are three theological assumptions on which the superstructure of men's alleged superiority to women has been erected. These three assumptions are: (1) that God's primary creation is man, not woman, since woman is believed to have been created from man's rib, and hence is derivative and secondary ontologically; (2) that woman, not man, was the primary agent of what is generally referred to as "the Fall" or man's expulsion from the Garden of Eden; hence all "daughters of Eve" are to be regarded with hatred, suspicion, and contempt; and (3) that woman was created not only *from* man but also *for* man, which makes her existence merely instrumental and not fundamental. The three theological questions to which the above assumptions may appropriately be regarded as answers are: (1) How was woman created? (2) Was woman responsible for the "Fall" of man? and (3) Why was woman created?

It is not possible, within the scope of this short paper, to deal exhaustively with any of the above-mentioned questions. However, in the brief discussion of each question which follows, an effort has been made to highlight the way in which sources of normative Islam have been interpreted to show that women are inferior to men.

How was woman created?

The ordinary Muslim believes, as seriously as the ordinary Jew or Christian, that Adam was God's primary creation and that Eve was made from Adam's rib. While this myth is obviously rooted in the Yahwist's account of creation in *Genesis* 2: 18-24, it has no basis whatever in the Qur'an, which describes the creation of humanity in completely egalitarian terms. In the 30 or so passages pertaining to the subject of human creation, the Qur'an uses generic terms for humanity (*an-nas, al-insan, bashar*), and there is no mention in it of Hawwa', or Eve. The word *Adam* occurs 25 times in the Qur'an, but it is used in 21 cases as a symbol for self-conscious humanity. Here it is pertinent to point out that the word *Adam* is a Hebrew word (from *adamah*, meaning "the soil"), and it functions generally as a collective noun referring to "the human" rather than to a male person. In the Qur'an, the word *Adam* (which Arabic borrowed from Hebrew) mostly does not refer to a particular human being. Rather, it refers to human beings in a particular way. As pointed out by Muhammad Iqbal:

> Indeed, in the verses which deal with the origin of man as a living being, the Qur'an uses the words *Bashar* or *Insan*, not *Adam*, which it reserves for man in his capacity of God's vice-regent on earth. The purpose of the Qur'an is further secured by the omission of proper names mentioned in the Biblical narration, Adam and Eve. The term *Adam* is retained and used more as a concept than as a name of a concrete human individual. The word is not without authority in the Qur'an itself.[5]

An analysis of the Qur'anic descriptions of human creation shows how the Qur'an evenhandedly uses both feminine and masculine terms and imagery to describe the creation of humanity from a single source. That God's original creation was undifferentiated humanity and not either man or woman (who appeared simultaneously at a subsequent time) is implicit in a number of Qur'anic passages. If the Qur'an makes no distinction between the creation of man and woman — as it clearly does not — why do Muslims believe that Hawwa' was created from Adam's rib? It is difficult to imagine that Muslims got this idea directly from *Genesis* 2, since very few Muslims read the Bible. It is much more likely that the rib story entered the Islamic tradition through being incorporated in the *Hadith* literature during the early centuries of Islam. In this context the following six *ahadith* are particularly important, since they are cited in *Sahih al-Bukhari* and *Sahih Muslim*, which Sunni Muslims regard as the two most authoritative *Hadith* collections and whose authority is exceeded only by the Qur'an:

• Treat women nicely, for a woman is created from a rib, and the most curved portion of the rib is its upper portion, so if you would try to straighten it, it will break, but if you leave it as it is, it will remain crooked. So treat women nicely.[6]

• The woman is like a rib; if you try to straighten her, she will break. So if you want to get benefit from her, do so while she still has some crookedness.[7]

• Whoever believes in Allah and the Last Day should not hurt [trouble] his neighbour. And I advise you to take care of the women, for they are created from a rib and the most crooked part of the rib is its upper part; if you try to straighten it, it will break, and if you leave it, it will remain crooked, so I urge you to take care of woman.[8]

• Woman is like a rib. When you attempt to straighten it, you would break it. And if you leave her alone you would benefit by her, and crookedness will remain in her.[9]

• Woman has been created from a rib and will in no way be straightened for you; so if you wish to benefit by her, benefit by her while crookedness remains in her. And if you attempt to straighten her, you will break her, and breaking her is divorcing her.[10]

• He who believes in Allah and the Hereafter, if he witnesses any matter he should talk in good terms about it or keep quiet. Act kindly toward women, for woman is created from a rib, and the most crooked part of the rib is its top. If you attempt to straighten it, you will break it, and if you leave it, its crookedness will remain there, so act kindly toward women.[11]

Elsewhere in my writings I have examined the above ahadith and shown them to be weak with regards to their formal aspect (i.e., with reference to their *isnad*, or "list of transmitters"). As far as their content, or *matn*, is concerned, it is obviously in opposition to the Qur'anic accounts about human creation.

Since all Muslim scholars agree on the principle that any *hadith* which is in contradiction to the Qur'an cannot be accepted as authentic, the above-mentioned *ahadith* ought to be rejected on material grounds. However, they still continue to be a part of the Islamic tradition.

This is due certainly, in significant measure, to the fact that they are included in the *Hadith* collections by Muhammad ibn Isma'it al-Bukhari (810-870) and Muslim bin al-Hallaj (817-875), collectively known as the Sahihan (from *sahih*, meaning "sound" or "authentic"), which "form an almost unassailable authority, subject indeed to criticisms in details, yet deriving an indestructible influence from the *ijma*, or general consent of the community in custom and belief, which it is their function to authenticate."[12]

But the continuing popularity of these *ahadith* amongst Muslims in general also indicates that they articulate something deeply embedded in Muslim culture, namely, the belief that women are derivative and secondary in the context of human creation.

Theologically, the history of women's inferior status in the Islamic (as well as the Jewish and Christian) tradition began with the story of Hawwa's creation from a (crooked) rib. Changing her status requires returning to the point of creation and setting the record straight. Given the way the rib story has been used, it is impossible to overemphasize its importance. The issue of woman's creation is more fundamental theologically than any other. This is so because if man and woman have been created equal by God, who is the ultimate giver of value, then they cannot become unequal, essentially, at a subsequent time.

On the other hand, if man and woman have been created unequal by God, then they cannot become equal, essentially, at a subsequent time. If one upholds the view that man and woman were created equal by God — which is the teaching of the Qur'an — then the existing inequality between men and women cannot be seen as having been mandated by God but must be seen as a subversion of God's original plan for humanity.

Was woman responsible for the "Fall" of man?

Muslims, like Jews and Christians, generally answer the above question affirmatively, though such an answer is not warranted by the Qur'an. Here it needs to be pointed out that the Qur'anic account of the Fall episode differs significantly from the Biblical account.

To begin with, whereas in *Genesis* 3 no explanation is given as to why the serpent tempts either Eve alone or both Adam and Eve, in the Qur'an the reason why ash-Shaitan (or *Iblis*) sets out to beguile the human pair in the Garden is stated clearly in a number of passages.[13] The refusal of ash-Shaitan to obey God's command to bow in submission to Adam follows from his belief that being a creature of fire he is elementally superior to Adam, who is an earth-creature. When condemned for his arrogance by God and ordered to depart in a state of abject disgrace, ash-Shaitan throws a challenge to God: he will prove to God that Adam and Adam's progeny are ungrateful, weak, and easily lured by temptations and thus unworthy of the honour conferred on them by God. Not attempting to hide his intentions to come upon human beings from all sides, ash-Shaitan asks for — and is granted — a reprieve until "The Day of the Appointed Time." Not only is the reprieve granted, but God also tells ash-Shaitan to use all his wiles and forces to assault human beings and see if they would follow him. A cosmic drama now begins, involving the eternal opposition between the principles of good and evil, which is lived out as human beings, exercising their moral autonomy, choose between "the straight path" and "the crooked path."

In terms of the Qur'anic narrative, what happens to the human pair in the Garden is a sequel to the interchange between God and ash-Shaitan. In the sequel we learn that the human pair have been commanded not to go near the Tree lest they become *zalimin*. Seduced by ash-Shaitan, they disobey God. However, in Surah 7: *Al-A'raf:* 23 they acknowledge before God that they have done *zulm* to themselves and earnestly seek God's forgiveness and mercy. They are told to "go forth" and "descend" from the Garden, but in addressing them the Qur'an uses the dual form of address only once (in Surah 18: *Ta-Ha:* 123); for the rest the plural form is used, which necessarily refers to more than two persons and is generally understood as referring to humanity as a whole.

In the framework of Qur'anic theology, the order to go forth from the Garden given to Adam or the Children of Adam cannot be considered a punishment because Adam was always meant to be God's vice-regent on earth (Surah 2: *Al-Baqarah:* 30). The earth is not a place of banishment but is declared by the Qur'an to be humanity's dwelling place and source of profit.[14]

There is, strictly speaking, no Fall in the Qur'an. What the Qur'anic narration focuses on is the moral choice that humanity is required to make when confronted by the alternatives presented by God and ash-Shaitan.

This becomes clear if one reflects on Surah 2: *Al-Baqarah:* 35 and Surah 7: *Al-A'raf:* 19, in which it is stated: "You [dual] go not near this Tree, lest you [dual] become the *zalimin*." In other words, the human pair is being told that if they go near the Tree, then they will be counted amongst those who perpetrate zulm. Commenting on the root *zulm*, Toshihiko Izutsu says:

> The primary meaning of ZLM is, in the opinion of many authoritative lexicologists, that of "putting in a wrong place." In the moral sphere it seems to mean primarily "to act in such a way as to transgress the proper limit and encroach upon the right of some other person." Briefly and generally speaking *zulm* is to do injustice in the sense of going beyond one's bounds and doing what one has no right to.[15]

By transgressing the limits set by God, the human pair became guilty of *zulm* toward themselves. This *zulm* consists in their taking on the responsibility for choosing between good and evil. As pointed out by Iqbal:

The Qur'anic legend of the Fall has nothing to do with the first appearance of man on this planet. Its purpose is rather to indicate man's rise from a primitive state of instinctive appetite to the conscious possession of a free self, capable of doubt and disobedience. The Fall does not mean any moral depravity; it is man's transition from simple consciousness to the first flash of self-consciousness ... Nor does the Qur'an regard the earth as a torture-hall where an elementally wicked humanity is imprisoned for an original act of sin. Man's first act of disobedience was also his first act of free choice; and that is why, according to the Qur'anic narration, Adam's first transgression was forgiven ... A being whose movements are wholly determined like a machine cannot produce goodness. Freedom is thus a condition of goodness. But to permit the emergence of a finite ego who has the power to choose ... is really to take a great risk; for the freedom to choose good involves also the freedom to choose what is the opposite of good. That God has taken this risk shows His immense faith in man; it is now for man to justify this faith.[16]

Even though there is no Fall or Original Sin in the Qur'an, the association of the episode described in *Genesis* 3 with fallen humanity and illicit sexuality, which has played such a massive role in perpetuating the myth of feminine evil in the Christian tradition, also exists in the minds of many Muslims and has had extremely negative impact on the lives of millions of Muslim women. The following comment of A.A. Maududi — one of contemporary Islam's most influential scholars — is representative of the thinking of many, if not most, Muslims:

The sex instinct is the greatest weakness of the human race. That is why Satan selected this weak spot for his attack on the adversary and devised the scheme to strike at their modesty. Therefore the first step he took in this direction was to expose their nakedness to them so as to open the door to indecency before them and beguile them into sexuality. Even to this day, Satan and his disciples are adopting the same scheme of depriving the woman of the feelings of modesty and shyness, and they cannot think of any scheme of "progress" unless they expose and exhibit the woman to all and sundry.[17]

Though the branding of women as "the devil's gateway"[18] is not at all the intent of the Qur'anic narration of the Fall story, Muslims, no less than Jews and Christians, have used the story to vent their misogynistic feelings. This is clear from the continuing popularity of ahadith such as the following:

The prophet said, "After me I have not left any afflictions more harmful to men than women."[19]

Ibn Abbas reported that Allah's Messenger said: "I had a chance to look into Paradise and I found that the majority of the people were poor and I looked into the Fire and there I found the majority constituted by women."[20]

Abu Sa'id Khudri reported that Allah's Messenger said: "The world is sweet and green [alluring] and verily Allah is going to install you as vice-regent in it in order to see how you act. So avoid the allurement of women: verily the first trial for the people of Isra'il was caused by women."[21]

Why was woman created?

The Qur'an, which does not discriminate against women in the context of creation or the Fall episode, does not support the view held by many Muslims, Christians, and Jews that women were created not only *from* man but also *for* man. That God's creation as a whole is "for just ends" (Surah 15: *Al-Hijr:* 85) and not "for idle sport" (Surah 21: *Al-Anbiya:* 16) is one of the major themes of the Qur'an. Humanity, consisting of both men and women, is fashioned "in the best of moulds" (Surah 95: *At-Tin:* 4) and is called to righteousness which requires the honouring of *Haquq Allah* ("the

Rights of God") as well as *Haquq al-'ibad* ("the Rights of creatures"). Not only does the Qur'an make it clear that man and woman stand absolutely equal in the sight of God, but also that they are "members" and "protectors" of each other. In other words, the Qur'an does not create a hierarchy in which men are placed above women nor does it pit men against women in an adversarial relationship. They are created as equal creatures of a universal, just, and merciful God whose pleasure it is that they live together in harmony and righteousness.

In spite of the Qur'anic affirmation of man-woman equality, Muslim societies in general have never regarded men and women as equal, particularly in the context of marriage. Fatima Mernissi has aptly observed:

One of the distinctive characteristics of Muslim sexuality is its territoriality, which reflects a specific division of labour and specific conception of society and of power. The territoriality of Muslim sexuality sets ranks, tasks, and authority patterns. Spatially confined, the woman was taken care of materially by the man who possessed her, in return for her total obedience and her sexual and reproductive services. The whole system was organized so that the Muslim *ummah* was actually a society of citizens who possessed among other things the female half of the population ... Muslim men have always had more rights and privileges than Muslim women, including even the right to kill their women ... The man imposed on the woman an artificially narrow existence, both physically and spiritually.[22]

Underlying the rejection in Muslim societies of the idea of man-woman equality is the deeply rooted belief that women — who are inferior in creation (having been made from a crooked rib) and in righteousness (having helped ash-Shaitan in defeating God's plan for Adam) — have been created mainly to be of use to men, who are superior to them. The alleged superiority of men to women which permeates the Islamic (as well as the Jewish and Christian) tradition is grounded not only in

Hadith literature but also in popular interpretations of some Qur'anic passages. Two Qur'anic passages — Surah 4: *An-Nisa':* 34 and Surah 2: *Al-Baqarah:* 288 in particular — are generally cited to support the contention that men have "a degree of advantage" over women. Of these, the first reads as follows in A.A. Maududi's translation of the Arabic text:

Men are the managers of the affairs of women because Allah has made the one superior to the other and because men spend of their wealth on women. Virtuous women are, therefore, obedient; they guard their rights carefully in their absence under the care and watch of Allah. As for those women whose defiance you have cause to fear, admonish them and keep them apart from your beds and beat them. Then, if they submit to you, do not look for excuses to punish them; note it well that there is Allah above you, who is Supreme and Great.[23]

It is difficult to overstate the negative impact which the popular Muslim understanding of the above verse has had on the lives of Muslim women. Elsewhere in my work I have done detailed analysis of this verse to show how it has been misinterpreted.

For instance, the key word in the first sentence is *qawwamun.* This word is most often translated as *hakim,* or "rulers." By making men rulers over women, a hierarchy akin to the one created by St. Paul and his followers in the Christian tradition is set up in the Islamic ummah. Linguistically the word *qawwamun* refers to those who provide a means of support or livelihood. In my exegesis of this verse I have argued that the function of supporting women economically has been assigned to men in the context of childbearing — a function which can be performed only by women.

The intent of this verse is not to give men power over women but rather to ensure that while women are performing the important tasks of childbearing and child-raising, they do not have the additional responsibility of being breadwinners as well. The root-word *daraba,* which has generally been translated as "beating," is one of the commonest root-words in the Arabic language, with a large number of possible meanings. That the vast majority of translators — who happen all to be men — have chosen to translate this word as "beating" clearly indicates a bias in favour of a male-controlled, male-oriented society.

The second Qur'anic passage which is cited to support the idea that men are superior to women is in the specific context of 'iddat — a three-month waiting period prescribed for women between the pronouncement of divorce and remarriage. The "advantage" men have in this regard is that they do not have to observe this waiting period, due to the fact that, unlike women, they do not become pregnant. (The three-month waiting period is to make certain that the woman is not pregnant.) That the intent of this verse is to ensure justice is made clear by its emphasis that "women shall have rights similar to the rights against them, according to what is equitable."

The reading of the Qur'an through the lens of the Hadith is, in my opinion, a major reason for the misreading and misinterpretation of many passages which have been used to deny women equality and justice. The following *hadith* is often cited to elevate man to the status of *majazi khuda* ("god in earthly form"):

A man came ... with his daughter and said, "This my daughter refuses to get married." The Prophet said, "Obey your father." She said, "By the name of Him Who sent you in truth, I will not marry until you inform me what is the right of the husband over his wife." He said, " ... If it were permitted for one human being to bow down [*sajada*] to another I would have ordered the woman to bow down to her husband when he enters into her, because of God's grace on her." The daughter answered, "By the name of Him Who sent you, with truth, I would never marry!"[24]

A faith as rigidly monotheistic as Islam, which makes *shirk*, or association of anyone with God, the one unforgivable sin, cannot conceivably permit any human being to worship anyone but God. However, this hadith makes it appear that if not God's, it was at least the Prophet's, wish to make the wife prostrate herself before her husband. Since each word, act, or exhortation of the Prophet is held to be sacred by Muslims in general, this hadith has had much impact on Muslim women. How such a hadith could be attributed to the Prophet who regarded the principle of *Tauhid* ("Oneness of God") as the basis of Islam, is, of course, utterly shocking.

In summation

Reference has been made in the foregoing account to the fundamental theological assumptions which have coloured the way in which Muslim culture in general has viewed women. That these assumptions have had serious negative consequences and implications — both theoretical and practical — for Muslim women throughout Muslim history up till the present time needs to be emphasized.

At the same time, it needs to be borne in mind that the Qur'an, which to Muslims in general is the most authoritative source of Islam, does not discriminate against women despite the sad and bitter fact of history that the cumulative (Jewish, Christian, Hellenistic, Bedouin, and other) biases which existed in the Arab-Islamic culture of the early centuries of Islam infiltrated the Islamic tradition, largely through the Hadith literature, and undermined the intent of the Qur'an to liberate women from the status of chattel or inferior creatures, making them free and equal to men. Not only does the Qur'an emphasize that righteousness is identical in the case of man or woman, but it affirms, clearly and consistently, women's equality with men and their fundamental right to actualize the human potential that they share equally with men. In fact, when seen through a nonpatriarchal lens, the Qur'an goes beyond egalitarianism. It exhibits particular solicitude toward women as also toward other classes of disadvantaged persons. Further, it provides particular safeguards for protecting women's special sexual/biological functions such as carrying, delivering, suckling, and rearing offspring.

God, who speaks through the Qur'an, is characterized by justice, and it is stated clearly in the Qur'an that God can never be guilty of *zulm* (unfairness, tyranny, oppression, or wrongdoing). Hence the Qur'an, as God's Word, cannot be made the source of human injustice, and the injustice to which Muslim women have been subjected cannot be regarded as God-derived.

The goal of Qur'anic Islam is to establish peace, which can exist only within a just environment. Here it is of importance to note that there is more Qur'anic legislation pertaining to the establishment of justice in the context of family relationships than on any other subject.

This points to the assumption implicit in much Qur'anic legislation, namely, that if human beings can learn to order their homes justly so that the rights of all within them — children, women, men — are safeguarded, then they can also justly order their society and the world at large. In other words, the Qur'an regards the home as a microcosm of the ummah and the world community, and emphasizes the importance of making it "the abode of peace" through just living.

In my judgment, the importance of developing what the West calls feminist theology in the context of the Islamic tradition is paramount today in order to liberate not only Muslim women, but also Muslim men, from unjust structures and systems of thought, which make a peer relationship between men and women impossible.

It is good to know that in the last hundred years there have been at least two significant Muslim male scholars and activists — Qasim Amin from Egypt and Mumtaz 'Ali from India — who have been staunch advocates of women's rights, though knowing this fact hardly lessens the pain of also knowing that even in this age characterized by an explosion of knowledge, all but a handful of Muslim women lack any knowledge of Islamic theology.

It is profoundly discouraging to contemplate how few Muslim women there are in the world today who possess the competence, even if they have the courage and commitment, to engage in a scholarly study of Islam's primary sources in order to participate in the theological discussions on women-related issues which are taking place in most contemporary Muslim societies. Such participation is imperative if Qur'anic Islam, which guarantees gender justice and equity, is to emerge in Muslim societies and communities.

Notes

1. Reference is made here to Surah 4: *An-Nisa':* 34.
2. Reference is made here to Surah 4: *An-Nisa':* 11.
3. Reference is made here to Surah 2: *Al-Baqarah:* 282.
4. Reference is made here to *ahadith* (plural of *hadith*, meaning "an oral tradition") cited in *Sahih al-Bukhari* and *Sahih Muslim*.
5. Iqbal, Muhammad, *The Reconstruction of Religious Thought in Islam*, Lahore: Shaikh Muhammad Ashraf, 1962, p. 83.
6. Khan, M.M., translation of *Sahih Al-Bukhari*, Lahore: Kazi Publications, 1971, p. 346.
7. Khan, M.M., p. 80.
8. Khan, M.M., p. 81.
9. Siddiqui, A.H., translation of *Sahih Muslim*, vol. 2, Lahore: Shaikh Muhammad Ashraf, 1972, p. 752.
10. Siddiqui, p. 752.
11. Siddiqui, pp. 752-53.
12. Guillaume, Alfred, *The Traditions of Islam*, Beirut: Khayats, 1966, p. 32.
13. For instance, see Surah 15: *Al-Hijr:* 26-43; Surah 17: *Bani Isra'il:* 61-64; Surah 18: *Al-Kahf:* 50; and Surah 38: *Sad:* 71-85.
14. Iqbal, p. 84.
15. Izutsu, Toshihiko, *The Structure of Ethical Terms in the Koran*, Mita, Siba, Minatoku, Tokyo: Keio Institute of Philosophical Studies, 1959, pp. 152-53.
16. Iqbal, p. 85.
17. Maududi, A.A., *The Meaning of the Qur'an*, vol. 2, Lahore: Islamic Publications Ltd., 1976, p. 16, n. 13.
18. This expression comes from Tertullian (A.D. 160-225), a Church Father from North Africa who wrote: "And do you not know that you are [each] an Eve? The sentence of God on this sex of yours lives in this age: the guilt must of necessity live too. You are the devil's gateway; you are the unsealer of that [forbidden] tree: you are the first deserter of the divine law, you are she who persuaded him whom the devil was not valiant enough to attack. You destroyed so easily God's image, man. On account of your desert — that is, death — even the Son of God had to die." From *De culte feminarum* 1.1, cited in Swilder, Leonard, *Biblical Affirmations of Woman*, Philadelphia: The Westminster Press, 1979, p. 346.

19. Khan, M.M., p. 22.
20. Siddiqui, p. 1431.
21. Siddiqui, p. 1431.
22. Mernissi, Fatima, *Beyond the Veil*, Cambridge: Schenkman Publishing Company, 1975, p. 103.
23. Maududi, A.A., *The Meaning of the Qur'an*, vol. 1, Lahore: Islamic Publications Ltd., 1971, p. 321.
24. Khan, Sadiq Hassan, *Husn al-Uswa*, p. 281.

Strategies from a lesbian perspective — the ethic of diversity

Rebeca Sevilla
International Lesbian and Gay Association, Peru

I am Rebeca Sevilla from Peru — and lesbian everywhere.

I am also a native Spanish speaker. But today I speak English because not everyone has headphones. I want to speak about the ethic of diversity, which is to meet each other halfway. So I will speak English. *Estoy segura que mis compañeras comprendan el sentido de esta decision para hacerlo en otro idioma.*

The rise of conservatism

Look at this issue through lesbian eyes. For lesbians the oppression has always been high. Lesbians usually live invisible, silent, secret lives. Sometimes lesbians lived openly for a time, but then soon came witch hunts, concentration camps, electric shock treatment ... and social rejection. Today we are speaking out. Not because there is less conservatism, but because there is a stronger women's movement. And a stronger lesbian movement.

Let's have a look at the United Nations world conferences on women. In Mexico in 1975 lesbians spoke out but were criticized by some feminist sisters. Too many women were at that time afraid to be labeled and discredited as lesbians.

In Copenhagen in 1980 lesbians organized informal workshops. A photographer caught some women sunbathing topless in a private garden. The photo became world-famous, with the caption "Lesbians in Copenhagen." Should we conclude that all women sunbathing topless are lesbians?

Before Nairobi in 1985, because of this photo, there was trouble about lesbians attending. But the International Lesbian Information Service (ILIS) was part of the NGO Forum program, and for the first time the lesbian issue was raised by a Dutch minister at the official UN conference.

Before Beijing the same story reemerged. There were rumors that lesbians would be refused visas, newspaper reports that the Chinese were most worried about lesbians taking off their tops and kissing each other. Police women were supposedly especially trained and issued with sheets to quickly throw over any such disturbance. (We lesbians do actually like to take off our clothes, kiss, and ... but mostly in private.)

Now we do have our own tent — and are also invited into major panels and commissions. Sexual rights are an important lobbying issue in the final UN document. This is a positive story, a story of gain for the lesbian movement — but also a story of the conservative reaction.

And here?

• Newspapers in China and elsewhere focused on the lesbian issue in a negative way. Lesbian information material in Chinese was removed from the tent.

• The European/North American tent did not want to announce a lesbian workshop, *but*

• The Cyprus tent invited the entire lesbian caucus to join their party.

• Young Chinese volunteers were interviewed — and said they knew from the Hite report that homosexuality exists, that they had learned a lot from the lesbian tent — and that lesbians are humans and that repression is not a solution.

The analysis

In fact, this Beijing conference — both the NGO Forum and the official UN Conference — is about the political battle between progressive and conservative forces. In all issues,

• human rights — violence against women
• economic issues — exploitation of women
• education, health, development issues
• reproductive rights — or oppressive family planning
• the Holy See as just one of thousands of NGOs — or as a major influence?

And being honest, there are some conservative forces within the women's movement too.

It is not so easy to know these days who is conservative and who is progressive. More economic and political insecurity means more fear — and therefore more fundamentalism. Women are the topic over which progressive and conservative forces are fighting. Can we control our own lives and our own bodies? Can we choose our own sexuality? The lesbian issue evokes tremendous emotional reaction, conservative backlash, because it is (quite correctly) the symbol of women's freedom and independence.

So often we hear that lesbianism is a "Western disease" that is "caught" by Southern women. But a look in their own histories shows that in all cultures and countries lesbians popped up every now and then. Today lesbian groups are active on all continents and in most countries in the world.

It is not Europe or the United States, but South Africa which has the most progressive legislation, with laws against discrimination and the possibility for lesbians and gays to adopt children. Nelson Mandela, the ANC, and the Lesbian and Gay Coalition worked together and understood that democracy also means fighting gender-apartheid and homophobia.

Most lesbians have to discover their own feelings in isolation, without information or role models. Many lesbians reject their own feelings at first. In cultures where women suffer clitoridectomy, incest, or arranged marriage, women have little or no control over their own lives or bodies. But still, we know, women love women everywhere — under any social, economic, or political condition. And now we are speaking out internationally about our lesbian lives, our lesbian love.

We are learning to be proud, not ashamed.

We are learning to be visible and loud, not secret.

We are not satisfied with a lesbian tent; we want to be included in the political agenda.

And therefore the conservative backlash

Of course, then, we can expect a conservative backlash — not only because of the general rise in religious, cultural, and economic fundamentalism, but because we lesbians are the *symbol* of the battle between the sexes, the symbol of the independent, autonomous woman. We do not need men. I am a lesbian. I have good friends who are men. But emotionally and sexually I prefer women.

This makes some men and some conservative political movements very nervous indeed. Because if women can choose to be lesbian, how then to control us?

And yes, it does also make some women nervous. Why? Because lesbians challenge any woman to think about her own choices and her own sexuality. How many of you today have been able to explore your own sexuality, to discover for yourself what you like or dislike? Young women, the next generation, can take this issue further and hopefully claim more freedom.

Solutions and strategies

I want to ask all women and progressive men to realize that democracy should be based on respect for differences, respect for different choices in life. Women's rights are sexual rights; therefore lesbian rights are human rights.

I want to introduce a new concept to you. I call it *the ethic of diversity*. We are all so different at this conference, from so many backgrounds. In order to avoid international conflict, in order to start solving problems in this world, we must develop an ethic of diversity. We need to meet — but more than that, to get to know each other, to ask each other questions. We need to discover what we have in common — but particularly to respect our differences. We need to put effort into meeting each other halfway and into learning from each other.

The ethic of diversity is different from religious ethics or political values, which we hear so much about, because the ethic of diversity does not claim one truth but aims to deal with differences, to respect and accept. The daily practice of this ethic means that we build networks and organizations which include everyone: indigenous women, Western women, straights, lesbians, bisexuals, women with visible or invisible abilities, migrants or refugees, rich women or poor women, women with AIDS — in fact, any of us. An ethic of diversity means building a culture of respect. That is a rich culture which will allow us to find new solutions to old problems, new solutions based on agreement and peace, not on fights. The ethic of diversity is a strong strategy to stop conservatism, because conservatism is based on fear, on greed, and on divisions between people. Developing an ethic of diversity — and especially a daily practice — is our challenge.

But I want to share with you something which worries me: Too many religions and political or economic systems have preached freedom but practiced oppression. The women's movement, too, sometimes shows seeds of intolerance, jealousy, and disrespect.

And now back to lesbian rights and some strategies:

• If you are a teacher, talk about sexual diversity and different lifestyles.

• If you are a health worker, don't assume that everyone is heterosexual. Ask me whether men or contraceptives are relevant topics for me.

• If you are working on human rights, work on the issue of women's rights and lesbian rights and violence.

• If you are working with media, include realistic reports about various aspects of lesbian life.

• If you are a lesbian, come out and speak out. And make a link with others, with other diversity issues. Lesbians have multiple identities.

• If you are involved in politics, fight this week, and in your own country, to ensure that sexual rights are part of any constitution — and that local, national, and international laws fight against homophobia instead of supporting it.

• If you are interested, join our Lesbian Parade tomorrow. Of course, this last strategy will not stop all conservatism, but I'm sure you'll enjoy it.

But remember, we don't want a tent or a parade. We want sexual rights — in all political documents, and in practice.

Conservatism within the Catholic tradition

Frances Kissling
Catholics for a Free Choice, United States

I am here to speak of conservatism within the Catholic tradition. The most important strategy to combat conservatism has begun and is exemplified in this very meeting — that is, to be open, to talk about the problems. The fact that the NGO Organizing Committee and the NGO Forum have recognized this problem is really the very first step that we need to take as women. They are to be applauded for this decision.

It is not easy for those of us as women and as justice-loving people sometimes to challenge the conservatism that is among us, for that conservatism often expresses itself in ways that are intolerant, violent, silencing, and provocative. But we need to stand firm, and we need to move forward on this question.

I come from the Roman Catholic tradition, and in some ways, talking about the rise of conservatism seems to me to be an anomaly, for there has always been conservatism within Roman Catholicism. There has also always been within Roman Catholicism a liberation perspective at the root of our church.

For me, the more interesting question is why governments tend to support the conservative side of religious thinking and to degrade and ignore the liberation side of conservative thinking. Why do conservatives in politics and religion seem to go together?

The second interesting question for me is — and I just want to raise these questions because, part of what we want to do is to dialogue with each other in this room and also out in the halls and the corridors and the streets, and we need to ask critical questions, and to know that we don't have all the answers — Why is it that conservativism always includes the attempt to control women's lives? Whether it is religious, political or cultural, there is always the attempt to rein in women.

The word "conservative" could be good or bad.

There are many things I want to conserve as a Roman Catholic feminist. I want to conserve respect for the moral capacity of women to make good decisions about every aspect of their lives. I want to conserve what I see as the vision of the way Jesus Christ operated in the world, including his respect, inclusion, and friendship with women and many different types of women. But when the Vatican in its present form talks about conservativism, what it wants to conserve is patriarchy, and this we cannot permit.

All of history is not good, and we need not conserve that which represents injustice, intolerance, discrimination, and degradation of women. In that sense, I want to talk about some of the strategies and some of the organizing principles that we at Catholics for a Free Choice operate by. I offer them as our way and our path, and I am sure that we all have much to add to this and that these are not strategies which work for everyone. In fact, that is the first principle, and I think Rebeca Sevilla spoke about this very compellingly. We are diverse; we have different backgrounds; we have different personalities; we have different gifts; and each of us needs to bring our gifts and our personalities and our inclinations into our political work, and we need to respect those who have different gifts than ours. That is the first principle that we try to work by.

The second principle is that, particularly in the Roman Catholic tradition, the other thing the church wishes to conserve is secrecy. Injustice and intolerance operate best in the dark. It is our job as feminists to take that injustice out of darkness and expose it to the light of day. For centuries, women and men in the church who speak for justice and who go against the current church thinking of their times are punished and suffer in silence. Indeed, our religious leaders are trained to submit: submission — supposedly to the will of God, but most often to the will of men — is ingrained in the early education of religious leaders within Catholicism.

We have learned that this works against freedom. For example, two years ago in Brazil, a Roman Catholic nun spoke out in a magazine and said, "Abortion is not a sin." She also said that because she believed in the preferential option for the poor, because she has committed her life to the poor, she is in favor of poor women's and all women's ability to make decisions about their reproductive health. She did this in a forthright, straightforward way. She is on her way to Belgium, punished by the Vatican. She is an eminent feminist theologian who has been told by the Vatican that she doesn't understand theology. They are sending her off from Brazil to Belgium to study theology. Can she learn theology only in Europe? Is there no theology in Brazil? Is she not wiser than these Belgian theologians? And she has been told that for two years she cannot write, she cannot speak in public, she cannot express her views. But we are here to serve as her voice and to let you know that she has been punished.

We also need in our struggles — and I think this is something the women's movement has learned very well — we need to use the media. This is another way of bringing injustice to light. The media is interested in our lives, maybe for good reasons, maybe for bad reasons, and it reaches billions and billions of people. We must be public in our disagreements, in our dissent, and in putting forward our positions. I have learned, as I have watched the Vatican operate in the last two years in various conferences, from the Rio conference on environment, to the population conference in Cairo, and to this very Conference we are at today, that the person who gets to shape the debate rules the discourse.

It is our obligation not simply to respond to the ridiculous charges about women by those who disagree with us, but to put forward the correct questions, to guide the media, government, and indeed, each other, by going to the root of these differences and asking the right questions. Why does conservativism, or patriarchy, or religious fundamentalism seek to control women's lives? We need to ask that question.

The other thing we need to do, and we know this for those of us who have tried all of our lives to move through and in society and to have a voice and to have power — and power is not a dirty word — we are entitled, we are responsible and obligated, to exercise power as women who work for justice. We need to do solid research. Our research and our scholarship needs to be impeccably accurate. One mistake and we will hear about that mistake forever. We put out 100 accurate statements, and one error condemns us. So we need to do something. We need to be perfect, or in this sense as near perfect as we can.

We also need to accept our imperfections, something that the hierarchy of the Roman Catholic Church seems to have great difficulty in doing. I often think that our biggest mistake is to put forward the vision of an omnipotent or perfect God. Indeed, if we understood the frailty of God, perhaps we would be more respectful of the frailty of human beings. In terms of the impeccableness of our research, we need to do that also in terms of history — which we at Catholics for a Free Choice have done. This helps us to challenge the statements of the Vatican. How many people really know that the Roman Catholic Church has no position on when the fetus becomes a person? The Church does not know, any more than anyone in this room knows. But such misinformation on the part of the Vatican leads to absolutism in terms of women's lives.

How many of us know that the Church is willing to give more latitude to politicians, to generals, to soldiers in deciding when and whether to take life and no latitude to women in deciding when and whether an abortion will be appropriate? How many of us know the lies the Vatican has put forward at this Conference? The Pope's spokesperson, Navarro Val, states that the document does not contain the word "mother," that the document is negative on the family. We need to publish the reality about the document and about women.

The next thing we need to do is not be divided. We are different; we work on different issues; we work in different forums. Some women have chosen to work within systems; some women have chosen to work outside systems. But we need to understand in terms of issues that all our issues are related. I say to Rebeca, the homophobia we see in the world, the hatred of lesbians, is rooted in the same hatred about women who choose to have abortions or use contraception. It is rooted in a principle that says the only purpose of sexuality is procreation, and that to seek pleasure in sexuality, to seek unity, to seek growth, to seek affection and love, to express commitment and ideals is not adequate without the willingness and the desire to procreate. I say this is a bankrupt principle that should not be conserved.

Finally, or close to finally, we need to listen to those who disagree with us, and those who disagree with us need to learn to listen to us. The hallmark of mature difference is the ability to recognize what is good in the positions and arguments of those who disagree with you. It is not to stereotype and mischaracterize the position of many. This is difficult, and we have tried hard to do this at Catholics for a Free Choice.

Finally, and next to finally, we need to commit to religious freedom. We are all free to find our spiritual paths, and we need governments that will permit us to do that. At the same time, we need to be sure that we do not allow those with narrow or even specific, even good, religious views to impose those views on all of us through the use of state power. We do not need to attack religion in order to be clear in saying that the role of government is to make it possible for all of us to practice our faith and to express our spirituality without state interference. We must be committed to that.

Here we must be committed to understanding that the Vatican sits in this body as a government, and that it is a religion. I respect it as a religion. I invite it to participate in the NGO Forum where it belongs. But I say it does not belong at the table of the United Nations. And now I want to quote John Paul II, the Pope. The hallmark of his papacy, the phrase that he used most often when he was installed as Pope and throughout his papacy, has been: "Be not afraid." I support that. We must not be afraid to speak the truth as we see it. We must not be afraid to take difficult positions. We must not be afraid of being marginalized. We must be courageous.

Now I quote Sister Teresa Kane, a Roman Catholic nun, who said, "The core of courage is rage." Let us also not be afraid of our anger. It is not wrong to be angry in the face of injustice. In fact, it would be a terrible shame to never experience righteous anger at the horrible injustices that we see in the world. If we can be courageous, if we can be open, we indeed can begin to conserve that which is good, that which is justice-seeking. And we can begin to defeat that which oppresses us.

Building a new house

Bisi Adeleye-Fayemi
Akina Mama wa Afrika at the London Women's
Centre, United Kingdom

They may allow us temporarily to beat him at his own game, but they will never enable us to bring about genuine change.

—from "The Master's Tools Will Never Dismantle the Master's House," Audre Lorde (1934–1993)

For us to be able to talk about strategies for dealing with the rise of conservatism, it is vital for us to understand the depths and interlinkages which make it possible for a global majority to be economically, politically, and structurally undermined by a coalition of conservative interests intent on preserving a status quo which guarantees them perpetual supremacy. These conservative interests have operated on a philosophy of total control; they permeate economic structures, political systems, religious thought, social issues, and all areas of human activity imaginable. As tools of operation they employ racism, xenophobia, sexism, misogyny, homophobia, and religious and cultural fundamentalism — pillars supporting a supremacist superstructure. Since those who control these systems are male, their tools of operation build a Master's House. Within this Master's House women are dispensable; their bodies and rights can be violated at will; they have few economic, political, legal, or religious rights; and any attempt to change this ordained order is violently resisted. It is also important for women in the Master's House to be co-opted into sustaining the culture and tradi-

tions of the Master in order to ensure his immortality. In addition, all elements not made in the Master's image are rejected.

The nature of contemporary global conservatism

I hold a European Union passport. Sometimes when I am passing through immigration points, I am asked, "Where are you from?" I tell my interrogators to look at my passport, but they say, "Yes, we know you have a British passport, but where are you *really* from?" This is what I have to say to that:

Where are you from?
Please don't ask me where I am from
I am here
Because you were here there and everywhere
So now I have a right
To be here there and everywhere.

I do not need to remind people of the centuries of slavery, colonialism, and imperialism which black people and other people of color all over the world have suffered. However, contrary to what conservative elements would have us believe, slavery and colonialism are not echoes of some rather forgotten, remote past, constantly invoked by frustrated minority leaders looking for an excuse to get their "sponging," "lazy," "single parent," "jailbird," "violent" minority constituents off the hook. Slavery, colonialism, imperialism, and neocolonialism are still very much alive, so much so that almost the entire global South and vast communities of the North are impoverished and lack access to basic resources and amenities.

Global economic restructuring has enabled international monetary institutions such as the World Bank and the International Monetary Fund to recolonize Africa through endless debt-servicing and the implementation of structural adjustment programs (SAPs), which have devastated entire political, economic, and social systems. SAPs have led to extensive cuts in services, unemployment, inflation, a sharp decline in standard of living, and a massive brain drain. Middle- and high-level managers, whom Africa needs badly for its recovery and development, seek a more conducive working environment outside Africa. According to a United Nations

Programme of Action for African Economic Recovery and Development (UNPAARED) report published in 1991, by 1995 there would be 400 million Africans living in poverty, of whom 260 million would be women. The perennial conflicts and wars which have beleaguered Africa over the past few years have left the continent in a state of despair. The causes of this conflict are as complex as they are diverse. The factors are a combination of struggles over resources, power, ethnicity, democratization, and a host of other variables. Then there are the foreign interventions by the world's superpowers, who used Africa as a battleground for ideological supremacy during the cold war. All manner of tyrants and despots were propped up in a race for doctrinal territory and showered with sophisticated military hardware and billions of dollars in loans, which were promptly salted away in Swiss banks.

This history has now caught up with us. It is payback time, and we are all caught in the most vicious cycle of human suffering and deprivation imaginable. African nations cannot afford to pay back the debts, hence the structural adjustment programs. African people are now using the stockpile of weapons they acquired years ago to wage endless wars; hence they constitute 75 percent of the world's refugee population of 15 million. Due to the collapse of health-care systems, Africans cannot deal with the scourge of HIV/AIDS that has devastated parts of East, Central, and Southern Africa.

All these complex issues are no coincidence. For every deficient system there is always a beneficiary. It is not surprising that due to the state of the African continent, there are a large number of African refugees, exiles, students, and migrants in various parts of the West. The same applies to Eastern Europe, Latin America, and Asia. This has amounted to a recycling of slavery and colonization on an even greater global level than in earlier centuries. There are currently millions of women working as domestics, cleaners, and factory hands, or trafficked into the commercial sex industry. The survival of entire communities in their homelands is dependent on them. The very same economic adjustment policies that the North tries to apply to communities in the South have not worked in their own countries, and the convenient scapegoats are the ethnic minorities, the poor, the single mothers, and any other "undesirables" who are regarded as threatening to their way of life. It is important to clarify here that my definition of the North in this context is the predominantly white, male, upper-class leadership and big-business interests of the multinationals. There is no homogeneous North in the same way that there is no homogeneous South; African people are now holding their own corrupt, collaborating leaders accountable.

Forging tools for a new house

My organization, Akina Mama wa Afrika, was started in 1985 as a support group for African women living in Britain. At that time there was a need to provide space for African women who required a culturally familiar environment in which to share their problems and seek help. After years of providing welfare and front-line services, we decided that we had lived in the Master's House long enough. We wanted to tell the Master that the roof was leaking, the door needed changing, and the sewage stank. We believed that in order to effect change, we needed to have a direct investment in how structures were created. So we started showing up at policy meetings, and from the polite stares we received when we started doing this work, it was obviously not expected that we would one day want to tell the Master to his face that we wanted to speak for ourselves. We now know there is no other way.

Our work in Akina Mama wa Afrika is now centered on advocacy, policy, and international outreach in an effort to bring home the global and make it relevant to the lives of all the women in our communities, be they in Europe or in Africa. Our history has taught us that our struggles are interlinked and interdependent. In order to counterbalance the immense pressures of these broad but converging conservative global interests, women all over might have to consider the following:

• Women need a thorough understanding of the systems which dominate their lives and deprive them of their fundamental human rights, including economic rights and a respect for bodily integrity.

• Women need to reconsider how to negotiate with structures which use religion as political weapons of oppression.

• Women need to build up their capacity to act as agents of change. In the post-Beijing process the global women's movement must devote attention to mobilizing resources to carry out plans of action and, at the same time, advocate for the resources being committed at the Beijing Conference.

• Racism, as well as other forms of discrimination, is still very predominant within the global women's movement. We must have the humility and integrity to come to terms with our own specific privileges wherever we are and assess how they impact on other women. Sisterhood might be global, but at the same time, sisters are not all the same, and they have different priorities.

• The feminist movement has been recognized as the most powerful social force in the world. It is therefore no surprise that the most powerful conservative elements — such as the Vatican, Islamic fundamentalists, Christian fundamentalists, pro-lifers, big-business economic interests, and other right-wing elements — will do all within their power to crush this movement that so threatens their powers and privileges. It is vital that women forge long-lasting alliances on the local, national, regional, and international levels.

• There are hardly any coincidences when global conservative forces work together; events and single issues seem always to complement each other. For example, the wars in Somalia, Rwanda, Liberia, Sierra Leone, and Angola all happening at the same time are no coincidence. It is also no hapless coincidence that Africa is being ravaged by HIV, if you consider the fact that Africa has the most dilapidated health-care system in the world and that the Roman Catholic church, which has millions of followers in the poorest parts of Africa, preaches against the use of condoms. The strategy, therefore, is always to see things in a myriad of contexts.

• We must seek accountability from our leaders, most of whom are male, and from the women who collaborate to sustain them. World communities need good governance, accountable to and representative of the people. No amount of charity, aid, or bilateral assistance can replace the responsibility of government to its people; neither can relief workers or peacekeepers be expected to stop conflicts.

On the road to Beijing, women were asked if they hoped to achieve anything tangible at such a massive, miscellaneous gathering. Some replied that the mere fact that large numbers of women would be gathering and exchanging experiences would be enough of an achievement. There was of course a deliberate effort to de-legitimize the women who would actually make it to this Conference, under the excuse that they do not speak for the vast numbers of women they were leaving back home. This is a familiar trick used by the international media.

Two years ago Gertrude Mongella, the Secretary-General of the Conference, said that if her mother in her village in Tanzania did not hear about Beijing, then she would believe she had not done her job properly. A few months ago I sent a message to my 70-year-old grandmother in Nigeria. She is a widow and a farmer; she lives in a rural area, is nonliterate, and has never heard of China. I told her about the Beijing Conference and what we were hoping to achieve. She got someone to write a reply, which I have translated from the Yoruba:

I am happy that in my lifetime something will be done about the plight of women. In our time, we were brought up to believe that men were more important than women and were just born to serve them till we die. I now know this is not true. There is nothing that is hard that does not eventually become soft. There is nothing inside a man's trousers that is more important than what is inside a woman's head. There is nothing that is impossible. May you go well and come back well, and may the spirit of our ancestors be with you.

My vision is a world in which women and men can forge new tools to build, not a Master's House, but a place where there will be respect for humanity and the dignity of humankind, a place where we will truly appreciate the world through women's eyes.

XI • Obstacles to Peace and Human Security — *Strategies*

Opening remarks

Dessima Williams, Moderator
Brandeis University, United States (Grenada)

We are now in the second phase of our plenaries, when we shift from analytical overviews to the search for strategies and mechanisms — strategies that women have been successfully using and that we think likely to work as we enter the 21st century. The importance of our strategy sessions is really to figure out, as part of our commitment, what new tools we take from here back to our respective arenas and homelands.

As we talk about strategies, let us be reminded that some women are insisting that we come out of here — from both the NGO Forum and the Fourth World Conference on Women — with more than words, with *commitments*. That is, we want all our governments to commit to improving the lives of women not only by upholding past commitments but also by initiating new ones, especially new and additional resources for women's development.

Of equal importance is the obligation we have here at the NGO Forum to match our call for government commitment with our own determination to implement viable strategies that are commensurate with our capacities.

This panel will explore strategies for the removal of obstacles to peace and human security. We know that when a woman's rights are protected, the security and the stability thus created produce ripple effects beyond her and into her family and other social institutions. In a perverted use of this positive nexus of relations between women and society, militarists have abused women's emotions and sexuality (for example, as "comfort women") to keep up the morale of soldiers. When women are not available, pornographic images of them are used for the same purpose. Can the so-called security of the state, purchased at the expense of women's rights and at a cost to society's values, be acceptable? Can it even work? Must not the very notions of security and state be redefined by women?

The 1994 United Nations *Human Development Report* proposed that human security, not that of the state, is the challenge of our day; that is, the economic, social, and political well-being of all human beings, individually and collectively, defines our present imperative. While this need not occur at the exclusion of the state, the report makes it clear that this is all too often the case. I would add that the military component of national budgets and the overprotection of the market and of physical property, to mention a few things, have often been placed ahead of the well-being of people. Structural adjustment programs (SAPs), debt repayment, and liberalization, all of which weaken the social fabric, and the sending of so-called "smart bombs" to kill people but leave buildings intact, are some of the things I am speaking about. Today, then, part of our charge is to explore strategies for the reversal of this pattern — how to put people's needs at the center of all our undertakings, including at the center of strategies for securing peace and human well-being.

In seeking real security on the eve of the new millennium, women have often brought strategies of peace to the public arena — dialogue, negotiations, addressing justice. Women have also played a pioneering role in seeking to implement peace strategies. The Women's International League for Peace and Freedom (WILPF), a turn-of-the-century pioneer in women's work for peace, is very worthy of mention here, alongside many others that have arisen since. Against great adversities of racism, sexism, classism, and violence, women's role in devising strategies for peace and security has been truly remarkable.

We turn now to our presenters. Let us hear their strategies with openness, so that we, too, may commit to trying them in our own environments as our societies search for human security.

The struggle for liberation in the Pacific

Susanna Ounei-Small
Pacific Concerns Resource Centre (PCRC), Fiji

My name is Susanna Ounei. For my entire adult life, I have been fighting for the liberation of the people of Kanaky, which the French colonizers call New Caledonia. Like my Pacific Island sisters in French Polynesia and East Timor, West Papua and Bougainville, I know well the cruelty of colonization, the degeneration it brings to the young people of our countries. I know what it is like to have my own relatives slaughtered for opposing their oppressors, and to have my sisters and brothers in the struggle condemned to a jail cell for daring to talk about a better life. When I was appointed as assistant director on the Decolonization desk of the PCRC-NFIP, therefore, I understood well what the people of the other colonies of the Pacific were talking about — self-determination toward independence. I doubt there would be one person in Kanaky, Bougainville, East Timor, or West Papua who has not had a relative killed, tortured, or imprisoned for political beliefs. As a Kanak woman, I also know the special kinds of degradation that colonization brings to women — the humiliation of rape, the violence of military occupation, the sadness of watching our children being butchered by the occupiers, or turning to drugs and alcohol, and yes, even abusing our own women because there is no future for them, no jobs, no educational opportunities.

In many ways, our struggle in the Pacific has become more difficult and more painful in recent years. Our colonial masters have introduced new economic development "partnership plans" designed to buy off some of our people and to divide the independence movements. It is a familiar story from many other parts of the world: A few puppets of the colonizers get rich, the money builds glittering tourist facilities and shops for overseas people, while people continue to live in slum housing, and nothing is done about improving basic health services, the water supply, or areas of the economy that might benefit local people. The colonizers also buy off our independent neighbors with promises of foreign aid, trade incentives and high-technology military equipment if they keep quiet about the injustices in the region. Meanwhile, structural adjustment and trade policies bind independent states, also, into a relationship of servitude. This provides ammunition for the colonizers' argument that we could not possibly survive without them.

Meanwhile, many countries seem to have given up on putting an end to Indonesian atrocities in East Timor and West Papua, as income from trade and arms sales unfortunately means more to many governments than do torture and displacement. It is this confidence in the complacency of the international community that has led France to decide to resume nuclear testing in the Pacific this year and to ignore the feelings of the people in the region and the cost to their health and their environment. As every year of colonization passes, the problems created by refugee camps, the settlement of outsiders into our territories, unemployment, poverty, and the psychological harm of hopelessness and racism become greater.

The women from the Pacific colonies have never accepted this abuse. We realize that it is our work in the villages and through activist networks that ultimately will bring liberation to our people. We also have a clear understanding of the kind of societies we want. As activists, we are working together throughout the region and with activists around the world to bring an end to these injustices. We demand that the end of colonization mean more than just a new flag and a new constitution. It must include an end to all economic exploitation and militarism in the region. And it also must include justice for women within our countries.

In order to explain what human security must mean for us, I need to give you a sense of what is happening in our occupied territories, and of what this has meant for our women and men.

New Caledonia was annexed by France in 1853. Since then, the Kanak people have been forcibly pushed aside onto tiny reserves while foreigners extract raw materials such as nickel from our land. We provide the third-largest source of nickel in the world. The majority is mined and sold by French companies to Japanese companies for manufacturing of all kinds, or used in France for the manufacturing of military arms and other equipment. Since the 1970s, the French government has been actively encouraging immigration by white French people and other foreigners in order to drown out the local population. Periodic revolts against French rule always meet with violent repression. For example, in 1988 the government responded to a revolt on the tiny island of Ouvea by sending in their elite 11th shock unit and killing 19 Kanak people, at least five of whom were executed after they had surrendered. For ten days leading up to the massacre, all communications with the island were cut, innocent civilians were tortured, and the entire population was terrorized. The military locked civilians up, tied them to posts, beat them, and tortured them with electric shocks. They also tried to break their spirit by humiliating them, stripping them naked in front of their brothers and sisters. My cousin had her period. All the men in the tribe saw her blood, which is taboo in our custom. It is a humiliation even to speak of this, but she told me that it was important for people to know what the French military did to them.

If Kanaky is colonized for its rich minerals, the colonization of French Polynesia centers on nuclear testing. When people talk about nuclear testing, it is important to remember that this is not just a question of environment. The French Government last year published a "White Paper" on defense which outlines French defense policy until the year 2010. I can't read it to you now, although I have an English translation here for you, and I encourage you all to read it to understand fully how France threatens international peace. The introduction by François Leotard, Minister of Defense, states clearly the French approach: "The defense of our values and ideals in new circumstances and in places distant from national territory will often be the front line of our security." And he states further that "nuclear deterrence remains one of its foundations." The paper makes clear the lack of confidence that the French government has in international cooperation and demonstrates the importance of international military power and control over its territories to its own national power. Nuclear weapons are the cornerstone of the French military regime, therefore, and they have become increasingly important in the post-cold war era. Nuclear testing is *militarism*, and the French have decided that their military prowess is more important than our health and safety. But it is equally important to keep in mind that nuclear testing is inseparable from colonialism. The French keep French Polynesia as a colony in order to test their weapons, because since the independence of Algeria in the 1960s they no longer can test them in the Sahara desert. This is what we mean to them: We are their testing ground. Without colonization there would be no nuclear testing.

Likewise, since 1975, just twelve days after the independence of East Timor, when Indonesia invaded the country, the Timorese have been fighting an armed resistance against the Indonesian army. The world needs to realize what it means for a people like the East Timorese, who number only 700,000, to have over 200,000 of their people killed within just a few years since the invasion of their country by Indonesia. Most recently, 200 young unarmed protesters were massacred in front of overseas television cameras in one single bloody day. Torture and rape are daily occurrences in East Timor. It is forbidden to speak the Timorese language. The leader of the resistance movement, Xanana Gusmao, currently is in jail in Indonesia. However, a very well organized underground movement links the resistance movement inside and outside East Timor. Most recently, UN-sponsored talks hold some hope, as Timorese resisters call for a gradual military pull-out, leading to a national referendum on independence.

Our 1.5 million brothers and sisters in West Papua also suffer from Indonesian colonization since 1963. Like the East Timorese, the people of West Papua have suffered massive loss of life, as well as having thousands of innocent people thrown into prisons, concentration camps, and re-settlement camps. A total of 30,000 West Papuans now live in refugee camps along the Papua-New Guinea border or have fled overseas. Meanwhile, Indonesia has opened the land's rich resources to mining by American companies, and is forcibly clearing the Papuans off their land to make room for the mines. The government also has instituted a massive transmigration scheme aimed at popula-ting the country with Indonesian settlers and drowning out the local population. We do not have sufficient details on all the killings and disappear-ances taking place in West Papua, but we know that these occur regularly.

When we look at these problems as women ac-tivists, we see many similarities — the violence, the deaths, the rapes in the name of economic and military gain and at the expense of people the col-onizers consider inferior, black, primitive people. We also see that because in every case the colon-izer hopes to drown out our population and to de-stroy our culture, women become a special focus of oppression through such methods as forced ster-ilization campaigns by the Indonesian government. We also emphasize that our human security must also include freedom from violence at the hands of our own men as well. Our analysis of neo-colon-ialism must also look at the role of women during the struggle and after independence. There are many things that are not ideal within Kanak society, for example, and the treatment of women is one of the worst. Domestic violence against women is com-mon, and so is rape — even gang rape. Within the movement too, women are expected to be secre-taries, cooks, cleaners, and mistresses, while the men make all the important decisions. I often am given a compliment by male activists when they say that I fight like a man. but I don't consider that a compliment: I am a woman, and I fight for liber-ation as a woman.

Dewe Gorodey from New Caledonia was sup-posed to be here. But mysteriously, both her pass-port and the passport of the Tahitian activist who had hoped to testify to you about nuclearization

disappeared on their way to my office before I could secure their visas. We can only conclude that this is a sabotage.

Dewe and I first began to think about women's struggle in Kanaky when we were in jail together in 1974. When we raised it in the movement, al-most everyone was hostile — men *and* women. We were accused of copying "women's libbers" in France and "dividing couples" and "dividing the movement." We were the extremists among the ex-tremists. Only a few men listened to us and sup-ported our ideas, and no political party seriously addressed the issue. Instead, they tried to undermine us and protect their power by creating low-status "feminine sections" to make cakes and sew dresses to make money for the party.

This is a difficult issue for many women acti-vists. We are supposed to avoid these issues for the sake of unity. But although we agree that we must fight for independence alongside our brothers, we want to be clear about what sort of society we are fighting for. We will not accept being looked upon as useless when we have played such an important role in the struggle, and have given our lives for independence, and seen our children punished by the authorities because of their mothers' activism.

We will not fight the violence of the colonizer in order to endure violence in our own homes. And yet, we also feel a great solidarity with our bro-thers. We recognize that all of us — women and men — are fighting a basic battle for survival at this stage, and we recognize that the colonizers will win if they manage to divide us.

What do we do, then? Victory will not come simply from attending conferences like this one. I believe that there is a special opportunity now in the Pacific colonies, because more than ever, peo-ple at the grassroots level are well aware of the in-justice of their situation. They are aware, but they are disorganized. They don't see any way out. We have to go back to our towns and villages and work with people, help them to organize them-selves. For example, I have been active in setting up women's cooperatives in Kanaky to show women what they can achieve together and to help them to transform their frustration with their op-pression into politicization. We need to talk with people, to tell them about other struggles happening around the world, to help them to understand about global economics, militarism, and all the other aspects of their condition that the colonizers do not want them to understand, and to teach them that there is no point in achieving liberation if we are going to turn around and colonize our own women.

At the same time, I strongly believe that it is only through our connections as activists that we will achieve true liberation. In the 1970s, I would not have said so. I would have said we should focus on our own situation first, and leave international meetings for later. But I have seen the good that has come from the pressure the international community has put on Indonesia concerning the massacres in East Timor, for example. One of the colonizers' main tactics is to isolate us, and we have to resist that.

As women, we know better than most that human security is not just independence, although it must include independence. It means freedom from military intimidation, and it means freedom from personal intimidation. It means control over the resources of one's land and control over one's own life. It means an environment safe from the hazards of nuclear poisoning and the diseases brought by foreign occupying armies. It will not be easy, but women know how to fight long and difficult battles. We will achieve true liberation, true human security, true protection of our human rights, and true dignity for ourselves and our children. We will achieve these things as activists united together in the Pacific and across the world. And in the process, we will teach our brothers to deserve their independence by the way they treat their women as well.

The unsung heroines of the conflict in Northern Ireland

Caitriona Ruane
Centre for Research and Documentation, Northern Ireland

Introduction

I would like to thank the NGO Forum for inviting me to address this wonderful conference. It is great to be here in China with so many women and men from countries all over the globe. I would also like to thank Chandra Budhu, who has been so patient, calm, and helpful to me. I am speaking from my own experiences, and obviously I am affected profoundly by those experiences. I am not neutral or objective; I do not believe that anyone is. I do not claim to represent all Irish women because no one person can do that. Ireland, like every other country, has a diversity of political opinions.

Brief history of Irish-British relations

Ireland and Britain have had a troubled history since British troops landed in Ireland in 1171. During those 824 years there has never been a time when there have not been British troops in Ireland. British colonialism has not been a happy experience for the native Irish or, indeed, for British soldiers. It has resulted in famine, mass emigration, hangings, slaughter, land wars, plantation, hunger strikes, floggings, rebellion, partition of Ireland, and untold suffering for the Irish and the British people. It is one of the oldest and most complex of all colonial conflicts, and it predates the development of capitalism.

Every subsequent development in Irish society was structured by the colonial process — urbanization, industrialization, the transition from feudalism to capitalism — each of these huge processes was given the colonial imprimatur. In consequence, decolonizing Ireland or healing the wounds attendant to the colonial process in Ireland is not an easy task. Every party to the conflict — Irish and British, settler and native, colonizer and colonized — has had its identity forged at the colonial nexus. The colonial legacy continues to structure

British and Irish lives in a way that is just as profound as gender, race, or class.

Ignoring this colonial legacy does no service to the prospects for peace, reconciliation, and political settlement of the Irish-British conflict. This is not to argue that colonialism explains every contradiction and nuance in Irish society. It is to argue, however, that without an analysis of colonialism and its effects on Ireland, the analysis of most aspects of division and conflict is both limited and flawed. The colonial legacy is complex; there are many colonial dimensions to Irish society and to Irish-British relations.

Ireland was partitioned in 1921. The South of Ireland is an independent state with an elected president and parliament. The North of Ireland is currently ruled directly by Britain, by British ministers, with no democratic control by local people. It is one of the most heavily militarized states in the world, with 30,000 armed troops, soldiers and police, garrisons, watchtowers, helicopters, and border fortifications. Emergency legislation has been used since the foundation of the Northern Ireland state in 1922. The state has accrued power to itself in a number of ways: emergency legislation, which includes seven-day detention; delayed access to solicitors; one-judge, no-jury courts with judges who are appointees of the British government. Since the foundation of the Northern Ireland state, there has been ongoing conflict and denial of civil liberties.

The last period of armed conflict, from 1968 to 1994, was the longest sustained period of conflict in recent times. The main political actors are the British and Irish governments, Nationalists (who want an United Ireland) and Unionists (continued union with Britain). The main military actors over the last 25 years are the British government, the Irish Republican Army (who want a United Ireland and British withdrawal) and the Combined Loyalist Military Command (who are loyal to Britain). Amnesty International and other human rights groups have alleged that there is collusion between British state forces and loyalist armed groups. As in all conflicts around the world, civilians have paid a very heavy price. Nationalists have been discriminated against and treated as second-class citizens.

The first prime minister of Northern Ireland publicly called it a Protestant state for a Protestant people. Many unionists see nationalists' demands for basic rights threatening their power, which of course it does. Middle-class unionists in particular have far too much power and privilege. South Africa is a good analogy.

Such a situation encourages the privileging of some groups at the expense of others — economically, politically, and militarily — in the interests of managing conflict and generating acquiescence, if not active consent, to the existing regime. The result is the institutionalization of divisions within and between both communities in the North and between both communities and their counterparts in the South of Ireland.

Founding of CRD

I began working in the North of Ireland in March 1988. I had returned home after working for three years in El Salvador, Nicaragua, and Guatemala. I wanted to work on issues of conflict in Ireland and link those with the issues and people I was working with in Central America. I co-founded the Centre for Research and Documentation (CRD), based in Belfast, which was founded by Irish people who had worked in Africa, Asia, and Latin America and human rights workers in Ireland.

The only "acceptable" analysis permitted in the media was that the IRA are the problem: if they would stop, we would have peace. There was little or no analysis of the root causes of conflict except by a few courageous journalists, politicians, and human rights workers.

In 1988 CRD spoke of the need for negotiations and that everyone should sit down and talk rather than fight. That statement may not seem very radical now, but at the time it made us many enemies. The longer I worked in the North of Ireland, the more I experienced directly and indirectly the almighty power of the British state. I had spent years condemning U.S. government policy in Central America, in the Philippines, in Iraq. Yet I was rarely accused of being anti-American. The minute we became critical of British government policy in Ireland, it was a different story. I patiently but firmly explained the difference between being anti-British and anti-British government policy.

CRD's human rights work

Over the past 25 years of armed conflict, the British government has "managed" the conflict. They have used the legal system, the media, armed troops, and incredible levels of militarization. They portrayed themselves as neutral peacekeepers between the warring tribes in Ireland. The British government is using "law and order" to fight the conflict. When challenged, they parrot, "we operate within the law, people must obey the law." The British government has one law for us civilians and another for their soldiers and police. Over the past 25 years, more than 15,000 IRA and loyalists have spent many years in jail. In fact, some Irish prisoners are going into their 21st year in English jails. Over the past 25 years, only four soldiers have been convicted of murder, and they are out after two years and reinstated into the British army. It is the same the world over.

I have been asked by the organizing committee to give you an example of a strategy used by CRD over the past ten years. I intend to focus on our human rights work. One of the strategies we have used is to expose the British government's blatant disregard and violation of human rights and support local human rights groups and victims and their families. CRD has worked on all human rights abuses by the state, regardless of the politics or religion or gender of the person.

Crossmaglen and Cullyhanna

Crossmaglen and Cullyhanna is a rural border area. It has been an area of intense conflict between the IRA and the British Army. Some people would argue that it is Ireland's equivalent of a liberated zone. It was too dangerous for the British Army to travel in armored cars or jeeps; they used helicopters. They built militarized forts, observation posts overlooking the town, state-of-the-art infrared cameras to spy on domestic and business lives. High-tech long-range listening equipment drops in on conversations. A high percentage of cancers in the area make local people worry about the use of such equipment. Elite British regiments, the infamous Royal Marines and Parachute regiments, are sent there. It is one of the worst areas for British soldiers to be stationed. Helicopters take off and land at all hours of the day and night in people's fields and gardens, in schools and health centers. The soldiers arrest people by helicopter, and they are brought to detention centers. The area has been labeled "bandit country" by the media and by many British politicians. This labeling is aimed at dehumanizing the men, women, and children in South Armagh — i.e., making them non-people.

In December 1990, 20-year-old Fergal Caraher was shot dead and his brother Miceal was seriously wounded as they were driving to a local pub for a drink at Christmas. The Army press office immediately put out a statement saying they had broken through an Army checkpoint and there were arms in the car, which later turned out to be totally false.

A few days after the shooting, we met with Fergal's mother and father and young widow and son. They were adamant that they wanted the soldiers brought to justice and the truth about the killing known. The Cullyhanna Justice Group organized an international tribunal on the shooting and invited international legal experts to sit on a panel. The local community worked with us day and night for four months. They went door to door to collect the £15,000 it cost. (There is no practically no funding for human rights work in the North of Ireland.) Invitation lists were drawn up. The press was contacted. Jurists were identified. The legal case was drawn up.

For two days in so-called bandit country, there was a people's court with a higher standard of justice than we have ever known in the North of Ireland. People listened to the 11 witnesses explain what happened on the day Fergal was killed. Professional actors reenacted the shooting, while helicopters hovered overhead. While all this planning was going on, the Army tormented the Caraher family. They raided the home; they punched the younger brothers; they threatened to shoot the sisters. They put a gun to Peter John Caraher's head and threatened to "blow his f-----g head off." They stopped Mary Caraher, Fergal's mother, and asked "if she wanted to buy a white Rover, it was going cheap in the barracks." This was the car her son was killed in. Despite all this harassment, the family kept going and organized the two-day inquiry. Two days after we launched the findings, the British government charged two soldiers with the killing. One year later, the family and international observers spent three weeks in a one-judge, no-jury court and watched a farce of a trial. The two soldiers walked free, to backslapping and cheers. One of the soldiers was back serving in the area afterward and gloated about having "one under his belt and pity it was not the two brothers."

After the inquiry, our offices were "mysteriously" broken into, and our only computer was taken. The bad publicity after the inquiry forced the British government to rethink their shoot-to-kill policy. They were obviously feeling under pressure. What did happen was an increase in death squad-type killings by loyalists. Our next strategy was to organize an international tribunal into the shooting of a young man by a death squad and expose the state's complicity in this shooting.

The strategy CRD has used is to highlight at the international level the British government's human rights abuses. We also support victims' families so that they become a part of organizing and speak for themselves. We put a lot of energy into organizing locally, leadership and human rights training, and working with women and children.

Our next major event, with Action From Ireland, which we have been organizing for the past few months, is an international conference on militarization and the international arms trade, its effect on people and countries all over the world. This will be held in Crossmaglen. We are using theatre, dance, arts and crafts, and international speakers.

We are organizing a vigil for all the people killed in this conflict and other conflicts in the world outside a massive military barracks. The main local organizer is Margaret Caraher, who was 20 years old when her husband was shot dead in 1990. She is now a very active human rights worker and mother to her son, Brendan.

Women's rights are human rights

Many of the people we work with on abuses of human rights are women. CRD and CAJ have worked on a beautiful quilt entitled "Women's Rights Are Human Rights," which many of you may have seen in the European tent. This quilt has 30 panels made by women's groups from all over Ireland, North and South. We all came together in a small border village and sewed the quilt together. This was an amazing experience for me, especially given the fact that I could not sew. The camaraderie, solidarity, and respect that existed between the women of different generations, politics, and sewing skills will stay with me always. It also taught me a valuable lesson: that is, in my rush toward feminism, I have not learned many of the traditional skills that my mother's generation has. Those skills are empowering and a very strong bond with an older generation whose voices were heard even less that ours are. Our quilt was finished one week before we came here, in another Irish border village, Cashel, County Fermanagh. In its short lifespan it has achieved more than 100 reports.

Women and conflict

How the women have suffered in this conflict, and how they have worked! They have worked to survive, to educate their children, to keep their children from joining military organizations, even when they themselves supported those organizations. Women gave birth, protected their children, visited them in jail, bought food, clothes, and book parcels for prisoners. A prisoner in jail cannot do without, no matter how bad the family finances are. They protested; they confronted armies; they demanded to know where their children were. They were strip-searched; their children were killed by IRA bombs and British Army bombs. On top of all that, many women suffered violence in the home. Now, because of the courageous work of organizations like Women's Aid, the Rape Crisis Centre, and people like Mary who spoke at the tribunal on Friday, the silence is being broken slowly but surely, and women are finding their voices and supporting other women.

I remember calling a friend of mine, after a particularly difficult visit to a jail in Belfast. I was telling Nora about the visit. She asked me what wing he was on and said, so matter-of-factly, "I have been visiting that jail for 55 years." Fifty-five years, week in, week out. She was herself interned without trial in the 1940s; she visited her three brothers in jail; she met her future husband on a visit to the jail; and she visited her son in jail. She hopes she will never have to visit her grandchildren in jail. She is now 73 years of age, and has spent her entire life working for prisoners' rights. The Nora McAteers and many others like her are the unsung heroines of this and every conflict. They did things that few people hear anything about but that mean the world to prisoners and their families, such as collecting a few pounds from an already overstretched community so the children of prisoners can have toys for Christmas. Our generation owes so much to the courageous women of previous decades. Women from all different communities in Ireland have major political and personal differences. However, women have been more open to listening, and accept that others have a right to political viewpoints without necessarily agreeing with them.

Peace process

On August 31, 1994, one year and three days ago, the IRA declared a cessation of hostilities. This was followed six weeks later by a Loyalist cessation. We have an historic opportunity to end the conflict and enter a new era of Irish-British relations. However, the British government still refuses to accept any responsibility for this conflict. They continue to parrot their peacekeeping role. They are still waffling on about their wonderful police force and act surprised when questioned about political prisoners. According to them, there are no political prisoners in the jails. The government still refuses to accept that it might have a part to play in the 16,000 armed British troops, the 13,000 police officers, the 120,000 licensed guns. The military fortifications are still in place along the border and towns and villages. A meager few have been dismantled.

One year into the peace process, we still do not have all-party talks, and there are grumblings in many areas and an increasing feeling of frustration and anger against the British government. They are still in military-victory mode, and everyone else is talking about compromise. They have not released one political prisoner from jails in England or the North of Ireland. Indeed, IRA prisoners in England have been subjected to extremely harsh conditions. Some of them are, as we speak, locked up 23 hours a day with no exercise. Patrick Kelly, one of these prisoners, had a cancerous growth on his back. The British government refused to give him proper medical treatment, despite doctors' advice that he should be moved for immediate medical attention. Eventually, after pressure by human rights groups and the Irish government, he was grudgingly brought to an outside hospital. Before, during, and after the operation, he was chained to a prison officer. For the first time in 25 years we have an opportunity to deliver lasting peace. Yet the British government is acting like a spoilt child that had its sweets taken away. How dare they? Do they realize that they are toying with our lives and our children's lives?

Conclusion

The last eight years have been the hardest, most emotional, most amazing years of my life. It was so much easier for me to deal with death and destruction in countries where war was "supposed" to happen. White Irish people "should not" be getting killed. The injustice and killings in Ireland brought all my inert racism to the fore and forced me to deal with it. Sometimes I, like many other political activists, feel tired and drained. I feel the problems are too great and our efforts useless. I had a little girl three years ago, Eimear, and this threw up questions and dilemmas for me that I never imagined. I felt fear, that awful cold feeling that sticks in the pit of your stomach and will not go away. It was one thing for me to make choices that would endanger my life. Have I the right to make choices that endanger my daughter's? I have made a choice, but did I make the right one? Should I be here, or should I be at home with her? I don't know if I have made the right choice. I look at her, so innocent, so beautiful. Do I warn her about the bad things, or do I give her a few untroubled years? The compromise I came up with is that I teach her to question and trust her own instincts, but I keep some truths from her yet.

The older I get, the fewer certainties I have. It

was so easy in my twenties. Things seemed so much clearer. Now in my early thirties, I have so few answers and a million questions. I seem to see the complexities more. When I am at my most uncertain and questioning everything I am doing, I feel I am trying to cling onto some of my beliefs. I go through the El Credo or the Creed, except it is a different one than I learned as a child. It goes something like this. "I believe violence against women and children is wrong. I believe working-class people all over the world are oppressed. I believe superpower policies are wrong and cause misery and destruction all over the world. I believe we in the North use up far too many resources. I believe . . ."

Suddenly "I believe" is not strong enough, and "I know" comes bounding into my mind. I know the arms industry is absurd, I know I am tired of seeing helicopters and military barracks, weeping mothers at grave sides, and holding Eimear's hand tighter as we pass a British Army foot patrol. I know the British government are not neutral in my country. I know I am a feminist, and it is great to be a feminist. And the questions come back. Would my mother-in-law and my mother call themselves feminists? Probably not; why not? Have I, have we, excluded them from our feminism? How can we make our feminism more embracing, more inclusive?

I want to see a new type of army, the type of army I have seen here in Huairou over the past week, an army of white, black, yellow, brown, and pink people, an army of political activists who are working on many different issues, an army that redefines solidarity and feminism. We are all struggling for change, loving, creating, giving birth to something new, something special. We are uncovering the horrors of the past and present, trying to make sense of them, to create a better present and future. Most of all, we are trying to support the survivors, saying to them: Yes, life is difficult, we cannot bring back what you have lost, but we can be there and tell you that what happened is wrong, and it should not have happened. And most of all, we will do our utmost to make it more difficult for it to happen again.

In Ireland we want justice, peace, and freedom, and we hope with all our necessary idealism and optimism that this time we are going to end this age-old conflict. We are not naive. We know it will be hard, and we have many struggles and disappointments ahead of us. We do not want freedom at the expense of other people struggling throughout the world today. Many of us are opposed to the fortress Europe that is gaining strength. We have free movement of capital but not free movement of people. We know what suffering is; many of us will continue our solidarity with many of you struggling for basic rights.

The year 1995 is the 150th anniversary of the Irish "famine," when more than two million Irish people died in their mud huts, ditches, and workhouses, and another two million were forced to emigrate while corn, cattle, and grain were exported to England by the boatload. We know what so many of you have suffered, are suffering, in East Timor, Rwanda, Tibet, Nicaragua, El Salvador, the Philippines, India, Sudan, Bosnia, South Africa, Brazil, Palestine, the Kurds, Guatemala, and the Third World in Europe and North America. We know, and many of us are in solidarity with you.

A citizens' initiative: Bringing soldiers home

Maria Kirbassova
Committee of Soldiers' Mothers of Russia, Russia

Young women, on behalf of the soldiers' mothers of Russia, I would like to thank all the women's organizations of China, the organizing committee of the People's Republic of China, and Mrs. Supatra Masdit and the organizing committee in New York for inviting me.

The history of war and peace is probably the most important theme for our small planet. I am so glad I can be here with you. I recall my youth when we had Chinese students who studied at our colleges. We remember them with very warm feelings; they are wonderful people. Even now at the end of my life, thanks to the organizing committee, I am here in China, and I am glad to see the exquisite Chinese culture. Everyone is so polite. Nobody pushes me; nobody speaks rudely to me. We are staying in a wonderful hotel near a beautiful lake. Nature is beautiful here. I would like to stay forever, but of course I will have to go back home to fight against violence and militarism in Russia.

Our committee was founded six years ago. It was a grassroots movement. We are an independent public organization of soldiers' mothers. Its history is connected with the fact that in 1984, with the war in Afghanistan, our soldiers were recruited into the army even out of college, which had not been the case before. My son had to join the army; I have one son and one daughter.

There was an interview with the academician Rauschenbach, who spoke against recruiting students from colleges. He said that the brain of the person is shaped at the age of about 20, and all discoveries are made by people before they are 30. If those who study humanities go through the school of violence which the army and the war represent, when they return from the army they cannot be real creators; they will only be able to take orders. Our six-year-long experience testifies to this fact.

The violations of human rights within the army are outrageous. Some young men returning from the army take revenge against society for not being able to protect them. Others become racketeers and gang members. Our leaders dream of imbuing all young men and all the ranks of young people with the idea that it is impossible to oppose the state machinery.

In April 1984, Mikhail Gorbachev, then president of our country, at the insistence of our scientists, again introduced a reprieve for students; they were not to be recruited into the army. At that time, the impetus for organizing our committee was the fact that our country had always been ruled by the military. Even now, under the constitution, the president of our country is the commander-in-chief. These military people who ruled our country when it was the Soviet Union — about 80 percent of our country worked for military ends — they

forgot that we mothers, and our husbands as well, we as taxpayers, feed the vast military machine. (The army was eight million at the time; now it is four million, according to the estimates of German analysts. The figures were published in September 1994 in one of our most influential newspapers.) They forget that we have some rights. When we give our sons to them to be soldiers, after bringing them up, they may go hungry in the army. They are very often beaten and humiliated.

In 1989 when we were confronted with this, we decided to fight back. As a result, thousands of young soldiers were able to return earlier than scheduled. That was the first fight we won against the establishment. That is why we said that women who give life to their children can do anything.

Mothers have never been for war. We do not bear our children in order to make soldiers out of them, not for war. Everyone helped us in achieving our first victory. It was possible thanks to perestroika, which our former president, Mikhail Gorbachev, started. It was thanks to the beginnings of the new independent society, to the offshoots of the civil society which appeared at the time.

Our committee is one such offshoot of democracy. We also have a newspaper for young people. I work for a TV studio. I went to the mass media, but only one journalist agreed to publish a small item saying that mothers would fight to return their sons to peaceful life. I can't tell you how much we have lived through in these six years; we represent such wonderful women. Now we have about 60 organizations throughout the country.

The war in Chechnya has stirred the country. About 80 percent of the country is against the war; we are not an empire of evil. When there was a Soviet Union, our people were kind; we had good education; there were social benefits. Now, with this collapse of the state, our people are going through a period of great difficulties, of psychological discomfort. Ten percent of the so-called new Russians have privatized all the riches of the country. The industrial potential has been deteriorating; pensioners are living in poverty; women don't want to get pregnant; women with higher education have to work as maids for the nouveau riche.

Those who are not connected with the establishment, according to our estimates, will get a majority of votes.

Our magazine, *The 20th Century and the World*, published an article which said that there is militarism and the military in central Moscow. There is a building we call the Moscow Pentagon, the headquarters of the army, the symbol of the militarism that has emerged in the party leadership and in industry and transport. It has always been at the helm of our country. Our people received about 20 percent of what they produced. All the rest was spent for military purposes. Even though our army now amounts to only four million, about 30 percent of the national income still goes to military purposes. This is taking place because even in all these years, working together with all the parliaments, we haven't been able to find out where our money goes — our own money pays for having our children beaten.

When the war in Chechnya began we had to organize a hotline to at least be able to tell parents whether their sons had been sent to Chechnya. This war is outrageous, it is an aggression against a colony. We should remember: Chechnya never voluntarily became part of the Russian empire.

In the 19th century, the Chechen people, under their leader, fought for 50 years for its freedom. After the revolution Chechnya was annexed, and after World War II the minorities were deported. In two hours they were all assembled, put onto trains, and sent to the steppes of Kazakhstan, where two-thirds of my own people died. I lived there only for a year. Then Nikita Kruschchev returned freedom to us, and we went back to our native lands. In my mother's stories our native land seemed to be something fabulous, a land of pastures. It is usually beautiful when it is green in spring at the beginning of summer, but in August, when we came back, it was all scorched. I understood it was my native land. When I went to Chechnya and stayed there for a whole month, I understood why the war affected so many people, why those mothers and children without any weapons tried to protect their country.

We wanted so much to help these people by any means, but we couldn't do anything. In December,

we organized protests, but nothing succeeded. The president of the Chechnyan Republic said that he would return the captured Russian soldiers to their mothers if the mothers came to fetch them. So the mothers went, together with Chechen women. They arrived on December 29, bringing a list of soldiers who had been captured on December 11, the date when Russia invaded Chechnya. When we stopped not far from one of the settlements, we saw officers who asked us to return because we couldn't stop the war. We said that nobody was listening to us in Russia; the people in the Kremlin did not want to listen to us.

As it turned out, during the Chechnyan war, we were in their way, we were an irritant. We received a copy of a letter from the soldiers' mothers to the president, and the person who answered said that they were concerned about mothers constantly going to Chechnya. Our committee held a nonviolent campaign of opposition, and many mothers were able to take back their sons from the troops that were being sent to Chechnya.

On January 8 we came to Grozhny and we left on February 7. Why did we stay there so long? Because the dead bodies of our soldiers were lying all over the city. It was so outrageous for the Muslims, for the Chechens, that when the generals of the two armies met, they begged that the bodies be taken away. Our military did not care; they wanted to conceal the number of casualties; they wanted to cover up their professional inadequacy.

We stayed in the cellar of the presidential palace in a dangerous district. The palace had been built in order to sustain heavy earthquakes. All kinds of weapons were used; fire was above our heads. On January 12, everything was shaken. We were near the hospital; we put on masks. Our wounded were a little bit further off. They used rockets; they wanted to attack the palace. They wanted every one of us buried there, though the Russian authorities knew that mothers of captured soldiers and representatives of the Committee of Soldiers' Mothers were there. They knew that there would be a tragedy. There were about 600 captured soldiers.

The Chechen people turned out to be very generous. The Russian women who came to Chechnya were very warmly welcomed, and it was heartwarming to see such generosity and compassion. It was sympathy toward the mothers. The Chechen soldiers told us that according to the code of military honor they couldn't even fight those 18-year-old boys. They said, "Okay. Take your sons away and send mercenaries or marines or someone else." That was, in fact, done later. Marines were sent to Chechnya, and the Chechen soldiers said that they were destroyed within three days.

We were in the basement of the presidential palace, and we were being bombed by the Russians. They were bombing Russian people in the basement of the palace, but our Russian television showed something quite different. But we know who gives us the truth. We only watch independent television.

We took 13 wounded officers and soldiers in armored vehicles. We did not differentiate between soldiers and officers; they are all our children, just the same. My deputy went with them. Later more mothers came. We asked if some people were surrounded and requested the release of those who were besieged. There was one such division. Over the course of a month about 100 captured soldiers were released.

Peaceful Chechen men were imprisoned in camps; I have visited many such camps where torture is used, including electric shock and dogs. I am not speaking from hearsay; I am describing what I have seen with my own eyes. There were Chechens who were beaten until they were blue, and some of them died of torture. The Chechen mothers asked, "How long can we stand it?" The Chechen general said, "We treated the Russian soldiers decently. They had the same treatment as our soldiers." Why do our sons return absolutely beaten? Due to corruption, parents often had to pay about two million dollars as ransom for their sons. When a Chechen father of six children was exchanged for one of the Russian soldiers, he had been subjected to electric shock and beaten. He was released, thanks to women.

Our march began on March 8, the day of women's solidarity. We went to Grozhny. The march was interrupted. We reached Grozhny a month later.

I would like to thank first and foremost the journalists who saved the mothers during this march. A courageous journalist from Germany was able to get through the lines to get back home and show the world how the soldiers' mothers were treated. I would like to thank all the German women who in those days supported us, and the women of Switzerland, of Denmark, of the whole world. We also had Buddhist monks from Japan, who used nonviolent methods. We believe in Mahatma Gandhi's principles and are his followers.

Dear women, let us work to make our planet free of nuclear arsenals by the middle of the 21st century, free of trade in arms and weapons. Let us have no more armies and transparent borders. We want soldiers to serve in the army only under contract. Let us do whatever we can to assure every person a dignified life according to Oriental philosophy. Every person has the right to live as they wish. The way to such an ideal society is to foster our international solidarity. We want to expand the activities of our committee to the whole territory of the CIS.

When foreigners come to Russia, they sometimes adopt our children, usually sick children. But what is also important is how countries behave toward Russia. Our country, with all the chaos displayed by its leaders and with so many weapons, can pose a real threat to the world community. I ask everyone to help the proud Chechen people to organize a Nuremberg-like trial. A wonderful woman from Germany organized a charity concert and collected money for our committee.

My colleagues in the committee never think in terms of who belongs to what national group. They said, "Let us give all this money to the Chechen mothers, the wounded children." So we decided to organize a committee, Save Your Children. Several German theaters organized committees, along with a number of other organizations, including the International Peace Bureau.

We can't understand why NATO should bomb Yugoslavia. We proposed a march from Grozhny to Yugoslavia; the Chechen and Russian women agreed. There is a tradition that a woman can take a white scarf and throw it in front of men and the men should then stop fighting. So when we reach the Yugoslav border, let us try that.

XII • Violence Against Women — *Strategies*

Opening remarks

Ijeoma Agugua, Moderator
High Court of Justice, Nigeria

In the African region, especially in those pronatalist societies such as Nigeria, the main strategies to be adopted in the struggle to eliminate violence against women are attention to the alleviation of poverty; changes in societal attitudes; enhanced legal literacy for women; adequate legislation to cover areas such as personal rights in marriage, property rights of spouses, equality of rights concerning children, family planning, tax relief claims, female circumcision, interstate succcession, and noninterference with property of the deceased, etc.

In the interpretation and application of existing laws, efforts should be geared toward gender sensitization of law enforcement agents such as the police, the enhancement of legal literacy of economically empowered women, and a substantially increased number of well-informed, gender-sensitive male and female judicial officers throughout the hierarchy of the Court. This will enhance sensitivity to, and provide for the just interpretation and application of, laws that aim at the elimination of violence against women.

In the interim, NGOs, women activists, and organizations should take up the prosecution of cases, especially appeals, or provide financial backup, or act as pressure groups to ensure that cases of interest to women's issues reach the highest Court in the land (e.g., the Supreme Court in Nigeria) so that judicial stands on such issues are clear and unanimous.

The Large Roof Concept and Life Cap

Kiran Bedi
Indian Police Service, India

Friends and sisters from all over the world, and sisters from India in particular, we have here a large Indian contingent, which is absolutely proportional to our size, and we have very dynamic women, which is both within and beyond our potential.

I come to you with two kinds of experiences: first as a police officer who is now in her 24th year of police work, and also as officer of an NGO. For many years I have run an NGO, because to me policing is not just detection but primarily prevention. Policing to me is the power to correct; it is the power to reform and the power to do. That is how I looked at policing from the year I joined the service. It is what I said in my acceptance speech for the Ramon Magsaysay Award. To be honest with you, the citation in no way rewards me for the gangs I arrested but for the crimes I succeeded in preventing, and the majority of these were crimes against women. So these are the two streams which drive me and bring me with all happiness to this Forum.

When I started to work on this plenary's subject of violence against women, I couldn't think of addressing this Forum only as a police officer. I had to address you as a woman in the police force.

Women are biologically vulnerable — and here we are talking about the majority, not the minority. A woman is biologically vulnerable, economically weak, and poor; often poorly literate, she becomes pregnant at an early age. She is not only poor, illiterate, and pregnant; she is also inadequate. Most poor women of developing societies are primarily worried about food, fodder, and water; they have no access to networks, and they have very limited mobility. Their mobility, in fact, is linked mostly to the collection of water and fodder. The media uses the woman as an object to help sell consumer goods, but it enhances her own thirst for consumer goods as well and leaves her very frustrated. It is a man's world where all hard political decisions are made by men, not by women.

I have a concept to offer. It is called LARC, which stands for Large Roof Concept. Once a woman comes under the roof, she has access to many opportunities. If she enters the door from *C*, she has a counselor; *L* leads her to literacy and legal aid; *VT* means vocational training; *F* is for finance; *A* is for access to health, information, and anything else, even political access; another *C* is for the coordinator; and *P* stands for police. You cannot keep the police out of this Concept. A woman entering the Large Roof Concept has access to a counselor, legal aid, vocational training, finance, access to information and health care, the coordinator, and the police.

I offer this concept of LARC because I have seen all along that *P* alone – the police – is not the answer to our problems. *P* (the police) has to be integrated into the Large Roof Concept and retrained to understand that Concept. *E*, the concept of education, has to include re-education of men, which will not come without such a Concept. We have got to integrate all this into LARC.

Where does LARC lead us? To another concept called the Life Cap. What is this? Life Cap stands for all I have said – for literacy, legal aid, health care, vocational training, access to finance, access to marketing, access to information, counseling, coordination, the police, the courts and criminal justice system, and political access. To me this is Life Cap. Without this Life Cap, I will be working in isolation. As long as I work in isolation, we will not achieve as much as we wish to achieve. We need to develop the concept together, because the Life Cap will change the woman from an easy victim to a difficult victim to a nonvictim to an empowered victim who can save other victims, and finally into someone who can help devel-

op society and mankind the same way you and I are attempting to do.

I personally think we need to work together — NGOs networking with government and with police, not government alone. I am for joined hands, not isolated hands. We can achieve a double win. Why wait until tomorrow? Let's start lobbying! Let's bridge the gap with the Life Cap!

Strategies of the women's movement for combating gender violence

Alda Facio
Instituto LatinoAmericano de Naciones Unidas para la Prevención del Delito y Tratamiento del Delincuente (ILANUD), Costa Rica

It is going to be very difficult for me to outline in fifteen minutes all the strategies we women in the movement have used to combat gender violence against us, because they have been as varied, different and complex as the violence itself is varied and complex.

To simplify my task of sharing these initiatives and strategies with you, I have classified them on the basis of those to whom the strategies are addressed. Thus we have different strategies depending on whether they are addressed to:

1. the victims
2. the government (the executive authority)
3. the mass media
4. the legal system (including the legislature and the police)
5. the educational system
6. the health care system
7. other NGOs
8. aid agencies
9. the international community (including the United Nations and its agencies, the World Bank, the Inter-American Development Bank, etc.).

This list gives an idea of the diversity of strategies and the complexity of the task. They are all needed, because experience has shown that if we do not work with all of these target audiences, we shall not be able to work well with even one of them. Of course, that does not mean that a given NGO working in the field of elimination of gender violence has to have strategies addressed to each of these sectors. It does mean that the women's movement must learn to coordinate itself better, so that the work done by each organization is complemented by the work of another. If better coordination were achieved, there would not be so much waste or so many misunderstandings.

In addition, within each of these strategies classified according to those to whom they are addressed, there are different strategies depending on whether they relate to investigation, immediate or long-term response, or the total elimination of gender violence, which to me means all those strategies aimed at promoting equality between the sexes. Here, too, we women in the movement need to learn to respect ourselves and to understand that all the strategies are necessary and, moreover, are interrelated.

Regarding what I have just said about my belief that the only strategies aimed at totally eliminating gender violence against women are those that are addressed to promoting equality between men and women, I should like to make a brief comment. I want us to think that if the lack of equality between men and women is the fundamental source of gender violence against women, only the elimination of discrimination against women will put an end to this violence. All the other strategies are really strategies for reducing the number of cases of violence, punishing those who commit them or providing support to the victims. In saying this, I am not saying that there should not be strategies addressed to reducing violence, punishing those responsible and supporting the victims, but that we need to understand that only measures which promote equality are what we can term measures for the definitive elimination of gender violence against women.

Of course, within the strategies designed to promote equality as well, we can make the same classification, since in order to achieve equality we shall have to have all the sectors I have referred to above as points of arrival.

In referring to equality between men and women, I am not interpreting equality as being based on women having to look and behave like men, but rather an equality whose roots are to be found in the Convention on the Elimination of All Forms of Discrimination Against Women — that is to say, an equality of results based on the fact that the treatment men and women should receive may be identical or may be different, but should in either case result in there being no discrimination against women.

Thus, in some cases, for equality to exist between men and women, men and women will have to be treated the same, but in many other cases, for there to be equality between men and women, men and women will have to be accorded different treatment, because our situations are not the same.

In short, I want to emphasize that only strategies aimed at achieving real equality — what many people call de facto and not merely formal equality — can be termed strategies for the elimination of gender violence. Of course, there is still much for us to investigate in relation to violence, and we still need to be able to give immediate responses to the victims. For this reason, I have decided to talk to you for the rest of the time available to me about the considerations to be borne in mind in legislating on the subject of gender violence. Nevertheless, I should like to stress that in my view, legislative strategies should never be the only ones. In addition, they should be employed with the greatest caution, because the legal system is highly patriarchal in nature, and generally speaking, even laws that have been proposed by women can be turned against us.

Considerations to be borne in mind in legislating on gender violence

Legislating to eliminate all manifestations of gender violence is a complex task. How can all the manifestations of gender violence be included in a law or even in a body of legislation? Moreover, how can laws really aimed at eliminating gender violence be produced and applied within a system that could in historical terms be evaluated as one that has contributed to keeping women subordinate to their fathers, husbands, brothers and even sons, as demonstrated by a study conducted by ECLAC. It states:

> Latin American and Caribbean women have been legally subordinate to men ever since the establishment of the civil and penal codes in each country. The road to achieving equality of rights with men has been slow, full of obstacles and resistance . . . Nevertheless, there remain in the legislation discriminatory aspects to be overcome, some of them very obvious, such as the absolute authority of the husband, which still exists in some countries, and others more subtle but not less effective . . . The legal rules reflect the dominant social values, and the law has the function of regulating interpersonal and intergroup relations, thus legitimizing the ideological content stemming, for example, from the patriarchal system — which serves as the symbolic foundation of social life, rating and appraising actions and conduct in general.

Latin American and some Caribbean legislation — inspired by Roman or Napoleonic law and embodying codes that endorse and promote violence against women by their husbands as a means of punishment and control — reinforces the concept of male ownership and authority. The laws support and legitimize the person exercising power, in this case the man, over the person occupying an inferior position, namely the woman, thus establishing a normative and judicial system which operates in a feedback loop with cultural values and becomes consolidated as a basic obstacle to overcoming the problem of violence against women, especially the violence to which they are subjected within the family.

Once it is recognized that the legal system is committed to strengthening the structures that keep women in subordinate positions, it is obvious that in order really to eliminate the gender violence that is reinforced or generated by the legal system, qualitative reform of that legal system is required.

Nevertheless, while it is true that more than legislative measures are needed, and that total overhaul of the whole legal system also is called for, it is also true that we cannot avoid making use of the law to contribute to eliminating, punishing, and even preventing gender violence.

Accordingly, while we have to use the legal system and while we have to fight for the promulgation of laws that punish the different forms of violence against women, we have to bear in mind in doing so that any legislative measure aimed at preventing, eliminating, or punishing gender violence must take into account, in the first place, the fact that gender violence covers all forms of violence that perpetuate inequality between men and women, and at the same time ensure the inferiority of everything associated with being female. Accordingly, any law that aims at eliminating one or more of the manifestations of gender violence must take into account the inequality between men and women. As a consequence, the law must acknowledge that the perpetrator and the victim of the aggression are not on an equal footing; they do not have the same power or the same freedom to decide to put an end to the abuse.

In contradistinction to past legislative practice, the best way of eliminating or penalizing a form of behavior is by describing what it actually involves. Thus, instead of producing a law called the "law on incestuous sexual abuse" — which leaves it obscure who is doing what and to whom — laws of this kind should be given titles that are more in line with what is actually going on, such as, for example, "Law to prevent and penalize incestuous sexual abuse of girls and boys." This makes it easier to identify that the juridical commodity being protected is not "morality" or "accepted standards of behavior," but the physical, sexual, and psychological integrity of boys and girls.

Another important point is to recall that the aim is not to put more men in prison, but to prevent violence directed against women. Accordingly, although in order to combat many of the manifestations of violence against women, it will be necessary to establish by law that they are unacceptable and will be punished. It is at the same time important to seek other means of depriving such violence of legitimacy.

The fact that gender violence impedes the advancement of women in all walks of life and denies them dignity and the right to lead their own lives has been recognized at both the national and the international levels. Moreover, it has also been recognized that this type of violence has repercussions on society as a whole in that, although women are normally the immediate victims, the family, the children, and even men may suffer from the consequences of this type of violence. From this standpoint, legislation against gender violence must place special emphasis on prevention and, where appropriate, on rehabilitation. Therefore, a law aimed at preventing, eliminating and punishing a given form of violent conduct by men against women must allow the woman invoking that law to decide on what measures she wishes to be taken to penalize the aggressor, and must at the same time help overcome the obstacles that prevent women acting with legal capacity. Enabling women to influence the action that will be taken is of the greatest importance in that, at the same time as the violence is being penalized, it contributes to improving and enhancing the status of women, which in turn contributes to preventing violence against them.

A law aimed at penalizing gender violence that takes the form of sexual harassment, for example, should not only institute a new category of offense but also should establish conditions in which working women and students do not see their employment or their studies endangered because they have filed a complaint against the perpetrator. The law should afford the victim of the harassment some participation in deciding what punitive measure or measures provided for by the law will be imposed on the perpetrator of the harassment, and should also provide for mechanisms that enable women to overcome their embarrassment at filing a complaint against any act apparently or really associated with sexual identity.

Given that this embarrassment is not an individual or personal problem of each woman but is imposed on all women by the patriarchal nature of society, the burden of overcoming it should not fall on each individual woman. Therefore, the law must also provide for measures which compel employers to maintain environments and create commissions that help the victim overcome it.

Serious thought needs to be given to the large amount that has been written about the impossibility of changing attitudes and forms of behavior by promulgating a law, especially in relation to "machismo." The conquerors of all eras have changed, and even totally transformed, customs and values of the conquered peoples by promulgating legislation, especially because they have the backing of the repressive machinery of the state to penalize forms of behavior that the conquerors do not find desirable.

If thought is given to this, it may be concluded that laws can indeed play an important role in eliminating attitudes and forms of conduct that society does not find desirable. If most men who beat their partners or most incestuous abusers were punished, the message could be imprinted on the collective awareness that these forms of behavior are not acceptable. In relation to gender violence, however, the message has rather been that acts of violence against women will be tolerated because everyone knows that neither rapists nor men committing aggression in the home nor incestuous abusers are punished.

Moreover, legal systems still exist which implicitly proclaim that there are circumstances that justify violence by men against women. For this reason, an essential means of combating violence against women is the repeal of all articles that mitigate or exculpate violence against women and the prohibition, in legal practice, of invoking precedents or arguments that vest it with legitimacy. For example, there is a need to repeal the articles that mitigate or eliminate the penalty for rape of a prostitute, and those that permit murder on grounds of adultery or injury of a spouse, etc., to go unpunished. There is also a need to expressly prohibit prosecutors and defense attorneys from investigating, putting questions about, or submitting evidence of the prior sexual experience of a victim of rape or defloration, because such questions reinforce the idea that rape is not punishable if the victim was not a virgin.

It is also important that, when any law aimed at penalizing one or more of the manifestations of gender violence is being drafted, great attention should be paid to language, because this is capable of facilitating or impeding understanding of the legislation by the population at large. Clearly, the way in which a law is drafted influences people's knowledge of it and the use they make of it.

Despite the fact that the law is not, of itself alone, capable of eliminating gender violence, it can make an enormous contribution to eliminating it, especially if it is legislation that takes into account all the components of the legal system and, still more important, if it takes into account that the aim is to eliminate a form of violence practiced against women because they are women, and, ultimately, if it is legislation which makes clearly explicit who are the victims and who are the aggressors.

I should like to conclude this analysis by reminding you that, in the case of gender violence as distinct from other forms of discrimination against women, there is an extremely clear commitment on the part of States to legislating for its elimination. There are many resolutions of the United Nations and OAS which require member States to do something to halt and eliminate gender violence. Many of these resolutions call for the inclusion of legislative measures among the measures to be taken. Nevertheless, given that the Inter-American Convention for the Prevention, Punishment, and Elimination of Violence Against Women explicitly refers to this duty, in the Latin American and Caribbean region there is no need to make reference to these other resolutions, since the Convention is binding on all member countries of OAS, and especially on those that ratified it.

Article 7, in subparagraphs (c) to (h), refers explicitly to the duty to legislate:

The States Parties condemn all forms of violence against women and agree to adopt, by all appropriate means and without delay, policies aimed at preventing, punishing and eliminating such violence and to undertake the following: . . .

(c) to include in their domestic legislation penal, civil and administrative rules, and such other rules as may be necessary, to pre-vent, punish and eliminate violence against women, and to take the appropriate administrative measures required;

(d) to adopt juridical measures to warn aggressors to refrain from harassing, intimidating, threatening, harming or endangering the lives of women in any way that impairs their integrity or harms their property;

(e) to take all appropriate measures, including legislative measures, to amend or repeal laws and regulations in force, or to alter juridical or customary practices, that lend support to the continuation or tolerance of violence against women;

(f) to establish fair and effective legal procedures for women victims of violence, including *inter alia* protection measures, timely hearings and effective access to such procedures;

(g) to establish the judicial and administrative mechanisms necessary to ensure that women victims of violence have effective access to compensation, reparation for damages and other means of just and effective redress;

(h) to adopt the legislative or other provisions necessary in order to give effect to this Convention.

As the above list makes apparent, all signatory States have undertaken to legislate to eliminate gender violence. This commitment requires the promulgation of laws which posit the reality of gender violence, not a supposed neutrality of legislation. I emphasize this because in too many countries the laws for the elimination of gender violence have taken as their starting point a misinterpretation of the right of every human being to equality of protection before the law and by the law, with the result that laws have been promulgated which make no reference to the sex either of the victim or of the aggressor.

This interpretation is wrong because the principle of equality calls for an equality of status. If two people who are unequal are treated as if they were equal, the result is lack of protection for the person who is at a disadvantage.

For this reason, the Convention makes it clear

that the protective measures must be consistent with the reality of gender violence, namely that the aggressors are generally men and the victims for the most part women and that, accordingly, the legislation must reflect this reality.

Distinguishing features of violence against women: Strategies at the national level

Shanthi Dairiam
Asia/Pacific International Women's Rights Action Watch (IWRAW), Malaysia

I run the International Women's Rights Action Watch for the Asia/Pacific, a program based in Kuala Lumpur, Malaysia. It is a program that focuses exclusively on monitoring the implementation of the Convention for the Elimination of All Forms of Discrimination Against Women and builds the capacity of women's groups to draw accountability from their governments with regard to their obligations under this Convention.

I have also worked extensively in other capacities on the issue of violence against women. I would like to share with you the perspectives we have gained in working on the issue of violence, especially the kinds of strategies we have implemented and the need for us to be political in the work we do, to be much more integrated and much more holistic.

To begin, it is perhaps over the last 20 years that violence against women has become a critical issue. The consciousness of violence against women as a human rights issue has coalesced only recently. We have to be very particular in our program in recognizing that we are talking about gender-based violence. There are certain features which distinguish gender-based violence from all other forms of violence, because there is a great deal of violence in the world today.

Gender-based violence is distinguished by the fact that there are particular manifestations of violence which only women experience. This is not common to other species. It is true even in contexts where there is a particular calamity or a particular situation that the entire community faces. For example, armed conflict is a national problem, but within that particular problem — whether it is internal conflict faced by particular groups or conflict across borders — women under these circumstances face different forms of violation than men. We are talking, therefore, about particular forms of violations that women face.

The other feature that distinguishes violence against women is that there is a certain dynamic between the violator and the one who is violated. First of all, in most instances of violence, it is men who are the perpetrators. In most instances, it is a form of control over the woman because of the inequality between men and women. This is clear whether it be sexual harassment in the workplace, wife abuse in the home, or situations of armed conflict where there is rape and custodial violence of refugees. Wherever it occurs, there is a situation of power or control that is manifested in the violations. Even where there may be no actual physical abuse, violence can take the form of threat, coercion, putting the woman in fear of violence — all these manifestations have a power dynamic.

One of the things we always see is that a choice is made by the perpetrator to use violence. I emphasize this point because in the strategies we engage in, very often we get confused by looking at the perpetrator more as a victim. In the groups I work with, the question often surfaces, "But this poor man, isn't there something psychologically wrong with him, and shouldn't we do something for him? Is he a victim or is he a perpetrator?" This is a critical question, and therefore I emphasize the point that men make a choice when they use violence against women.

The third factor that we have to be cognizant of, and that should therefore inform the kind of strategies we engage in, is this: The vulnerability of women and the fact that they are at risk of violence puts them in situations where they can be easily manipulated or where their freedom and will are taken away. The vulnerability spans women's differing socioeconomic status. It spans both material and ideological dimensions.

The material dimension involves the context of economic dependence, the lack of social security, and other things women would need to lead independent lives in comparison to men. Even in contexts where women belong to the same socioeconomic class, they are at greater risk than men of the same socioeconomic status.

The ideological dimension of the vulnerability lies in the fact that the whole social environment is hostile to women who try to break away from situations of violence, because the environment is male-dominated. The social structure is male-dominated; the institutions such as the criminal justice system and even the bureaucracy that could put in place certain kinds of policy reforms — all these structures are male-dominated, and therefore not in any way supportive of a woman's need to be independent and free of a violent situation. This is another aspect of the vulnerability of women and it exposes them to greater risk. These are factors which distinguish gender-based violence, and they have to underpin any solutions we seek.

Strategies to combat violence against women have been put in place at many levels. In the international arena, there has been the development of international structures and mechanisms, human rights law, and policy; conceptual thinking has changed.

The United Nations itself, from the time of the World Conference at Copenhagen, has begun to articulate the fact that violence against women is a serious issue and that certain programs and policies need to be in place to curb this problem.

The most recent strategy has been the Declaration Against Violence, which came out in 1993, and the Convention on the Elimination of All Forms of Discrimination Against Women (CEDAW). Although it does not have a specific article on violence, the CEDAW committee prepared General Recommendation 19, indicating that violence as an issue can be addressed through various articles of the Convention and obligating state parties to the Convention to report on incidences of violence within their countries and what they are doing to combat this problem. At the international level and at the regional levels, there have been

many strategies.

What I would like to focus on are strategies at the national level. A proliferation of programs has been taking place over the past decade or 20 years. These strategies have been in place largely through the efforts of women's groups. In cases where the state has come in with a response, it has been mostly in the area of legislative reform. Even legislative reform has been put in place because of the demands of women's groups or the women's movement.

Looking at these strategies, we can divide them into broad categories. This has been our experience in Malaysia as well. The first category of strategies has been in the area of services for women who have been abused. The two most common forms of abuse have been wife abuse and rape. In particular, the support services in Malaysia have been for victims of domestic abuse. The services began with a battered woman shelter.

Services of this nature accomplish goals at two levels: (1) They provide a safe place that takes care of the immediate needs of the abused woman, the immediate need for safety and shelter; and (2) they provide support on the less tangible level of giving a message that wife abuse is not legitimate.

I believe this message has gone out, because there has been opposition to some extent. The providers of such services had to face a certain amount of conflict from the community. When the shelter was being set up, there was a lot of criticism from many quarters which said that women would not come and expose their families to shame and ridicule. But women did come.

We have a shelter which provides immediate support. Unfortunately, there have not been similar services set up for victims of sexual abuse. It is a problem, because when women want to break out of an abusive situation, unless we support it and make a stand against this, it will not happen. These supportive services are essential.

The second level has been legislative reform. Regarding both rape and domestic violence, there has been a lot of legal reform — in particular, criminalizing wife abuse. The third level of strategy has been in research, to identify forms of violence, and in the education and training of law enforcers, the judiciary, legislators, and the public.

Briefly, I want to share the weaknesses of these strategies. We have not addressed the vulnerability of women to violence in any of these services. The fact that they are socially and economically weaker and that there is male dominance at every level in institutions has not been addressed. Inequality and discrimination against women are issues that underlie the manifestation of violence against women: there has been no consistent or persistent long-term strategy to combat that. Programs have been set up to take care of immediate needs, to provide individual solutions to individual women, to have a campaign when there have been gross violations. Therefore, strategies have not been integrated enough, not been holistic enough, and not sustained enough. Where there has been legislative reform, it has not been followed through. Implementation has not been monitored to see how effective the law enforcement is, to see whether the infrastructure enforcing the law has the resources to implement it. Sometimes we do not have enough policemen to investigate. Therefore, the police forces and welfare services have to expand. Resources have not been allocated in these fields.

Third, the issues of violence have not been used adequately to mobilize the support of women themselves. There has not been a follow-up program to make them conscious of gender inequality and discrimination. Again, women activists have not recognized their own vulnerability to violence; very often, they have done something for a group of women who are more vulnerable than themselves. But I think we are all vulnerable, and we have to recognize the discrimination that we all face and eradicate it in all its forms.

These are the areas that we still need to move on. I do believe that the women's movement has made tremendous gains in this field, in particular in identifying violence against women as a violation of human rights. We need to move more strongly toward state obligations and community responsibility, and to remove responsibility from the individual woman who has to cope with the violence. The responsibility has to be put squarely on the community and on the state and other institutions that are around us.

Between protection and empowerment: Strategies against trafficking in women

Lin Lap-Chew
Foundation Against Trafficking in Women (STV),
The Netherlands

INTRODUCTION

In the early 1980s, mass tourism was becoming the alternative paradigm for development in many regions of the world. Women's organizations, development NGOs, and various action groups, especially in the developing countries, were awakening to the fact that not only the natural resources but also the human resources, namely the young women, of their countries were being traded for foreign exchange.

In the Netherlands there had been sporadic actions and publicity against tour organizations offering sex tours as package deals, sometimes with a "bride" included in the price. Travel brochures and advertisements offered "exotic" women from Thailand and the Philippines as by nature subservient and eager to please rich white males.

The organizers of these sex tours even suggested that their customers could assuage their conscience with the idea that they were doing a kind of "development aid" by buying the sexual services of women in developing countries. A group of Dutch and Asian women who were beginning to address this issue were enraged: This was imperialism, sexism, and racism rolled into one. The issue symbolized the total exploitation of womankind: sexual, economic, and cultural.

When news of an organized sex tour leaving from Amsterdam leaked out, they organized a demonstration at the airport which was synchronized with a demonstration at the Bangkok airport when the tour arrived there.

This event launched a joint campaign in the Netherlands and Thailand against prostitution tourism and trafficking in women both publicly and politically.

START-UP STRATEGIES
IN THE NETHERLANDS

The first essential step was to get the issue on the political agenda. The time, 1982, was opportune: the Ministry for Social Affairs had organized a study conference to gather the opinions of women's organizations across the board as part of the process of formulating state policy guidelines to address the issue of gender violence in the Netherlands. The group participated in the workshop on prostitution and succeeded in getting the Ministry to commission an official investigation into the phenomenon of what was perceived to be the reverse side of prostitution tourism: trafficking in women *into* the Netherlands for prostitution.

In 1985 the report of this investigation was published, entitled "Investigation into the nature, global scale, and channels through which women are trafficked into the Netherlands." The researchers, Buys and Verbraken, could not find any statistics to indicate the scale on which trafficking into the Netherlands was taking place, because no one had been addressing the issue systematically until then and there were no records in police or court files. Nevertheless, they were convinced of the reprehensible nature of trafficking in women:

> [T]rafficking in women is definitely not a marginal phenomenon … it transpires in a clearly criminal sphere, whereby deception, coercion and violence are used to transport women to the Netherlands, and to bring them into prostitution and keep them in prostitution. The victim is in a situation of exploitation, in violation of all basic human rights and of the right to sexual liberty, physical and emotional integrity.

This report signified political recognition of the seriousness of the issue and paved the way for the establishment of an NGO which would coordinate the various aspects of action to combat trafficking in women. The Foundation Against Trafficking in Women (STV) started work in 1987, with the tasks of organizing victim support services, informing the public, and developing policy.

An event which served as an impetus and learning experience for formulating local strategies and which opened channels for international contacts and cooperation was the Global Feminist Workshop to Organize Against Traffic in Women, held in Rotterdam in 1983 (report by Barry, Bunch, and Castley, 1984). Already, then, all the various manifestations of violations of the human rights of women had been identified and discussed, including trafficking in women for work as domestics, for marriage, and for prostitution, and plans were made to work at all levels.

THE NATIONAL STRATEGY

However, STV decided that the first necessary step was to build up a strong national program. The issue was complicated, and action had to be taken at various levels; most important of all, the need was felt to establish direct contact with women who had been victimized in order to gain insight into their real needs and issues and, as much as possible, to facilitate their speaking up for their own rights.

At that time, in the Netherlands as in most countries, trafficking in women and minors was simply defined as unlawful and punishable. In the Dutch penal code, the maximum sentence for trafficking was five years. This legislation had been in existence for nearly a century, and trafficking was typically equated with "bringing a person into prostitution"; the crime of trafficking was not precisely defined, and there were no guidelines as to the punishable elements. Thus, as mentioned earlier, there were very few cases listed under "trafficking in women" in police and court files.

Litigation was thus one area where concrete action could be taken. Legal proceedings against traffickers would serve three purposes:

• The victim could obtain some sense of redress if the trafficker was convicted;

• Creating precedents would help clarify the issues involved in trafficking and lead to more effective detection and prosecution of trafficking organizations; and

• This could be a very concrete manner to mainstream public awareness of the issue and keep it on the political agenda.

The problem was how to encourage and enable women to press charges. Most women we talked to were afraid of reprisals and terrified that news of their predicament would reach their families back home. At the same time, foreign women found working in prostitution by the Aliens Police were simply being evicted and sent back to their countries without any investigation being made into how they had gotten into the business in the first place. Needless to say, they did not even get time to recover, much less to consider pressing charges.

So the first campaigns undertaken by STV in 1987 and 1988 were aimed at refining the instruments for addressing trafficking in women at the levels of legislation and litigation:

First, to obtain a ruling under the Aliens Laws to prevent migrant women who may have become victims of trafficking from being deported before investigations have been done

• In August 1988, a special ruling — paragraph B22 (now B17) — was inserted into the Dutch Aliens Law. It stated that "at the least suspicion of trafficking, a woman should be allowed time to consider pressing charges. When she has done so, she should be allowed to stay in the Netherlands until the whole judicial process has been completed." This was necessary in order to encourage women to indeed press charges, which in turn would build up jurisprudence in prosecuting cases of trafficking. It was also necessary in order to allow women time and safety to recover from the bad experience they had gone through and to consider their options for the future.

• In 1993 this provision was extended to witnesses who were willing to testify for the prosecution in cases of trafficking.

Second, to sharpen the judicial definition of trafficking in order to facilitate prosecution of traffickers

• In 1989 the Attorney General's office formulated a new definition, stating that a person is guilty of traffic in persons when he

A. forces another person into prostitution by means of

1. violence; or

2. the threat of violence; or

3. by abusing the ascendancy (authority) derived from actual relationship; or

4. by misleading another person (deception); or when he

B. undertakes any action under such circumstances which he or she knows or could reasonably suspect, may bring the other into prostitution.

The following explanation was added: "Abuse of ascendancy derived from factual relations is assumed if the prostitute is in a situation which is not equivalent to the normal conditions for an independent prostitute in the Netherlands." This definition introduced the element of the "dependency" of the victim-survivor on the defendant as a probable basis to assume that trafficking has taken place. Later another qualification was added: that of "transporting a person across borders." In 1994 the relevant article in the Dutch Penal Code (art. 250) was changed to include this definition. The maximum sentence for trafficking was raised from five to six years. In cases involving minors, severe physical violence, and organized trafficking, the maximum sentence is ten years.

The success of these campaigns was due to the fact that two women — one from Indonesia (Adek) and one from the Philippines (Nena) — who had been trafficked into prostitution in the Netherlands in the early 1980s bravely filed charges, persisting in the face of slanderous character attacks and intimidation from the traffickers.

Their cases were exemplary: Adek's case illustrated the difficulties that victims of trafficking faced if they were sent home immediately, while Nena's case showed the reluctance of the judiciary to prosecute trafficking and the difficulties of successful litigation based on the then-inadequate definition of trafficking. They spoke before Parliamentary committees, to the media, and at meetings. The publicity and political value generated by these cases were crucial for the first successes achieved in the field of government policies.

The 1993 extension of the B22 (B17) provision to include witnesses was obtained after an intense lobbying campaign to prevent a prostitute from Colombia, who had reported a case of trafficking, from being deported. She had gone to the police when she could not stand seeing her Polish colleagues being physically assaulted and coerced, and in return she was locked up in prison and threatened with immediate deportation.

In 1992 STV evaluated its work and structure, choosing to remain a small organization but to extend its influence through an extensive network, like a spider in a web. In this way, we would be structurally obliged to consistently seek cooperation with others in every project we undertook. At present the general strategy of STV combines elements of anti-violence programs and pro-rights campaigns, based on the following principles:

• direct work with the women concerned as much as possible supporting them to speak up for themselves

• cooperation with others addressing related issues,

• continuing analysis and evaluation of the situation

• alertness to the prevailing conditions and timing for launching projects and campaigns.

Main areas of work

Work is done in the following five main areas:

Organizing social support and practical assistance for the victim-survivors

This includes safe shelter, legal aid, finances for basic needs, medical services, and counseling. This forms an essential element of the program. Through direct contact and in the process of assistance, firsthand insight is gained into the motivations and the dilemmas of women who have been deceived or coerced into prostitution, or who find themselves working under unfree and exploitative conditions. To date, STV has assisted about 750 women, in the beginning mostly from Asia, South America, and Africa, but in the last three years, more and more from Central and Eastern European countries (CEECs). Last year 69 percent of women assisted were from CEECs, double the number of the preceding year. STV has published a book describing the methodology developed for victim support work and is currently integrating the support work into the programs of mainstream social work institutions, shelters, etc.

Advocacy work and campaigning

This is done in the fields of legislation and litigation, social policies, migrant women's rights, prostitutes' rights, and assistance programs and to strengthen political commitment to combating trafficking in women. The interest and welfare of the women concerned is the basis of advocacy work and political campaigning. As much as possible, cooperation is sought with other organizations working on the same or related issues at national, European, and international levels.

Documentation and information services

These are tailored to inform specific relevant groups in the society and are aimed at increasing public awareness of the issue. STV publishes a quarterly magazine, *Keerzijde*, which carries current news and national and international developments in legislation and policies concerning trafficking in women, as well as thematic articles. Occasional publications are produced when appropriate or necessary.

Training and educational programs

These are organized to enable interested and qualified persons to participate in the various works of the Foundation or to initiate their own activities.

Prevention

This is done through collaboration with diverse organizations in specific countries on concrete issues, projects, and cases:

• cooperating on research projects, conferences, and seminars;

• supporting and participating in prevention initiatives undertaken in sending and receiving countries (currently two such projects are in progress in Poland and the Czech Republic); and

• participating in training seminars in sending and receiving countries.

STV can report a reasonable degree of success in these different areas of work. More and more people who should be able to reach us are now able to. The number of clients referred to us for assistance increases every year, and they are being referred to us not only by the police but by various other organizations and individuals. The number of cases that get to court is increasing slowly but surely, and more police districts are placing priority on investigating trafficking. We are in general overwhelmed with requests for advice and information and invitations to participate in conferences, give talks, etc., which means that there is growing concern for the issue as well as acknowledgement of our expertise.

INTERNATIONAL STRATEGIES AND A GLOBAL NETWORK

After five years of building up an effective national organization, STV was ready to participate in building up a strong international lobby to influence policies at European and international levels. Although we had developed considerable international contacts since the beginning of STV and had participated in important European and international conferences, the pressures of daily work did not allow more consistent follow-up activities. It was only in 1993 that international work became structurally programmed.

This work started with participation in the World Conference on Human Rights (WCHR) in Vienna in June 1993. STV presented testimony at the Global Tribunal on Women's Human Rights and cooperated with three other organizations to hold a workshop.

This cooperation was the beginning of a new international network, and the cooperating organizations — the Foundation for Women in Thailand, the Asian Women's Human Rights Council, the Human Rights Committee of the Council of Churches in the Netherlands, and STV — were later again present at the formation of the Global Alliance Against Traffic in Women (GAATW).

The lobby was part of the international women's movement for the recognition of women's rights as human rights. As you all know, the women's lobby was tremendously successful!

Along with all other forms of violence against women, trafficking is specifically mentioned in the Vienna Document and Program of Action adopted by the WCHR in June 1993. Paragraph I/18 states:

Gender-based violence and all forms of sexual harassment and exploitation, including those resulting from cultural prejudice and international trafficking, are incompatible with the dignity and worth of the human person and must be eliminated. This can be achieved by legal measures and through national action and international co-operation in such fields as economic and social development, education, safe maternity and health care and social support.

The inclusion of gender violence (including trafficking in women) on the human rights agenda is a political victory. It implies the recognition that keeping women in a subordinate position is a politically construed reality, which is maintained by patriarchal interests, ideologies, and institutions, and can therefore be dismantled. Strategically, nation states can now be held accountable for their efforts, or lack of efforts, to suppress gender violence.

At the end of 1993 STV launched an international project, utilizing the preparatory events leading up to the Fourth World Conference on Women as strategic lobbying moments. The objectives of the project are to extend the international network and identify partners working from the same principles of respect for human rights, in order to form a really strong lobby for pro-rights measures to prevent and combat trafficking.

Since then, the most important event has been the launching of GAATW in October 1994 in Chiangmai, Thailand. This happened during an international workshop organized jointly by the Foundation for Women in Bangkok, the Women and Autonomy Centre in Leiden, and the Women Studies Department of Chiangmai University, where 75 women activists, social workers, researchers, policy makers, jurists, and civil servants met to evaluate their work and formulate new strategies. The participants, coming from 22 countries and representing some 40 organizations, recounted experiences of women being trafficked within Southern regions, as well as to Western and Northern countries.

One sad but unanimous conclusion was that

there seems to be an explosion of trafficking; that trafficking routes crisscross each other faster than we can document them; and that the demands of the "consumers" are getting more and more cruel and degrading, while the trafficking networks are becoming more organized and violent in their business. Furthermore, the workshop also concluded that national governments in both sending and receiving countries play a significant role in exacerbating the situation by:

• promoting migrant labor exports without any regulations or supervision to protect the rights and welfare of the workers;

• neglecting to secure the rights and protection of migrants, particularly women migrants, in their respective states, thus rendering them dependent on third parties and middlemen; and

• denying women migrants opportunities to work in the formal, regulated sectors by upholding repressive immigration and migrant labor laws.

GAATW advocates a *pro-rights framework* to analyze and strategize against trafficking in women. Member organizations of the alliance in different countries are engaged in victim support work, running crisis centers, educational and informational work in prevention projects, and advocacy for women migrant workers' rights and for better legislation and policies. Because of the transnational scope of the problem, one of the priorities of the Global Alliance is to facilitate the exchange of information and practical experiences and cooperation where needed and possible.

Another important event in which GAATW members participated was the International Conference on Trafficking in Persons held in the Netherlands in November 1994. This Conference was jointly organized by the Department of Law of International Organizations of the University of Utrecht, the Netherlands Institute of Human Rights, and the Centre for Human Rights of the University of Limburg. Forty-one experts from all over the world discussed measures, within the framework of human rights, to combat the traffic in persons. The main conclusions of the Conference, which reiterate most of the conclusions of the conferences mentioned earlier, were:

• The traffic in persons is a worldwide phenom-

enon, often highly organized, dramatically on the increase, and taking new forms.

• The traffic in persons mainly affects women.

• The issue of traffic in persons should be dealt with in the international socioeconomic context.

• The traffic in persons is not only for purposes of prostitution; any form of forced labor in the formal and informal spheres should be eliminated.

The following international measures were suggested:

• Trafficking in persons should be prosecuted even when the actions that make up its component parts take place in different countries. Therefore, there should be strong national and international cooperation between departments of justice and the police, and between state agencies and NGOs working in direct contact with the persons concerned.

• An international standard should be developed to secure the protection and well-being of trafficked persons.

• The various international legal human rights instruments offering points of reference to combat traffic in persons should be applied and strengthened. Various existing international legal human rights instruments offer points of reference and should be examined further and, if necessary, improved and strengthened. The most relevant ones are Articles 6 and 19 of the Convention on Elimination of All Forms of Discrimination Against Women (CEDAW), the International Covenant on Civil and Political Rights, the Convention on the Rights of the Child, and relevant ILO Conventions (those concerning migrant workers' rights, forced labor, and freedom of association). The problem with all these international instruments is that they do not have strong monitoring mechanisms or the possibility of receiving individual or group complaints against violations.

• Individual complaint procedures should be developed and included in CEDAW and in the International Covenant on Economic, Social, and Cultural Rights.

• The Commission on Human Rights should establish a thematic Special Rapporteur or a thematic Working Group on Traffic in Persons to complement the mandate of the Special Rapporteur on Violence Against Women.

• The Commission on Human Rights should continue to support the mandate of the Special Rapporteur on the Sale of Children, Child Prostitution, and Child Pornography.

• The usefulness of the Working Group on Contemporary Forms of Slavery should be reviewed and, if appropriate, strengthened.

• The adequacy of the Convention for the Suppression of the Traffic in Persons and of the Exploitation of the Prostitution of Others (1949) in the fight against traffic in persons should be assessed. As the only Convention dealing explicitly with trafficking, it has proven to be ineffective for the simple reason that we are seeing today a dramatic increase, instead of a decrease, in the problem it is meant to address. It is also no longer adequate to address the contemporary situation, since it does not define trafficking in persons and does not address contemporary manifestations of trafficking in women.

Putting trafficking in women on the women's agenda

Two positive recent developments are the adoption of the Convention on the Elimination of Violence Against Women (CEDAW) by the UN General Assembly in December 1993 and the appointment of a Special Rapporteur on Violence Against Women in April 1994, in whose mandate "forced prostitution and trafficking" are included as issues to investigate.

The imminent lobbying moment is this Fourth World Conference on Women. The paragraphs on trafficking in the final Draft Platform for Action (document A/Conf.177/L.1, dated May 24, 1995) are reasonably acceptable, compared with the text in the first draft. The most important points included in the Platform for Action, and *not* bracketed, which means that they should remain unchanged in the final document, are:

• an expression of "pressing international concern" for the failure to suppress trafficking;

• a recognition that the 1949 Convention for the Suppression of the Traffic in Persons and of the Exploitation of the Prostitution of Others has not been effective, although the Draft Platform for Action does not go so far as to ask for review of the Convention itself;

• recognition that different forms of prostitution exist, by the inclusion of the word "forced" in the crucial contexts;

• a call to address the root causes of trafficking;

• implicit acceptance that trafficking occurs in more situations than prostitution, e.g., in "forced marriages" and "forced labor"; and

• a recommendation to cooperate with nongovernmental organizations to provide victim support.

Typically, the paragraphs which call on states to commit resources for the implementation of these good intentions are still bracketed!

Dutch state policy: Liberal but not liberating

As the saying goes, one's strength is also one's weakness. STV has to be constantly alert and avoid the pitfalls created alongside the achievements.

Although there is now a clear legal definition of trafficking, making it easier to prosecute cases of trafficking, and also a policy to provide victim support, there are still several limitations to the Dutch state policy:

• Despite original allusions to the human rights of victims of trafficking, the Netherlands' policy on trafficking is motivated principally by the expediency of criminal prosecution of the traffickers. Under such a policy, the woman is interesting only as victim and complainant. As soon as she has given all the necessary information, she is no longer needed and is given notice of deportation.

• Increasingly restrictive immigration policies throughout western Europe have led to more stringent bureaucratic control procedures to prevent any unlawful channeling of resources to "illegitimate aliens," which leads to ridiculous but painful scenarios for the women involved, although they are entitled to all social benefits for the duration of their stay in the Netherlands as complainants and witnesses for the prosecution. Moreover, the imminent decriminalization of prostitution in the Netherlands will be accompanied by a bureaucratic ruling leading to the exclusion of women from countries outside the European Community from working in prostitution in the Netherlands. This, we fear, will lead to a situation in which Dutch and

EC prostitutes will be legal, regulated, and protected, while foreign prostitutes will be illegal, unprotected, and thus even more vulnerable to traffickers.

• Trafficking, under the Dutch Penal Code, is limited to trafficking for prostitution, and the special ruling in the Aliens Circular and the victim support services that have been developed are not accessible to domestic workers who have been subjected to trafficking practices.

REPRESSIVE REPERCUSSIONS

The danger of states resorting to restrictive measures that further curtail the rights of women is ever-present; there have been many examples in the past.

At present we are alarmed at the news that the Government of the Philippines, instead of developing ways of protecting workers, has put restrictions on permits for domestic workers to work abroad.

And, more recently, one woman from Poland and one from Lithuania, on returning to their respective countries after filing charges of trafficking in the Netherlands, have been banned from traveling abroad for five years.

CONCLUSION

The strategy of STV lies "between protection and empowerment." Protection alone presumes weakness and need and does not appeal to the autonomy and power inherent in every individual; empowerment is an ideal still to be striven for. The most important principles underlying STV's strategy are:

1. All actions must be based on a consistent regard for the human rights — control of her own mind, body, and life — of the woman concerned.

2. Strategies must be based on a clear and regularly reviewed analysis of the different issues involved, in order to be real and practical.

3. The women concerned should be involved as much as possible in designing solutions to their problems; their interests and needs are the basis of action.

4. Empowering strategies and positive actions are preferred above repressive measures, which tend to have negative repercussions on the women involved and, sometimes, on all women.

5. There should be collaboration with others working on the same or related issues, on the basis of shared interests and/or pooling of resources and expertise.

XIII • Media, Culture, and Communication: Challenges and Opportunities — *Strategies*

Opening remarks

Kamla Bhasin, Moderator
Food and Agriculture Organization (FAO), India

I have been writing songs with and for women and children on issues related to women, ecology, human rights, and so on. It is an honor to welcome you this morning. For me, it has been extremely empowering to be in Huairou for this Forum. I have been feeling something like what a drop of rain must feel when she falls into the sea, where she suddenly feels so big, so strong, so powerful, part of a vastness which connects from one continent to another.

If others are also feeling the same, I would say, relish every moment of the days left here in the Forum and cherish these memories, because this is one of the most historic gatherings of women in the world and probably will be the last in this century where we gather in such strength.

I'll be doing two things: one, as a moderator, just putting the thematic, the problematic in front of us, reminding us what has happened and what we need to do. Then I will share a little bit about the strategy we have used in India, which is the use of songs, the use of the oral media.

The theme of our plenary, as you know, is "Media, Culture, and Communication: Challenges and Opportunities." We are talking this morning about strategies. We will be focusing on initiatives and strategies used by women and women's organizations over the past decade to bring about change. We will be talking about the methods used, reviewing them, talking about their efficacy, and also talking about the weaknesses we might have faced.

Let me just do a quick recap of the challenges we face. We have been saying that most communication, media, and cultures are part and parcel of the overall economic and political system; they are not separate. You can say that the media are like a flute, which has no voice or music of its own. The flute plays the music of the people who get hold of it. And as we see, most media are controlled, used, and manipulated by those in power locally, nationally, and internationally.

Therefore, the challenge before us is not only to control and change media but also to transform the unjust and unsustainable, in which 20 percent of the people control 80 percent of the resources of all kinds, including information technology and media. Our first problem, we have said, with media is that mainstream media are "man-stream": patriarch-controlled, made and oriented to patriarchy and to perpetuate patriarchy. They are tools of countries and classes which have grabbed political and economic power, and they serve the interests of these. The increasing centralization and control of media make them undemocratic, and they wipe out diversity; they wipe out cultural diversity to such an extent that we Indians and Bangladeshi now are forced to have a staple diet of *The Bold and the Beautiful* and *Santa Barbara*. Whether we like it or not, we have to get to know Donald Duck and O.J. Simpson.

Mr. Julius Nyerere once said, "It is very unfair that we Kenyans and Africans cannot vote for the president of the United States, because we hear about his election 24 hours a day, as much as a U.S. citizen does." But most U.S. citizens don't even know who Julius Nyerere is, and this is cultural hegemony.

The other problem related to sustainability is that the media are perpetuating consumerism of the worst kind. The American Dream is becoming a nightmare for the majority of the people of this world. It is breeding so much unrest, showing cakes to people and taking bread away from them, showing them luxuries and robbing them of their basic resources, be it the rain forests of Brazil or the coal mines or the people's labor in all our countries.

The increasing violence of media and the increasing monologues of media: women are challenging not only the patriarchal nature, they also are challenging the neocolonial nature, the imperialistic nature, of media. We have done this over the last several decades; we have used many strategies. Many of us have gone into mainstream media, have joined the boys, and have tried to see whether we can look at the world through women's eyes.

The others have created alternative media, and if you look at the NGO Forum, everywhere you can see the outburst of creativity which has taken place in the women's movement globally. Huairou today is the site of all kinds of examples of alternative media we women have created. We have created feminist songs, feminist theater, magazines, posters, books. We have created radio programs, television programs. We have made films. We have made kangas and quilts giving our messages, postcards and T-shirts, orchestras and circuses — everything to communicate, to reach out to others, to heal the wounds inflicted by the other media, to present our views, our perspectives.

We are also now getting into the electronic media in a big way. Satellites are being used by women. Satellite networks are being used to lobby, to be heard internationally, to make a difference at the global level. Through our media friends we have challenged not only patriarchy, but all other hierarchies — hierarchies of nations, of classes, of races, of castes, of gender, and of sexualities. Our media is full of challenges to these things.

We have been trying to do away with the duality between media creator and media user, the subject of media and the object of media. Our strategies have been different depending on our location, our specific situation at the level at which we are functioning, whether it is local, national, or international. It is now time to take stock of these; it is now time to ask: Have our media reaffirmed women, women's wisdom and knowledge? Have our media encouraged and unleashed women's creativity? Have our media empowered women and all the other marginalized groups in the world? And have we empowered human values? Because empowering women, according to me, is not enough, because I believe there is no sense in only changing the sex of the cancer cells, we have to fight cancers. Have we changed human values through our media?

Those of us who have been successful in mainstream, "man-stream," media, have we been able to retain our feminist principles? Have we been able to deal with technology and make it participatory? Or have we also gotten to copyrights rather than the right to copy — which is my definition of copyright?

We in India, at my group, have used songs to communicate. We use songs because women sing songs all the time in our culture, and in most cultures of the world they have been doing that. We use songs because ours is an oral culture. Almost 50 percent of our people are very wise, very intelligent, but nonliterate. We use songs because they create a feeling of community. They empower; they energize; you can join together almost immediately. What did we do with songs? All the analysis we got from feminists on violence, on dowry, or on structural adjustments — these are woven into songs. These messages are put into simple songs using folk tunes, and sung sometimes with ten women, if we are in a small group, or sometimes with 50,000 to 60,000 people.

Songs are the basis of building any community, and for me, the 21st century will again belong to communities. It is grassroots-level democracies which will have to flourish once again if we have to fight globalization, homogenization, centralization of power, and control. Songs, we have found, are an excellent medium to do that. They do away with the hierarchies of the creator and the listener. And, in fact, when I say I am a songwriter, I am wrong, because I find I actually never write a song. A song is born from the warmth and energy of the movement. As a songwriter, all I have to do is merge with the movement, and I find the words of the songs floating around, the analyses floating around. You just have to pick them up like flowers and weave them into a song, and the garland is ready. They are born of the movement; they go back to the movement. That is the dialectics of these songs.

I will just give you one example, because language and time are basic barriers this morning. On structural adjustments, we were trying to understand what was happening to our countries, so we constructed a song:

There is Pepsi Cola,
There is Coca Cola,
All kinds of cola,
But there is no water
When I open the tap.

Mr. Dunkle of the Dunkle fame,
And Cargill, the multinational,
They are uncles and aunts of our government,
While they thrive our people die of hunger

Friends, I could go on and on, but I have the responsibility to introduce to you the panel.

Reaching across the miles of ocean: Satellite communication at the University of the South Pacific

Ruby Va'a
University of the South Pacific (USP), Fiji

Greetings from the South Pacific. Kia orana, bula vinaka, namaste, kona mauri, halo long yufala everiwan, yokwe, omo yoran, fakalofa atu, malo e lelei, talofa lava.

To be invited to speak at this prestigious forum is a great acknowledgement of the work we are engaged in at the University of the South Pacific (USP). I am pleased and privileged to have been given this opportunity to inform you about our use of the satellite for distance and continuing education. Thank you to the NGO Forum '95 organizing committee.

The problem

Ours is a region of 32 million square kilometers, of vast expanses of water and isolated island nations on land masses that take up only a tiny fraction of that waterland. The provision of higher education for the USP region is the mission of the university, which faces tremendous constraints related to access, equity, and cost-effectiveness. The university's solution to better serve its member nations is distance education. The offering of higher education by distance mode has taken university programs and services to the village. It has also made the institution visible to its owners. But how could the problem of island isolation — given the great distances and the poor and costly transportation (air and boat) — be overcome in order to facilitate distance teaching? How could we reach our regional centers regularly, immediately, and interactively? Could there be direct and cost-effective interactions between distant students and on-campus course tutors, or would any such communication be constrained always by the high costs of long-distance telephone calls?

This paper outlines the USP satellite network as a communications strategy to address the problems of distance and isolation, effectively reaching across the miles, linking the university to the four corners of its region and the parts of the Extension operation with one another.

The context

The University of the South Pacific belongs to 12 countries of Polynesia, Melanesia, and Micronesia: Cook Islands, Fiji, Kiribati, Marshall Islands, Solomon Islands, Nauru, Niue, Tokelau, Tonga, Tuvalu, Vanuatu, and Western Samoa.

A comparison with the outline of China or the United States will give some idea of the area of the USP region. In her award-winning video *The Divided World*, Dr. Claire Matthewson presents the region's great diversity in physical geography, population size, economy, education, social and cultural aspects, and political standing. For instance, the atolls of the Republic of Kiribati are numerous, low-lying, and scattered across four time zones. The Independent State of Western Samoa comprises seven islands of volcanic origin, all within an hour's ferry ride of one another, while it takes 20 minutes to drive around the phosphate-rich island of the Republic of Nauru. The total population served by the USP is less than two million, with country populations ranging from 1,500 in Tokelau to 700,000 in Fiji. The multicultural and multilingual (more than 300 languages) mix means more barriers. Most people still have neither access to electricity nor a telephone nor a reliable postal service. Inter-island transport is fraught with difficulties; regionally it is conducted mostly by air and domestically more often by boat, which in some cases is quite irregular — for example, Tokelau is serviced by boat from Western Samoa at best once a month.

The USP was established in 1968 to serve the higher education needs of 11 countries. In 1988 the Marshall Islands became the twelfth. The university has two campuses: the main campus in Suva, Fiji, and the other in Apia, Western Samoa.

As a dual mode institution, the USP teaches both face-to-face and at a distance. The distance program is the responsibility of University Extension, which interfaces with students and local communities through the Regional Extension Centers, physically present in all member countries except Tokelau.

Distance education at USP

Two years after the university was established, it was apparent that an alternative to face-to-face (on-campus) teaching was needed, since many potential students could not leave their jobs or families. Hence, in 1970 a few teacher education courses were offered for study by distance education, and Extension Studies was born. In 1976, 15 credit courses were offered; today in 1995 the distance program has grown to 150 courses for pre-degree and undergraduate students. Study programs include Agriculture, Accounting, Education, Law, Librarianship, Management, Marine Studies & Ocean Resources, Tourism, Pacific Languages, and the usual science and social sciences. Study materials for the distance mode are mainly in the print medium. Student enrollment has grown from 1,300 in 1976 to almost 14,000 in 1994.

Dr. Matthewson refers to the distinct pattern of enrollment with regards to gender: from 12 percent females in Melanesia to 60 percent in Polynesia. A recent study on access barriers of women in distance education in the USP region has revealed that this proportion has not changed much.

Continuing education at USP

Hand in hand with distance education is another program known as continuing education, which operates through University Extension and its Extension centers network. Continuing education is the noncredit offering. It includes short-term courses and workshops in which participants learn new skills or upgrade existing professional ones. The regional programs include, for example, community nutrition, preschool teaching certificate, nonformal early childhood education, early childhood education, and caregiving for the disabled; the national programs include such areas as basic English, basic bookkeeping, creative writing, fabric dyeing, guitar playing, computer awareness, shell jewelry, flower arrangements, national and foreign languages, pottery, and video production. An average of 6,000 participants complete continuing education programs each year.

The strategy

Both distance education and continuing education use the USP Educational Telecommunications Network (USPNET), the satellite facilities which encompass the whole USP region and provide the means for direct (live) dialogue.

Using INTELSAT, USPNET is an audio teleconferencing system linking nine countries — five by satellite and four by high frequency (HF) radio. Since May of this year, the network has been extended to a tenth country through the generosity of PEACESAT. Hence this audio medium is used extensively for satellite tutorials for distance courses; for networking, training, information sharing through guest speakers, and advocacy in the continuing education program; and for administrative functions of both aspects of the University Extension and the USP as a whole.

The satellite network has facilitated meetings of regional groups such as the Pacific Island Regional Association of Distance Education (PIRADE),

Community Nutrition Certificate tutors and participants, South Pacific Regional Environment program (SPREP), women's interest groups (e.g., Women in Media), Pacific church groups, librarians, and also UNESCO and WHO. It has made possible live debate and discussions among participants in a session and facilitated the presentation of a paper to a conference in New Zealand from a participant in Suva. Through the satellite, there has been an international teleconference between Vancouver, Solomon Islands, Fiji, and Brunei.

In distance education, tutors and students participate in tutorials just as occurs on-campus, except they cannot see one another. Extension Headquarters in Suva coordinates the regional distribution of study materials, examination papers, mailbags, and assignments and receives centers' queries, which include additional orders of study materials, enrollment, students' unreturned assignments, problems about exam papers, difficulties with course materials, and staffing matters. This has provided a means of immediate contact and allowed the interchange of views. Interviews of potential regional staff have often been facilitated by the satellite network. During the period February-June 1995, there were about 400 hours of satellite tutorials.

The idea

To be able to operate across such huge distances successfully, a viable means of communication is required, allowing immediate feedback to queries and enabling discussion on matters of common purpose. In 1971 the United States National Aeronautics and Space Administration (NASA) offered its Applications Technology Satellite (ATS-1) for free use by the people of the Pacific, and USP immediately joined the Pan-Pacific Educational and Communications Experiments by Satellite (PEACESAT). It was soon realized that there was tremendous potential in the outreach progam, and so in 1974 the USP applied for some independent satellite time and the USP network (USPNET) was established. In 1977 access was increased to 24 hours a week.

So useful had the network been that when ATS-1 went out of service in 1985, rigorous negotiations for the use of INTELSAT occurred, and

USPNET was silent for only about one year. In 1986 the network resumed operations. Access is now seven days a week.

The difficulties

The initiative has not been ideal. There have been problems with the technology, both in installation (due to lack of funding) and in maintenance. In the days of ATS-1 reception was often unclear, voices faded out, and communications became quite irritating. When INTELSAT came into use, four centers were left out of the network: one due to inability of the University to meet the high cost demanded by the local company, and three due to lack of facilities in those countries. Until the PEACESAT agreement this year, Kiribati has been off the air. Three other countries have been linked up through HF radio.

A serious implication was that for all sessions, written transcriptions needed to be circulated, particularly for the sake of Kiribati. Indeed, all tutorials are recorded on audiotape and distributed to centers for outer-island students and others who have little access to the facility. Most times also, at least one Center is not on air due to local power failure, a public holiday in that country, or very poor transmission, especially for the HF systems. Furthermore, communication is not continuous as on the telephone, since there is only a single channel in one-way use, so that users need to switch off their microphones and go "over to" the other person. In addition, the system is affected by other unidirectional media, such as radio and TV broadcasts, and there is much static disturbance.

Another problem has been the four time zones of the region and its division by the international dateline. Regional group usage has been limited to Tuesdays to Fridays, 9:00 a.m. to 6:00 p.m. Fiji time. For instance, Monday 5:00 p.m. in Fiji is Monday 4:00 p.m. in the Solomon Islands and Vanuatu, Sunday 6:00 p.m. in Western Samoa, and Sunday 7:00 p.m. in the Cook Islands.

For distance education, access varies: It is easy for those near the USP Center and impossible for those on outer islands or in rural areas. Most countries outside Fiji, even those within five kilometers of the Center, have low access because after-hours local public bus transport is nonexistent and taxis are very costly. This has limited satellite tutorials to Tuesday through Friday, 11:00 a.m. and 5:00 p.m. Fiji time. Students have also reported difficulties with employers being reluctant to release them during the day; hence, audiotape copies of satellite sessions are made available. Finally, using the technology itself presents barriers for those uncomfortable with it, and two booklets have consequently been developed to guide both students and tutors.

The successes

Offering satellite facilities for teleconferencing by international, regional, and other groups and organizations has been seen as an important contribution of the University to the general development of the region. In a study on the effect of satellite tutorials, Gillard and Williams (1986) found that students viewed the sessions as valuable aids to learning. Satellite tutorials have been reiterated by students as helpful to their learning, and Center staff hold the view that better technology leading to better reception will without doubt increase participation. In continuing education, networking via the satellite has been viewed as very useful by the users and has provided the opportunity for live discussion and immediate feedback.

Finally, the extensive use of the facility for administrative purposes has given those out in the region a feeling of belonging and being a part of the whole operation, in addition to ensuring a cost-effective means of communication.

The lessons

I had been with Extension for a few months when the satellite facilities came to a halt, yet even that short period had impressed upon me the positive effect of the network. During the time between the end of ATS-1 and the beginning of our use of INTELSAT, it felt as if we were in a vacuum. Without doubt, satellite communication has been of tremendous importance in the University's presence in the region, in the distance and continuing education programs, and in forging links across the social, political, and geographical barriers of island isolation, diverse cultures and values, and oceans.

I understand that one of the education issues highlighted at the ESCAP ministerial conference and the NGO Forum at the World Summit for Social Development was reducing educational disparities between males and females. The satellite network has enhanced the learning of distance students despite the many barriers. And since distance study has increased opportunities for education of those constrained by family ties and financial difficulties, particularly women, this communications strategy has played an indirect role in increasing the access of women to higher education. However, the use of satellite tutorials must be planned with care as late sessions have been found to be inconvenient for women, although the audiotape recordings alleviate this problem to some extent. Such a strategy can be useful if applied with careful planning and consideration of the users.

The satellite has proven cost-effective and has become successful in the support activities of an operation that spans millions of kilometers. It has supported the USP policy of providing both higher and continuing education to the people of the South Pacific where they are. In networking the medium has been used for discussions; for sharing information and resources; for advocacy, involving audiences and guest speakers participating in discussions on issues of concern; and for providing participants in adult education the opportunity to improve their quality of life through the weekly tutorials and meetings. The Continuing Education program has also used the satellite for training Access Barriers co-researchers and field workers based at USP Regional Centers in the use of the research questionnaire.

Finally, the USPNET would not be the success it is if not for the regional cooperation shown by the national telecom companies and the fruitful communication of those who spearheaded the initiative.

The future

It is my view that the satellite medium is a powerful and effective communication tool. In the developing nations, financial constraints severely limit development activities. At the USP, the satellite has effectively reduced communication costs, which would have been prohibitive if we had depended only on the telephone and fax facilities. Despite the limitations of audio-only, power failures, public holidays, fear of technology, and time zones, the satellite has reduced the miles of ocean to mere inches of sound waves. There is no doubt that successful communication transcends all barriers and that the use of satellite communication has removed the barriers of isolation and prohibitive costs. I would not presume to offer a solution to your deliberations.

And so I leave you with this short verse, begun in Suva, Fiji, last week and finished in Beijing this morning:

> *ours is a region of voices echoing across the*
> *ocean*
> *seeking to find land to bounce back from*
> *ours is a region of dots, little dots of islands*
> *trying to keep above that ocean*
> *trying to emerge clear*
> *of the chaos of development*
> *ours is a region of peoples needing to find*
> *a line, a link, a means*
> *to connect them to the world*
> *and each other*
> *uniting into one voice*
> *empowered, encompassing, endless!*

References

Gillard, G.M. and Williams, A.I. "Improving Satellite Tutorials at the University of the South Pacific." *Distance Education* 7: 2 (September 1986).

Matthewson, C.C. "The USP's Divided World." Paper presented to the Canadian Association for Distance Education Conference, Vancouver, 1994.

University Extension. *South Pacific Women in Distance Education*. Suva, Fiji: University of the South Pacific, 1995.

Vaa, R. "A Case Study on Information Technology at the University of the South Pacific," in *Pacific Regional Seminar on Information Technology*. Port Moresby: Commonwealth Association of Science, Technology and Mathematics Educators, University of Papua New Guinea, 1988.

Wah, R. "The University of the South Pacific Education Telecommunications Network." Paper presented at the International Symposium on the Impact of Higher Education on Social Transformation in Asia and the Pacific, Chiba City, Japan, 1992.

Electronic networks and the participation of civil society in global processes

Magela Sigillito
NGONET; Third World Institute, Association for Progressive Communications (APC), Uruguay

Introduction

In recent years, electronic communication has been seen as an almost magical tool for solving all our communication and information woes. It is being used in a context of growing globalization and has contributed to that process. It has permitted an increase in communication between people who are geographically distant but who have common problems, and it has promoted and facilitated the possibility of global problems being treated globally. NGOs have used electronic means to communicate among themselves, establish networks, receive and disseminate information, and influence decision-making processes.

The disparity between North and South and between women and men, in terms of access to and use of this technology, is clear. These inequalities are reflected not only in access to communication channels, but also in the information distributed via those channels.

Can electronic communication be a tool for empowerment of organizations in the South and particularly for women? Or will it be one more element to further increase the inequalities between North and South, between men and women? We at NGONET believe that it is a useful tool and, if used with our own realities in mind, can be an element for strengthening the activity of civil society and its ability to impact on decision-making processes worldwide. The experience of recent years would seem to confirm this.

Communications infrastructure

While Internet is a reality in industrialized countries, in the Third World, access to electronic communication still has its problems. The situations are diverse: In some countries, poor quality telephone lines hamper access. In others, there simply is no Internet connection. In others there is one, but the costs are high. This means that some of the newly developed information tools — for example, the World Wide Web (WWW) and even Gopher — are of little use for Southern users. Moreover, the communication protocols developed in the North only allow for transmission of standard ASCII characters, which means that the same ease and quality of transmission cannot be achieved with information in languages using other characters (French, Spanish, Portuguese, Arabic, Chinese, etc.).

Access to the South's information

Due to the communication difficulties in the countries of the South, the volume of information generated in the Third World that is available in the electronic network is significantly less than that coming from the countries of the North. During the Earth Summit, some 5,000 pages of information circulated in electronic networks, of which only 1,000 came from the South. The weakness of our information structures means that in most Third World countries, it is easier to obtain a document produced by a European or North American researcher than a document produced in another Southern country, and at times even in the same country. Furthermore, most information circulating electronically is in English, which limits its use by non-English speakers.

Women's access to electronic networks

Technological designs are developed with the possible user in mind. The sexual division of labor places men in the majority of jobs where decisions are made as to the technological designs to be developed. When there is a woman among them, she has often acquired "male logic." These individuals necessarily think with a male mind, so that the technology is conceived for men, even if this is not a conscious intention, and is designed to be used with male logic. Thus, the technology is gendered.

Another problem to be underscored is the paradox reflected in the excess of information produced in the North that is available electronically, which becomes a sort of informative avalanche, so to speak, and whose result is disinformation and the scarcity of information produced in the South. In fact, it is often difficult to find and determine what information is really relevant.

In conclusion, the difficulties in accessing electronic networks, the high costs of communication, the predominance of English, the avalanche of information from the North, and the scarcity of information from the South, together with the fact that technology is gendered, imply a need for creative solutions adapted to our needs.

Strategies

Despite all these problems, electronic communication offers enormous advantages over other means (telephone, fax). It is cheaper, permits communication instantaneously or in very little time, and it is democratic to the extent that it allows for horizontal communication and debate among all those using it. Nevertheless, this democratic nature is valid only if we think in terms of who has access to the network. If we know how to use it, it will be a tool for empowerment. If not, we will generate a new disparity between those who have broad access to information and communication and those who do not.

The experience of the different initiatives involving electronic communications among Southern NGOs — among them, NGONET — has shown that "small nodes" can be set up to run and become economically sustainable after a year in Third World countries with a very small initial investment. Capacity-building through the training of operators and users is a key component of success in a project like this, but the crucial factor is the availability of the information that users need.

The Association for Progressive Communications (APC) has played a key role in the establishment of these "small nodes" in Southern countries. APC is an electronic network devoted specifically to serving NGOs and activists. It has more than 50 member networks and offers a vital tool for communication among thousands of nongovernmental organizations, activities and educators in 133 countries — many without direct access to Internet — and a tool for sharing information among organizations and individuals.

Moreover, to surmount access difficulties, it is vital to have intermediaries who access the information generated at the international level select and transmit it in a language and format appropriate for the audience to whom it is directed, and at the same time identify and disseminate the information generated in our countries at the national and local levels. This implies a conception of horizontal communication and the existence of a back-and-forth flow of information that are contrary to the pyramidal and hierarchical communication model providing for transmission of information from a single point to a mass of passive receivers.

Women must have access to the information we ourselves produce, and at the same time must disseminate our points of view so as to influence decision-making processes at all levels. This technology can be an appropriate means, if we manage to get beyond the barriers that hinder its use. To do so, we feel it is necessary to strengthen the ties among women so as to move ahead with the training of other women and decisively take collective ownership of these tools, so as to use them to our benefit, exchange ideas and viewpoints on issues that concern us, and surmount the obstacles that remain.

A good example of this type of activity is the Program for Support to Women's Networks of the Association for Progress of Communications (APC), which over the last two years has promoted the incorporation in electronic networks of women's organizations in more than 30 countries within the framework of the preparations for this Conference. Right now it has two communication rooms installed in Beijing (one for the NGO Forum and the other for the Fourth World Conference on Women) and provides services including communication, information, and training on the use of this technology.

The NGONET experience

Civil society can influence global processes only if it has appropriate and timely information and the communication channels that make it accessible. In fact, decision-making processes worldwide, although they may seem distant from the problems of Third World citizens, have a real impact on their everyday life. At NGONET, we select relevant information on these processes and seek to transmit it in a language understandable to Third World women and men. At the same time, we collect information produced locally and nationally and disseminate it internationally.

This implies the development of communications strategies that take the following aspects into account:
• that the South is in no way excluded;
• that Southern women are not excluded; and
• that the issues of interest to civil society in the South appear on the agendas for discussion.

Considering the aforesaid difficulties and challenges of developing a communications strategy in our countries that will effectively contribute to increasing men's and women's understanding of international processes and promote their participation in those processes, NGONET combines the use of electronic mail with conventional means. We disseminate information by electronic mail, fax, diskettes, mail, and radio, and at the same time promote electronic communications. Furthermore, taking into account that English is the language of global negotiations and that those who do not read and write English only have access to a tiny part of the information, we translate relevant information.

For example, during the preparatory process for this Conference, we disseminated information features in four languages (Spanish, French, English, and Portuguese) via electronic mail and regular mail. These features were prepared by women in different Third World countries and were geared to publicizing the achievements made by women at earlier United Nations conferences. Radio programs were also transmitted to Latin America. The NGONET document server — which can be consulted using a simple electronic mail message — contains both the official documentation of the World Conference on Women and the information produced by women's groups.

The NGONET document server is a means that makes it possible to bridge the technological gap between North and South, allowing anyone having electronic mail, even if not directly connected to Internet, to retrieve information. We understand that we need a focus using a "least common denominator," which is electronic mail and the tools that have electronic mail as their basis: mailing lists, electronic conferences, document servers, etc. At the same time, we believe that the South's possibilities for access must be stepped up by developing appropriate tools — in particular, software to work with less sophisticated machines and low-quality telephone lines.

Conclusion

In conclusion, electronic communication exists and is being used, albeit in an uneven manner. It can be an empowerment tool, or it can generate greater disparities between men and women, and between North and South. The challenge we now face is knowing how to use it in keeping with our realities and needs.

We should change the prejudice of the Western media

Xiong Lei
Capital Women Journalists Association, China

I am very glad to to be able to talk at this Forum. I longed to have such an opportunity, because I'm eager to share with you our experiences. Because of the language barrier and because we lack the experience of participating in such an international gathering, few Chinese women can have the opportunity to talk at such a Forum. That is why I'm happy to be here to speak to you.

First I'd like to say something about what we women journalists are doing in China; then I'd like to make some comments on the Western mainstream media from the perspective of a woman journalist in a developing country.

Media used to be a male-dominated world in China. We did not have a woman journalist until the end of the last century, when a woman assisted her uncle in running a newspaper. Then we had a women's newspaper around 1905. But for a long time since then, women journalists were still rarely seen in China.

Today there are many women journalists in China, and we feel so equal with our male colleagues that many women journalists — and I myself — took for granted our entering this trade. But this doesn't mean that we have no problems here. During our preparations for this Conference, many of us found that because we were born and grew up in cities and because we had received a good education, we tended to neglect the problems confronting rural women in the poverty-stricken areas. So some women journalists launched a magazine especially for rural women, and its circulation has reached 160,000 in a little more than two years. Some women journalists were not satisfied with our environmental situation and wrote some very good investigative reports on our environmental problems, which have drawn attention from both the government and the people. We also conducted a nationwide survey on the status of women journalists. Those who are interested in this survey can come to our workshop on women and media.

Nor were we satisfied with China's mainstream media coverage of women. We conducted a survey on the ten leading newspapers in China and found that women represented less than 4 percent of the front coverage in these newspapers. So we sent the findings to these newspapers' editors-in-chief. Of course, all of them are men. We conducted a sort of opinion poll among them, asking them if it is necessary to increase the coverage of women. Most of them said yes, and we felt very much encouraged. I think that to change the media coverage of women, we cannot only run some alternative media but must also establish a kind of cooperative relationship with our male colleagues in the mainstream media and make a change together with them.

But none of these activities of ours get any publicity in the Western mainstream media. Why? I feel there is a strong prejudice, a strong bias, not only against China but also against all the developing countries and against women. The Western mainstream media always look for troubles. Take this NGO Forum, for example; more than 25,000 women from all over the world are here, discussing various issues we are concerned with. We are concerned with these issues because we want to make our world better. But the Western mainstream media just ignore us and focus their attention on some minor things, such as the collapse of a section of wall, some car accidents, and a few Tibetans in exile. This reminds me of the male owner of a newspaper chain in the United States, whose name was Hearst. During the Spanish-American War, he told one of his reporters: "You furnish me a story, and I furnish you a war." Today many Western media people are doing the same here. They love trouble — so that if there is no trouble, they will make some.

The theme of this Conference is equality, peace, and development. But in Western media coverage of the developing countries you can feel the strong inequality. We want to build up peace in the world. But the Western mainstream media always look for conflict. If they are so interested in conflict, how can the world have peace?

In the process of development in the developing countries, there are bound to be problems, shortcomings, and mistakes. It is easy to criticize them. But it is difficult to build a new world. I want to ask those Western media: When you make criticisms, what positive comments and constructive suggestions have you also made?

There is still a long way to go before the developing countries have equality in the Western mainstream media. I think we need a change here. First of all, we should change their prejudices. It is not easy to change their attitude immediately. But I think we should take advantage of this Conference and Forum to unite and create enough pressure for them to make a change.

Women should be heard: Expertise as well as experiences

Laura Flanders
Fairness and Accuracy in Reporting (FAIR),
United States

Thank you very much. I am speaking to you on behalf of the media watch group FAIR. I would like to start by thanking all the members of the NGO Forum who have made this program possible. And I would also like to thank our hosts, the Chinese people.

I have the privilege of living in New York City, the media capital of the world. So, of course, thanks to all the radio stations, television networks and newspapers to which I have access, I am lucky enough to know absolutely nothing about your ideas and your way of life. And that is part of why I am here.

I should not have to travel halfway around the world to hear from the Chinese people. The words of your government leaders and your businessmen seem to get through just fine. Nor should any of us really have to make this expensive trip to hear from the women at this Forum. It is ironic that so much of the press coverage of this event has focused on the difficulties that women are having getting heard and seen in Beijing. The problems here are nothing in comparison to what most women face every day trying to be taken seriously by media in their hometowns. This NGO Forum is not just the largest gathering of women in history. It is probably the largest gathering of marginalized experts the world has ever seen.

Unlike some women's media watch groups, at FAIR we do not believe in women's issues. We are against the very idea that men and women have mutually exclusive areas of concern. What we call for is reporting that covers the world as it is — more than half populated by women, with ideas and experiences and bodies that matter — regardless of their race, their age, their sexual orientation, their political power, their physical abilities, or their class.

Consider any topic, whether it is the global economy, health care, education, human relations, or how to avoid war. You are the experts because you, as people who are focused on women and the marginalized, are paying attention to the majority of people on the planet, the very people who are on the cutting edge of current policy. In many cases, it is an edge that does not just cut, it kills. And you would think that would make your information good to share.

So here you are, 20,000 or more of the world's most rarely heard-from experts, all gathered more or less conveniently in one place. Being discussed here are some of those key issues, some of them the very issues that the boring men in suits discuss on television every night. The press are here, a lot of them, and I am glad. As a reporter myself, my sympathies are with you. I wish you well. But what do we get? Stories about justice, equality, and how women are moving an international agenda from the bottom up? Hardly.

I turn on my TV in the hotel room and read a U.S. paper and what do I find? The same U.S. media that remained tight-lipped when Ronald Reagan approved sales of police equipment to China's internal security force, and praised Vice President Bush's visit here in 1985, are suddenly concerned about security levels and whether Hillary Rodham Clinton is disrespecting human rights by coming to a rights conference. People think the media's sound bites are short; that is nothing in comparison to their memory. Has anyone seen *Time* magazine this week refer to the fact that in 1985, their editors selected Deng Xiao Ping as "Man of the Year"?

Sure, there are traces of the discussion that is happening here, but those traces are edged out by the same government and establishment faces and the same rhetoric that always dominate the news. We call what is happening here "wildlife reporting." People like yourselves who represent vast popular movements may get captured in a short or two — speaking at a demonstration or waving a fist into the air. But you are not allowed to set the agenda. You are not invited into the television studios to sit on the comfortable chairs like the generals and the bankers. They get to explain

themselves in a number of paragraphs. You get to shout a slogan in the street. And then, having been exiled to the margins, you are called "marginal" or "not representative." It is a cute trick. And it happens over and over again.

What has changed in twenty years? Well, women get into a few more pictures. This weekend's *Herald Tribune*, for example, put two women from this Forum on the cover (September 2-3). But the women were gagged: in the picture and in the paper. Look inside for the follow-up story, having read the caption, and there is not a word from the two protesting Tibetans. It was interesting over the past few days to watch how the big cameras came into this hall when celebrities were talking or when women were telling their personal stories, but left when women were giving analyses of things like the global economy or the rise of the right.

We want women seen, but we also want them heard — women's expertise as well as their experience. We are not just bodies; we are also minds; and some of you can argue the pants off some of the establishment's stuffed shirts.

These days there are more women in the industry, but unfortunately, as we have seen here, without other changes, adding female reporters does not necessarily guarantee a sea change in the coverage. A woman in front of the camera may be a good new role model, but gender parity without a broadening of the political spectrum will help only the individuals who scramble to the top.

We also have to be more subtle in our call for more women opinion-givers. The same issue of the *Herald Tribune* this weekend published an opinion piece by a woman — what a concept! But the author, Camille Paglia, who seems to believe that only Americans worry about reproductive rights or homophobia, is not a women's rights expert or an activist. She is an art critic who has made a name for herself echoing old familiar arguments against the movement for women's rights. She once said that "feminism misses the blood lust in rape, the joy of violation and destruction." The call for women pundits needs to be more sophisticated. We need to say which ones.

It is no academic question who gets to speak in

mainstream media. The people who frame the media debate are often framing political policy and public opinion. Take crime, for example. In the United States, the number of victims of violent crime decreased by 9 percent from 1981 to 1990, but in the same period, the number of stories about street crimes soared. The most common victims of violent crime are black men, who are 50 percent more likely than white men and two-and-a-half times more likely than white women to be the victims of violent street crime. Yet U.S. newspapers are full of racially coded stories about "suburban victims" of "urban crime" — the "suburbs" being a code word for white, the "city" the symbol of people who are not. In opinion polls now, the public put "fear of crime" close to the top of their list of worries, and politicians get support to invest the public wealth in prisons.

Meanwhile, corporate crime is doing the big-dollar damage: banking scandals, tax fraud, and stock cheating, swindling people out of billions. But predominantly white, male corporate criminals do not feel the heat because crime in the suites does not get the same coverage as crime in the streets. As a result, there is little pressure to put the corporate crooks in jail. A greater diversity of viewpoints of the subject of crime could at least open up this debate, if not get it back on the rails. So, at FAIR, we look at who gets to talk.

We monitor the media: we record the national news off the television every night and watch as much of it as we can bear. We read the newspapers and news magazines and produce data on who is participating in the public-opinion-shaping debate.

FAIR's first study was of a single influential program called *Nightline*. It is a nightly news-discussion show broadcast nationally by ABC. We recorded forty months of programs and compiled statistics on who got to speak in the studio discussion. What we thought was bad, we found out was even worse.

The most frequently featured guests on *Nightline* during that period from 1985 to 1988 were Henry Kissinger, Alexander Haig, Elliot Abrams, and Jerry Falwell: one former warmonger now a corporate consultant, a laid-off member of Ronald Reagan's cabinet, a cabinet member who

was found guilty of lying to Congress, and an evangelical minister who manipulates people's religious beliefs to promote a rollback of feminism and civil rights. We also found that 89 percent of the guests were male and 92 percent were white — not a big surprise. And 80 percent were representatives of professional groups, corporations, or government.

Faced with that data, the host of that program responded, "Ours is a news program . . . we go to people involved in making the news." And that spoke volumes about how the media defines news and power. "Is it only what people in D.C. do?" we asked reporters, and the project got attention around the country. We have done several similar studies since, and the idea has also been taken up by other groups.

The goal of this sort of study is an expanded debate. FAIR is not interested in preventing the airing of viewpoints with which we disagree; we are working for the inclusion of more. A more pluralistic media would be nice. It would certainly be more entertaining. But that is not the point either. The slighting of public interest and minority viewpoints is dangerous. This spring, for example, we watched in horror while the mainstream media looked for Arab terrorists in their effort to explain the bombing of the federal building in Oklahoma City.

And when a white Christian man was arrested in the case, the *New York Times* ran headlines like "New Images of Terror . . . A suspect, a white drifter, evokes new fear." Right-wing terror is hardly surprising to those who have been on the receiving end of it for years. The sort of coverage that followed the Oklahoma City bombing showed the price we pay for racism, homophobia, and sexism in the news: it is information. The pale image of the suspect would hardly have been "new" to mainstream viewers if the media had been doing their job covering hate crimes. But they have been looking the other way.

In the U.S. today, there are right-wing demagogues who provide easy solutions to real problems by pandering to popular ignorance and prejudice. In my hometown, New York City, the most popular host on the most listened-to station routinely refers to African-Americans as "savages." He once urged New York City cops to show up at the gay pride parade with machine guns "and mow them down." A man who broadcasts weekly to over 20 million people calls advocates of human rights for women "Feminazis." And the mainstream media's alternative to that? Respectable "polite" debate about the intellectual inferiority of black Americans and the threat that gay men and lesbians may pose to the military and the family — as if we do not have families. When the *New York Times* published a graph to illustrate "other bombings in America" the day after the one in Oklahoma City, the chart spanned four decades and dozens of incidents, but none of the 40 officially documented bombings of women's heath clinics made it onto the list. None of the attacks on civil rights offices or gay and lesbian homes. Not one.

As a lesbian, the fact of invisibility is painful, but to me and my friends at FAIR, my invisibility is not the only problem. Ignorance is, and hate. This is not just bad reporting, it is reporting that is costing lives, and as we know, bigotry breeds bigotry, or it can.

Rather than damning reporters to hell, as some right-wing critics have done, we engage with journalists directly, and we begin, at least, by appealing to their higher natures. We are not asking you to do us any favors, we say; we are just asking you to do good reporting, better reporting. And we come to them with ideas.

After a short study of several weeks of the media's coverage of NAFTA, the North American Free Trade Agreement, we found that working women were not being heard. Female business owners showed up a couple of times and some U.S. women politicians, but women workers were not cited even once, although women workers are the largest single group likely to feel the effects of the not-so-free free trade pact. Women were the majority of workers in the multinational factories that were at that time likely to expand under NAFTA and the most vulnerable workers facing layoffs in the United States if the jobs were relocated south. Covering them was not doing us any favors, we told journalists. It is just covering news. We suggested that perhaps they might want to take a break

from quoting representatives of the World Bank and the International Monetary Fund. Just to relieve the boredom, if nothing else, why don't you talk to the folks at a grassroots organization like MADRE, a 12-year-old women's group that works with women in Central America, or the National Labor Committee, a labor group that works with unions in the U.S. South. And we offered names and numbers of suggested guests and a documented case that was hard to ignore.

Just recently, a number of stories have focused on the impact of NAFTA on workers in Honduras. We do not know whether our work helped, but it certainly did not hurt.

We try to correct the record by writing opinion pieces and letters to the press, to editors, publishers, even members of the company's corporate board. And we help give people tools to do the same. But even while we are doing all that, we know that media institutions are not about to change. The industry is an industry, and it is serving its corporate interest just fine, thank you. The *Wall Street Journal* is not about to see the light and say okay, you are right, we are wrong.

In 1986 when we started FAIR, a few months after the Nairobi Conference, media institutions were owned by a small and shrinking number of powerful businesses. Now the number is even smaller. In 1986, 29 corporations dominated broadcasting, publishing, and cable. By the end of 1993, the number was down to 20. Some have estimated that before the end of the century, an oligopoly of about half a dozen hugely profitable giant firms will have consolidated control of the mass media worldwide.

Today, newspapers can be published simultaneously on five continents and a single satellite beam can carry information to half the globe. As one speaker put it this week, now CNN brings you the world — and all of it in 30 minutes — whether you want it or not. The way that CNN covered the Gulf War affected not just Americans but Europeans and Australians as well, even people in whose neighborhoods the U.S. bombs were being dropped.

Media companies are no longer the businesses in your neighborhood, vying with one another for your support. They are major political players on the national and even international scene. For example, if current merger plans go ahead, soon two out of three of the world's richest television networks would be controlled by nuclear power companies, both of which have the U.S. military as their most important client. Can you expect plenty of critical reporting on the issue of military spending on NBC and CBS? I don't think so.

Media moguls have become even more explicit about the fact that they pursue corporate profits, not the public interest. The head of Tele-Communications International, the man who is currently poised to have a virtual monopoly over the U.S. cable industry, recently scoffed at the notion of ever developing a media system that would serve the public interest. Private corporations are not set up to serve the public interest, he said. "One would be fired as the CEO (the Director) of a profit-making company if one did that." So that is settled.

And the corporate interest puts profit first. As the head of the Disney Corporation put it recently, after announcing his plan to buy up ABC, which also owns the sports network ESPN, "There are many places in the world, like China, India, and other places, that do not want to accept programming that has political content, but they don't have a problem with sports and the Disney kind of programming." In other words, you can make a lot of money downplaying reality.

The world as reported by multinational corporations like these is certainly not a world where women and marginalized people get many starring roles. So, we produce our own independent media: a syndicated column, a bimonthly magazine called *EXTRA!,* an activist newsletter, and a weekly syndicated radio program called *CounterSpin*, which is now heard on about a hundred college and community radio stations in the United States and Canada and on shortwave from Radio for Peace International. We also have a Web page and exchange information with reporters and others online. And in all the work we do, we applaud hard-hitting independent journalism that cuts against the conventional grain. High-minded reporters who do that sort of work usually get pretty discouraged in the mainstream, so we think it is our job to highlight work that challenges the establishment and keeps people doing that job.

If anyone asks me what they can do about the problems we are facing, I say step one, support your local independent media, whether it is a radio station or a newsletter or a flyer or a storyteller. Unfortunately, the means of communication have become far too expensive for freedom of press to belong only to those can buy one. So we have more to do as well. We have to fight for our right to communicate and for the means of mass communication to be used for conversation, not control.

In the 1930s, it was determined that under U.S. law, the airwaves, like the air and the water, belong to the public. With the growth of cable and telecommunications, that principle, long unenforced, is in danger of dying a quiet, unreported death. Internationally, the first United Nations General Assembly declared freedom of information the "touchstone of all freedoms to which the UN is consecrated." The individual and collective right to communicate is "an evolving principle in the process," UNESCO declared in a study in 1979.

But no enforcement mechanism has ever evolved to protect that evolving principle.

Looking to the future, I'll make a proposal. Since the international women's conferences began, we have seen an environmental movement grow up to protect and share the scarce resource that is the planet; seen a women's and human rights movement built to protect the invaluable resource of human potential, all our people. What we need now is a global movement to assert the public's right to the resource of information and communication. We are entitled to exist in each other's lives, and not just once every ten years. And we are entitled to feel that we are not alone, because obviously, we are not.

What is holding us back is lack of access. But so, what else is new? Like any right, the right to communicate is not given. Like any right, it has to be won.

The Boston Women's Health Book Collective

Nancy Miriam Hawley
The Boston Women's Health Book Collective,
United States

Greetings from all the members of the Boston Women's Health Book Collective, which has created books on women's health and sexuality. I am one of the founders of the Collective and co-author of two books. In May 1969 I offered the first workshop, entitled "Women and Their Bodies," as part of a women's movement conference in Boston, Massachusetts. Some of us who worked on this project to gather and disseminate information on women's health and sexuality had been active in other political movements and knew about the political processes of advocacy for human rights; others were learning for the first time.

Unlike what some of you might imagine, we didn't set out to write a book, rather to get answers to questions for ourselves about health and sexuality issues that concerned us as young women in our twenties, as wives, and as mothers. The book came later. The information we were learning was so important and empowering that we shared it with friends, family members, colleagues — anyone who would listen. We offered courses in local colleges. The model was expansive. We passed on what we learned, and the women we taught became the teachers of other women. Women came together in schools, in day care centers, in churches, and in temples to study about our bodies and talk together about our lives.

The presentation we gave on women's sexuality was original and unique — the first ever taught about women, by women, and for women. That first evening was electric as we gathered in a room at the Massachusetts Institute of Technology. In retrospect, this male bastion of science and engineering was an unusual setting for women to speak about what had previously been unspeakable: women's anatomy, sexual pleasure, orgasm, and masturbation. This presentation and others in the series, which included topics such as birth control, pregnancy and childbirth, postpartum issues, violence against women, common health problems, nutrition, and the medical care system, were compiled into papers. Due to popular demand, these papers became a 112-page newsprint book that we personally raised money to publish with the New England Free Press. The phenomenal success of this "underground" publication (over 250,000 were sold, mainly by word of mouth, before commercial publication in 1973) demonstrated women's profound need for clear, comprehensive information about our bodies as well as about health and medical care.

Collective ignorance about the most elemental aspects of anatomy, physiology, and reproduction, coupled with the growing anger of many women about frequent mistreatment by a mostly white, privileged, and male medical profession, helped to spark numerous initiatives, from self-help groups to women-controlled health centers. Women taught one another how to do cervical self-exams, shared information about self-help treatments for vaginal infections, established advocacy groups which sought to make medical institutions and professionals more responsive to women's needs, joined local health planning boards, and even became involved in the training of medical students (for example, the teaching of pelvic exams).

At one point I predicted that we'd sell a million copies of the book — an outrageous suggestion at that moment — but we've exceeded that prediction several times by now!

Expansion beyond our national borders

In the United States next year we will celebrate the 25th anniversary of *Our Bodies, Ourselves*. This ground-breaking book about women's health and sexuality has sold over 3.5 million copies worldwide and now appears in about 13 different foreign-language editions. New adaptations of the 1992 edition of *The New Our Bodies, Ourselves* are now under way in several regions of the world. Some examples are:

• In Thailand, Indonesia, and China, women's groups already have secured financial support from the Ford Foundation to support key aspects of their work.

• In Latin America, women's groups in over a dozen countries will be collaborating to produce a Spanish-language edition — again, with support from the Ford Foundation.

• In Russia, an edition is forthcoming, published by Progress Publishers in Moscow; a single American woman provided most of the funding for the Russian adaptation.

• In Turkey, two women have approached us through the World Health Organization in Geneva about their interest in producing a Turkish edition.

• Women in Poland, Hungary, and other Eastern European regions have contacted us about beginning projects in their countries. We have been in contact with women from Armenia, South Africa, Korea, Latvia, Lithuania, and elsewhere.

One main reason for our being here at the NGO Forum is to meet with women from all over the world who are involved with translation and adaptation projects based on *The New Our Bodies, Ourselves*. The expansion continues into electronic media (including radio, TV, and movies) and into computer technology. We are negotiating for a CD-ROM version of our book and currently communicate with women all over the world through the Internet, e-mail, and soon the World Wide Web.

For many years our Women's Health Information Center, based in the Boston area, has been another channel for health and sexuality information and activism. This center houses a large and varied collection of resources on women's health. Women staff members disseminate information all over the world. We welcome visits, telephone calls, e-mail, and faxes.

Women's health and sexuality: Public health and human rights models

Knowledge is power, and the people and institutions that benefited from women being uninformed or misinformed about our bodies, health, and sexuality were not so eager for us to empower ourselves. So what made *Our Bodies, Ourselves* so successful also made it controversial. Information that had been locked away in doctors' offices or in medical books was now readily available to women on a mass basis. We were openly discussing our

life experiences as women with other women, often for the first time. We also, through graphic illustration and real-life self-help demonstrations, began to demystify a woman's body. With plastic speculums we could now see ourselves as only our gynecologists had seen us before.

We continually made the links between health and sexuality. We went beyond information sharing to analyses and critiques of the ways things were for women.

• We fought and continue to fight ways women were and are discriminated against by men and by institutions.

• We addressed and continue to address the right of access to available and affordable health and medical services as a human right.

• We spoke and continue to speak about the right to refuse services that negatively affect our health and sexuality.

• We worked and continue to work for the right to evaluate, criticize, and help establish appropriate services for women.

• We stressed and continue to stress the right to sexual self-determination and to claim one's own sexual identity.

• We supported and continue to support the right to refuse sex and the right to have sexual pleasure.

We do not separate women's health from women's sexuality. We do not protect our health without protecting our sexuality. Issues such as reproductive choice, AIDS, PID, STDs, violence against women, and mental, physical, sexual, and mental health issues such as depression and addiction are all our issues.

Our Bodies, Ourselves first emerged out of women's need to demystify medical care and to redefine and reclaim female sexuality rather than leave it up the judgments and writings of male experts. Our collective ignorance about the most elemental aspects of anatomy, physiology, and reproduction made it difficult to have a positive impact on the health and medical care institutions around us. Over the years, those of us working in the field of women's health advocacy have learned a great deal not only about specific aspects of health and medical care, but also about the central importance of a public-health perspective. Put simply, although medical care is important, our health and well-being are affected far more by our living conditions — where we live, where we work, the food we eat, the air we breathe, the water we drink, the violence in our homes and communities, and the overall level of stress in our lives. All of these issues must be addressed to realize meaningful improvement in the health and well-being of ourselves and our communities.

The transformative nature of our work

Talking at a personal level is one of the most important ways to contribute to social change. As Judy Norwegian and Wendy Sanford have said, "We believe that starting at the personal level generates the motivation, energy, and skills for large political movements. Certainly it has been the source of our group's continuing and energetic public presence in the struggle for women against organized sources of oppression." Women who don't consider themselves feminists have used our book for making changes, both small and large, in their lives — for instance, asking a friend to accompany them on a visit to the doctor or deciding to move out of an abusive relationship into a battered women's shelter. The presence of this kind of work in the culture can and does change the culture. It changes both expectations and a sense of entitlement. Every time we meet or hear from a woman who says, *Our Bodies, Ourselves* changed my life," we know this is true.

The issue of censorship

Even in the richest and freest country we experience attempts to censor our work. The groups that tried to ban our book in the 1970s couldn't do it. But they had a chilling effect. The librarians under attack sometimes selected other, less controversial, books. We know that censorship takes place all over the world. In the United States we don't assume we're free. Censorship is a violation of human rights — one reason we resist and persist to counter censorship. Gloria Steinem speaks about media acting as a censor. To move forward means addressing the media.

There are people in the media who have ana-lyzed how the media (including TV, radio, newspapers, and magazines) is owned by fewer and fewer corporations — under two dozen in the U.S. The effect is that if a critical article is written about the corporation that owns the media, the media won't publish or produce it — whether that media is owned by that corporation or by a parent corporation. This is a significant reason for us to be concerned about the increasing centralization of power. We have megamedia conglomerates that concentrate power in fewer and fewer hands. So it's harder to find a forum to publicly air, for example, our critiques of pharmaceutical companies that produce drugs of questionable value to women both in the North and in the South.

When we in public interest groups do decide to work with corporations to alter their harmful practices, we have to be alert and struggle to stay focused on our own agendas.

Our present agenda

At this time, the agenda for us as health activists includes creating a national health program that will provide universal coverage for all people residing in the U.S., regardless of citizenship. The issue of undocumented immigrants is a human rights issue. We are concerned, especially in these times when conservative ideology emphasizes seeking individual rather than collective solutions, to work for an agenda of universal health coverage, and we continue to stress our global interconnections. After all, that is the basis of this Forum and of the UN Conference.

In continuing to be advocates for women in the areas of health and sexuality, we must find new ways as well as the ways that are already successful in countering the pernicious economic and political backlash that is attempting to destroy social programs and wipe out the gains we have made for women, children, and families, and for minorities. In the process, we highlight and reject the beliefs of groups, individuals, and institutions that would still curtail women's human rights. We strongly reject fundamentalist tenets that would restrict women's role in society. We are critical of institutions and governments that place the highest priority on achieving demographic targets without looking at what women want.

Basically, what we still need is what we offered at the start:

• up-to-date critical information about women's health and sexuality;

• access to a variety of resources, including education, money, safety, and social support; and

• the ability to make informed choices about our lives.

We at the Boston Women's Health Book Collective continue to offer our book as a manual on women's health and sexuality as a major resource for women's empowerment.

We remain strongly committed to feminist publishing and documentation. In this way, we aim to keep the information in all presentations of our book — both paper and electronic — current, critical, and balanced, in both providing accurate information and allowing women to speak directly about their own experiences. For example, instead of establishing and maintaining family planning programs that offer only provider-dependent, long-acting methods of contraception (such as implants and injectibles), we believe that family planning programs should always offer an array of women-controlled choices — especially barrier methods, which prevent not only pregnancy but also the transmission of life-threatening sexually transmitted diseases. Even when we're not looking at HIV or PID, we're looking at levels of infection that can cause infertility, and while not life-threatening, infertility can have a devastating impact on a woman's life.

While the diaphragm — tried and true tested birth control — does not protect against the AIDS virus, it is a good method for helping prevent gonorrhea, chlamydia, and possibly other STDs. Until recently, the only method effective in preventing HIV was the male condom; now we have the female condom, which is a feasible method for many women.

Implications for the future

Our work is ongoing. The fact that we are gathered here in Huairou at this Forum is a testament to that. We must keep advocating for women's human rights in all arenas. Health and sexuality is one arena that is central to ensuring women's physical, mental, and spiritual well-being throughout the world.

We need everyone's energy and participation — especially that of younger women who will be able to carry on the work for women's rights after we are gone. We want all men — young, middle-aged, and older — to join us: men who benefit from living and working with girls and women who are healthy, strong, and confident.

We celebrate the 25th anniversary of the women's health movement, and we are working together with the National Women's Health Network and with the National Black Women's Health Project to create an event that acknowledges all of our anniversaries and to plan for the next decade of the women's health movement.

XIV • Institutional Mechanisms and Financial Arrangements — *Strategies*

Opening remarks

Rounaq Jahan, Moderator
Columbia University, United States
Center for Policy Dialogue (Bangladesh)

As you know, the main purpose of the strategy plenaries is to take stock of our past work, identify problem areas, and think of new strategies. Some of you who were present two days ago in the strategy plenary on governance already know me, but for the newcomers I would again like to introduce myself. I am a citizen of Bangladesh, but like many of you, I consider myself a world citizen. I have developed this identity from my involvement with the international women's movement, and I am one of the few fortunate women who have participated in all of the three previous World Conferences on Women.

Again, like many of you, I have led a rather nomadic life. I started my career as a university professor in my own country, but the involvement in the international women's movement led me to join the United Nations. Failing miserably as an international bureaucrat, I am back again to academia, reflecting and writing on the experiences of the last 20 years. My latest book, which I have titled *The Elusive Agenda*, will suggest to you how I assess the last 20 years.

Gender equality mandates institutional and financial arrangements for its implementation, and that is one of the major strategies we have pursued since Mexico. The so-called national international machineries were established after Mexico. We asked for the establishment of these institutions, but now after 20 years, we all feel frustrated by the record and experiences of these institutions. Yet we are in a dilemma. Few of us are willing to argue that these institutions are useless and that we should abolish them. Instead we keep on saying,

let us strengthen them. We feel that these institutions are in some ways set up for failure, so we want to completely overhaul the institutional framework.

The limitations of these institutional and financial arrangements are known to all of us. The special machineries still remain largely marginal, and organizations are still far from mainstreaming women's agenda. In fact, mainstreaming itself is a double-edged strategy. How would we mainstream as we also challenge and change the existing mainstream? How would the gender focal point of the World Bank and the chair of the OECD/DAC WID Expert Group question and work to change the ideological assumptions of the unbridled market economy that their organizations are imposing on the rest of the world, which is destroying the livelihoods and human security of millions of people? How would the special machineries — national and international — mainstream institutional responsibility, yet keep a focus on women's agenda? What concrete measures can be taken to ensure accountability for gender equality mandates?

Our speakers have long been involved in promoting gender equality in their own institutions. They are all intimately aware of the achievements and failures of their own organizations. Some of them are as frustrated as we are by the lack of progress, but none of them has given up the struggle. They are our allies inside the system, and we need to support them through our honest questioning, demanding, and keeping up the pressure outside the system. If there is one lesson we have learned, it is that the inside-outside alliance strategy has worked best for promoting our agenda.

The pressure from women: Fire on the top, fire at the bottom

Remedios Ignacio-Rikken
PILIPINA; Center for Asia-Pacific Women in Politics (CAPWIP), Philippines

My favorite metaphor to describe what in some way I had the privilege of initiating in the National Commission on the Role of Filipino Women (NCRFW) is cooking our traditional rice cake, *bibingka*. We put "fire on the top" and "fire at the bottom." The structures and mechanism we have installed within government and which are continuously being improved — these are the "fire on the top." The efforts of women to organize in order to push, to demand, to urge government to do something — these are the "fire at the bottom."

The time allotted for this sharing does not allow me to tell *how* things were done. We have time only to share *what* has been done and is now in place and *what else* needs to be done.

Ensuring implementation of GAD policies: Operational issues

• How to work with the bureaucracy
• How to get into the mainstream mechanisms
• How to build commitments and capabilities
• How to get the resources
• How to gauge performance
• How to measure impact
• How to build a supportive environment

If I cannot finish all these in the time given, at least you know what the elements are, and we can discuss them outside this hall.

NCRFW's four-point program

In August 1986 we recommended to the President that the Commission stop organizing women directly and also stop doing projects and programs with them, which the NCRFW had been doing since 1975. The Commission's job is to mainstream women's concerns in major agencies, which essentially means questioning every program and project as to its impact on women and men. With this policy the Commission has basically only a four-point program:

• to build its capability to give training on gender awareness and sensitivity and to do advocacy work;
• to study the formulation of gender-responsive planning;
• to study the mechanism that must be instituted for the implementation of such a plan; and
• to develop the necessary database to serve its own needs and that of its own constituency, legislators, and other government entities.

The vision is for the Commission to become the national authority on women and that, being recognized as such, its opinion must be sought on all policies and laws affecting women.

On training and advocacy: We have developed modules and materials that respond to the needs of critical groups such as gender advocates, decision makers, planners, trainers, statisticians, etc. Initial five-year funding comes from CIDA in Canada. To assure ourselves that training continues after the five years, gender-skills training is institutionalized into the regular functions of the official training institutions of government, such as the Development Academy of the Philippines and the Local Government Academy. At the same time, networks of accredited gender trainers on the national and local levels are encouraged. Likewise, mentoring schemes are being established to mobilize "advanced" agencies in support of those who are encountering difficulties in their gender mainstreaming work. Regarding our database: In cooperation with UNIFEM, ESCAP, the ADB, and our official statistical offices, we are in the final stages of setting up a system that will develop and continuously refine a set of gender-responsive database indicators.

Mainstreaming in planning: Complementary strategies

1. MTPDP

August 1986: We were appointed to office too late to influence the formulation of the Medium-Term Development Plan of the Philippines (MTPDP). Chairperson Leticia Shahani of the Commission fought for the inclusion of one sentence in the macro chapter: ". . . women constituting one half of the population must be effectively mobilized."

With this in place, our first strategy was to see that in the update of the MTPDP, every chapter would have significant statements of concern on women. This practice was institutionalized with the approval of seats for women representatives in the approving committees and in the drafting committees of the national planning process. These women representatives ensured that priority policy measures emanating from women were articulated during the deliberations and were subsequently reflected in every chapter.

2. PDPW

The second strategy was the decision to write the Philippine Development Plan for Women. Again I have no time to share with you the process that we went through (which to me is the more exciting part) in formulating the PDPW. The important elements, however, were:

• The President and the Cabinet approved Sectoral Working Groups (SWGs) on Development Planning for Women.

• NGOs and women's groups participated in three- to five-day consultations on rural women; women and education; family; health; labor; law, policy, and action; research; sexual exploitation; arts and culture; media; and community organizing, and this was the start of the GO women appreciating the world view of these groups.

• All parties, including NCRFW commissioners and staff, undertook gender-awareness and sensitivity training as part of the process.

Maybe a little note on the process: I would like to emphasize that in all our consultations and training programs we explicitly required of ourselves to listen, truly listen; to foster the spirit of openness that breeds respect and friendship among the participants; and to adopt an attitude of faithfulness to the participatory process that made all our encounters both consultative, inclusive, educational, and — in spite of the dissonance created — fun.

The result is that people love to come to our exchange and training programs, and they become allies in what we would like to see happen in their agencies. And this policy paid off. In the history of the presidential Cabinet, the PDPW was the first major document that was approved in one presentation.

3. PPGD

Regarding the Philippine Plan for Gender-Responsive Development 1995-2025 (PPGD): Legally the PDPW covers only 1989-1992, and since we have gotten development planning for women situated within the national planning system, the same process was observed in putting together PPGD, which is now ready for approval by the President and the Cabinet.

Programming and budgeting

President Aquino issued Executive Order 348 approving and adopting the PDPW, which enjoined all government entities to ensure implementation; mandated NCRFW and NEDA to monitor its implementation, assessment, and updating; and urged NGOs and private entities to give their assistance. But most important, it called for the creation of an appropriate focal point in all government entities and gave the source of funds.

Here I would like to emphasize the attitude that the Commission projected in helping establish these focal points. At first we had to correct the impression that most agencies had: that what they were being asked to do was assist the Commission to do its work. First we had to show that what was being defined was their responsibility toward gender and development, and then to clarify that the job of the NCRFW is to give assistance — that we are a partner ready to help, not a watchdog. As this became clear, our presence was not only welcomed but sought, and we are now allies in building the capabilities of GAD focal points in line agencies. These are small groups of highly motivated, GAD-skilled people in government agencies, who were initially trained by NCRFW on gender issues and whose main task is to catalyze, coordinate, facilitate, monitor, and provide technical assistance to the various units of an agency in the process of gender mainstreaming. Presently there are 75 GAD focal points at national and subnational levels, and new ones are in the process of being formed. Focal points are encouraged to build internal and external mechanisms, including alliances with constituent women and sectoral gender specialists, to support the mainstreaming work of their agencies.

A note on future needs: As we went deeper into assisting agencies, we realized the need for gender specialists by sector, such as agriculture, and that much more needs to be studied if we want to continue to be effective in this work. So far, the discipline of gender studies is very general in character. For a start, what we did was advocate the need for gender and development studies in the University of the Philippines College of Agriculture. Now they have a group of women and men developing themselves into gender specialists in agriculture.

About our materials: We have a training kit that we give to GAD focal points. Other materials that we prepared in cooperation with NEDA, practitioners, and academics include "A Primer on the GAD Focal Point: Guidelines for Developing and Implementing Gender-Responsive Programmes and Projects" and "Gender and Development: Making the Bureaucracy Gender-Responsive (A Sourcebook for Advocates, Planners, and Implementors)," which is a study of six line agencies. We have developed other materials to guide field workers, such as "Gender Awareness Through Theater Arts, Games, and Processes." Last September we had a mob attending our sharing "Handling Gender Sensitivity for Men: Strategies and Methodologies."

Final remarks

Why did I resign after eight years in government? I am proud of what I helped establish in the National Commission on the Role of Filipino Women, the "fire on the top." Now I am back in NGO work — helping light the "fire at the bottom" — but in a completely new field: women in politics and decision-making at different levels. Already I have evidence that the policies, programs, and structures I have explained above will only benefit women as they organize and demand change. But now we are also talking of public power. In this conference we, the Center for Asia-Pacific Women in Politics, are coordinating five

regional workshops on "Why Women? What Politics?" to culminate in a global congress on September 6.

See you in the next World Conference. I am confident we will have something different to report — a quantum leap.

Gender on the World Bank's agenda

Minh Chau Nguyen
The World Bank, United States

It is a pleasure for me to be here for three reasons. First, on a personal level, I am pleased to join you at a Conference that gives women from around the globe the chance to come together and celebrate looking at the world through women's eyes. Second, as a World Bank staff member, I am speaking for an institution that is evolving and reaching out and has something to contribute to the advancement of women's status. And finally, my colleagues and I — some of whom are men — are here to listen and to learn. We plan on carrying the messages from Huairou back to Washington with the hope that the World Bank can move more aggressively to turn the arguments for gender equality into action.

While various governments and agencies are working toward gender equality, our respective mandates differ. The World Bank is a multilateral organization responding to some 180 countries who are our shareholders. You can imagine the difficulties in reaching consensus among so many differing views.

These difficulties were evident when our gender policy was being approved in April 1994. The governing board finally agreed that there were three compelling reasons for the World Bank to consider gender issues as key to economic growth and poverty reduction. First, it is now recognized that when we say investing in women is good economics, we are talking hard-nosed economic facts, not "soft" emotional issues. Second, the study we prepared for this Conference has also shown that there is no trade-off between growth and equality; rather, inefficiencies resulting from gender inequality hamper growth. This is quite an eye-opener to many economists, who always think in terms of trade-offs. As one of those economists myself, all I can say is, I have seen the light. Finally, growth is not an end in itself — the quality and sustainability of growth also matter. Investing in women ensures the quality and sustainability of growth, as it affects the welfare of future generations and the environment they live in.

The case has been made, but how do we go from arguments to action?

For many of you who are not familiar with the Bank, let me explain our mandate. The World Bank assists developing countries in three areas: by providing advice and technical assistance; by lending for policy reforms; and by lending for investment purposes. How does gender fit into these three functions?

• In terms of advice, I have to admit that I can count on one hand the number of governments that have asked the Bank to provide advice on gender equality. However, our international experience is valuable because we can demonstrate to governments what works and how it works. We have what we call an Institutional Development Fund that provides grants to strengthen the capacities of national machineries. In Tunisia, for example, the Fund was used to strengthen the monitoring and evaluation capacities of the Ministry of Women's Affairs by bringing Canadian expertise, coupled with World Bank experience, to Tunisian staff.

• In terms of policy lending for policy reforms, the Bank is well known for its Structural Adjustment Programs (SAPs). But the macroeconomic measures that are introduced, and which are necessary to the success of these programs, are just part of the picture. For example, in Honduras, land reform that ensures the right of women to own land is part of the policy package. In Pakistan the adjustment supports a shift of government expenditures toward primary levels of social services,

where the use by women and children is the greatest, and away from tertiary levels. While I am at it, let me put the record straight. In the 334 SAPs the Bank has introduced since 1980, never has a loan been made conditional on a government's cutting expenditures on health and education. On the contrary, 60 percent of the loans recommended that the government maintain — or increase — spending on health and education. And 40 percent of these programs made the loan *conditional* on the government's maintaining or increasing social expenditures.

• In terms of investment lending, very little is known about the changes that have been taking place in the World Bank's portfolio. The Bank has tripled its lending for human development during the last decade — from 5 percent of total lending to 15 percent. We are now the largest international financier of education, health, nutrition, and family planning, with 50 percent of our projects targeting women. But we are hard at work in more than just these sectors; for instance, we have programs that target women in agriculture, water supply, and urban development as well. At present, more than one-third of the Bank's lending portfolio has specific actions targeting women. The Bank, together with other donors, has recently launched a $200 million microenterprise program to help viable intermediaries provide credit to the poor. The majority of the beneficiaries of this program will be women.

As you can see, the World Bank is changing because it is learning. The challenge now is to accelerate this learning process.

How do we do this?

First, I think *vision and a commitment from management are very important.* It gives me great pleasure to stand here today and share with you the vision of our new President, a man who said, and I quote, "The gender issue is one which I've embraced for over 20 years and is very dear to my heart." Mr. Wolfensohn has been on the job only a few months, and yet he has made it a point to be here to dialogue with you and share his beliefs with you. I am optimistic for the future of gender issues in the Bank.

Second, *we need to lift gender issues from the project level to the policy level*. Two key areas here are (1) the legal and regulatory framework that governs the development of women's capacities and opportunities; and (2) public expenditure. The allocation of public expenditure is normally gender neutral. However, its use could have a gender bias. We have developed a methodology, explained in the World Bank report "Toward Gender Equality: The Role of Public Policy," to highlight this point.

Third, *participation is becoming a key factor in our work*, and it is through this means that the voices of women can be heard. We have begun to see signs of the difference the participation of women can make. For example, the Bank supports a water supply project in Azerbaijan, which was designed with the help of women's committees. This was quite simply the most logical approach to take, since the project's main beneficiaries are the region's women. Or take Morocco, where rural women helped to define development priorities; now the Government of Morocco and the Bank are trying to incorporate these women's concerns into lending operations.

Last but not least, we are now in the process of institutionalizing the exchange of views between NGOs, communities, and Bank staff. We will begin this process this year by bringing NGOs and Bank staff together to discuss various issues, such as user fees, land reform, and credit for women. The purpose is to reach out and learn from each other.

I would like to conclude by reading the poem that inspired the cover of the report we prepared for the Fourth World Conference on Women:

I am the woman who holds up the sky
The rainbow runs through my eyes
The sun makes a path to my womb
My thoughts are in the shape of clouds
But my words are yet to come.

It is my responsibility at the World Bank, with your support, to make sure that women's words are not only given a voice, but listened to as well.

Strategies for gender equality in Norway

Grete Berget
Royal Norwegian Ministry of Children and Family Affairs, Norway

Our goal is to achieve an equal distribution between the sexes of rights, duties, and benefits, including an equal opportunity to participate in and influence society. This also means more choice for both women and men in education, occupation, career, family life, political participation, sports, culture, and other fields of interest.

Health, education, and income are basic needs that must be satisfied before choice can appear meaningful to the individual. The Norwegian government has had a deliberate strategy and has intervened systematically through policy reforms and affirmative action, and we have improved women's capabilities as well as facilitating and encouraging economic and political participation by women.

Norwegian women have experienced marked changes in political influence over the past decade. In 1995 the prime minister is a woman, as are close to 40 percent of the cabinet ministers and state secretaries (deputy ministers). About 40 percent of the members of parliament are women. At the last general elections in 1993, all three candidates for prime minister were women, the leaders of the three largest political parties. Following the election a woman was for the first time appointed to the position of President of the Storting (Parliament), a position next only to the King.

Quotas are by far the single most important factor in the high level of female representation in politics in Norway. The Gender Equality Act requires no less than 40 percent representation of both sexes in publicly appointed boards, councils, and committees. This is not binding for political parties. Nevertheless, it is an effective guideline, and all major political parties have adopted quota systems in their internal bodies and election lists.

There is also a strong tradition of women's organizations and feminist research and of the fruitful coalition between these groups and women politicians up to the highest levels. Feminist ideas have had a major impact on public opinion and on political parties, and most political parties have established women's branches.

It is our experience that having a high number of women in governance *does make a difference*. The most obvious result seen in my country is the new significance accorded to and the progress achieved in the field of family policy, particularly with regard to opportunities for reconciling work and family responsibilities. Since 1986 parental leave has been expanded from 18 weeks to 42 weeks, with full wage compensation. The time-account scheme and the fathers quota are other important reforms in this area, both of which have been implemented during periods otherwise characterized by economic recession.

Finally, it is our impression that women, due to their multiple responsibilities, tend to take a more holistic approach to politics. Mainstreaming has become an important strategy in our efforts to promote gender equality.

Mainstreaming of the gender perspective implies a recognition that women's issues are not concerns primarily outside or on top of existing organizations, structures, or resources. The gender perspective should be taken into consideration and allowed a decisive voice in all important matters. It is our experience that much can be done to improve the situation of women without extravagant expenditure, through reallocation of means and gender-sensitive planning.

To sum up: A legal framework for gender equality, investments in education and health, and measures to facilitate economic independence through labor market participation and social security are results of firm political commitment and policy reform, including the use of affirmative action and an active mainstreaming policy. The results include high levels of women's labor-market participation and political representation and have gained us a ranking, second only to that of Sweden, by the Gender Empowerment Measure presented in the UNDP *1995 Human Development Report.*

Moving positions forward: Strategies for gender and development cooperation

Carolyn Hannan-Andersson
OECD/DAC Expert Group on Women
and Development; Swedish International
Development Cooperation Agency (SIDA),
Sweden

INTRODUCTION

I have been asked to talk about institutional development: how to ensure that everyone working with development cooperation mainstreams a gender perspective into their work. What this entails is a massive shift of responsibility from the few gender specialists within agencies to top management and all personnel and consultants. This is obviously no easy task.

The establishment of a strategy for institutional arrangements is an essential ingredient in overall strategies for gender equality within bilateral development cooperation agencies. It is important, however, that an institutional strategy not be developed as an end in itself; rather, it should aim to address problems that have been identified and to facilitate achievement of objectives.

It is not possible to separate operational strategies from institutional strategies, since shortcomings in institutional strategies hinder achievements at the operational level, and constraints at the operational level require the development of appropriate institutional arrangements. Thus, although the focus of my presentation is on institutional arrangements, it is necessary also to take a look at the operational constraints and potentials.

The experience I will discuss here is from bilateral development cooperation. However, the findings have relevance for mainstreaming a gender perspective in other forums. I am not offering a blueprint for success. There can be no blueprint, since institutional contexts and organizational environments/cultures differ greatly.

ASSESSMENT OF PAST STRATEGIES

As part of preparations for, and follow-up to, the UN Conference on Women and Development in Nairobi in 1985, many bilateral donor agencies developed comprehensive policies and strategies for women and development, including institutional arrangements. Ten years later, reviews of these policies and strategies are being undertaken to take into account the considerable evolution at both conceptual and operational levels over the past decade. Most notable is the assessment of the policies and programs of OECD/DAC members (CIDA and OECD/DAC)[1] that was carried out as part of the preparations for the Beijing conference. These assessments focused on a broad range of policy, strategy, and institutional development issues and had the objective of providing insights into past experience as a contribution toward the development of strategies for the future.

The results of the DAC assessments have shown that there has been considerable innovation in relation to the development of conceptual approaches, policy development, the revision of project/program planning procedures, and adaptation of institutional structures. The assessment confirms that once official mandates on women/gender were in place, DAC members were able to make commendable efforts in relation to developing specific policies and strategies for women in development (WID)/gender.[2] Many of these are at the cutting edge in relation to conceptual, methodological, and institutional development, for example, in relation to mainstreaming, the role of men, etc.[3]

A substantial base has been developed in donor agencies for implementing policies on gender — a base which includes adoption of policy mandates; formulation of country and sector-specific strategies; employment of specialists, and establishment of institutional structures for gender such as desks, units, etc.; development of methodologies and instruments such as guidelines and checklists; and the development of training programs.

However, despite these many positive developments, the reviews of policies and strategies of the past decade have pointed to many constraints. The major failing has been in relation to the necessary broad shift in responsibility for mainstreaming gender from gender specialists to management and operational levels.

The institutional implications have become much clearer over the past decade — in particular, the important linkages between operational constraints and institutional arrangements. Several serious constraints in relation to policy, practice, and outcome that must be addressed within institutional strategies have been identified.

In my presentation I will address some of the major constraints. It should be kept in mind that the presentation will, of necessity, involve generalizations. There are many differences between individual agencies based on a broad range of factors — ranging from simple issues, such as the length of time that efforts for WID/gender have been undertaken, to more complicated factors, such as differences in development cooperation models and economic and political influences.

The political commitment to gender equality is, of course, of particular relevance. Some bilateral agencies have gone further than others in relation to operational and institutional strategies. However, the constraints identified in this presentation probably exist in all individual organizations, but to a greater or lesser degree.

CONSTRAINTS

Operational constraints

The major operational constraints identified are:

• A major gap remains between expressed intentions (in gender-equality policy statements and mandates) and actual impact on development cooperation policy, practice, and outcomes.

• The lack of impact of gender-equality policies on overall policy development within agencies is a particularly serious hindrance to further advancement. Moving forward in relation to mainstreaming at the program level is dependent on mainstreaming gender into all policy development.

• A gender perspective is still not considered

systematically throughout the project/program cycle. Procedures and documents relating to particular "events" in the cycle often remain gender-blind, as do the outcomes of these events.

• The attention given to gender equality is still too often more descriptive than operational. There is a serious lack of concrete goals, strategies, and measurable targets.

• Despite the rhetoric on mainstreaming, the issue of gender equality often remains "separate." Analyses, profiles, methodology development, and sometimes even training are inadequately linked to the mainstream. Thus, even when inputs are good, the overall long-term impact, especially at the level of policy development, remains weak. This negates the insight that gender equality is a prerequisite for, and indicator of, development. It confirms the false perception of women as a "special-interest group" that can be dealt with separately. It also confirms the negative impression among many agency staff that gender focus is an "add-on" rather than a perspective that can provide new and important insights to improve their work.

• There have often been drastic "policy swings" on gender equality — for example, in relation to its prioritization, resource levels, and so on — which seem, despite glossy policy statements, to indicate a lack of overall commitment. Few other issues in development cooperation have been subjected to swings of such intensity. This has resulted in problems in relation to the continuity and stability that are so necessary to the development of strategies, methodologies, and instruments within agencies.

Institutional constraints

All the above constraints can be linked to failings at the institutional level. The three major constraints there are the following:

• Responsibility for mainstreaming is not broadly shared within agencies but is still placed de facto with specialist units and individuals. Even where agency rhetoric talks of a spread of responsibility, the reality is that the attention accorded gender is far too extensively determined by personal commitment. Few, if any, accountability mechanisms are developed; there are no demands and few incentives.

• One of the main reasons for the failure to take on responsibilities and for the lack of accountability is the very weak role played by leadership. Few signals are given concerning the importance of gender equality to development. No demands are made, and progress is not monitored from top-level management.

• Gender specialists in agencies are in an extremely vulnerable situation, although impressive efforts have been made by under-resourced and often low-status individuals and units. The problems experienced by these gender specialists include lack of personnel, financial resources, and strategic alliances; inadequate access to crucial information; and lack of close links to the policy level and management. The greatest constraint of all, of course, is the fact that gender specialists are still often given all the responsibility. There has been an ambition in many agencies to move forward on all fronts, with the main actors being the gender specialists — a strategy that is both impossible (given the limited resources) and incorrect (given the need for the agency as a whole to "take on" the task of the mainstreaming of gender). This puts gender specialists in an even more vulnerable situation — a "damned if you do and damned if you don't" syndrome.

EMERGING POTENTIALS

To move forward, it is important also to be able to identify existing potential. There have been some positive changes in development cooperation over the past decade, which have given rise to new potentials for mainstreaming a gender perspective at both policy and program levels.

• There is a general increase of emphasis on the overall policy level, which can lead to clearer goals and targets and facilitate a much-needed focus on gender at the policy level.

• There has been a shift of emphasis toward a more "people-centered" approach. The greater the focus on people and sociocultural aspects, the greater the potential for working with gender.

• The attempts to link the micro levels and macro levels and to bridge gaps between sociocultural issues and economic issues provide great potential for overcoming the "separateness" of gender issues.

Links with institutional development

Taking advantage of these new potentials requires some adaptation of institutional strategies, particularly for gender specialists.

• It will be increasingly important to develop strategic alliances, particularly in relation to policy development and macroeconomic issues.

• As more attention and resources begin to be given to sociocultural issues and poverty issues (incidentally, probably due to the insights gained from efforts to mainstream gender), there is a need to see that gender equality is integrated into all analyses and all policy and program development. This will require more active cooperation with sociocultural specialists.

MOVING FORWARD

Dealing adequately with the constraints identified and taking advantage of these new potentials requires some adaptation of institutional strategies, in particular in terms of ensuring a real shift in responsibility away from gender specialists to personnel/consultants.

Increasing the role of all personnel and consultants can be achieved through competence development (focused on awareness, commitment, and skills); development of clear and measurable strategies and targets; and further development of methodologies and instruments, including accountability mechanisms.

To ensure further development in relation to the much-needed shift in responsibility, strategic inputs are required from both management levels and gender specialists. I would therefore like to concentrate on these two areas in the remainder of this presentation.

Management roles

Top management must in future take on more active responsibility and show clear leadership:

• Leadership should send out more positive signals that gender equality is a priority issue.

• There should be more active monitoring of policy and strategy development, operational procedures, and outcome.

• Mechanisms for accountability should be developed, focusing more on positive incentives than on sanctions. A few more "pats on the back" for good work with gender would go a long way toward promoting more interest in mainstreaming gender.

To facilitate more active roles of management, the following improvements are also needed:

• Gender policies and strategies must be more concrete, with clear goals and measurable targets. Simple monitoring systems should be established for regular follow-up and reporting to top management. Investment of time and resources of gender specialists in this area can pay great dividends.

• Increased political pressure from outside the agency — with more demands made on management — should be facilitated by developing strategic alliances with those working with gender equality in national organizations and in political pressure groups. Gender specialists can play a role

---

There are some positive signs of changes in relation to shifting responsibility within organizations. I give here two examples:

With the Swedish International Development Cooperation Agency (SIDA), all divisions are expected to develop action plans that give clear goals, strategies, and targets and to focus on roles and responsibilities, including the development of competence and accountability mechanisms.

Within OECD/DAC, the recent High-Level Meeting (1995) endorsed a proposal that called for increased demands on DAC members to mainstream gender (including institutional arrangements) as well as to develop clearer operational strategies and lines of responsibility for gender within the DAC itself, which will result in a concrete Gender Plan for the DAC and all its subsidiary bodies.

in stimulating increased pressure from outside the agency.

• Competence-development programs on gender and development, with focus on policy issues, should be developed for management levels.

The role of gender specialists

First, it is necessary to state categorically that gender specialists — units and individuals — are still required in development cooperation and will be for a long time to come. To move positions forward, it is necessary to ensure the following in regard to specialist resources within an agency:

• They should be sufficient in number (a critical mass).

• They should be strategically placed within the organization to have access to information and potential for impacting on important processes and to play an effective advisory role. This would include placing specialist resources at the overall policy level so as to impact on policy development as well as concrete programs.

• They should have a clearly identified mandate with a focus on catalytic, advisory, and supportive roles rather than operational roles.

• They should be sufficiently competent, i.e., highly qualified.

The importance of policy-level gender advisers

The establishment of gender advisers at the policy level should be a future key strategy. It has been suggested in the preparation of the Platform for Action, for example, that the placing of a high-level adviser in the Secretary-General's office would be a means of moving positions forward within the UN. This proposal has led to some discussion as to whether this threatens or jeopardizes the mainstreaming goal.

It is important to state categorically that having gender specialists at a high-policy level in no way threatens mainstreaming. On the contrary, it creates new possibilities for mainstreaming gender equality into overall policy development, which facilitates translation into concrete inputs at the program/project levels. It can improve the status of the issue since such advisers tend to have higher status and better links to, and support from, management. That, in turn, enables them to be more active in setting priorities and making demands. However, this positive impact is conditional on the gender advisers at this level having high levels of competence.

The question of mandate

Given the need to encourage stronger management roles and a shift of responsibility within the organization, a major challenge will be to review critically the role of gender specialists in this new context. It is not possible for a handful (at best) of gender specialists to move positions forward on all fronts, as has been attempted in the past. Aspects of the roles and responsibilities of specialist units is taken up in the Platform for Action.

However, its approach is not far-reaching enough. There has not been enough questioning or discussion of the limitations of current roles and the need for new strategic roles, given the focus in the Platform for Action on mainstreaming and high-level management roles. It cannot be assumed that the roles of specialist bodies should simply be renewed and their resources increased. Efforts must be made to assess the most effective role for specialists at all levels. The focus must be on catalyzing, not on doing.

A new type of gender specialist

If resource levels are to remain unchanged, it will be necessary to develop clearer priorities and to focus scarce resources specifically on development of a clear policy and strategy, methodologies, and instruments necessary to ensure a real shift of responsibility, including an increase of management responsibility.

A new type of gender specialist is required in situations where the level of specialist resources is inadequate and unlikely to be increased. Specialists — especially when they are a scarce resource — cannot be "doers" but must really concentrate on catalytic and advisory roles to facilitate the taking on of responsibility through the agency. Key strategies will be:

• building strategic alliances, both within and outside the agency;

• identifying and focusing on the most prioritized entry points;

• developing adequate links to and support from top management;

• undertaking leadership training to acquire the status necessary to play a more active role in establishing priorities and making demands.

Strategic alliances need to be identified in the area of policy development in general and macroeconomic issues in particular. In addition, as increasing attention and resources are given to sociocultural and poverty issues — incidentally, probably as a result of the insights gained from efforts to mainstream gender — there is a need to see that gender equality is integrated into all analyses and policy and program development. This will require more active cooperation with sociocultural specialists. The added value of such increased linkages would be the elimination of the problem of the "separateness" of gender as an issue in development cooperation.

More drastic solutions needed?

The invitation to make a presentation to this plenary included a call to be provocative. I gladly take the opportunity in presenting the following scenario: What would happen if — within an agency — there were no possibilities for additional gender-specialist resources, few attempts to shift responsibilities within the organization, little evidence of management commitment, and no support for the focusing of limited gender resources on a few priority areas rather than struggling to cover all areas? Is the correct response "business as usual," or is it time to recognize that continuing in the same manner may actually be doing gender issues a disservice?

Put provocatively, gender specialists — in this context — could actually constitute a serious constraint to long-term development, despite the very positive work they may do, if their presence hinders a clearer shift of responsibility to management and operations units. Agencies will continue to be "let off the hook." By struggling with inadequate resources, gender specialists will help agencies to "keep face" without having to make a real commit-

ment. In this context, there may be a need for more drastic changes.

It is my hope that it will not be necessary to look for drastic solutions. If the Platform for Action adequately explores the full implications of the paragraphs on mainstreaming which conclude each of the critical areas of concern, it should include discussion of strategies to ensure responsibility at the highest management levels, development of competence (awareness, commitment, and skills) and accountability for all personnel/consultants, and new roles for gender specialists. Hopefully, after the Beijing Conference, the agencies themselves will take up the challenge posed by the new thinking around institutional arrangements by:

• ensuring that management and operational levels are made aware of the extent of their responsibilities in relation to mainstreaming gender and develop the capacity to take on these responsibilities;

• identifying the limits of the responsibilities of gender specialists and defining new, more strategic catalytic roles for specialists which facilitate a shift in responsibility within agencies.

Notes

1. For more information on OECD/DAC see the box in the Annex. The findings of the DAC assessment presented here are largely based on the results of ths assessment taken from the Overall Assessment Report (CIDA/OECD-DAC, 1994).

2. The terminology "Gender" will be utilized in the report. While DAC Expert Group on Women and Development documentation continues to utilize "WID," an increasing number of members utilize gender analysis and planning.

3. Although it is not generally well known outside development cooperation circles, the work with women/gender in relation to development cooperation has been at the cutting edge in terms of identifying men's roles, the need for a gender approach, and in relation to the "mainstreaming" approach. Discussions with women in partner countries have already gone beyond the "mainstreaming" approach as presented in the Platform for Action, i.e., discussing going "beyond participation" to focus on a transformation of the agenda. This involves changes in both structures and processes of development in order to include the visions, goals and strategies of women as well as men.

References

CIDA/DAC Expert Group on Aid Evaluation. 1994. *Assessment of DAC Members' WID policies and programmes. Overall Report.* December.

DAC. 1995. *Gender Equality: Moving Towards Sustainable People-Centred Development.* Paper endorsed at the High-Level Meeting held in Paris, May.

Jahan, Rounaq. 1995. *The Elusive Agenda. Mainstreaming Women in Development.* Zed Books, London.

Ministry of Foreign Affairs. 1995. *A vision for gender and development. The outcome of an Expert Group.* Workshop, January 30–February 3. Stockholm.

SIDA. 1994. *The further development of SIDA's strategy for integration of a gender perspective in development assistance.* Stockholm.

SIDA. 1995. *Gender equality in development cooperation: Taking the next step . . .* Stockholm.

SIDA. 1995. *Review of Documents Related to SIDA's Strategy on Gender and Development (Prepared by Johanna Schalkwyk).* Stockholm.

Annex

The OECD/DAC Expert Group on Woman and Development is a formal expert group within the Development Assistance Committee (DAC) of the Organization for Economic Cooperation and Development (OECD/DAC). It was formally established in 1984 and has been a major catalyst for attention to women and development in the programs of DAC members, as well as in the work of the DAC itself and its subsidiary bodies; for example, those working with statistics, environment, urban development, evaluations and participatory development, and good governance. In relation to the efforts of DAC members, the Expert Group has focused on exchange of experience among members as well as development of instruments and methodologies.

Two important instruments developed by the Expert Group include Guiding Principles for Women and Development *and* Statistical Reporting System for Women-Oriented Aid Activities. *These two instruments were trailblazers at the time of their initiation, but both are now in need of revision to reflect the experiences gained over the past ten years. Both these instruments will be revised in the near future on the basis of the new thinking emerging from the Beijing Conference processes.*

The Guiding Principles reflected the new thinking of the time; i.e., the consensus that efforts for women in development were not only good for women but also contributed to improving the quality of development cooperation by taking into account the socioeconomic roles of women as well as men. The guiding principles did not, however, explicitly state that gender equality is a goal in itself. The principles recommended action in three major areas — development of mandates, policy guidelines, and plans of action. The implementation of the principles was monitored on a regular basis.

The Statistical Reporting System, which focuses on the planning phase, was innovative when developed because it emphasized the need to consult with women, to identify constraints to women's participation and strategies for overcoming them, and to make use of WID or gender expertise.

The High-Level Policy Meeting of May 1995 endorsed gender equality as a strategic development objective. This will lead to concrete positive changes within programs of member countries. There will also be positive changes within the DAC itself, beginning with the development of a Gender Plan covering all DAC activities.

XV • United Nations Agencies — Gender Equity Strategies

Opening remarks

Karina Constantino-David, Moderator
Harnessing Self-Reliant Initiatives and Knowledge,
Inc. (HASIK); PILIPINA, Philippines

Over the past decades, much has been achieved by our initiatives, although much remains to be done. The call for gender equity — from the streets, from communities, from academe, and from the women's movement all over the globe — has permeated government discourse. The United Nations has played a significant role in mainstreaming gender equity concerns from the Mexico and Nairobi Conferences up to the present Forum in Beijing.

But for gender equity to be truly a reality, conferences, declarations, and conventions must be backed up by concrete implementation. Each UN agency must therefore not only pursue programs and policies, it must also be able to make gender equity a major concern within the procedures and structures of the agency itself.

This afternoon we have women representing four UN agencies who will share with us their accomplishments and frustrations, their battles and their victories in the field of gender equity strategies. How has the UN concretized the vision of gender equity? Has gender equity remained an "add-on" concern, or has it finally taken root as a non-negotiable bottom line in all UN programs, policies, and procedures? What has been accomplished so far? How have these been done? What can we look forward to?

Words versus deeds

Angela E.V. King
United Nations Office of Human Resources
Management

This is indeed a historic time for the United Nations, when women and men representing over 180 nationalities have come together to celebrate the contribution of previous UN conferences and forums on women, and at the same time to look forward with a critical eye to practical measures leading to the achievement of true balance and equality for women throughout the world and in the secretariats of the UN system by the end of this century.

When equality is achieved in the United Nations, it will mean not only equality for women but for all staff, irrespective of gender, and will contribute to the enhancement of the organization as a whole. Moreover, to be credible, it must be equality with no concessions, securing the Charter's admonition in Article 101 of maintaining the highest standards of efficiency, competence, and integrity for all UN staff. We know there are detractors who preach that equality will mean a lowering of standards. There are excellent women available both inside and outside the organization.

Let us take a lesson from the Cairo Conference, which concluded decisively that once women are empowered through equal access to employment, education, and training, the society as a whole will benefit economically, politically, and socially. Let us mark this 50th anniversary year by a determination on the part of member states and the organization to meet the challenge by finding and placing these women in strategic central positions at all levels throughout the system.

At the outset, tribute needs to be paid to the

NGO Forum for sponsoring this event. For nearly two decades since the Mexico Conference in 1975, this Forum, through its persistence and intellectual toughness, has brought women together from all over the world to chart the way forward, especially for this Fourth World Conference on Women being held in Beijing.

Over the past 25 years the impetus to improve the status of women in the Secretariat has stemmed from three main sources:

• *Governments*, particularly those which have served on the Commission on the Status of Women since 1946.

• *The leadership of top managers* who had the courage to be bold on this issue. Here I include the current Secretary-General and certain institutions such as the Joint Inspection Unit, which, with its first report on women in 1977 (prepared by Inspector Earl Sohm), signaled that in the view of what was then an all-male bastion, women throughout the system of UN bodies and organizations were at last worthy of a separate report, as they were acknowledged to be an important feature of the organization's effectiveness and credibility. Indeed it showed that there were effective, proven strategies by which their status in the organization could be advanced through equal access to opportunities for promotion, decision-making, and training as well as a better opportunity for recruitment other than to the General Service and the lowest levels of the professional grades. The tradition pioneered in the Joint Inspection Unit by Earl Sohm has been more than continued by the careful research and powerful presentation of the only woman member of the Joint Inspection Unit, Professor Erica-Irene Daes. Her recent report has put the Secretariat starkly on notice that more comprehensive actions must come.

• *Women staff members themselves* who, through the Group of Equal Rights for Women, started in 1971 as a pressure group and continue today to focus on key issues for the advancement of women.

My task here today is to comment on some of the main obstacles to the advancement of women in the United Nations and on what the Secretariat is doing toward meeting the goals of the Charter and the resolutions of the General Assembly by improving the organization's chances of gaining access to a greater portion of the world's human resources, that is, the 51 percent of its population who are women. I will show that while appearing to be "strategies of words," some deeds have occurred, and that there is concrete expectation that strategies will be transformed into real action. These strategies have been firmly placed in the context of the policies for management change, managerial responsibility, and accountability that are the hallmark of the modernization of human resources of the United Nations called for by the Secretary-General in 1992.

Six problem areas for women were highlighted in a recent report of the Joint Inspection Unit related to unmet targets:

• slow promotion

• lack of high-level appointments

• lack of attention to the General Service and related categories

• uneven distribution of senior women in the various departments

• poor representation of women from member states as measured by the number of women heading Permanent Missions: down from 8 to 5 (Jamaica, Kazakhstan, Liechtenstein, Trinidad and Tobago, and the United States of America) of the 185 member states, or only 9.2 percent

• lack of career planning.

I am pleased to report that progress has been made in some of these areas. For example, although the target of 35 percent of posts (subject to geography) set by the member states will not be met by December 31, 1995, there is every reason to believe that with managerial intentionality the percentage — which had risen to 33.8 as of the end of August 1995 from 32.6 in December 1994 — will reach over 34 percent by 31 December of this year. With regard to the number and percentage of women in decision-making and policy-making positions — always a measure of progress — while the target of 25 percent women at the D-1 level and above will not be reached this year, I am also happy to report that the percentage had moved from 14 in June 1994 to 16.9 in August 1995. We are here dealing with just over 300 posts. Only 15 countries exceed the UN in this regard, including the Scandinavian countries, the Netherlands, Dominica, Zimbabwe, Seychelles, and the United States, as shown by *The World's Women 1995*. So, indeed, the targets have set the stage for the United Nations to lead rather than follow the majority of its member states.

In yet another area, that of promotion, we are pleased to report that the number and rate of women promoted to the P-5 (senior officer) and D-1 (assistant director) levels has increased steadily since November of last year. Over 50 percent of all promotions have gone to women staff, and 45 percent of all those recruited over the same period are women. This trend promises to continue.

The "Strategic Plan of Action for the Improvement of the Status of Women in the Secretariat (1995-2000)" was presented to the General Assembly at its 49th session last year in document A/49/587. This Plan is firmly in place and provides a sound foundation by which the administration, member states, and women staff can map and monitor progress and charter ways forward.

The Plan of Action covers goals and objectives for meeting targets and for the first time clearly enunciates the goal of reaching 50 percent by the year 2000. This is 10 percentage points higher than the goal declared in the 1992-1997 medium-term plan of the organization, which projected reaching 40 percent by the end of the century with a modest target of "at least 1 percent increase of professional women per annum." This shows a quantum leap in what the management now regards as the possible and the desirable, which would have been laughed at six or seven years ago.

The Plan also stresses the need for clear opportunities for all categories of staff for career development, succession planning, more innovative hiring practices, a more practical and updated roster of women and men candidates with due regard to the projected occupational needs of the organization, and the introduction of regular instead of ad hoc reviews of General Service staff who have not been promoted for long periods.

This Plan of Action, which is very comprehensive, also encompasses strategies for setting up women's rosters and databases, networking and executive searches for women, skills inventories of existing women staff, more creative recruitment missions, career counselling, mobility, and training. In addition, the often overlooked area of harassment, including sexual harassment of both women and men, is being addressed, and existing mechanisms for investigation and disciplinary action tightened.

Perhaps the most innovative part of the Plan is to link it with mechanisms for introducing a new management culture. This involves a radical change in approaches, attitudes, and ways of thinking among all levels of management and provides as a measurement tool a system of performance appraisal for all members of staff up to the Under Secretary-General level.

The training for this new system started a month ago and in a year's time will cover nearly one-third of the organization's staff, or approximately 5,000. The remaining 10,000 staff will be trained in the following year. The appraisal form itself contains as a major new feature an assessment of the extent to which managers have encouraged gender and cultural diversity within their departments and offices. For the first time, the results could provide the data required not only to monitor but also to change the attitude of senior managers, which until now has been one of the major stumbling blocks to progress for women in the organization. There are now ongoing training programs for senior managers, male and female, from the P-5 level and above, which include gender-sensitivity training.

The Strategic Plan of Action also looks at other aspects of a woman's life. Staggered hours were recently introduced, and greater attention has been paid to the impact of family on the work of all staff. Initiatives are under way throughout the UN system for reviewing existing policies and formulating recommendations on issues such as the concept of the family, child care, career development, flexi-time and flexi-place, personal leave, and the establishment of support groups. Many of these initiatives are commonplace in many work environments in industrialized countries. Many of these programs would allow greater flexibility to working women, who have dual responsibilities toward the family and the workplace.

On this occasion, I believe we can also report positively that there is a transformation of the commitment level from the very top.

The Secretary-General led the way in his statement to the General Assembly in his first year of office, 1992, that the 50 percent target had to be met. Top leadership in Administration and Human Resources are also fully committed to undertaking any necessary action to meet the stated goals.

The Focal Point for Women, who with the Office of Human Resources Management has full responsibility for developing and monitoring the Strategic Plan, is entrusted with reviewing existing policies and commissioning new initiatives with regard to the status of women in the Secretariat. There is continuing focus, in the Secretary-General's annual report on the work of the organization, on the need to improve the status of women.

Women are participating more than ever before in peacekeeping, administration, and in the political and nontraditionally "women's" fields such as the environment, food provision, and refugee programs, which will ultimately lead to an evening out of what has been rightly deplored as the concentration of women in a few areas.

And finally, for the first time in its history, the Administrative Committee on Coordination, comprising the heads of all the organizations and bodies of the UN system, with the Secretary-General himself as Chair, discussed in Vienna in February 1995 the role of women in the organization and took the time to examine seriously what strategies for improvement could be adopted.

The committee issued a landmark statement which, if properly publicized and monitored, will set the tone for changing attitudes to the way in which women currently participate throughout the United Nations system in a way which can set a realizable example to member states.

At this turning point, when we launch and endorse action and support that will determine whether the tone and nature of our discussions five years from now, in the year 2000, will be triumphant or recriminatory as to whether the women of the world and the organizations of the system are dealing in words rather than actions, may I end with the following:

• Commitment must continue to come from the top.

• Attitudes at all levels must change.

• Managerial accountability must be a reality, and sanctions have to be imposed where there is no compliance.

• Women must bear the responsibility for charting their own careers; they must keep up the pressure on the administration and never give up.

• Women outside the United Nations who are interested in working for the organization must take an active role and apply.

• Male staff should no longer feel challenged, but rather the opportunity to share professional and collegial growth with women staff at all levels should be welcomed.

• The administration, whose record has been marked by inconsistent spurts of enthusiasm and planning, has to sustain its determination to meet the targets and to provide the underpinning of the Steering Committee on the Improvement of the Status of Women, the Focal Point, and other mechanisms to reach full equality with excellence, including the necessary resources to ensure that we concentrate not just on words but also on deeds.

Should these goals be accomplished, then I believe that women in government, in NGOS, in the private sector, and at all levels of society will feel that the efforts of the Fourth World Conference on Women in the sector of advancing women in decision-making will not have failed.

Copies of the booklet "Employment Opportunities with the United Nations" may be obtained from the Director, Specialist Services Division, Office of Human Resources, Room S-2527, United Nations, New York, NY 10017, USA.

UNDP: Giving organizational force to the rhetoric

Rosina Elizabeth Wiltshire
United Nations Development Programme (UNDP)

What is UNDP doing in this? At an organizational level we reinforce what Angela King identifies as the overall strategy for the UN. As our specific goal, we focus on poverty elimination and equality as the central elements; and the advancement of women constitutes one of the four major dimensions of the overall framework. What are some of the key elements of the program framework?

One is increasing women's participation at the highest level of decision-making. We recognize that you cannot achieve at the country level what is not happening within the organization. In other words, you have to begin at home if you are going to be effective in achieving the objectives you set out. To promote this we have passed a policy, which has been reinforced and accepted by our senior management committee, to promote equality of women within UNDP at the highest levels of decision-making, with specific targets, monitoring mechanisms, and accountability mechanisms. I would say to all of you now we need your assistance, the assistance of the networks in identifying women who have skills and capabilities for filling positions in a range of areas. Get your curricula vitae in. To make this work, the pool of women has to be there. Often the positions have to be filled at quite short notice, but the men have their systems in place for identifying possible candidates. We have some systems, but we have to make them more effective. At the organizational level, that is what we are doing.

Our efforts are complemented at the country level by ensuring that we move from our old focus of interfacing specifically with government as the major partner — as the only partner really, and the primary partner defining the country's program priorities and implementation mechanisms — to greater emphasis on civil society as another major partner. So it is government and civil society, with a focus on women's groups. It is recognized that if you set the program priorities, and women's perspectives and priorities are not in there from the identification phase, then by the time you get to the program implementation phase you have already missed the boat.

Therefore, we have attempted to move beyond the old way of doing things, and — I must be honest — it is not easy to turn around the entire historical way of organizational functioning. It takes time, and we recognize that it takes time, and we recognize that we have a far way to go. But the commitment is there, the policy framework is in place, and the monitoring and accountability mechanisms are in place, so we see the way forward.

We also have a specific program focus on promoting women at higher levels of decision-making. We are working with women parliamentarians and with our governance division to facilitate the processes of building women's capacities to participate in decision-making, and also identifying women in decision-making who are interested in making a difference in this regard and in promoting technical cooperation among different countries, so there is a critical mass there of women who are planning and working their strategy together.

The second major program for us is strengthening legal and policy frameworks so that they promote equality. Here I give an example of Latin America, where our Latin America bureau has been working to devise model legislation which is gender sensitive, and also working with the governments. The draft document is almost complete and it is being discussed in workshops at the ministerial level, at the parliamentary level. The model, whether it is accepted or not, is diffused, and elements of it will begin to shape the legal frameworks of the countries in which we work.

Economic empowerment is the third major area, and promoting equal access to resources is an important focus. I will give you an example. We were recently in Nepal, where we participated in a group activity of businesswomen whom UNDP was supporting, in collaboration with UNIFEM, who had been given credit to set up their own businesses. I am not talking about microenterprises. It is a concept of women and their potential as businesspeople which goes beyond their working only at the smallest level. We are not necessarily dealing with large amounts of money, but it gives them capacity, gives them the base so they can break into businesses which include export businesses. In Nepal, a country in which women constitute very few of the literate, you had a group of women who were supporting another set of women in the rural community, whom we were also supporting in silviculture.

We had provided the women in silviculture an income-earning capacity and management capability too. The middle-class businesswomen recognized that they could not get credit on their own because there is a whole series of laws relating to land ownership that militated against their getting credit. The businesswomen who were breaking into the international market linked with the rural women as a network, so that while they couldn't get credit as individuals, they could get credit as a group.

The fourth area is capacity-building. Across all these areas we are training, both within UNDP and within our country offices, with our partners, building gender capacity for analysis, policy, monitoring, and evaluation.

I will end by saying that all of this requires effective monitoring and evaluation. We have specific overarching monitoring and evaluation mechanisms, and we are working with our division of evaluation and strategic planning to ensure that the UNDP systems integrate monitoring and evaluation of the gender dimensions and the gender impact of our work, how many women are benefiting. What are the gender dimensions across the board such that it is not just the project monitoring? It's the overall organizational monitoring of our programs, program directions, resource allocations which are being put in place.

We are involved in a task we hope will bear fruit in the very near future. We want to enter the 21st century with a system that is transformed. We recognize there is a commitment at the very top of the organization to this transformation of the system. There is a woman in senior management, in the formal group that keeps the organization accountable, who says we have to look at ourselves, we have to put a mirror up to watch ourselves, to identify where we are falling short and where we need to do better. That is at the informal level. At the formal level, the system is putting mechanisms in place — in budgeting, in monitoring, in evaluation, in programming, in project design, in partnering — which are designed to give a pragmatic practical force to the rhetoric that has characterized organizational change and gender mainstreaming.

Effective gender equality strategies

Misrak Elias
United Nations Children's Fund (UNICEF)

I am very pleased to be with you this afternoon and to share UNICEF's experience with gender equality strategies that have worked for us. Instead of going through our programs, I would like to use only two examples, one example of capacity-building for mainstreaming gender in programs and another example of advocacy strategies we have used in initiatives for girls through the life-cycle approach.

UNICEF's gender and development mandate comes from three different areas.

UNICEF's main mandate is the well-being, development, and protection of children, and ensuring that their rights are upheld. With this, we have a duty and responsibility to eliminate gender disparities between boys and girls.

The second mandate comes through the adult caretakers of the children. Women are key actors in the development and well-being of children. We have added the new dimension of having men as key actors in the development and well-being of children.

Throughout, women are seen as fundamental actors in development, peace-building, and the transformation of society; our mandate calls for promoting gender equality and the empowerment of women and girls.

Capacity-building for gender-responsive programs

The first strategy that we use to make sure our programs integrate a gender perspective is to not only address the needs of women but also to include women as decision makers. We call this capacity-building for gender-responsive programs. It calls for a move from policy to action, because our policy — dating from 1985 and updated in 1987 and again in 1994 — mandates us to integrate or mainstream gender in programs. In order to do that in a more systematic manner, we thought that we should have a conceptual framework to use in all our programs — in Africa, Asia, Latin America, and the Middle East. Accordingly we identified, developed, and adopted the Women's Equality and Empowerment Framework.

Using this framework, we designed training packages which we tried out with UNICEF colleagues as well as experts from various regions. Once we improved the framework as a tool, we thought we should also build a consensus, and focused on training as the entry point for transforming our programs such that they integrate a gender perspective. In recognition of the important role of training, the UNICEF executive board mandated that by 1994, 80 percent of UNICEF program training staff should be trained in and conversant with gender analysis. Taking this as a basis for our initiative, we developed various strategies for translating this training package into reality.

One challenge we faced was in-house expertise. We realized that we did not have all the necessary experts to do gender training in-house, so we looked for partners, consultants who would work with us. We asked our colleagues in various countries and regions to identify gender experts who knew the situation within their countries so that they could be partners with us in bringing about this change in our programs. In this way, we identified a global network of gender experts within as

well as external to UNICEF. By first bringing them together in 1993 and providing them with an orientation program — first to the UNICEF programming approach and second to the process and approach we have adopted for gender training — we thought we could achieve the basis for launching intensive and extensive training.

I said that training is the entry point for programs because if we focus on training alone, it will not bring about the necessary transformation. We thought that after the training, these experts — whether external consultants or colleagues serving as gender focal points within UNICEF — would work with our program officers, be it in health, education, nutrition, or other areas of focal development, so that a gender perspective would be integrated into programs and projects and so that women would be decision makers in the various projects we have at the community levels. This is done through follow-up technical support to what we call the country programming process.

UNICEF does not operate by having projects by themselves. We have five-year country programs, which are developed and agreed upon between UNICEF and the governments. These five-year country programs also include partnerships with NGOs within the countries. It is a long process which begins with a study called a "situation analysis" of children and women within that country.

We ensure that technical experts work closely with the country program team and the governmental partners in order to ensure the integration of gender. In so doing, the gender and development section and headquarters, the regional offices, and the gender focal points in countries act as catalysts, provide expert technical support, and promote intersectoral cross-fertilization.

The training process involves the development of two modules. The first, lasting about four and a half days, is for training UNICEF program staff, government counterparts, and NGO partners. The second, lasting one day, is for training senior management and policy makers. We are a decentralized organization working within communities, and this training reflects that.

What are our achievements? In going through this process, we were not able to meet the 80 percent target set up by our executive board. However, within a period of two years we have managed to have 223 workshops globally, we have managed to train over 1,000 UNICEF staff, and we have managed to train close to 8,000 government and NGO partners.

To determine the effectiveness of this training, the next task was assessment, which took place over a two-year period. First, we commissioned a background paper and asked our partners, the global network of experts who worked with us, to assess the entire process. In a review meeting we learned how to continue with our successes and make corrections where mistakes had been made.

What are some of the lessons and challenges we faced through this process? The first one was that we really have to work hard to make sure the link between training and program transformation is systematically followed up. By just giving training, change does not happen. To do this, we have to strategically choose our entry points at various stages of program development.

For example, it could be the situation-analysis study, the strategy development, the country program, and also the program plan-of-action preparations. Then we have to follow up, not only with document preparation but in actual implementation of programs. For this, the development of monitoring and evaluation indicators is critical. I cannot say we have done this fully, but we have developed some of these tools and think that by next year, we will be in a better position to use concrete indicators to measure progress.

We also took to heart the lesson that having separate gender training is not sufficient. Gender training should be integrated into other training activities and other meetings or initiatives taken cross-sectorally. For example, if there is a workshop in education, then the gender perspective should be part of it.

Another lesson we learned has to do with skills development as the main focus of our entire training package in gender analysis and gender planning for mainstream programs. We have not focused much on the personal values and attitudinal changes necessary to change practice. We now believe we need to make a major change in those as well.

Another major lesson we learned was that what we do in our programs needs to be reflected internally within UNICEF. We cannot preach to others what we don't practice, and normally that is the situation for many of us. What kind of organizational commitment do we have? In many situations, when it comes to gender equality, organizations have good pronouncements in terms of policy and good intentions in terms of strategy, but the resources, commitment, and priorities may not measure up to expectations. So we felt it was very important to increase organizational commitment and change the organizational structure.

The next lesson is that we have to develop a system of accountability and responsibility mechanisms. All country programs have to mainstream gender, but what ensures that the UNICEF country representative actually complies with the policy? This is something we really need to work on. Unless there are individual and program-level accountability and responsibility mechanisms, it is very difficult.

For this, we need to talk of management support. I am very pleased to say that Carol Bellamy, as a woman head of an agency and a committed feminist, points the way toward greater effectiveness for us in the future. Many of us at UNICEF who are committed to gender issues are very excited about this new development.

So, to sum up the first part, that is capacity-building for mainstreaming gender, we have three challenges for bringing about the necessary transformations:

• transformation of programs,

• necessary changes in organizational, institutional environment, and

• changes in the personal values, attitudes, and practices of UNICEF staff as well as the other partners who implement programs within communities.

This is the first strategy that we believe has managed to bring about positive results, even though we would like to do more. I told you about the 80 percent target for training more than 1,000 UNICEF staff. We have managed to reach only 33 percent, so there is a long way to go.

Girl child initiatives

Now I would like to share with you the second strategy we have adopted to bring about changes through advocacy. This has to do with the initiative for the girl child. As some of you recall, concern for dismantling gender discrimination by taking action at the roots with a girl child initiative came from Asia, when it declared the 1990s as the decade for the girl child. UNICEF took this initiative from Asia and globalized the whole concept through the booklet "Investing in the Girl Child." The executive board of UNICEF has said we should increase our efforts to ensure gender equality between the boys and girls in our constituencies. So in order to globalize priority action for girls, we have to come up with certain elements that would appeal to large numbers of people. Allow me to explore several aspects of this area.

The concern for gender is universal, but the dimension we have added is the realization that gender discrimination can be eliminated only if tackled at the roots with action for girls. To help this process along and gain adherents, we have promoted conceptual and methodological approaches which are still evolving.

One of these is the life-cycle approach, which postulates a diversity and difference of issues and concerns at different stages of a woman's life cycle. For example, the issues for children of 0-5 years are very different from the issues of adolescent girls of 13-18. In the 0-5 category, the main focus is nurture, care, and stimulation. The main concern is to ensure that girls are not fed less and not neglected and that their health is maintained. The main focus in the 6-12 age category would be ensuring that girls get equal opportunity for education, develop their self-esteem, and do not get overloaded with work; in Africa and many other parts of the world, girls become little women in many senses, taking on the work burden of their mothers from age six onward.

We advocate that in order to break the cycle of disadvantage for women, we have to focus on the early stages of life. Throughout the Decade for Women, the focus was on adult women. We are saying that unless we look at women holistically from birth through old age, we cannot tackle the problem and will be attempting to find piecemeal solutions.

This brought about a concern for intergenerational influence. If we are talking about equality for little girls and adolescent girls, we are talking about the influence of earlier generations. What is the role of yesterday's girls — now adult women — in promoting either equality or disadvantage for their daughters? We believe that the values, attitudes, and practices of women should change, but that's not enough.

Men, too, influence this process. Here is where the gender dimension comes in. There need to be changes in the values, attitudes, practices, and gender roles of men as parents in the upbringing of boys and girls as well as in communities and nationally. In order to bring about greater adherence to this concept, we rely on alliances and partnerships in various countries, regions, and globally.

The role of NGOs has been very critical and central in this process. At the international level, there is a working group on girls which is a coalition of international NGOs; this has been instrumental in putting at the forefront of the global agenda the concepts of the life-cycle approach and taking action for girls.

In many regions, again, NGOs have done very important work. To use the example of Africa, FEMNET — the African regional coordinating group — as well as FAWE have played a central role in bringing the issues of the girl child onto center stage. Within civil society, academics, human rights activists, and development practitioners have been very much in partnership to bring about this change. Governments have also been at the forefront.

As these alliances and coalitions developed, there was a focus on the girl child initiative. There are several important issues — from adolescent health to education to female genital mutilation to sex-selective abortions — but the focus of many agencies, many organizations, and many people now has been on educational opportunities for girls. The World Bank has said that girls' education is the single best investment in development. Various international agencies, such as UNESCO and USAID, have taken up the issue of girls' education as a priority. Preparations for the FWCW have provided the impetus for building up this coalition of NGOs and governments. Actually, it was the initiative of NGOs in the Asia region that put the girl child's concerns on the Asian Platform for Action; it was again the coalition of NGOs and governments in Africa that first initiated the chapter on the girl child in the African Platform for Action; it is the alliance of the Group of 77 that placed the girl child on the Global Platform for Action.

These are important, positive developments that are being increased, tallied, and transformed every day. The latest development, which I find very exciting and rewarding, is the participation of young women and girls themselves in setting the agenda. I am sure all of you are aware of their work in the Youth Tent here in Huairou and their participation in the Conference. This means that not only adult women and adult men will be speaking about the needs and concerns of young women and girls, but that girls themselves are articulating and speaking about their own needs and concerns. I think this is an exciting and healthy development, and this Conference has created a new milestone in the participation of young people in setting the agenda for the 21st century. We are very pleased to be part of this process.

An integrated response to population and development

Ana Angarita
United Nations Population Fund (UNFPA)

UNFPA is a crucial player in the effort to implement the International Conference on Population and Development (ICPD) strategy to empower women and give them full and equal partnership in the population and development process. The principles at the core of the Programme of Action — the need for gender equality and equity — spell out an integrated response to population and development challenges in the decades ahead. UNFPA's efforts in the area of women, population, and development have been at the vanguard of the organization since its inception. As far back as 1975 the Fund issued guidelines for incorporating women's concerns into population and development activities, making it one of the first UN agencies to take such an initiative.

In the intervening years, UNFPA has deepened its commitment to the area of women, population, and development, particularly in the delineation of explicit and integrated strategies to improve the critical importance of women's status and roles in population and development. Growing attention has been given to women's needs, including special measures to increase their participation in programs and the benefits they receive from program results.

With the establishment in 1986 of its Special Unit for Women, Population, and Development, the Fund strengthened its efforts to (1) ensure women's involvement both as beneficiaries and participants in all UNFPA programs and projects and (2) support activities aimed specifically at benefiting women and improving their status. The Special Unit was reorganized in 1991 as the Women, Population, and Development Branch of UNFPA's Technical and Evaluation Division. Guidelines were again revised to strengthen the objectives of "complete and total integration of women's concerns into all population activities and the increased participation of women in all projects supported by the Fund."

UNFPA continues to fine-tune its policies to make them more gender sensitive and has embarked on a number of initiatives that have significantly enhanced its capacity to deal with issues concerning women. These efforts include a new emphasis on field-level programming and a holistic approach to country programming based on macroeconomics and sociocultural factors — a major step in mainstreaming women into the population and development process. UNFPA has also strengthened its linkages with NGOs by identifying and supporting grassroots groups that promote women's issues and enabling them to play a more active role in the development process.

In 1995 the Women, Population, and Development Branch of UNFPA was renamed the Gender, Population, and Development Branch to reflect the full variety of gender-sensitive concerns that need to be incorporated into programs, including male participation and responsibilities. The Branch has been given additional staff to enable it to fully and effectively discharge its functions. Recognizing that gender issues and concerns have expanded beyond women-specific activities to include gender equality and equity, participation of both men and women in all aspects of population and development, and the role of men in achieving women's empowerment, UNFPA has issued revised guidelines for the Gender, Population, and Development Branch.

With the objective of providing technical assistance to governments, UNFPA in 1990 established eight country support teams (CSTs). Each CST has a gender, population, and development advisor.

Implementing the ICPD Programme of Action

With the Programme of Action (specifically chapter 4), UNFPA has further focused its approach on gender issues and concerns rather than on women's issues *per se*. UNFPA will ensure that gender concerns will be an integral component of all its program areas and that women, women's organizations, and other groups working for women's needs are involved in the planning, implementation, and monitoring of the program activities, especially those related to reproductive health and family planning. The Fund is strongly committed to vocal advocacy on behalf of women's issues, even in areas where our mandated role and financial support are limited. UNFPA will, in collaboration with other UN entities, support countries in formulating gender-sensitive action plans to implement the Programme of Action.

For example, the Fund has provided support for management training programs for women and women's microenterprises that are linked with reproductive health and family planning programs and for supporting the strengthening of institutions

and organizations dealing with gender issues, including NGOs. Such activities have been carried out in collaboration with programmes of other organizations, including the International Labour Organization (ILO), the United Nations Development Programme (UNDP), the Food and Agriculture Organization (FAO), the United Nations Development Fund for Women (UNIFEM), and the Centre for Development and Population Activities (CEDPA). UNFPA will also extend its cooperation to ensure that governments effectively implement the Convention on the Elimination of All Forms of Discrimination Against Women (CEDAW).

As part of the interregional activities to promote gender equality and provide information for policy and program development, UNFPA has funded a number of research activities which have been carried out with other UN agencies and international NGOs. Important policy-oriented research activities were carried out with The Population Council on family structure, on female headship and poverty, and on family and population policies in Egypt, Kenya, India, and Ghana. Other activities under way are:

• working closely with UNIFEM within the context of CEDAW to include reproductive rights of women as a human right;

• assessment of mainstreaming of gender in country programs and projects;

• a research project with The Population Council on male involvement in reproductive health; and

• establishment of gender training centres.

UNFPA will also be concentrating its efforts on advocacy. Activities will be of two types. The first will address gender equality and equity, education of women, reproductive rights, protection of the girl child, and the role of males in matters of sexual and reproductive health and in the family. The Fund will also work as an advocate for human rights and development issues such as education, poverty, basic health services, empowerment of women, and people's participation, all emanating from the ICPD Programme of Action and agreements reached at other UN fora.

Since 1987 UNFPA has been convening a panel

on gender, population, and development. The last one took place in April 1995 to discuss UNFPA's future directions in the area of gender and population, taking into account the outcome of the ICPD. The Executive Director also decided to establish an NGO advisory committee to explore various aspects of UNFPA policies and programming. Participants at the first meeting recommended, *inter alia*, that UNFPA strengthen its partnerships with NGOs and the private sector at the country level and use its position as a convener to bring governments and NGOs together in their common efforts to implement the ICPD Programme of Action.

At another level, UNFPA has taken various institutional actions to ensure vigorous attention to gender concerns by all UNFPA staff. Last June, as part of a global meeting at headquarters, UNFPA country directors and program officers participated in gender training. It was quite a challenge.

We will continue to update our gender training for staff, including compulsory training for all senior staff. The overall objectives of these workshops are to create gender awareness — in particular, the strategic and analytic shift from a narrow women-in-development concept to a broader gender focus — and to ensure that gender issues are mainstreamed.

The Fund is also proud to say that in promoting the status of female staff and meeting a gender balance, 44 percent of our professional staff and managers are women. So far, we are the leading UN agency in meeting the target of 50 percent.

Just a few days ago, an International Meeting of Parliamentarians on Gender, Population, and Development, sponsored by UNFPA, was held in conjunction with the Fourth World Conference on Women in Beijing. This meeting, which took place in Tokyo, was attended by more than 90 parliamentarians from 57 countries. A Call to Action to Governments was made on the following issues, among many others:

• integrating gender perspectives in development strategies;

• implementing policies and programs to improve the legal, health, social, and economic status and rights of women;

• advocating for women's empowerment and gender equality; and

• maintaining or increasing funding levels for women and gender-related programs, especially during periods of budget reduction and under structural adjustment and economic recovery programs.

I would like to end by quoting a young woman who participated in the global youth meeting "Voices of Young Women," held in July in Washington, D.C., and convened by the Centre for Development and Population Activities (CEDPA) in collaboration with UNFPA. What she said was this: "Young women are like tea bags. The minute you put them in hot water, you see how strong they are."

PART III

COMMITMENT TO THE FUTURE:

Accountability and Action

Opening Address

PART III • ACCOUNTABILITY AND ACTION

Opening address

Hillary Rodham Clinton
First Lady, United States

I feel so much at home and so much a part of this group. I only wish that in addition to the enthusiasm and interest amongst all of the NGOs gathered here, the weather had been more cooperative this morning, and I greatly regret that we were forced to move this occasion indoors in order to avoid any of us drowning out there. But I am very sorry that not everyone who wished to be with us this morning was able to get in, and I hope all of you will convey my personal regrets to anyone who was turned away or disappointed because of the size of this auditorium.

It is a great pleasure for me to be here, and I want to start by thanking Supatra and Irene for their leadership in this extraordinary and historic enterprise. But I also want to thank all of you who are here, because I know from looking at the lists of people who have come, of knowing personally many of the Americans who have come, that in this auditorium and at this Forum, there are thousands and thousands of women and men who every day work to make lives better in their communities for all people. And that is the greatest contribution any one of us is able to make, and that is why the United States and many other countries so strongly support the efforts of NGOs and have worked very hard to ensure that NGOs could participate in this Forum. As many of you know, our government and other governments recognize the important role that NGOs play in policy and planning, in development and implementation and monitoring of programs that advance the progress of women.

I wanted to come here to Huairou to salute you for your dedication to a cause greater than all of us. I know that many of you went to great efforts to be here. I know many were kept from attending this Forum. I know that for many of you who did get here, getting here was far from easy. Many of you did not even know until the last minute that you would be permitted to travel here, and others bore great personal expense in order to come. In addition to the weather, which is not in anyone's control, and is always unpredictable, I know that you have had to endure severe frustrations here as you have pursued your work, and I also want to say a special word on behalf of women with disabilities who have faced particularly challenging circumstances. But I mostly want to thank you for your perseverance, because you did not give up, you did not stay away. You are here, and the fact that you are will make a difference.

In the days and months and years to come, even though you may not be physically present in Beijing at the Conference during these ten days, the wisdom that is accumulated here, the experience, the energy, the ideas are on full display. Thanks to your resourcefulness, your tenacity, your sense of purpose, and your spirit, you are playing an important role in this Conference, and you will be the key players in determining whether or not this Conference goes beyond rhetoric and actually does something to improve the lives of women and children.

As I said yesterday, the faces of the women who are here mirror the faces of the millions and millions who are not. It is our responsibility, those of us who have been able to attend this Conference and this NGO Forum, to make sure that the voices that go unheard will be heard. This Conference is about making sure that women, their children, their families, have the opportunities for health care and education, for jobs and political participation, for lives free of violence, for basic legal protections, and yes, for internationally recognized human rights, no matter where they are or where they live.

Time and time again, we have seen that it is NGOs who are responsible for making progress in any society. Some of us never knew that we were NGOs 20 and 25 and 30 years ago. That was not even a phrase that any of us had ever heard. We were people working together on behalf of all of those rights which we care about and hold dear. But when one looks at the progress that has been made throughout the world, it is clear that it is the NGOs who have charted real advances for women and children. It is the NGOs who have pressured governments and have led governments down the path to economic, social, and political progress, often in the face of overwhelming hostility. Again, NGOs have persevered, just as you have by coming here and staying here and participating in this Forum. What will be important, as we end the Forum and the Conference at the end of this week, is that it will be NGOs who will hold governments to the commitments that they make. And it is important that the final Platform for Action that is adopted be distilled down into words that every woman, no matter where she lives or how much education she has, can understand. I think we should want every woman, no matter where she is, to believe that there are women all over the world who care about her health, who want her children to be educated, who want her to have the dignity and respect that she deserves to have.

I think of the faces that I have seen in my own country; I think of the women who do not have health care because they cannot afford it in the United States of America. I think particularly of a woman I met in New Orleans, Louisiana, who told me that because she did not have enough money, she was told by physicians in our country that they would not do anything about the lump in her breast but would merely wait and watch, because if she had insurance she would have been sent to a surgeon.

I think about the woman I met in a village outside Lahore, Pakistan, who had ten children, five boys and five girls, and was struggling as hard as she could to make sure her girls were educated, and wanted help to get that job done. I think of the faces of the beautiful women I met at SEWA, the Self-Employed Women's Association, in India. All of them had walked miles and miles, some of them for 12 and 15 hours, to get to our meeting. I listened as they stood up and told me what it had meant that for the first time in their lives, having a little money of their own, they could buy their own vegetable carts, they could buy their own thread and materials, so that they could make an income for themselves and their families.

I think of the women in a village in Bangladesh, a village of Untouchables. I think of how those women, who were Hindus, invited to their village for my visit women from the neighboring village, who were Moslems. I think of how those women sat together under a lean-to, Hindus and Moslems together in one of the poorest countries of the world. So many of those women told me what their lives had been changed to because they had become borrowers that were now part of the Grameen Bank microenterprise effort. I think particularly of the play that their children put on for me to see, a play in which the children acted out the refusal by a family to let a girl child go to school, and how finally through efforts undertaken by the mother and the sister, the father agreed that the child could go to school. And then further down the road from that village, I stood and watched families coming to receive food supplements in return for keeping their girl children in school.

Those are the kinds of women and experiences that happen throughout the world, whether one talks about my country or any country. Women are looking for the support and encouragement they need to do what they can for their own lives and the lives of their children and the lives of their families. The only way this Conference will make a difference to these women is if the results of the Conference are taken and distilled down into one page perhaps, which states basic principles that you and I would perhaps debate and understand but may not be easily communicated. If that is done, then to carry that message into every corner of the world so there can be sharing of experiences. When I came home from Bangladesh, I visited Denver, Colorado, to see a program that is modeled on the Grameen Bank, helping American women who are welfare recipients get the dignity and the skills that they need to take care of themselves and their children.

So despite all of the difficulties and frustrations you have faced in coming here and being here, you are here not only on behalf of yourselves, but on behalf of millions and millions of women whose lives can be changed for the better, if you resolve along with all of us to leave this place and do what we can together to make the changes that will give respect and dignity to every woman.

I know that today at the women's Conference there is a special celebration of girls. The theme is investing in today's girls, tomorrow's women, and the future. We know that much of what we do, we are doing not for ourselves, but we are doing for our daughters, our nieces, our granddaughters. We are doing it because we have the hope that the changes we work for will take root and flower in their lives. When I was privileged to be in New Delhi, India, I met a young woman who I think spoke for many, many women, and someone asked me yesterday at the Conference if I had a copy of the poem which this young woman wrote. And I said that I did, and she asked if I could read it today, and I said that I would. Because this was a poem about breaking the silence, the silence that afflicts too many women's lives, the silence that keeps women from expressing themselves freely, from being full participants even in the lives of their own families. This poem, written by a young woman, I think is particularly appropriate since we are celebrating today the future of girls. Let me read it to you:

Too many women in too many countries speak the same language of silence. My grandmother was always silent, always agreed. Only her husband had the positive right, or so it was said, to speak and to be heard. They say it is different now. After all, I am always vocal, and my grandmother thinks I talk too much. But sometimes I wonder. When a woman gives her love, as most do generously, it is accepted. When a woman shares her thoughts, as some women do graciously, it is allowed. When a woman

fights for power, as all women would like to, quietly or loudly, it is questioned. And yet, there must be freedom if we are to speak. And yes, there must be power if we are to be heard. And when we have both freedom and power, let us not be misunderstood. We seek only to give words to those who cannot speak — too many women in too many countries. I seek only to forget my grandmother's silence.

That is the kind of feeling that literally millions and millions of women feel every day. And much of what we are doing here at this Forum and at this Conference is to give words to break the silence, and then to act.

When I was at Copenhagen for the World Summit on Social Development, I was pleased to announce that the United States would make an effort to enhance educational opportunities for girls so that they could attend school in Africa, Asia, and Latin America. Today, that effort, funded with U.S. dollars, is being organized in countries throughout those continents by NGOs.

There are so many ways we can work together. There are so many things that must be done. And let me just end with a postcard that I received from a woman who, with many, many others, wrote me her feelings and thoughts about this Conference. I don't know this woman, but she wrote to tell me that she wanted me to carry this card to Beijing. And she went on to say, "Be assured of many prayers for the success of the conference, to better conditions for women and children throughout the world."

She put on this card a prayer, and the prayer was written in many languages. It's a prayer that applies to and can be said by many, if not all, of the world's religions. And I want to end with that, because I think that in many respects what we are attempting to do requires the kind of faith and commitment that this prayer represents:

O God, creator of the heavens and the earth, we pray for all who gather in Beijing [and I would add Huairou as well]. *Bless them; help them and us to see one another through eyes enlightened by understanding and compassion. Release us from prejudice so we can receive the stories of our sisters with respect and attention. Open our ears to the cries of a suffering world and the healing melodies of peace. Empower us to be instruments in bringing about justice and equality everywhere.*

That is my prayer as well, and with my thanks to all of you. I believe we can take the results of this Forum and this Conference and begin to translate them into actions that will count in the lives of girls and women who will have never heard of what we have done here, but whose lives can be changed because of what you have done coming here. Thank you all very much.

XVI • NGO Structures and Accountability — *Strategies*

Opening remarks

Pak Po-Hi, Moderator
Korea Institute for Social Information & Research,
South Korea

GENERAL PREMISE

Nongovernmental organizations are often perceived as a weaker counterpart of government organizations. This, however, is a misconception. Historically NGOs have consistently been in the forefront of social change; they have often seen beyond the present and so given rise to new thoughts, new modalities of life, new laws and institutions. NGOs and GOs are but two institutional manifestations of us, the people. They are our instruments for purposeful action.

GOs and NGOs can form well-balanced and cooperative partnerships; they can be in conflict with each other; the former can dominate the latter. These relationships may reflect cultural differences or be related to levels of socioeconomic development. In the typical Asian society with patriarchal and/or authoritarian traditions, government has tended to dominate the nongovernmental sector. In the typical Western society with individualistic mores, on the other hand, the notion of government as the servant of the people is well established, and the position of NGOs vis-à-vis government is correspondingly stronger.

Even in the Asian context, however, as people grow in economic abilities, are exposed to alternative values, or are faced with conditions requiring them to take charge of their own fate, such as times of extraordinary disaster or war, the nongovernmental sector has been known to emerge dominant in relation to the government, regardless of cultural context or tradition.

In the Asia-Pacific region, the democratic ideology that swept the region following World War II has perhaps had the most powerful influence on the emergence of NGOs, including women's organizations. Such international instruments as the Universal Declaration of Human Rights — as well as numerous conventions or protocols dealing with racial, gender, and minority discrimination and people's rights to life, work, culture, development, and so on — have worked as catalytic agents in many Third World countries, encouraging or even requiring them to introduce egalitarian and democratic values and establishing the people as the real masters of their nations.

But perhaps the most significant agent of change in the Third World has been the growth of people's power itself. As they have grown increasingly better educated, people have grown in knowledge and information resources. Grown healthier thanks to better health care, they have had more energy to tackle their own affairs and to produce more and better goods and services for their well-being. With improved, independent economic resources, they have been able to stand up better to unnecessary external controls and have come to expect their statutory rights to be respected and honored.

The threats posed by the global ecological imbalance — spreading mass poverty and ceaseless tribal, racial, religious, and/or national wars and conflicts — have constituted another important factor contributing to the growth of NGOs in the past few decades. These threats and challenges are beyond the capacities of the GO sector alone to meet. The NGO sector must not only actively collaborate with the GO sector but needs to take new initiatives in responding to these global issues as only the NGOs can, free from the sorts of institutional constraints that GOs usually suffer from.

CHALLENGES

If NGOs in general, and NGOs for women in particular, are to rise to the challenges stemming from the pressing world situation, they must undergo profound changes. They must metamorphose from government-dependent entities into leading forces for social and economic change. In general, NGOs are only loosely organized, resource-poor, and lacking in expertise. Overcoming these weaknesses is an important precondition for the continuing efficacy of NGOs, and the following would seem part of the requisites that they must fulfill in this connection.

Context awareness

Each NGO has its own goals and objectives, whether social, economic, cultural, political, religious, or issues specific to one population group. It can therefore carry out its work independently, without paying too much attention to what is going on in society at large or in the world as a whole. In the long run, however, an inward-looking organization loses its effectiveness by becoming either irrelevant to the changing needs of the society of which it is a part or unable to mobilize the necessary resources and institutional support from the relevant community. To better pursue its particular goals and objectives, an organization must see where and how it fits in with the overall configuration of the developmental and/or problem-solving needs of a given society or of the world, and it must adjust its goals, objectives, and modes of operation to changes in those needs.

Systemic linkage

NGOs need to be in touch with one another to avoid functional overlaps and waste of resources and to collaborate in areas where their interests and functions cannot but overlap. NGOs also need to be in touch with the government sector. The latter may be the former's client or its source of financial and technical support. On the other hand, the two may just be concerned parties with reference to a particular issue or subject. In any event, each needs to know what the other is about and why. They need to have a working relationship based on mutual understanding, acceptance of differences, and basic trust. To achieve such a working relationship, there must be regular and sufficient information flow between them, the operation of organizations needs to be as transparent as possible, and their credibility must be beyond question. These, indeed, are part of the prerequisites for effective partnership between the NGO and GO sectors.

Intrasectoral solidarity

NGOs are not simply service organizations. Many of them come into being as straightforward pressure groups to protect the interests of certain groups within the population, which may be women as a whole or some segments thereof, or to advance particular causes. While varying degrees of schism among NGOs cannot be avoided for this reason, there are many times when and many areas where they need to speak with one voice and act as a body in relation to the GO sector or the business community.

Policies and measures related to the environment, the family, consumer issues, women's rights, and basic social services are examples of areas where the concerns and interests of NGOs for women can well coincide. Because of these common interests and solidarity, it is usual for NGOs to group themselves under one or more interorganizational coordinating bodies. Problems can arise in this connection, however, if the coordinating body does not adequately encompass the diverse interests of its constituents or if there is more than one coordinating body in a given sector and little communication or collaboration between the bodies. These situations must be avoided if the NGO sector is to be influential vis-à-vis government or the business community. Frequent and regular dialogue, consultations, and issue-oriented workshops could help air differences of view and position and evolve alternative perspectives congenial to the entire sector.

Routinization of NGO networking and NGO-GO collaboration

One or more consultative bodies should be formed among NGOs and between the NGO and GO sectors to facilitate their collaborative efforts.

In the past, the concerns that the various NGOs and GOs have endeavored to address have tended to be sectoral, and the means employed too fragmented to be effective. Past efforts to overcome these shortcomings have been ad hoc and loosely structured. Interorganizational cooperation needs to be more systematic in the future.

The consultative bodies should be formed at both the national and local levels, and the various population groups directly or indirectly concerned with given issues should participate in the consultation process. In a well-functioning democracy, the parliament and local legislatures perhaps could represent the totality of the nongovernmental sector, both NGOs and the business community. Experience has shown, however, that the workings of these formal institutions are too slow to respond to the rapid changes of our time and do not always adequately represent the interests of all concerned. It is important that NGOs, GOs, and the people at large have proper opportunities to put their heads together and come to some agreement about what should be pursued as priority goals at the national and local levels and what proposals should be sent to relevant legislatures for sanction and budgetary support. It is necessary that they jointly follow up on parliamentary decisions regarding their proposals and on the implementation of funded proposals.

Many matters of interest need not go to the legislatures at all and can be dealt with by the consultative bodies themselves. This will apply to many government regulations, administrative practices, and styles.

Setting priorities for NGO networking

NGO concerns and interests are quite diverse at any given moment. Nevertheless, they cannot be addressed and/or solved all at once, and certain issues and problems need to be dealt with before others. Environmental destruction is one example. Human-resource development is another. Women's full and direct participation in national and global decision structures is still another. In intra-NGO networking and NGO-GO cooperation alike, it is important that the foci of joint efforts be as clear and uncluttered as possible. Of the hundreds of specific action proposals in the Platform for Action, it must be sorted out which proposals require collaborative efforts among NGOs or between NGOs and GOs and which would be most amenable to such efforts, and these should be made the priority agenda for networking.

The grass roots as the foundation of NGOs

Many NGOs are top-heavy and without solid support bases at the grassroots level. Yet it is the amount and vitality of grassroots support that can make an NGO influential and effective. Any effort directed toward advancing the cause of women must first and last be responsive to the development needs of grassroots women, be firmly grounded in their support, and be ultimately accountable to them. No women's organization that leaves out the majority at the grass roots can effect substantive changes in the lives of women as a whole. Nor can such an organization justify its call for gender equality because gender equality is none other than a call for solidarity among all people, regardless of their biological or socioeconomic status.

Resource mobilization

If NGOs are to be effective in pursuing their goals, they need to have an independent organizational footing worthy of respect and trust, and such a footing can best be attained and sustained if they command independent financial resources. NGOs usually start out with independent wherewithal. In the course of their evolution, however, they tend to become dependent on government subsidies and thus lose a good part of their initiative in policy-making and program-setting.

NGO dependence on government subsidies has been almost unavoidable in many developing countries, where government regulations restrict GO fund-raising and no institutional incentives are provided for private donations. In some countries it is the government itself that becomes the fund-raiser, scooping up most of the available goodwill among the populace that otherwise might go to NGOs. Limited government budgets for humanitarian affairs are one reason why this has happened. The question of trustworthiness of individual NGOs has been another reason. Whether government is more trustworthy in the management and disbursement of funds raised is of course open to question. But even leaving this question aside, one wonders why governments, having the power to collect taxes for their work, should seek donations outside the official channels. Among other things, this had the effect of drying up NGOs' sources of support and thus keeping them tied to government apronstrings.

In view of the need for future expansion of NGO roles, their resource base should be enlarged and made fertile through such means as liberal tax deductions for private donations to accredited NGOs, tax exemptions for income-generating enterprises conducted by NGOs, and policy and/or legislative support to joint fund-raising operations by NGOs such as exist in some countries in both East and West. This last is meaningful from the standpoint of not only assuring participating NGOs a regular work budget but also strengthening their mutual ties.

A member-based NGO: Building in accountability

Ela Bhatt
Self-Employed Women's Association (SEWA)
Cooperative Bank; Women's World Banking, India

As you know, there are NGOs and there are NGOs. Oxfam is an NGO, the Red Cross is an NGO, and the village-level adult education class is also an NGO. So we are of all sizes and all forms and all profiles. Which NGOS are we talking about? We here represent thousands of NGOs from around the world. We deal with many issues, such as economic participation, women's health, safe drinking water, the education of our girls, human rights, violence in the home and outside, and structural adjustment programs. So all of us here have

formed organizations and have joined organizations to make a difference in the world of the women of the world.

Let me start with India. In India, which is my country, there are dedicated women doing social work in remote corners. Today's voluntary workers clash with firms and have moved to big-time deeds, and the profile has changed. There are no firm figures about how many NGOs are registered within my country, but a rough estimate puts the figure at around 30,000, with the focus increasingly on poverty alleviation and on poor people.

The NGOs have done commendable and frustrating work in the areas of health, the environment, rural development, nonformal education, banking for rural people, and almost all the subjects. Taking note of this work, the government invites the NGOs to the policy forums for advice and also provides them with funds for necessary purposes.

With the changing times, there are some NGOs whose profiles and styles have changed. Some of us have become more professional in approach; we recruit modern, educated views and use modern communication techniques. The criticism against us is that the present-day NGOs are a far cry from the earlier, barefoot *kopi wallahs* who dominated the Independence movement and that we are moving on the fast track with as much haste as the elite of the corporate world. So we should be conscious about the criticisms of us as well.

Another question is asked: How right is it for the government to shun its own duty to solve the people's problems? The government is happy because they are unable to deliver the goods and can use NGOs as their alibi. NGOs have become a sort of undesignated state; some have become agents of Western power.

Of course, there are no answers to this and I don't wish to give any answers, either yes or no, right or wrong. But in such cases, again the main question is of accountability. To whom should the NGOs be accountable: to the government or the donors or the common man for whom they are working? Today we deal with the issues that face all of us as nongovernmental organizations, regardless of our cause or sector of activity. These are questions of how we choose to build the legal, organizational, accountability, and financial sections of our organizations and how these sources affect what we do, how we do it, and how effective we are in achieving our objectives — in particular, who owns our organizations; who has the power to decide on the policies, strategies, and programs of our organizations; how are those whom we seek to help involved in the ownership and decision-making processes of our organizations; who provides the funding; how does the way we get money affect what we do and how we do it; how do the legal, organizational, and financial sections of our organizations affect what we do, how we go about our business, and how effective we are in achieving our objectives? So these are the core questions that we need to constantly ask our own organizations.

Our experience is in SEWA, the Self-Employed Women's Association, which is a trade union of women workers in the unorganized sector having a membership of about 250,000 in India. Our union and our experience in the union say that the strategies for action should include the members. That is, the organization is member-based, and when we have a member-based approach, then from the start we are able to involve them in built-in accountability. I, for one, believe that our effectiveness as NGOs is greatly increased when we have member-based organizations and when these members come from the groups we intend to serve. If we are in the business of building credit and selling services for poor women, then poor women should be the leaders, the members, the owners, the decision makers, and, if possible, the managers.

For example, in SEWA Bank, most members of the board are poor women — who happen to be street vendors, rag pickers, used clothing sellers, agricultural workers, and so on — and these women own the bank and run the bank. These women are tough. We have visitors, and when they ask what is their role as board members, they say, "To make sure that the loans are repaid."

When women's savings groups decide at what interest rate they will lend to one another, they choose such high rates because they know how much it costs to run a program and how vulnerable

financial resources are. At the same time, these women make sure that the services of SEWA Bank respond to the needs of poor women. In SEWA we started with savings, moved to small loans for businesses, and now have loans to buy land and build homes in the woman's name. So our task as an NGO is ultimately to empower people, to empower the women, and thereby to build up people's own organizations.

Another example is our Women's World Banking. We have pioneered the capitalization of growth. We need to get external funders to provide finance, not so much for our operating costs but more to provide core capital or endowments for our institution. We should try to negotiate that all funding goes toward our general program and not into specific, donor-designed projects. We should negotiate that 50 per cent be used to form a capital or endowment fund for our activities. This means that after seven or ten years, we would have invested sufficient earning income to cover our core costs. In this way we can survive and grow as a self-determined organization instead of begging the donors each year, spending the funds, and starting all over again.

So, as women, we need to make financial mechanisms that ensure our organizations are sustainable and self-determined. Today's need is for a long-run risk-taking attitude by all institutions, by all NGOs, public or private. It must be clear that all NGOs and institutions bear their origin in society, in the people. They exist for the development of society; otherwise, they do not have a right to survive.

Accountability and the international networks

Patricia Mercado
Grupo de Información y Reproducción Elegida
(GIRE); Mujeres Trabajadoras Unidas (MUTUAC),
Mexico

First I must begin by saying there is no satisfactory translation for this concept of implementing and carrying out accords that I refer to in English as "accountability." For those of us who use it with a feminist perspective, accountability signifies not allowing the realization of a single motion on the part of governments, international agencies, multilateral groups, or UN conferences to develop, implement, and evaluate policies and programs that concern the lives of women — such as the one that is taking place at this moment — without our being there to guarantee the greatest benefits for individuals and/or families and/or communities.

When I speak of "us," I am referring to the NGOs that work in favor of women's empowerment. Our novel experience of accountability is centered on basic reasons: the first — and its priority is explicit — is the social force and public opinion that we can generate in the demand and implementation of policy, or in the compliance of an international agreement. The second is our own technical capacity to generate information, the indicators of evaluation, and the opportunity to produce in the moment proposals and counterproposals.

The possibility of demand, implementation, and monitoring of policies is given by the working capacity and mobilization of different women's networks, some tied to specific issues, others to social sectors or to regions or countries, and also for the capacity to empower ourselves through training and education, and in doing so, to build alliances with other progressive movements like our own.

To be able to develop strategies that maintain the needs of women in all moments of decision-making is one of the most difficult challenges that our global movement will face in the coming years. In the new settings where the feminist and women's movements are active, an international decision can achieve an important cascade effect, nurturing national processes that in turn will nurture local and municipal processes. Beyond reaching accountability, there is also a need to implement, at the national level, tri-partisan meetings in which governments, international agencies, and local NGOs will participate.

Without a doubt, we owe much to the international networks for the changes that have taken place in the United Nations, especially in its opening to civil society. These networks are important in preventing the ideas of some countries from being imposed on others without the benefit of open and democratic discussions concerning the priorities of all.

One important element for achieving accountability is to be involved in the initiation and development of policy, especially when it is a result of an international plan of action, and to say at the end, in a critical manner (which is not the same as a response), what happened and what did not, and how that transpired. An example: In Mexico, we have decided that every group should keep a record of any government action on the recommendations of the Programme of World Action of the International Conference on Population and Development.

In addition, as NGOs, alone or in networks, we have to make our own experiences concrete, in order to establish better and greater elements of judgment for evaluation. In that way, we define the demand for how we want a determined action to be carried out, drawing from information that stems from our own models of implementation.

There are also original mechanisms, and even some with a sense of humor, such as that of an organization of citizen participation that called for the "adoption" of a legislator so that through that distant relationship people could monitor whether or not their needs were being met as promised in the election campaign.

The strategy of accountability needs precision. We cannot disperse ourselves nor disperse our human or financial resources, which of course are always scarce. It is a question of priority to know in what manner to choose the program, the policy, the international accord, the concrete recommendation of the large world meetings upon which we will build our work of accountability. To realize a good selection of priorities, we need to evaluate the forces that we contend with and the obstacles that we face. It is crucial to realize a rigorous analysis of the interests that propel us as NGOs or networks, of the previous experiences we have accumulated, of the possibilities for alliances, of the agents which intervene, of our technical capacity, and of the human and financial resources that we have available.

Further, we need to move public opinion in our favor, and we need to understand that to pursue accountability (demand, follow-through, supervision, proposals, implementation) requires a great deal of media attention. If there exist important contextual moments where the diffusion of action through the mass media is counterproductive, this should be the exception and not the rule. Public opinion should be informed by our presence; we have to create the social need to know of the news generated by organized women who work daily for the advancement of their rights.

Our technical capacity to generate proposals and indicators for evaluation is strongly tied to our experience and to our knowing how to take advantage of the incredible growth of our movement. To develop accountability we must close the gaps that separate the women dedicated to grassroots work from those who have developed an enormous experience in the implementation of public government policies. Now many of them are irreversibly our allies (and I say this with much affection) just as those who through their intellectual and academic work are researching the problems that affect women and, in general, re-analyzing problems from a feminist and gendered perspective.

The networks are an incomparable structure for the strategy of accountability, especially now that public policy is marked by international, national and local contexts. Having women working in the same line of action on the three levels will (a) build fronts and (b) build bridges between the different spaces and diminish the margin of escape for the decision makers.

Globalization and/or internationalization of de-

cision-making with respect to socioeconomic and political policies is a fact. It is also a fact that during the last 20 years women have been building a powerful movement, extremely creative and active. This process has been marked by an international character with a democratic perspective.

We have exercised a form of open and flexible organization and communication that allows all the initiatives to express themselves in spaces like these and others. This process has been nurtured by the new forms of technology that facilitate the communication between people and groups, making possible both coordination and decentralization.

The international and national networks are built on a foundation of diverse interests, goals, and camps of actions; some are built on perfectly defined objectives, and others promote new global perspectives. This great qualitative advantage of our movements allow us to develop a strategy of accountability through the formation, relevance, or affiliation of international networks to the women's movement.

Nonetheless, it is necessary to admit that in all our networks there exist tensions. We will have to unravel the conflicts with ethical proposals that demand, on the one hand, the need to be very clear and transparent in our leadership, and on the other, offer the capacity to grant our confidence to fellow women who voice and represent obligatory references for different women. Women need us. In order to transform society, the process for making policy and the process for carrying out accountability, we must develop alliances of confidence among ourselves and recognize that together we can walk a great distance before our political differences separate us.

We need democracy and efficiency, we need to form and confide in committees that transcend our local or national boundaries without centralization that reduces participants to simple efforts. We need active people and groups to gather information — information that each time is closer to our reach, since now it reaches not only one person's desk, but rather all our offices and homes, via electronic communication. We have to clearly establish the rules of the game so that they will be respected in every accorded space in order not to wear ourselves out or anger ourselves. Spending energy on conflicts reduces our strength to keep building our creative capacity. We must remember each day that for all the differences we have among us, what unites us is greater than what divides us. I will close by saying that the gains far exceed the risks in these types of strategies and structures; nonetheless, the ability to lose momentum is great, for the road is not easy. In addition, the "public" space is not accustomed to negotiate while being watched by us, and for us that place is not "strange."

Our movement is forceful and irreversible. The development that the Fourth World Conference on Women in Beijing is producing at this moment is an example of our strength. Women's capacity to pressure and lobby the international networks and the distinct national groups and networks is enabling the Platform of Action to be a great advance for our demands. The fundamentalist forces and the Right are finding themselves, however paradoxically, face to face with a great wall — us.

Resources are for all of us

Kicki Nordström
World Blind Union (WBU), Sweden

It is a great honor for me to have the opportunity to give my point of view about NGOs and accountability.

I am blind from birth. I cannot see you, but you can hopefully hear me. I am going to read my speech in Braille, which is my written language. I want you to listen to my message.

The world today has almost six billion inhabitants. More than half of them are women. Women and children together are about 75 percent of the total population in the world. Our accountability here in Beijing is to represent those three billion women. In other words, each participant in this Conference is representing 50,000 other women in the world!

Ten percent of the world's inhabitants live their lives with various disabilities that make a great impact on daily life. More than half of them, about 300 million, are women. My accountability is especially to represent women with disabilities, and we want you, all the women here at the NGO Forum and the UN Conference, to share this responsibility. We all have to use this opportunity and accountability to change the life conditions of our sisters.

Many disabilities are caused by violence, war, lack of child care and health care, lack of money, lack of proper food, injustice, and unfair priorities. Those "lacks of" can mostly be referred to hierarchic structures and sex. While men often get their needs covered, women have to wait. The hierarchic system is first the abled men, then the abled women; after that you find the disabled men and, last of all, the disabled women.

This is not a question of organizing the society — this is a question of the will of those who have the power. Women of all ages, cultures, classes, and colors need to consider that we have to work together to change the rules of the game.

Women's right to equal participation is a question of democracy. No country or organization should call itself democratic unless there is an equal share of power between men and women. The ancient Greeks, who claimed they were the first to practice democracy, did include women in their decision-making. During the last 3,000 years since then, the democratic process has developed very slowly. Everywhere in the world, women are waiting for a real democracy to arise.

Women from the developing countries have worse, bigger, more difficult, and more complex problems than women from the industrial world, but our goals are the same.

To illustrate the injustice, I will give you some figures about the conditions in the world:

• 25 percent control the 75 percent economically, culturally, and politically;

• 66 percent of the daily work in the world is done by women;

• 10 percent of this work is paid in cash; and

• 1 percent of all property is owned by women.

The problem with today's democracies is still the same as with the ancient Greeks: the male part of the population, unquestioned, have put themselves into the position of handling trade, politics, financial matters, and resources.

It is my belief that all resources have to be used for all of us. Even the resources of women have to be used — to create equality, development, and peace. Without a real change, women in the developing countries will remain the poorest, the most quiet, the most unprivileged, and the most under-stimulated among all mankind. Isn't this is a waste of resources?

Women's interests should be given high priority in all aid programs. To break the pattern, these questions have to be put on all governmental agendas as well as on the agenda of this UN Conference. This is not only a statement but also an urgent request!

We women around the world will no longer remain silent and patient. We want to share power and responsibility. The world must be aware of our demands. And we are prepared to be accountable. But we know that this power will not be given to us unless we ask for it. We also know that those who are privileged are not aware of it. A life of dignity — a home of their own, access to health care, education, and literacy, food of proper nutritional value — is something they take for granted.

We women will call your attention to our fight for equality and democracy, for human rights in all areas of the world. Every government must recognize women and let us participate fully in every aspect of society. This Forum is only one step toward our goals. We have much more to do and a long way to go!

Watch out! Women are on the move! We disabled women are part of this movement. And nobody can stop us!

NGO transformation into political actors: Issues of conceptualization and accountability

Florence Butegwa
Women in Law and Development in Africa (WILDAF), Uganda

Introduction

The last two decades have seen a tremendous rise in the number and nature of nongovernmental organizations all over the world. The tremendous contribution of these organizations to the development of their communities and countries cannot be denied. Their contribution to the progressive realization of democratic processes at all levels is undeniable. Their role in the promotion of peace, conflict resolution, and the welfare and protection of refugees and internally displaced persons has been and remains commendable. Their role in human rights education and monitoring, in documenting and reporting human rights violations is unique and indispensable. Their role in articulating demands for equality and a life of dignity for the women of the world is innovative and highly commendable.

Many of the NGOs playing these various roles can trace their origins to a need to address and respond to immediate needs of specific communities or constituents. Many NGO programs were designed from a welfare conceptual framework. Members of the organizations had resources, skills, or knowledge that the beneficiary community or group did not have, and they were genuinely committed to helping the latter. It was assumed that after this "assistance," the beneficiary community would be better off either economically, legally, health-wise, environmentally, or in other spheres covered by a particular program.

The last decade, however, has witnessed a broadening of NGO activities from service-giving to political activism and power sharing. Many NGOs no longer restrict themselves to providing services such as legal aid, counseling, credit, training, education, immunization, etc. Increasingly they are organizing, consciously and strategically, to influence policies at local, regional, national, and international levels. They are organizing to advocate for space for women to participate in decision-making processes and to speak on their own behalf. At the local level, for instance, women's NGOs have successfully lobbied to be represented on local authorities and committees. At the national level, NGOs have successfully lobbied for legal reform. At the international level, nongovernmental organizations have asserted, with increasing success, the right to access and contribute to and/or to influence policy formulations in a wide range of areas, from human rights to disarmament.

This kind of transformation has been an exciting feature of the political scene in the last few years. It has also caused some confusion and anxiety among public officials, so-called beneficiary communities, and members of the organizations themselves. In some cases, structures and the decision-making process have been able to adjust. In others, the transformation has caused monumental tensions.

I would like to attempt to look at the implications and challenges of this transformation.

From beneficiaries to constituents

Perhaps one of most fundamental challenges is for nongovernmental organizations to start regarding and relating to the communities they work with as constituents rather than just beneficiaries. This is at the core of the transformation of NGOs into political actors. No NGO ever says that it is advocating for change on its own behalf. The change is sought for the benefit of either women in general or a particular class or category. These women are said to be voiceless, thereby justifying our advocacy effort on their behalf. In many cases, the communities which we work with are voiceless because we consciously or unconsciously make them so.

Our political advocacy programs are designed in such a way that they do not empower the communities to become political actors on their own behalf. We fail to raise among our people the political consciousness that they have a right to participate in decision-making processes, and to work

with them to find ways of making this a reality. I think that it is a disservice to the people we work with just to give them technical assistance, food, medicine, and legal aid, and not work with them to raise their political activism. The latter would enable them to hold leadership within their communities accountable and to seek appropriate solutions to problems. They get a voice.

Transforming the relationship between an organization and its constituents requires significant adjustment of organizational outlook, decision-making processes, problem identification, and program design.

Members of the organization have to accept the fact that they do not have the answers and/or solutions to problems. The constituents are often in a better position to decide what can work, given the social and economic environment in which they live. Organizational structures have to change to accommodate a power-sharing role with the constituents. Executive boards and committees become facilitators of decision-making at the community level and of the consultative process which would enable the constituents to play a genuine role.

Without this transformation, the women's movement and its political role remains vulnerable to accusations of elitism. It remains isolated from the majority of the women we claim to advocate for. Our hard-won advances in legal and policy reform are at times rejected by the very women on whose behalf we were sure we were working.

Shifting accountability from donors to constituents

The kind of transformation I am advocating implies the shifting of accountability from the donors to the constituents. It is an unfortunate reality that many current programs are donor-centered. A lot of NGOs are influenced in choosing issues to focus on by the availability of funds for those issues. Donors will tend to seek a realignment of program focus to fit in with their priorities. The constituents are often out of the picture.

This approach does not lend itself to the relationship I am advocating. Programs should be based on what the participating communities see as priority needs after a participatory problem-analysis process. Donors should be more willing to respect the wishes of the people whom they are assisting.

We also as nongovernmental organizations need to move toward identifying and pursuing ways of increasing self-reliance and sustainability. Greater use of the human resources within the communities where we work is one way of not only empowering the community and ensuring sustainability but also reducing reliance on donor money for staff.

While we routinely submit reports to donors, we rarely think NGO accountability to our constituents demands that we report to them on what we did or did not do, or what it cost us to do it. That accountability builds a stronger relationship in which constituents feel part of the organization and increases the opportunities for mass mobilization for political action at the local, national, and even international level.

Right now, in many programs, the NGO and the donor decide criteria for measuring progress or success. Accountability to our constituents would require that *they* decide what they would regard as progress, what they see as obstacles, and how they would like the program to respond to the obstacles.

Concern for formalities and structures

Our concern for and emphasis on the constitutions and organizational charts and chains of command is often absurd. The constitution is revered to the point that it is often the biggest obstacle to democracy and efficiency within an organization. An example can be found in one organization where the constitution provided that the chairperson shall convene general meetings of the members. The chairperson never convened any such meeting, despite (and perhaps because of) serious problems in the organization.

As you can imagine, the members expressed their dissatisfaction among themselves and never to the chairperson. Every time an attempt was made by the members to convene a general meeting, the chairperson said it was unconstitutional, and there was monumental paralysis. No meeting could be convened to amend the constitution or to vote the chairperson out of office. The constitution ceased to be a facilitative tool.

The point I am making is that democracy within organizations requires flexibility in our structures and regulations. All of these are made to facilitate efficient programming and a sense of belonging among members and constituents. If they cease to do that, they should be discarded or adapted to the new needs. This is particularly crucial as we move into the arena of political activism.

Conclusion

In conclusion, I would like to say that politics can and should be defined broadly. Influencing policy and decisions by leaders at all levels can be done by a small number of people, even in a single NGO. But women's political power and its sustainability will depend on and be strengthened by our numbers and the political activism of women at all levels. As we move from Beijing, it is the challenge of every NGO represented here, and those which were not able to come, to increase women's power by raising political consciousness and enabling women to speak for themselves and negotiate space for themselves at all levels.

Let us recast our efforts to build a power base as we offer services, as we train, as we distribute food. Let it be a measure of pride when a community can organize to put pressure on the local council to offer better services. Let it be our aim to see women, though our facilitation, tell their local member of parliament that she or he will not get their votes unless certain needs are certified. That is the kind of power which will lead to change and equality for the women of the world.

The need for governments to take responsibility

Lorena Peña Mendoza
Moviemento de Mujeres Melida Anaya Montes,
El Salvador

I am a member of the Executive Committee of the women's organization Melida Montes and a National Deputy to the Congress of El Salvador for the party Frente Farabundo Marti para la Liberación Nacional.

First of all, I wish to thank the organizers of the NGO Forum on Women for the opportunity to see, hear, and participate in this incredible experience.

I will do my best to share with you some of the experiences of Salvadoran women with nongovernmental organizations, feminist as well as mixed (composed of men and women), and some questions that we believe need to be thought over.

In the first place, we believe that feminist organizations need to work for change, from short-term to long-term, to better the conditions of women's lives on the economic, social, and political level, and to better the position of women as well, which means to empower us. In this sense, we regard it as very necessary to promote changes in public policies, in the policies of states, which nowadays is difficult because of the evasion and diminution of social responsibilities on the part of states.

Taking account of the situation provoked by the politics of adjustment, privatization, etc., we regard it as equally necessary to fight for immediate improvement within the framework I have referred to. The other decisive element is to promote, support, and awaken the consciousness and attitude in each and all of our women, since we are the women changing and creating change, the only ones who can activate, mobilize, and push for change on a global level. Nobody will do for us what we the women cannot do.

With these ideas, the various groups and feminist organizations have organized, have created institutions, networks, and associations, and each of us works in what motivates us most, in projects of economic development, in education, in human and civil rights, in legal assistance, in health services, in the clarification of legislative initiatives, in grassroots organizations.

At this date I am able to confirm that we have achieved some results, such as making violence against women more visible and by promoting changes in legislation; making the situation of the maquiladoras — women in factories — more visible. In my country these factories are like concentration camps, practically without any rights for the workers, who are exposed to violence, social insecurity, persecution of trade unionists, etc. We have drawn attention to abused women, supported the demands of women against husbands who do not recognize their sons and daughters. We can account for experiences with banks, small women's banks, and microenterprise projects.

And on the level of the political struggle, we have united all the groups, and we are building a common platform in which practically all the demands from the women of all sectors are expressed. This platform is called Women '94, and it is our guide for political action and for action for our rights.

At this point, the issue of women is already a permanent issue of debate in my country. There is growing strength in the discussion, and this is positive. However, I want to submit to you the following points to think about.

Our NGOs, when all is said and done, always depend on the priorities, time lines, objectives, etc., that are determined by our counterparts in Europe and the United States. It is incredible how much work is demanded from us in a minimum of time, at the lowest cost, without taking into account the quality we try to achieve in our work. This results in our running to reach the goals of our counterparts in the First World, while on many occasions we lose the possibility of doing a more conscientious and effective job. Therefore, I suggest looking for better terms that are more related to what we can give.

Second, I want to propose other points for reflection. Governments now state that they are in accord with NGOs, that they are promoting development. I am uneasy that in time the state will take no part in its obligations regarding health, employment, education, credit, and the overall needs of women. Because of this, I suggest that NGOs should not only look for funds and support for our programs from the state, the governments. This requires a different mentality, different forms of action on our part.

Third, I think that NGOs have demonstrated much capability in attending to different types of problems. We are generating experiences. However, these don't translate sufficiently into proposals for public policies that promote change in the areas of credit, health, and so on.

Another point that concerns me: Nowadays certain global politics seem to support our right to control our lives, our bodies, our overall development. But, in reality, we have to be more careful and more curious, since I have seen that the only rights that are recognized are those that make the process of globalization, adjustment, and privatization more viable, forgetting the essence and the source of our demands. And many multinational organizations are offering funds to our NGOs, but we must evaluate the funds for their conditions and consequences.

As a woman of the Third World, I am convinced that we are obliged to demand that any form of aid in development will at least return to us part of the riches that are extracted from our peoples each day. I believe that we have to concern ourselves with searching for correct goals in relation to governmental organizations and nongovernmental organizations that support our movements and our NGOs, and above all, we are obliged to have a clear political view.

From another point of view, it seems most important to me that whatever the specialty of the NGO, each NGO must seriously work to incorporate in its program a gender focus. It is not enough that the programs be only for women.

It is not enough to enable women technically. We must seriously attend to the work of generating changes in attitude and consciousness, to generate changes in the communities where the women live: to diminish the violence and generate new relationships among women, and between men and women, in the communities where we develop our projects. We have to be sure to take into account the domestic work of the majority of women. We must promote changes in the self-esteem of each of the women who participate in our events. Contrary to their success in economic and other projects, they nevertheless continue being violated in their homes, continue being psychologically dependent on their husbands, and their capacity to influence their communities does not increase. Because of this, we must keep a more concrete focus on gender in our plans.

I do not wish to conclude my remarks without commenting that in El Salvador, we women are living in a critical situation. Peace has arrived; the armed conflict has ceased. However, there is still no peace for women. The new economic plans of the region that are offered to us are suspension of public health services (which already are very limited), suspension of public education, increase in employment in factories, bankruptcy of agricultural production, a practical negation of the possibility of obtaining credit at reasonable interest (in reality it is practically impossible for women to obtain credit of any kind).

Therefore, we have a high level of impoverishment among women, the majority of whom are in the "informal sector." In that sector, a majority live on a monthly income of $75, and 28 percent are single mothers, heads of household. There are 270,000 children — boys and girls — who are working.

Recent data indicate that one out of six women have been abused or raped. With that, I want to say that in the NGOs, we need to do much for women. However, we also have to see to it that the government clearly commits itself to the implementation of public policies: providing special credits and technical assistance for poor women in the country and the cities; creating health services, especially services for the reproductive health of women; defining new labor laws to guarantee labor rights for women workers in the factories; overcoming the impunity of aggressors and abusers of women.

The state must promote necessary education reforms to provide children with a nonsexist education; ensure that investigations and the census specify their data by sex; promote campaigns to raise consciousness on the social status and human rights of women. We must demand that the male-oriented language of official texts of the governmental organizations be changed. We have to look for political support for the execution of economic and social programs of development for women, specifically projects for women as well as mixed projects.

I feel that we have to work to see that the governments that come together in the Conference will not solely speak about abortion. It is clear that I support the legalization of abortion. But it seems to me that we have to put pressure to reach consensus on those issues I have just mentioned, along with clearly defined compromises, and mechanisms for the implementation and control of policies NGOs have fought for.

XVII • Intergenerational Dialogue

Opening remarks

Amy Richards, Moderator
Ms. Foundation, United States

Part of the reason I am here today is because Gloria Steinem could not be. I am also here because I am a young woman who has greatly benefited from working intergenerationally — primarily with Gloria, but also with many others. I wish there were more mentors like Gloria, who sees mentoring as a two-way street. She believes in me and my ideas and encourages me to explore new areas and ideas. This belief is evident in the way that she feels she learns as much from me as I do from her. I don't know if that is exactly true, but I like the idea.

Although Gloria is not here in person, I know she is here in spirit, and her letter is just one example of that.

The other participants in this dialogue — both seasoned activists and new voices — speak not only of mentoring but also of empowerment, feminism, and finding fresh ways to work together.

Letter to NGO Forum

Gloria Steinem
Ms. Foundation, United States

Dear sisters of all ages:

I had hoped I could be with you today, but part of the reason I am not is the very fact that the international women's movement has grown so big. No longer do a few activists in each country feel we have to be everywhere. Instead, we can each choose what we can uniquely do — thus better serving our sisters. In my own case, what I can uniquely do right now lies in my own country.

My decision was confirmed when I moderated a press conference in Washington for a coalition of many of the U.S. organizations going to Beijing, and I noticed that reporters still directed many questions to me, no matter how often I pointed out that there were younger women who were more representative of their organizations. So you see, perhaps the world media will introduce more new women to their readers and viewers at home if some of us "golden oldies" aren't around.

Courtesy of your kindness in letting me send this message, I would like to make three of the points I had hoped to make when we were together:

First, feminism is not about telling other women what to do, but about helping one another gain the power to make our own choices. We must work together to create that power and to expand possibilities. For in the long run, it matters less what we decide than that we have the power to decide. It's especially important to remember this goal of empowerment when we are working intergenerationally in order to offset the temptation of older women to feel we know best — even though we ourselves will never dwell in the land of the future — and the temptation of younger women to put their elders into the role of mother or grandmother — even though each older woman is a unique individual human being.

Second, one of the best things older generations can do is to lead by example. After all, no matter what our age, we're more likely to do what we see than what we're told. Mothers are much more likely to have daughters who respect themselves if we have objected as much as possible to husbands and bosses who didn't respect us. We are much more likely to have daughters who refuse to limit their humanity if we ourselves have refused to limit ours — including by any self-destructive addiction to the consumerist props of "femininity" that our economic systems may be pushing. And we are infinitely less likely to see a next generation repeating the divisions of race and class, sexuality and ability, if they have seen even a few of their elders valuing people for their unique selves.

Mothers know how to use the power of leading by example. Only a few male leaders — for example, Gandhi — seem to know, much less to use this approach; that is, to live as we wish others to live. We as women can introduce this intergenerational family paradigm of leadership — in public and political life.

Third, I remind my age peers — or anyone past 30 or so — that the great joy of working with girls and younger women is that they awaken within us an earlier part of ourselves. If we let it happen, we can re-enter the cells of the little girl or young woman we once were, before we were as socialized or damaged as we were to become. She is within us still.

I have seen women whose spirits were broken by long years of violence or unchosen childbearing, by female genital mutilation, or by the pervasive Western training in so-called "femininity." Yet they refound an original and true self that had existed before those sufferings. They discovered within themselves the seed of an unbroken spirit.

We have much to learn from each other. I look forward to hearing what is said at this meeting. If you have any doubts of its importance, remember: Even the toughest-minded physicist now admits that the flap of a butterfly's wing can change the weather hundreds of miles away. And today's meeting is a very, very big butterfly!

My heart is with you.

Weaving solidarity

Cristina Alberdi Alonso
Minister of Social Affairs, Spain

I believe everything women have accomplished so far has been thanks to the efforts of all women, thanks to the feminist movements, and thanks to the parallel NGO Forums which have been present at the four World Conferences on Women held in Mexico, Copenhagen, Nairobi, and now Beijing. Throughout these parallel forums, we have been weaving solidarity among all the women of the world.

We all share common problems, even though we live in distinct realities; some of us are in better economic situations or have better access to political participation. There also are many common points of discrimination. There is no country in the world where women, in any way, have the same opportunities as men. That is why we must have solidarity.

The task before us is fundamental, and it is fundamental to eliminate poverty, that feminization of poverty. Of the 1.3 billion people living in poverty, 70 percent are women. And to eradicate poverty, we must work together, we must have economic resources, we must have equal opportunities, and we must include the perspectives of women in all development programs.

This is fundamental because it is necessary to work for women in the areas of health, nutrition, and education. If we don't have the tools of good health and nutrition because since infancy we were denied equal treatment as women, and if we don't have the educational and formative tools to make our voices heard, in the home and in public spaces, then it will be an even greater struggle to build a better world. And the inclusion of education in the Platform for Action, denied to us for centuries, is one of the achievements; it is one of the fundamental aspirations that we as women hold.

Reflections on a life: Working for equality, development, and peace

Helvi Sipilä
Secretary-General of International Women's Year (1975) and of the First UN World Conference on Women, Finland

The written program introduced me as past international president of Zonta International. I probably represent one of the oldest generations present, and although I held the Zonta International position from 1968 to 1970, it would be more interesting to the audience to know that I was Secretary-General of International Women's Year in 1975 and of the first United Nations World Conference on Women, held in Mexico City.

As the panelists were invited to tell about themselves and their lives and as I considered my long life, perhaps different from that of most of the other panelists, I decided to concentrate on questions which still seem to be the important goals for women — "Equality, Development, and Peace" — which have been stated as goals since the First World Conference in 1975, at which the first World Plan of Action for the next ten years was adopted.

The first goal was and remains equality, especially equality between the sexes and how we experience this in our own lives. Equality between men and women is still lacking, especially in the political and economic fields and particularly in leadership positions. What is therefore still needed

is empowerment of women, at least to the extent that they have influence on matters concerning themselves.

Women often lack self-confidence and do not always accept leadership positions. The question is often asked whether leaders are born or trained; my answer is that even a born leader benefits from having role models and training in leadership at different levels.

I was born on my mother's 44th birthday. The midwives at the hospital told her, "Your daughter is certainly going to be a leader. When she cries, everybody cries. When she is quiet, no one else makes any noise." That was a famous joke in my home. But my first role model was also my mother, from whom I apparently learned a lot of things concerning self-confidence, responsible leadership, and care for other people. I could say the same about my father. Their example provided my first training in the role of a responsible citizen and a responsible leader whose goal was justice.

My own experience of leadership was greatly enhanced by my active role in the organization of Girl Guides and Girl Scouts, from my school and town to the national and the world level. The best parts of the program were the continuous training and the necessity to care for others.

Justice also was an important goal during the three decades that I worked as an attorney-at-law in an office of my own, of which I was a founder and director.

Leadership in national and international organizations brought me to United Nations activities, first as a member of the UN Commission on the Status of Women from 1960 to 1968. At CSW I was vice-chairperson for several years and, in 1967, its chairperson.

At that time I learned what responsibility means at the world level, where you have the opportunity to serve humanity as a whole. You can try your best in different ways, but at least you must be loyal to the cause you have accepted to serve. This principle can show the way toward growing responsibilities, which was true in my case during the many years I served as Finland's representative at the UN General Assembly, including finally, in 1971, serving as chairperson of one of its main committees.

A new way was opened when I was once again serving as Finland's representative on the Commission on the Status of Women and participated in its session in Geneva in 1972, where we made the recommendation to the General Assembly that 1975 be declared International Women's Year. But before the General Assembly of 1972 began its work, I was appointed by the UN Secretary-General to be the first woman in the world to hold the post of Assistant Secretary-General of the United Nations — and later, Secretary-General of International Women's Year and the 1975 World Conference.

Although I retired in 1980 from the position of Assistant Secretary-General, I continued to act as a UN consultant for a few months in order to promote the UN Fund for Women, now called UNIFEM, which assists women in their own efforts in the developing countries. This is the work in which I am still involved as a full-time volunteer.

Of the three goals of International Women's Year, we have been unable to achieve much in the third — that of peace — which means increasing women's contribution to the promotion of friendly relations among nations and to safeguarding world peace. From all that we see around us in the world today, women are still only objects, not subjects, in questions of war and peace. I hope that all of us, and the younger generation in particular, will concentrate on this question. There is no equality in a vacuum, and to the detriment of humankind, it is still missing in this most important field.

Our right to be as one in community

Pauline E. Tangiora
Rongomaiwahine Affiliation, Maori Network
of Indigenous Women, New Zealand

Nga mihi tuatahi Ki te Atua
E mihi ana Ki nga mate Haere Haere Haere
Te rangi e tu papa Kei waho, tena Korua
No reira
Tena Koutou Tena Koutou Tena Kouta Katoa

This is called *a Mihi*. In the language of my people, I have acknowledged those who have passed on in all of our families, the people of the land in this country of China of whom we are the guests; and in the language of our people we have greeted this house and those who are present here today. I feel very humble standing here with such a gracious panel. I don't think we've got an intergenerational gap at all, because when we see these young women, they are not the women of tomorrow, they are the women of the here and now.

I would like to suggest to those who have their pens and books: Shut your books, put your pencils in your pockets, and listen. Because we come from a tradition of oral listening, and if something's going to mean something, you hear it, you remember it, and you keep it within your heart. Maybe this is the time in your life to try that, because if we can't feel and hear, then we do have a generational gap. Sometimes we forget to listen to our younger people because we want to be the person who has the power; and power is nothing if we don't walk alongside our young people, our fathers, our husbands, our sons, and our daughters.

We come from an indigenous community, and the universality of human rights does not allow indigenous *communities* to be indigenous peoples. Human rights only gives the human right to an individual, and our indigenous women are not individuals. They are part of indigenous communities. Sisters and those brothers we have here today, listen to the cries of our women, our young women, and our old women, our men. We cannot be separated from that which is a whole, that which is the spiritual part of us, the land, because it is from the land that we come. It is from the land that we get the source of our water, our food. It is from the sun who makes us flourish and grow, and it is the cries of the sun that give us the rain. And all those things make us what we are. So our young women in indigenous communities work with us and are not divorced from us.

However, the colonization of the last 500 years has colonized the minds of our women, and they have moved into the cities, away from the groups which both the young and the old need to support each other. When our children come to us, they come within our community. There is no difference in respect. The respect that the old get only comes with the respect which we the elders give to our young people. If we can't listen and give respect to our young people, then we have the problems which recolonization has enforced and at this moment is enforcing in genocidal acts on indigenous peoples as we sit here and listen to each other today.

It is time that we open our minds to the indigenous and tribal peoples of the world. May I remind you it is *peoples*, not people or populations, because the "s" on "peoples" gives us our inherent right as women, young and old, to be as one in community. It is this united effort of universality which is breaking down the communication of groups, of family, of extended community. In the indigenous world, there is not a generational gap, because when you are a family, you are a family tribally, and then internationally. As indigenous peoples, you are responsible for each other. When we come together, we need to remember to look at our sisters. When I look at European young women here today, they are mine; I don't see them as another group, another culture, because I look at them as a part of the fruits of life which the Creator has given to us through man and woman.

I think I'd like to pay special respect to our elder who has just spoken before me, because it is the elders who have paved the way. As I look around, I look at the women that I have met over the last ten years, and I am sad that I see many of them have passed on; but they are the ones who have paved the way for us to be here in Beijing.

I have to tell you I didn't want to be in Beijing. In fact, I said I wasn't coming, in solidarity with those who couldn't get visas. I was told I had no choice, that as a woman of the community, it was my job to do as I was told. That came from younger people internationally as well as in my own area. You see, who makes the story that we have a generation gap is the media. All the media here today, I invite you to make a front page about the beauty of the young and the old, the male and female together.

The other day I had a very deep experience while listening to a tribunal on the crimes that have happened to women over the past 50 years. While I was waiting, someone said to me, "You're a feminist. I've heard all about you." I said, "Oh, yes. How do you mean I'm a feminist?" She said, "Well, you know, you're a feminist. Everybody around the world knows you're a feminist." And I said, "Well, would you like me to explain what I see as being a feminist?" And she said, "Well, not really, because we know you're a feminist." And I said, "Well, all right. I'll accept that, because I know that I'm the most perfect feminist, because I have 15 children, 47 grandchildren, and three great-grandchildren. That's why I'm a feminist."

I think we've got to stop labeling a certain thing as A, B, or C, because it's causing divisions among us. What we have to do and learn to do is to respect the right of every woman to be who she wants to be and lead the life she wishes to. Because it's the word "respect" that will enhance the quality of life of the young women we have here into the next millennium. We as women cannot divide ourselves; we as women cannot put up the walls, but we must make sure that our diversities enrich and respect one another.

Tena Koutou Tena Koutou Tena Kouta Katoa

A program to empower teenagers

Roxan Graham
Teens in Action, Jamaica

The goal of our organization is to empower teenagers, to give them strength and encouragement, and to reinforce them to rise above social and economic problems. The idea began with the brutal gang-rape and hanging of a 13-year-old girl by her very own peers. This brutal event was much more than a warning to the community, as well as to the society at large, of the crucial links between violence, solutions, and poverty. It was a call to action and social organization requiring the participation and tolerance of the entire community.

Teens in Action is a direct response to this call for action to address the social needs of the community's young women. The way I see young women implementing the commitments made here include these methods:

• to educate and explicate, through drama and theater, the problems that affect young women, such as rape, drug abuse, parent-child conflict, and so on;

• to conduct workshops that will function as a medium for young women to discuss issues affecting them and together find possible solutions;

• to provide peer counseling sessions that can cover a wide range of topics, including AIDS awareness and education;

• to ease social pressures and encourage the right attitudes toward self-development, such as the promotion of healthy and supportive relationships between teenager and community;

• to inform, train, and motivate young women, making teenagers aware of their mental and physical potential;

• to organize external and internal training programs in group dynamics, group relationships, and self-management that will prepare the teenagers for the wider society and its expectations; and

• to encourage interest and respect for the physical environment through conversation and consideration.

As the next generation, we young women need to have all the contemporary technological equipment readily available to us so that we can communicate effectively. For example, we need computers to receive e-mail and to be part of the Internet, because without information we cannot inform, educate, and move on.

Thank you for listening.

Intergenerational conflict: The shared path

Anabel Santos
Mujeres Jovenes, Spain

To speak of intergenerational dialogue we have to ask ourselves if there are generational conflicts and what resolutions for action can be set forth by young women. If intergenerational dialogue is critical in all spaces, it is even more critical in the feminist movement.

It is difficult to speak of intergenerational dialogue in general, since the subject is specific to distinct cultures; the realities vary from region to region. We don't all come from the same background; to be a girl, to be a woman, a young woman, does not mean the same in Asia, Africa, the Pacific, North America, or in the Arab world.

In some regions, female development moves directly from girlhood to womanhood; nonetheless, we have to emphasize the developmental stage of young women. What we are is established by our generation; therefore, from all parts of the world we can reflect on what happens in the different regions of the world. What is happening to young women, where do we locate ourselves within the feminist movement? Do we have dialogue with women of different ages?

We live in a period when it is difficult to debate equality between men and women, yet the most important social structures like the family, the school, and the media continue to promote a socialization slanted in terms of sex. This is the society in which we move, grow, and live as young women. The differences are not as explicit as those of ten years ago; nevertheless, perhaps today in some parts of the world there are subtle forms of discrimination, yet these are very dangerous. The change in attitudes and values is slow. We must bear in mind that it is difficult to participate in a social context developed by males for males.

It is extremely important that we speak of intergenerational dialogue. We want to listen and be listened to, we want to enrich our journey with your experience and enrich the shared path with our contributions. We have our own voice, our own specific needs with distinct solutions; furthermore, we are the next generation and we need to be considered.

Young people today are not the young people of yesterday. Our problems are different. We have the historic legacy of feminism, but we can stand before an apparent equality and still suffer problems like those of a decade ago. Progress for legal equality was made in some countries, but we are a long way away from true equality. Day after day we find ourselves confronted by the difficulty of the rise of dependent relatives.

There is no equality when we enter the working world. We don't have the possibility of exercising our reproductive rights; the educational system is sexist. It is almost impossible to find young people in decision-making capacities, and all of this is happening in the wake of a discourse that leads us to expect progress. It is true that we have progressed, but there remains a lot more to be done, and we have to do it with the help of all generations. We have to ensure that we don't regress, we can't leave out a single generation.

Young women accept your guidance, you are the example for all our actions. We have the testimony in hand, and together we can carry it toward our goal. The intergenerational pact is necessary and vital, in case we find ourselves detained by a double glass ceiling: one that we endure for reasons of gender, and one that we will have to endure for reasons of age. We will all lose, and above all, we will lose the objective that we all hold for development and equality. But to reach our goals we young women need resources.

There are 4,500 of us young women at this Forum, but we are many more young women throughout the regions working toward the same objectives. For all these women, I want us to work together daily, and I want the NGOs to create jobs for young women. Until now, history has been written by men and we were invisible — it was as if we did not exist. Today women are everywhere, even though we are a minority in relation to men. If we support each other, we will increase the reforms for those who come after us, spreading change everywhere.

For these young women, and from this moment on, we should move toward an intergenerational pact, extending the Forum's campaign to bring a sister to Beijing, to launching a new campaign to make young women visible, to motivate them. We should take positive action. The future of women depends on the intergenerational bond that we create among us.

Toward a realistic portrayal of our debate

Misha Schubert
Victorian Women's Trust, Australia

It is a great honor for me to be speaking to you today, an honor to be speaking alongside these older women who have achieved so very much for the advancement of women in their lifetimes. And an honor to be speaking with — and of — the exciting new generation of young feminists who have an equal imperative.

An intergenerational dialogue is a fitting subject for the final plenary of this historical Conference. At the point at which we begin to turn our viewfinders outward and look to implementation of the resolutions of this event, we come together as many generations — to chart our progress, to share a vision, and to close the gaps of information between women. What a truly powerful objective!

My peer speakers have already outlined some of the social and economic issues for young women which must be addressed by the women's rights movement. For my part, I hope to convey some of the structural and strategic issues for young women in organizing to achieve change in the issues of our lives. I also hope to give you a sense of the passion, fire, and determination of young women, and our current and future stakes in the women's rights movement.

There are a couple of key issues that we have seen come to the fore during the youth organizing part of the program of this Forum. Some of those debates have been quite instructive in coming to an intergenerational forum and starting to talk with our older sisters, our mothers, and our grandmothers about the ways in which we want to come to this movement and the impact that we would like to have on it — also about the ways in which we would like to work with older women to take forward and implement the goals and the strategies you started out with when you began your time as activists in the women's rights movement.

So first, I wanted to address the issue of whether there are gaps — and whether they are generational gaps or much larger gaps — in how we see the women's rights movement and whether we embrace it fully. For in our national movements, and even at this Forum, there is often a perception that young women aren't taking enough of a leadership role from older women. One of the criticisms that they have of us is that perhaps we aren't visible enough, or that we are not strong enough in proclaiming our association with the movement to which they have dedicated their lives. That's pretty much a falsification as far as we see it. Certainly the thousands of young women who have been active at this Conference have by presence, word, and action let it be known that they are very proud to be a part of the movement older women have helped to shape. We want to work with you to carry on and to implement in a clever, strategic, far-reaching way the kind of goals you have set about

achieving for women in your own countries, amongst women of your own religions, sexual orientation, race, ethnicity, and class. I think a critical reason that perceived gaps between us or the work we are undertaking often occur is because of our reliance on mainstream media to communicate with one another. And part of what we need to do as an essential strategy for linking older and younger women is to go to the heart of that problem and to target the ways in which feminists and feminist concerns — and images of women and girls generally — are represented through forums of the media. In doing so, we may actually achieve more realistic portrayals of our debates and our issues in mainstream media forums, reaching not only one another but also the broader mass of people who help to shape societal change, and to bring them to an understanding of the kind of change we are trying to effect.

Another key topic that has come out of the youth debates and programs has been the issue of how we embrace diversity and stem the forces promoting its erasure — moving past tokenism, moving past words, coming to a realistic process of bringing all women into one movement. Part of the initial emphasis in that debate talked about the importance of unifying all women under the one banner. We actually found that a very difficult way to conceptualize our strategic and structural objectives, because participants were continually characterizing diversity as a negative trait and were saying that "despite our diversity [it being a bad thing], we were all able to come together and work on the same issues." We felt that this wasn't a realistic or clever method of looking at or of capitalizing on diversity. Perhaps a more useful way of looking at the issue is to acknowledge that we are all immensely diverse, and that it pays no respect to our own intellect to pretend that we don't have differences in views on every issue which affects women, and differences in the ways we work and in the styles we choose to implement those agendas. Perhaps a better way of negotiating this issue is to say: "Let's embrace diversity, let's give each other voices to disagree with one another, always paying one another the respect that is needed to maintain cohesiveness." By *that* process of being honest and strong enough to debate openly our differences of perspective, we may just come to a greater level of conviction about the ways in which we think we should be working, and also come to a greater understanding of other women's concerns, rather than just trying to sweep our differences under the carpet in order to create unity.

I think that has some really important interconnections with what we are trying to do here also: to concede that perhaps women of different ages do see things differently, according to their particular historical site of activism. And that's okay. We don't need to see things in the same way. What we do need to do is work together on those issues that we do agree upon, to achieve and implement our agendas, and that is why debates like this (although slow in happening until a relatively recent period of our history as a movement) are really crucial to our beginning the work of better understanding our differences, and working through them and with them to achieve a greater level of emancipation for women.

Another critical issue of which I am aware is that young women have not been accorded their rightful place in decision-making forums. This has not only occurred as a general pattern, but also within the organizations and institutions of feminism and the women's rights movement. One of the things we would say to women who are already in relative positions of power and resource control in organizations is this: "Let us in, train us, utilize our energy, utilize our enthusiasm." We want to work with you, but as you must know and remember from your early days, to do so without resources is a very, very difficult thing indeed. It is not impossible — as we have learned from our sisters who are living every day in sites of armed conflict, and they are a lesson to us all — but it is a difficult task. If we are to be a clever, pragmatic, strategic lobby in the interests of women, then one of the things we need to do is to recognize that we must bring resources to those women who all too often don't have them and to concentrate our energies first on those women who have least.

To challenge a few stereotypes about the ways in which young women operate, I think there is often a criticism that we are either inactive or apa-thetic or, worse, that we just don't understand. I am here to tell you that we *do* understand and that we want to be a part of this movement. Our styles of activism are sometimes different (but not as often as media portrayals support), and part of the debate in Australia has been led by a school of thought that argues that because young women aren't in the media, therefore they aren't actively organizing as feminists in the community. I think that really invalidates some ingenious styles of activism that young women have brought to the movement — that is, to integrate their activism in their daily lives and to actually use every conversation, every social choice, every decision about how they interact with people and live their lives, to make political statements, and to actually capitalize on some of the rights older women have won for us. Sometimes there has been hostility to this from a few high-profile older feminists who intimate, "Isn't it terrible that they are using these freedoms and these rights, or that they are ungrateful, or they don't acknowledge us?" So it becomes important for us as younger feminists to point out that we do acknowledge, that we are respectful of the work of the women who have shaped this movement before us, and that we appreciate the rights that older women have won for us.

I think there are some other key benefits older women can capitalize on, in *their* objectives, by involving young women in their work. It is important to balance the disadvantages of youth which other young women have outlined — about not being taken seriously, about not having a rightful space or resources, about the particular forms of discrimination and denial of rights experienced by young women and girls — with some of the positives. The benefits of youth include an enormous wealth of energy, a creativity, a determination to actually find out *why*, a mischievousness, an irreverence, and a cheekiness that allows us to ask the questions other people can't. And we would like more opportunities to use these qualities, quite frankly. So give us opportunities to work in our ways with some of these assets and shields of youth to develop a multifaceted strategy in achieving our aims and objectives.

To finish up, I wanted to try and get a little pragmatic. I think part of the difficulty of these debates is inevitably that we identify problems, we talk about why these situations occur, and we cleverly and coherently formulate arguments about why these things are unjust. But moving on to the next step — working out good, clever strategies to actually alter those stumbling blocks — is a difficulty. It is a sticking point that we confront continually. So I will end with a couple of quick suggestions about ways in which we might work together more cohesively.

One is that within women's organizations we need to self-examine and to be really rigorous about ensuring that we have a genuine diversity of women receiving resources from our organizations, that we don't stick with what we know because it is easier and safer. This entails constantly asking ourselves the hard questions about whether we really make space for women of a diversity of backgrounds, whether we provide an adequate level of resources for a diversity of women, or whether we merely fulfill the obligations of rhetoric and assuage conscience.

A second strategy is committing personally to patiently unraveling stereotypes between women, to setting ourselves a personal goal of seeking out women of backgrounds unlike our own and asking each other how we see the world in order to sharpen our own knowledge of each other's issues and struggles and to challenge our own preconceptions. I have been on an incredible learning curve doing just that at this Conference, and I think it is one of the most important tangibles that we can draw from these opportunities.

Third, we need to commit ourselves to work together on our key issues, capitalizing on the inherent strength of diversity by coming together as a wide-ranging group of women who have different connections into the societies we are trying to change.

Rather than suggesting one site of activism and one style of doing things, we should actually acknowledge that women work in different ways, and that these are often the *best* ways to get information through to their communities and their interest groups. It is therefore important to have a diverse movement in order to realize our gains much sooner.

The final strategy is about mentoring. That doesn't just mean older women mentoring younger women but also women with more experience and insight in a particular area mentoring other women. This distinction is important to allow ourselves to have roles both of mentor and mentee, to step in and out when we feel we need greater levels of encouragement and enthusiasm and insight and support in the work we are doing.

So there are a few perspectives and some accompanying strategies. I look forward to hearing the views of our older sisters before responding to the challenges facing us. I wish you success in your feminist endeavours and hope that you will share your victories and inspiration with us when we meet again in 2005. May the forces of common sense and of justice hold sway!

LIST OF CONTRIBUTORS

Robin Abrams is a vice-president of Apple Computer and Managing Director of Apple in Asia. She is one of the world's highest-ranking women executives in the computer industry. Formerly she held senior executive management positions at Unisys and other high-tech companies.

Bisi Adeleye-Fayemi is a cultural anthropologist and gender-and-development specialist. She has spent the greater part of her life in Nigeria, and is currently the Director of Akina Mama wa Afrika, a nongovernmental development organization for African women based in the UK. She has also worked as a journalist and teacher.

Reine-Brigitte Agbassi-Boni, with Winrock International since April 1992, first as the Regional Coordinator for African Women Leaders in Agriculture and the Environment (AWLAE) and more recently as Regional Coordinator in West Africa, has been a consultant to international agencies on women in agriculture and worked with the Ministry of Agriculture and Livestock in Côte d'Ivoire. She was also a technical advisor to the Minister of Women's Promotion, concerned with rural development matters.

Ijeoma Agugua currently serves as a High Court Judge in Nigeria. She is a life member of the Federation of Women Lawyers (FIDA), a member of the Judges Forum of the International Bar Association (IBA), and a member of the Nigerian Association of Women Judges.

Cristina Alberdi Alonso has been Spain's Minister of Social Affairs since 1993. She is a feminist lawyer working on women's rights and judicial reform. In 1975 she organized and led with other women lawyers a legal collective to defend women and advocate for the reform of discriminatory laws.

Anita Amlen is Secretary-General of the Swedish Federation of Liberal Women and the Director of the Swedish NGO Forum Office. A social worker by training, for the past 15 years she has held many different positions in politics. She has worked extensively on aid issues around the world, with special emphasis on Africa, and particularly with the women of South Africa.

Ana Angarita is a national of Colombia. She joined the United Nations Population Fund (UNFPA) in 1990 as Programme Officer of the Latin America and Caribbean Division. While in the LAC Division, she was the focal point for all women/gender-related matters. In June 1995 she became Technical Officer of the Gender, Population, and Development Branch.

Aung San Suu Kyi has been a pro-democracy opposition leader in Myanmar (formerly Burma) since 1988. Educated in Burma, India, and the UK, she worked at the United Nations in New York and Bhutan prior to returning to her homeland. There she founded the pro-democracy party, the National League for Democracy, and in 1989 was placed under house arrest by the military junta. In 1990 her party won a major electoral victory, but was kept from assuming power. She received the Nobel Peace Prize in 1991. She was released in July 1995.

Edith Ballantyne, Secretary General of the Women's International League for Peace and Freedom from 1969 to 1992, after which she was elected international WILPF President. She was President of the Conference of NGOs in Consultative Status with ECOSOC (1976-1982), Secretary and later President of the NGO Committee for Disarmament (Geneva), and Secretary of the NGO Sub-Committee on Racism and Decolonization (a post she has held since 1972). In 1995 she received the Gandhi Peace Award for "Promoting Enduring Peace."

Kiran Bedi is India's highest-ranking female police officer and is currently Delhi's Inspector General of Prisons. She has held positions as Deputy Commissioner of Police and Deputy Director of the Narcotics Control Unit. In 1994 she received the Ramon Magsaysay Award for Government Service in recognition of her leadership and innovations in crime control, drug rehabilitation, and humane prison reform.

Marta Benavides has worked in support of peace and human development all her life. A biologist, educator, theologian, and ecologist, she is working cooperatively with rural people to facilitate and cultivate sustainability for El Salvador and the Central American region. She belongs to the Ecumenical Ministries for Development and Peace (MEDEPAZ) and is currently Director of the International Institute for Cooperation Amongst Peoples in El Salvador.

Grete Berget was appointed Minister of Children and Family Affairs in 1991. She was educated and worked as a journalist from 1978 to 1988, when she became the Information Director at the Prime Minister's office. In 1989 she was the Political Counsellor to the Prime Minister. She was very active in the labour movement.

Rosalie Bertell, an epidemiologist who has worked in environmental health for almost 30 years, founded the International Institute of Concern for Public Health in Toronto, Canada, which together with Dr. Bertell received the Right Livelihood Award in 1968 for research on nuclear pollution and health. She has worked with communities in crisis for pollution since 1975, including Bhopal and Chernobyl. In 1993 she was named to the United Nations Environment Programme Global 500 Honour Roll.

Marina Beyer was raised in East Germany and is a biological and behavioral scientist. She has been active in the peace movement since the early 1980s and founded the East-West Women's Network (OWEN), where she now works.

Kamla Bhasin, a social scientist, has been involved since 1972 with issues related to development, education, gender, and the media. Since 1976 she has worked with the FAO's Freedom From Hunger Campaign/Action for Development, supporting innovative NGO initiatives, organizing training workshops, and facilitating networking between NGOs and the women's movement. She has written songs for the women's movement and songbooks for children.

Ela Bhatt is a founding member of Women's World Banking and Chairperson of its Board of Trustees. She founded the Self-Employed Women's Association and the Self-Employed Women's Association Bank. Appointed to the Indian Planning Commission, she also served as Member of the Upper House of the Indian Parliament and as Chairperson of the National Commission on Self-Employed Women. Among her many awards, are the Right Livelihood Award, the Ramon Magsaysay Award, and the Susan B. Anthony Award.

Charlotte Bunch, feminist author and organizer, was a founder of Washington D.C. Women's Liberation and of *Quest: A Feminist Quarterly*. She is Director of the Douglass College Center for Women's Global Leadership and a professor in the Bloustein School of Planning and Public Policy at Rutgers University. The Center coordinated the Global Campaign for Women's Human Rights at the 1993 United Nations World Conference on Human Rights in Vienna and coordinated the women's human rights caucus and other activities for the Fourth World Conference on Women.

Linda Burnham is co-founder of the Women of Color Resource Center and currently serves as its Executive Director. WCRC organized a group of more than one hundred women to attend the NGO Forum, where the organization focused particular attention on the issues of women and homelessness, and ethnic and racial minority women's organizing worldwide. Burnham is also an editor of *CrossRoads* magazine.

Florence Butegwa is currently the Regional Coordinator of Women in Law and Development in Africa (WILDAF), a pan-African NGO bringing together individuals and organizations working to promote respect for women's rights in Africa. She is a lawyer by profession and a former lecturer at Makerere University, Kampala, Uganda.

Winnie Byanyima was the first woman flight engineer in Africa and is associated with many science and technology initiatives and institutions. She was Uganda's Representative to UNESCO from 1989 to 1993. A Member of the Ugandan Constituent Assembly, she is Chair of the Women's Caucus. From 1981 to 1986 she participated in the struggle to remove the dictatorship in Uganda and restore democracy

Cheryl Carolus is currently the Deputy Secretary General of the African National Congress (ANC) and is the first woman to occupy one of the top six positions in the history of the ANC. She was a founding Executive Committee member of the United Democratic Front (UDF) and of the United Women's Organization, the first nonracial women's organization. She also served as the Secretary of the relaunched Federation of South African Women.

Hillary Rodham Clinton served as staff attorney for the Children's Defense Fund and later for the Judiciary Committee of the U.S. House of Representatives, for which she worked on the Watergate impeachment proceedings. She taught law at the University of Arkansas and was First Lady of Arkansas for 12 years. She chaired the Arkansas Education Standards Committee and founded the Arkansas Advocates for Children and Families. As First Lady of the United States, she headed the Task Force on National Health Care Reform.

Karina Constantino-David is the Executive Director of the NGO, HASIK (Harnessing Self-Reliant Initiatives and Knowledge, Inc.) and President of CODE-NGO, the national coalition of more than 3,000 development NGOs in the Philippines. She is also Professor of Community Development at the University of the Philippines and a member of PILIPINA, the National Movement of Filipino Women.

Annie Delaney is Home-based Work Coordinator with the Textile, Clothing & Footwear Union of Australia. Her previous experience includes community development, community education, training, and teaching. Her community, political and campaign work have focused on the areas of domestic violence, immigration and refugees, equal pay for women, and workers' and women's rights.

Shanthi Dairiam is Director of the International Women's Rights Action Watch—Asia Pacific. She has been involved in human rights issues regarding violence, reproductive rights, legal rights, and development policies for women on a national, regional, and international level for 15 years. Currently she is involved in a program in Malaysia to combat violence against women, focusing on legal reform.

Duan Cunhua has been the President of Sumstar Group Corporation since 1993 and an advisor to the China Women Entrepreneurs Association. She is also a member of the National Committee of the Chinese People's Political Consultative Conference, China's highest consultative body. Formerly, she was Vice Minister of China Light Industry.

Misrak Elias is Senior Advisor in the Gender and Development Section of the United Nations Children's Fund (UNICEF) and served as the UNICEF focal point for the Fourth World Conference on Women. She joined UNICEF in 1988 in the Eastern and Southern Africa Regional Office in Nairobi, Kenya. She started her career in 1970 as Assistant Professor at Addis Ababa University and later was a consultant and WID Programme Coordinator at ESAMI (the Eastern and Southern Africa Management Institute) in Tanzania.

Ramabai Espinet, originally from Trinidad, is Professor at the School of English Studies of Seneca College in Ontario; her teaching interests include postcolonial Caribbean and women's studies. She is a writer and performer whose poems and papers have appeared in numerous publications. She is Director of OSICC (the Ontario Society for Services to Indo-Caribbean Canadians) and a member of the Canadian Research Institute for the Advancement of Women.

Alda Facio, a feminist lawyer and writer, is Director of the Women, Gender, and Justice Programme of the United Nations Latin American Institute for Crime Prevention. She is the correspondent for the Latin American Feminist Mothers (INFEM) Press and also a member of the International Women's Rights Action Watch.

Toujan Faisal is the first and only woman Member of the Jordanian Parliament. For 18 years, she served as producer/presenter at JTV. During that time, she also held the posts of Head of the Cultural Section at JTV, Director of Training and Development Communication, and Media Consultant to the Minister of Social Development.

Sally Field attended the Fourth World Conference on Women and the NGO Forum as the Honorary Chair of the Save the Children delegation. She is an actress, a two-time Academy Award winner (*Places in the Heart* and *Norma Rae*) and also an Emmy Award winner.

Laura Flanders is Executive Producer and host of *CounterSpin*, a nationally syndicated radio report from Fairness and Accuracy in Reporting (FAIR), a media watch group in the U.S. She writes a column on women and the media for FAIR's publication *EXTRA!* and contributes to a number of other publications. She has been an international correspondent for a PBS series on the Pacifica radio network and was Senior Producer/co-host of *Undercurrents*, an investigative radio program on WBAI, a Pacifica radio station.

Eva Friedlander, an anthropologist by training, has extensive research experience in South Asia and the United States with expertise in issues of gender-and-development, international health, disabilities and aging. She worked at the NGO Forum organizing the Program of Plenaries, prior to which she was at the United Nations Development Fund for Women (UNIFEM). She is a member of, and represents, the International Women's Anthropological Conference (IWAC) at the United Nations.

Roxan Graham is twenty years old and hails from Jamaica. A high school graduate, she has special training in drama in education, group dynamics and leadership, and peer counseling. She is a member of Teens in Action where she serves as a peer counselor.

Carolyn Hannan-Andersson has an academic background in social anthropology and social/economic geography. She has worked with gender-and-development as a researcher, consultant, and development cooperation official since the 1970s. Currently she is Gender Advisor for the Swedish International Development Cooperation Agency (SIDA), and is the Chairperson of the OECD/DAC Expert Group on Women and Development.

Raufa Hassan is the General Secretary of NGO Networks of Women in Yemen. She was a radio and television broadcaster and is now a professor of social change and women's studies at Sana'a University in Yemen. Between 1984 and 1986 she worked as Deputy Director in the Ministry of Education and Culture. In 1990 she ran as a candidate for Member of Parliament and has used the experience to mobilize other women to run for political office.

Riffat Hassan is a tenured Professor of Religious Studies/Humanities at the University of Louisville, Kentucky. She was also head of the delegation of the Religious Consultation on Population, Reproductive Health, and Ethics, an NGO based in Washington, D.C. She has been intensively involved in developing feminist theology in Islam since 1974 and has participated in Jewish-Christian-Muslim interreligious dialogue since the 1970s.

Nancy Miriam Hawley is one of the founders of the Boston Women's Health Book Collective and a co-author of *Our Bodies, Ourselves* and *Ourselves and Our Children*. With her husband she co-directs Cogswell Associates, a psychotherapy and consultation practice in Cambridge, Massachusetts.

Remedios Ignacio-Rikken, appointed by President Corazon C. Aquino as Executive Director of the National Commission on the Role of Filipino Women (August 1986-May 1994), spearheaded the Philippine Development Plan for Women (1989-1992), the first-ever blueprint to mainstream women's concerns in development. Now she is back to NGO work, organizing women in politics with the National Movement of Filipino Women (PILIPINA), a partner of the Center for Asia/Pacific Women in Politics (CAPWIP)

Rounaq Jahan is a Senior Research Scholar and an Adjunct Professor of International Affairs at Columbia University. She is also a Senior Fellow at the Centre for Policy Dialogue (CPD), Bangladesh. She was a professor of Political Science at Dhaka University from 1970 to 1993 and headed the women's programme of the International Labour Office (Geneva) from 1985 to 1989 and the United Nations Asian-Pacific Development Centre (Kuala Lumpur) from 1982 to 1984.

Françoise Kaudjhis-Offoumou has been a lawyer affiliated with the Côte d'Ivoire Bar Association since 1987. She teaches law at the National Insitute of Social Work. She was in charge of judicial affairs at the Department of Women's Affairs (1982-1987, and currently is President of the International Association for Democracy in Africa (AID-Afrique).

Vesna Kesić is a Croatian journalist, human rights and peace activist, and coordinator of the women's human rights group B.a.B.e. (Be active, Be emancipated) in Zagreb.

Nighat Said Khan has been an activist all her life and has been associated with various political movements, particularly the women's movement. She is a founding member of Women's Action Forum and a founder of the ASR Resource Centre, a socialist feminist group. ASR is involved in activism, training, teaching, publishing, and making documentary film. Her academic background is in economics and sociology.

Angela E.V. King is Deputy to the Head of the UN Office of Human Resources Management and Director of Staff Administration, Compensation, and Classification. She is also a member of the High-Level Steering Committee on Improving the Status of Women in the United Nations. Since 1964 she has served the United Nations in various posts. As Chief of Mission in South Africa from 1992 to 1994, she is one of only two women to head a United Nations peacekeeping, peace-making team.

Maria Kirbassova founded the Committee of Soldiers' Mothers in Russia in 1989. Since then, the Committee has become an umbrella organization for many similar committees all over Russia.

Frances Kissling has been president of Catholics for a Free Choice since 1982. She is a co-founder of the Global Fund for Women and the International Network of Feminists Interested in Reproductive Health and Ethics. She has served as the Treasurer of the International Women's Health Coalition. A founder and treasurer of the Religious Coalition on Population, Reproductive Rights, and Ethics, she is presently on the Executive Board of the American Public Health Association.

Yoko Kitazawa is a founder and member of the Pacific/Asia Resource Center (PARC) and is on the Editorial Board of AMPO. She was also a delegate of the Japanese government to the General Assembly of the United Nations.

Winona LaDuke is Program Director of the Seventh Generation Fund's Environmental Program. In 1988 she won the Reebok Human Rights Award and with the proceeds launched the White Earth Land Recovery Project, where she serves as Campaign Director. She is a board member of Greenpeace USA, co-chair of the Indigenous Women's Network, and a member of the Mississippi Band of Chippewa of the White Earth Reservation.

Lin Lap-Chew, a human rights activist, has lived in the Netherlands since 1973. In 1982, together with a group of Dutch and Asian women, she pioneered programs to address sex tourism, trafficking in women, and forced prostitution, resulting in the formation of the Foundation Against Trafficking in Women (STV) in 1987. At STV she facilitated the founding of the Global Alliance Against Traffic in Women in Thailand. Currently she is coordinating a comprehensive international report on trafficking in women.

Hilda Lini is the first and only woman Member of the Parliament of Vanuatu. She is also Vice President of the International Peace Bureau. Trained as a journalist, she was formerly the government minister responsible for health, water supply, population, and the rights of children. An activist with organizations within and outside Vanuatu, she led the Pacific region NGO delegation to the Cairo Conference (1994) and the Nairobi Conference (1985), and was the spokesperson for Pacific region NGOs at the Copenhagen Conference (1980).

Supatra Masdit was elected to Thailand's Parliament six times from 1979 to 1995. She served as Minister attached to the Prime Minister's Office from 1988 to 1990, the first woman Member of Parliament appointed as Cabinet Minister. The title "Khunying" (Lady) was awarded her by the King of Thailand for her outstanding contributions as a public servant. In 1989 she spearheaded the formation of a permanent National Commission on Women's Affairs, ensuring that NGOs were appointed to all its working committees.

Miria R. K. Matembe, a lawyer, has been a Member of the Ugandan Parliament since 1989 and a Member of the Constituent Commission which drafted the new constsitution for Uganda. She was also a Member of the Constituent Assembly which promulgated the new constitution. She is a founding member and former Chairperson of Action for Development (ACFODE), a member of Women, Law and Development in Africa (WILDAF), and other women's NGOs. She is Uganda's representative to the Inter-Parliamentary Union.

Yayori Matsui is a feminist journalist/activist and worked for the *Asahi Shimbun*, a leading newspaper in Japan, for 33 years until she retired in 1994. She is now the Director of the Asia-Japan Women's Resource Center, and is also Coordinator of the Asian Women's Association, Japan, which she founded in 1977. In 1994 she was East Asia Coordinator of the Asia Pacific NGO Working Group.

Patricia Mercado is President of Mujeres Trabajadoras Unidas (MUTUAC), United Working Women, and General Coordinator of the Information Group on Reproductive Choice (Grupo de Información en Reproducción Elegida, GIRE). She was a grantee of the MacArthur Foundation and Coordinator of the Latin American and Caribbean Campaign to Decriminalize Abortion.

Swasti Mitter is the Deputy Director and a Professorial Fellow at the United Nations University for New Technologies (UNU/INTECH) in Maastricht, the Netherlands. She is the Coordinator of 'Monitoring the Impact of Technological Changes on Women's Work in Asia', a collaborative research project involving 28 women workers' organizations from eight Asian countries. The project, funded partly by UNIFEM, aims to give women a voice in the industry and technology policies of their own countries.

Minh Chau Nguyen, an economist, is currently Manager of Gender Analysis and Policy in the Poverty and Social Policy Department at the World Bank, which she joined after one year of teaching at the University of Washington. She leads a group responsible for formulating the Bank's policy on gender and for technical support to the country departments in mainstreaming gender concerns in both policy and investment operations of the World Bank.

Kristina (Kicki) Nordström has a background in social anthropology. She has been Chairperson of the World Blind Union's Standing Committee on the Status of Blind Women since 1993 and has served as a politician in the City Council since 1986. She is also a member of the Central Board of the Swedish Association of the Visually Impaired.

Helen O'Connell is a writer and advocate on women's rights, gender and development, and aid issues. She works as the policy and education coordinator at One World Action, a UK NGO. She is also President of Women in Development Europe (WIDE Network).

Esther Ocloo is the 1990 recipient of the African Leadership Prize for a Sustainable End to Hunger. The first person in Ghana to start a food processing factory, in 1975 she received an Honorary Doctorate in science from the University of Science and Technology at Kumasi. She held positions as Executive Chair of the Ghana National Food and Nutrition Board, President of the Ghana Business and Professional Women (1981), Vice President for Africa of its international (1985-1989), and Chair of the Board of Women's World Banking.

Susanna Ounei-Small is the Assistant Director of the Pacific Concerns Resource Center, which is the secretariat for the movement for a free and independent Pacific. She was involved with the Beneath Paradise Project, a documentation center organized by eight countries in the region. She is also a political activist for the independence of New Caledonia and an organizer of the women's movement for the Pacific region.

Lorena Peña Mendoza is a member of the Executive Committee of the women's organization Melida Anaya Montes. She is also a National Deputy to the Congress of El Salvador for the party Frente Farabundo Marti para la Liberación Nacional.

Jacqueline Pitanguy is a sociologist, and founder and Director of CEPIA in Brazil, an NGO working on women's rights. She is the former president of the National Council for Women's Rights and has published extensively on women's issues.

Pak Po-Hi is a social development specialist, currently Chairperson of the Board and Director of the Korea Institute for Social Information and Reseach (In-Sirch). She is also a member of South Korea's National Women's Policy Commission and an official delegate to the Fourth World Conference of Women. She served as Social Affairs Officer at the secretariat of the United Nations Economic and Social Commission for Asia and the Pacific (ESCAP) from 1979 to 1988.

Judy Rebick is the co-host of *Face Off*, a CBC Newsworld television national debate show, broadcast every weeknight. She is also a lay member of the Ontario Judicial Council. From 1990 to 1993 she was president of the National Action Committee on the Status of Women, Canada's largest women's group, with more than 500 member groups. In 1993 she led grassroots opposition to government proposals to amend the Canadian Constitution.

Amy Richards is Chair of the board of Third Wave, a national organization for young activists. She is also a research and editorial associate to Gloria Steinem and works with *Ms.* magazine, the Ms. Foundation for Women, and Voters for Choice. Her writing has been published in *Listen Up! Voices from the Next Feminist Generation*, *The New Internationalist*, and *Who Cares*. She also has been an active supporter of people with disabilities.

Marcia Rivera is a Puerto Rican social scientist who since 1992 has headed the Latin American Council of Social Sciences, a federation of over 100 research institutes throughout Latin America and the Caribbean. Trained in economics and sociology, Dr. Rivera has published extensively on development issues from a gender perspective. She is a member of Development Alternatives with Women for a New Era (DAWN) and is the regional coordinator of work on alternative economic frameworks.

Amelia Rokotuivuna has been a leading activist for peace and for the advancement of women in the Pacific over the last three decades. She was on the staff of the YWCA of Fiji and served as its National Executive Director from 1973 to 1977. From 1992 to 1995 she was Programme Secretary for Advocacy for the World YWCA based in Geneva, Switzerland. Currently she works with the Asian-Pacific Development Centre.

Caitriona Ruane is co-founder and currently Coordinator of the Centre for Research and Documentation in Belfast in Northern Ireland. She worked and lived in Nicaragua and El Salvador from 1983 to 1987. She was an observer at the elections in South Africa in 1994.

Irene M. Santiago was Executive Director of the NGO Forum on Women, prior to which she was Chief of the Asia/Pacific Section of the United Nations Development Fund for Women (UNIFEM). A co-founder of PILIPINA, a national feminist organization in the Philippines, she was also founding Chair of the Center for Asia/Pacific Women in Politics.

Anabel Santos is President of the Association of Young Women in Spain. She is actively involved with both the feminist and youth movements in Spain. Her particular focus is on creating equal opportunities for both women and men.

Misha Schubert is currently Co-Convenor of the Young Feminists Group of the Women's Electoral Lobby, a member of the National Young Women's Task Group of the YWCA of Australia, and the Victorian Women's Trust "Woman of the Future" award recipient. Formerly she was State and National Women's Officer of the National Union of Students, Education Vice-President of her campus student association, and youth delegate to innumerable forums.

Mab Segrest, a lesbian writer and organizer, is on the board of the Center for Democratic Renewal, which monitors far-right groups and hate violence in the United States. She organized against white supremacist groups in her home state of North Carolina as staff member for North Carolinians Against Racist and Religious Violence from 1984 to 1990. She is currently Coordinator for the U.S. Contact Group of the Urban-Rural Mission, a program of the World Council of Churches.

Gita Sen is Professor of Economics at the Indian Institute of Management in Bangalore, India. She is a development economist whose research focuses especially on gender-and-development. A founding member of Development Alternatives with Women for a New Era (DAWN), she is currently Research Coordinator of DAWN's project on alternative economic frameworks.

Rebeca Sevilla founded the Feminist Self-Awareness Group for Lesbians (GALF) in Lima, Peru. She joined the coordinating collective of the Peruvian Feminist Movement in 1990. From 1988 to 1993 she served as head of the Homosexual Movement of Lima (MHOL) and from 1992 to 1995 as Secretary-General of the International Lesbian and Gay Association (ILGA).

Magela Sigillito is currently the coordinator of NGONET, an international NGO information-sharing network on global issues. During preparations for the World Summit on Social Development (WSSD), she headed the NGONET New York office in charge of information dissemination to Southern NGOs. At the International Conference on Population and Development (ICPD), she was Information Coordinator of the NGONET-APC information and communication room and liaison with the United Nations.

Helvi Sipilä is an attorney-at-law, having founded and directed her own law office in Finland from 1943 to 1972, during which time she was active in UN affairs. She was the UN Assistant Secretary-General from 1972 to 1980, the Secretary-General of International Women's Year and of the First UN World Conference on Women in 1975. She has played a leadership role in a number of national and international NGOs.

Pamela Sparr works as an economist in the Women's Division of the United Methodist Church General Board of Global Ministries, where she is responsible for advocacy, education, and organizing activities related to economic and environmental justice and works with members of the United Methodist Women as well as other groups inside and outside the Church. Her specialty is macroeconomic policy and gender concerns. She is a member of the Alternative Women-in-Development working group in Washington, D.C.

Gloria Steinem is a writer, editor, and feminist organizer. She is a Consulting Editor for *Ms. Magazine*; the President of Voters for Choice, a bipartisan political action committee that supports candidates working for reproductive freedom; and a current board member and founding President of the Ms. Foundation for Women, a national multiracial women's fund that supports grassroots projects to empower women and girls.

Estela Suárez Aguilar is from Argentina, a member of Association Mutual Siglo XXi. She has been a researcher at the Regional Multidisciplinary Research Center (CRIM) of the Autonomous National University of Mexico (UNAM) since 1990. From 1975 to 1989 she was a professor in the Faculty of Economics, UNAM. She is a co-founder and member of Mujeres Trabajadoras Unidas (MUTUAC; United Working Women), established in 1984.

Maria Suárez Toro is a Puerto Rican/Costa Rican feminist. A producer/activist in communications at Feminist International Radio Endeavour (FIRE) since 1991, she has taken part in all the major UN conferences since the Earth Summit in 1992, doing communications work to promote a gender perspective in their agendas. Formerly a teacher in bilingual education in the United States, she also worked on literacy programs for adults and was Coordinator of the Education Secretariat in the Central American Human Rights Commission (CODE-UCA).

Zenebeworke Tadesse, a sociologist by training, was a founding member and the first Executive Secretary of the Association of African Women for Research and Development (AAWORD). She was until recently Deputy Executive Secretary of the Council for the Development of Social Sciences in Africa (CODESRIA) and Editor-in-Chief of *Africa Development*, a quarterly journal. Presently she does freelance work on urban poverty and gender issues in Africa.

Pauline Tangiora has been involved in peace and security issues, focusing on the effects of war and the impact of multinationals on the environment since the 1960s. At the Vienna Conference on Human Rights, she served as an Indigenous Representative, calling on governments to respect the community rights of Indigenous Peoples in order for all of humanity to coexist. Residing in Aotearoa, New Zealand, she is active in lobbying the government on environmental biodiversity and conservation from a holistic perspective.

Sunera Thobani has been President of the National Action Committee on the Status of Women (NAC), Canada's largest feminist organization since 1993. As a member of the India Mahila Association, she helped organize against the sex-selection clinics in British Columbia. She is also a founding member of South Asian Women's Action Network (SAWAN), and in 1993 she served as a member of an Oxfam-Canada sponsored pre-election observer delegation to South Africa. In 1994 she received the Indo-Canada Chamber of Commerce Humanitarian of the Year Award.

Ung Yok Khoan has been the Coordinator of Amara, a network of Cambodian women for peace, since 1994. She began her career as a primary school teacher, interrupted in 1975 by the advent of the Pol Pot regime. In 1980, as a refugee on the Thai border, she began to work as a teacher trainer. From 1982 until she left the border camp in 1991, she was President of the Women's Association.

Ruby Va'a is Acting Deputy Director of University Extension at the University of the South Pacific. There she is also Head of Distance Education and Coordinator of Instructional Design and Development in the Distance Education Unit. She is active in promoting women's education and assists in generally raising the quality of women's lives through involvement with the Fiji Association of Women Graduates (an affiliate of the International Federation of University Women), an NGO which she helped found.

Virginia Vargas is a feminist activist and theoretician from Peru who served as the regional coordinator of the Latin American/Caribbean for the NGO Forum. She founded the Flora Tristan Center in Peru and is a founding member of various feminist networks, such as Entre Mujeres and Development Alternatives with Women for a New Era (DAWN), at the regional and global level. She also teaches at the Institute of Social Studies at the Hague in the Netherlands.